Praise for *Essays in Biography*

"Erudite . . . eloquent . . . opinionated . . . edifying and often very entertaining."

—*Publishers Weekly*

"The acclaimed essayist . . . presents a provocative collection of essays that [is] . . . guaranteed to both delight and disconcert."

—*Kirkus Reviews*

"[He] brings to biography a genius of discernment."

—*Choice*

"Mr. Epstein's essays are brilliant distillations. . . . "

—Carl Rollyson, *Wall Street Journal*

"*Essays in Biography* . . . is smart, witty and a pleasure to read."

—Jonathan Yardley, *Washington Post*

"This . . . collection of biographical essays . . . [is] unabashedly personal, and flavored throughout by a wit that never stays in the background for long. [What Epstein calls a] 'heightened sense of life's possibilities' is . . . what a reader may take away."

—*Boston Globe*

"Joseph Epstein['s] . . . style and wit make his subjects come alive. . . . [He is] the dean of contemporary essayists."

—*Washington Times*

"Epstein is a gifted storyteller, a discerning critic, and a peerless stylist. . . . It's fair to say that a variety of over-used adjectives—witty, urbane, intelligent—are in this case quite appropriate."

—*Weekly Standard*

"[Joseph Epstein is] one of the few living writers whose every book I try to read promptly. He is never—really never—less than a pure thoughtful joy."

—Brian Doherty, Senior Editor, *Reason*

"Epstein writes suave, free-wheeling, charged essays."

—Robert Fulford, *NATIONAL POST*

"[Joseph Epstein's] personal mission statement, apparently, is to instruct and delight. . . . This is a book you can pick up and skip around in with pleasure and profit."

—Christopher Flannery, *CLAREMONT REVIEW OF BOOKS*

"The joys of reading Joseph Epstein are many. . . . Readers consistently find wit, whimsy, and learning at the most accessible and enjoyable level."

—Larry Thornberry, *AMERICAN SPECTATOR*

A Literary Education

A Literary Education

Joseph Epstein

The essays in this book were previously published
in journals and anthologies. Original publication
information can be found on page 499.

Axios Press
PO Bo 457
Edinburg, VA 22824
888.542.9467   info@axiosinstitute.org

Library of Congress Cataloging-in-Publication Data

Epstein, Joseph, 1937–
   [Essays. Selections]
   A Literary Education / Joseph Epstein.
   pages cm
   Includes bibliographical references and index.
   ISBN 978-1-60419-078-6 (hardcover : alk. paper)
   I. Title.

PS3555.P6527A6 2014
814'.54--dc23

                                                    2013044959

In memory of
Mitchell Watkins
(1937–2013)

Also by Joseph Epstein

Essays in Biography (2012)
Gossip: The Untrivial Pursuit (2011)
The Love Song of A. Jerome Minkoff and Other Stories (2010)
Fred Astaire (2008)
In a Cardboard Belt!: Essays Personal, Literary, and Savage (2007)
Friendship: An Exposé (2006)
Alexis de Tocqueville: Democracy's Guide (2006)
Fabulous Small Jews (2003)
Envy (2003)
Snobbery: The American Version (2002)
Narcissus Leaves the Pool: Familiar Essays (1999)
Life Sentences: Literary Essays (1997)
With My Trousers Rolled: Familiar Essays (1995)
Pertinent Players: Essays on the Literary Life (1993)
A Line Out for a Walk: Familiar Essays (1991)
The Goldin Boys: Stories (1991)
Partial Payments: Essays on Writers and Their Lives (1988)
Once More Around the Block: Familiar Essays (1987)
Plausible Prejudices: Essays on American Writing (1985)
Middle of My Tether: Familiar Essays (1983)
Ambition: The Secret Passion (1980)
Familiar Territory: Observations on American Life (1979)
Divorced in America: Marriage in an Age of Possibility (1974)

Contents

Introduction

A LITERARY EDUCATION is my thirteenth collection of essays. The first, *Familiar Territory*, was published by Oxford University Press in 1979. Initially my essay collections were divided between what I thought of as literary essays and familiar essays; the former were essays about other writers, the latter about the world at large, or at least those things in it that captured my fancy at the time. Most of these essays originally appeared in intellectual magazines. I have been privileged in having magazine editors ask me to supply them with essays, and even more privileged in having had a generous response to these essays from readers. As an essayist, I am quite without complaint, which hasn't been easy for someone with a naturally complaining nature.

I have also been fortunate in the criticism my essays have encountered. I have taken my knocks and occasional smashes, but far and away most of this has been kindly and generous, and some of it has come from writers I myself much admired: Philip Larkin, Karl Shapiro, and John Gross, William Barrett, Sidney Hook, and J. F. Powers, to name only the dead among them. I have been compared to great essayists, to Michel de Montaigne, Charles Lamb, William Hazlitt, Max Beerbohm, and H. L. Mencken. I have been praised lavishly, called the best essayist writing in English, though, true enough, often with the word "arguably" qualifying this praise ("Arguably Epstein is . . ."). I have read so often sentences that begin "Arguably Epstein is . . ." that I have contemplated changing my name from Joseph to Arguably Epstein. As for the attacks on my essays, I have been able to take comfort in the fact that most have seemed to me unjust; and in the matter of literary criticism, as Mencken once remarked, it is only justice that hurts.

As for my own opinion of my quality as an essayist, it is simple enough, and comes down to the feeling that I could have done a lot better. I fear it is in the nature of writing always to feel that one could have done better, though sometimes I have reread an essay of mine written twenty or thirty years ago and think it not utterly disgraceful. Paul Valery, who said so many smart things about writing, claimed that he never finished a poem; he merely abandoned it. By which he meant that even after long labor he could not discover ways to make the poem as good as he hoped it might be. So it is for every writer who values craft, and thinks the badge of craftsman, even with its artisanal ring, among the highest of compliments.

An essayist is an amateur, in two primary senses of the word. He is, first, distinctly not an expert; and he is, second, a lover. Unlike the critic, or even the novelist or poet, there is nothing professional about the essayist. He comes to the world dazzled by it. The riches it offers him are inexhaustible. Subjects on which he may scribble away are everywhere. The essayist need not be an optimist, but a depressed essayist—and I can provide names of some now at work on request—is badly miscast.

At the same time, the essayist ought to be skeptical if not gloomy in outlook. He should distrust large ideas, and especially idea systems. He should view all theories as mistaken until proven true, which over the centuries not all that many have. Life for the essayist is so much richer, so much more various, than any theory or even idea can hope to describe. The best essayists, in my reading, are the laughing skeptics.

This is the second book of essays that I have published with Axios Press. Four or so years ago I received an email from Hunter Lewis, the founder of Axios, thanking me for the pleasure my essays have given him over the years and offering to print any essays of mine that have not previously appeared in earlier of my books that I deemed worth reprinting. Talk about an email that made my day. A man of his word, Hunter Lewis brought out a volume of my essays to which he suggested the title, after Lord Keynes, of *Essays in Biography*. His firm also produced far and away the handsomest of all the twenty-odd books I have thus far had published.

A Literary Education, the second Axios volume, is not united by the biographical or any other theme but instead covers the range of my interests and preoccupations as an essayist over a writing career that spans more than fifty years: education, language, the arts, magazines, intellectuals, the culture. Whether, taken together, the essays in this volume comprise a consistent and interesting outlook on the life of my time is not for me but for my readers to say.

I published my first essay, "A Stillness at Little Rock" in the *New Leader Magazine* in 1959 at the age of twenty-two. A publishing scoundrel, in Henry James's phrase, I have scribbled away continuously ever since. The most recent essay in this book, "You Could Die Laughing," appeared in 2013. If my luck continues to hold up, I hope to be able to publish further essays after this book makes its entrance into the world.

Luck is the right word, for, as I look back upon my career, it has been one of great good fortune. By my early thirties I had jobs—editing a magazine, teaching at a university without having any advanced degrees—that allowed me lots of free time for writing. I have never suffered anything like a writer's block. (Pause here to touch wood.) I have at one time or another written for all the notable magazines in this country and in England. I have had no difficulty getting books published by reputable publishers. I have not made vast sums of money through my writing, certainly not enough to gain me an honorable discharge from the financial wars, but it has provided me with a decent income over the past forty or so years. Best of all, I have acquired a small but hardy band of regular readers who fortify me and encourage me to persist. They, these readers, are the greatest reward of all.

—Joseph Epstein

Part One

A Literary Education

A Literary Education:
On Being Well-Versed in Literature

(2008)

S YDNEY SMITH, the early-nineteenth-century clergyman, wit, and one of the founders of the *Edinburgh Review*, once remarked that, if the same progress as had been made in education were made in the culinary arts, we should today still be eating soup with our hands. Quite so. Sydney Smith's simile holds up all too well in our time. New ideas and reforms continue to crop up in education—from the installation of the elective system more than a century ago at Harvard to the advent of digital technology throughout the educational system in recent years—each, in its turn and time, heralding fresh new revolutions in learning. One after another, these revolutions fizzle, then go down in flames, leaving their heralds all looking like some variation of what Wallace Stevens called "lunatics of one idea."

Meanwhile, things continue to slide: standards slip, curricula are politicized and watered down, and, despite all the emphasis on schooling at every level of society, the dance of education remains locked into the dreary choreography of one step forward, two steps back. Education remains education, which is to say a fairly private affair. No matter how much more widespread so-called higher education has become, only a small—one is inclined to say an infinitesimal—minority seems capable of taking serious advantage of it, at any rate during the standard years of schooling.

Let me quickly insert that, when young, I was not myself among this minority. As a student in the middle 1950s, I attended the University of Chicago. No teacher in whose class I sat has ever remembered me upon meeting in later years, and this for good reason: My plan during my student days was to remain as inconspicuous as possible; I was sedulous only in the attempt to hide my ignorance, which was genuine and substantial. But more than mere ignorance was entailed. I somehow could not bring my mind to concentrate—to "focus," as we say today—for long on many of the matters at hand.

A teacher in command of all the standard academic locutions—those "if you wills" and "as it weres," with a *mirabile dictu* and other Latin tags thrown in from time to time at no extra charge—might stand authoritatively at his lectern setting out eight reasons for the emergence of the Renaissance. As he did so, all I could think was what induced him to buy that hopeless necktie he was wearing, and might that be a soup stain prominently in the middle of it, and, if so, made by chicken noodle or minestrone? At examination time, I recalled only five of the eight reasons for the Renaissance, and wound up with a C, which did not stand for charming.

Classrooms can, of course, sometimes kill great subjects, and also splendid books. Recognizing this, Willa Cather insisted that her own books not be made available in school editions, for she feared that students, reading them too early and under the duress of formal education, would never return to them in later life when they were more likely to be truly ready for them. As delivered in conventional classrooms and lecture halls, education is not available to everyone, including sometimes quite bright, even dazzlingly brilliant, people. Henry James was never very good at school, and neither was Paul Valéry; Marcel Proust performed mediocrely at the Lycée Condorcet. W. H. Auden failed to come away with a First at Oxford. Sainte-Beuve said of Pascal, who was an authentic genius, that "it was easier for him to make discoveries for himself than to study after the way of others." Was there something wrong with these men, powerful artists and philosophers all, or something wrong with education, as it is usually construed and practiced?

I had a cousin named Sherwin Rosen, who, before his death at the age of sixty-three, was the chairman of the Economics Department at the University of Chicago, a department that for more than thirty years now has been dominant in its discipline. At his memorial, one of my cousin's older colleagues, Gary Becker, a Nobel prizewinner, remarked that Sherwin came close to being washed out of the PhD program in economics at the University of Chicago. The reason, Gary Becker said, is that my cousin was slow in response to questions in seminar rooms. He didn't have confident answers at the ready; his replies tended to be halting, faltering. But then a day or two, sometimes a week, later, Sherwin would return to the professor who had asked him the question and quietly reveal the defect in its formulation. "What this taught me," Professor Becker said, "is that too much in formal education has to do with quick response, with coughing up information quickly, and not enough leeway is allowed for reflection and brooding in the thoughtful way that serious subjects require."

I like this anecdote because it subverts normal notions of how education should work. After thirty years teaching in a university, I came to have a certain measured suspicion, sometimes edging onto contempt, for what I called (only to myself) "the good student." This good student always got the highest grades, because he approached all his classes with a single question in mind: "What does this teacher want?" And once the good student decides, he gives it to him—he delivers the goods. The good student is thus able to deliver very different goods to the feminist teacher at 9:00 AM, to the Marxist teacher at 10:00 AM, to the conservative teacher at 11:00 AM, and just after lunch to the teacher who prides himself on being without any ideology or political tendency whatsoever.

A T THE UNIVERSITY OF CHICAGO, I was obviously neither a "good student," in the nugatory sense I have just described, nor a seriously passionate one of the kind I most valued as a teacher. Without any gift for pure science or foreign languages or appetite for the often arid abstractions and embarrassingly modest conclusions of social science, when the time came to choose a field of concentration, I felt I had nowhere to go but to become an English major. (When a student in the Lionel Trilling story "Of This Time, Of That Place" tells the professor who is the story's protagonist that he used to be an English major, the professor, in the only humorous remark I have discovered in all of Trilling's writing, replies: "Indeed? What regiment?")

ALMOST EVERYONE OF ANY IMAGINATION wishes he could do a second draft on his education. The reason for this, I suppose, is that we are put through our education well before we can have any grasp on what education is really about. The Duc de Saint-Simon, the greatest writer of memoirs the world has known, noted, with chagrin, that "I had a natural love for reading and history. . . . I have often thought that, had they encouraged me to make it my serious study, I might indeed have made something of myself." In his autobiography *Old Men Forget*, Duff Cooper, the English diplomat, remarks,

> Had I devoted as much time to my school work as I did to promiscuous reading I might have obtained some scholastic distinction. But I had a stupid idea that hard work at given tasks was degrading. Brilliant success without undue application and, if possible, combined with dissipation was what I admired.

As for me, had I to do it over again, I should have studied classics, learned Greek and Latin, to be able to read Herodotus and Thucydides, Tacitus and Horace, in the languages in which they wrote; then I might have ended my days, like the Victorian gentlemen in the Max Beerbohm drawing, translating Virgil's *Georgics* into perfect English hexameters.

At the University of Chicago in the days I was a student there, English studies had shed their philological center. A student once had to study Anglo-Saxon, Old Norse, Old French, and linguistics, on the notion that these subjects served as a kind of hard-core scientific basis for literary study, but no more. Still, the underlying, the reigning, assumption behind most undergraduate courses was that one would go on to graduate school and a career as a university teacher of English.

English at Chicago in my day was dominated by a school of critics known as Aristotelians. This meant that many works read under their supervision tended to be twisted through the wringer—perhaps mangler is the better word here—of Aristotle's *Poetics*. The results were not often enlightening, and never exciting. The physicist Wolfgang Pauli used to respond to the inadequate answers of his less than brilliant students by saying, "That isn't even wrong!" I suspect that, had Pauli popped into one of these English Department classes at the University of Chicago during my day there, he would have exclaimed, "That isn't even dull!"

The one grueling standard the English Department set its students was two lengthy reading lists, to be read outside of regular course work, that an undergraduate English major was tested on at the end of his or her junior and senior years. These lists included all those books that, given any choice, a student would be pleased to elude: Milton's *Paradise Regained*, Hobbes's *Leviathan*, Spenser's *Faerie Queen*, Locke's *Second Treatise on Civil Government* are some of the items on these lists that, with a slight shudder, I can still recall. There were ninety or more books on the two lists combined. The assumption behind these reading lists must have been, you call yourself an English major (of no known regiment), you ought to have read the books required by such a pretension. I rather doubt that today any school could get away with asking so much extra work of its students. But then the difference between Harvard and the University of Chicago, it has been said, was that of the two schools Harvard was more difficult to get into, the University of Chicago much more difficult to get out of.

To give some notion of the randomness, the almost accidental, nature of education, which has always impressed me, I would say that the most significant course I took at the University of Chicago was a badly conceived one that was, in effect, a history of the development of the novel. This course was ill-taught by an under-confident instructor not yet thirty. The reading equivalent of a dance marathon, in ten weeks the course went—at the rate of a novel per week—from *The Princess of Cleves* through *Ulysses,* with stops along the way for Jane Austen, Stendhal, Dostoyevsky, Flaubert, Mann, and Proust. What do you suppose a boy of twenty gets out of reading *Swann's Way*? My best guess is some-where between 15 to 20 percent of what Proust put into it.

Yet still but nonetheless and however, something about this course lit my fire. From it I sensed that, if any inkling about the way the world works and the manner in which human nature is constituted were to be remotely available to me during my stay on the planet, I should have the best chance of discovering it through literature, and perhaps chiefly through the novel. The endless details set out in novels, the thoughts of imaginary characters, the dramatization of large themes through care-fully constructed plots, the portrayals of how the world works, really works—these were among the things that literature, carefully attended to, might one day help me to learn.

At nineteen, I read with genuinely heated excitement Max Weber's great essay *The Protestant Ethic and the Spirit of Capitalism*, quite blown away by the astonishing intellectual connections made by its author. I felt my spirit scorched reading Freud's *Civilization and Its Discontents*. Weber's and Freud's are ideas to the highest power, yet they were—and here I hope I do not sound condescending—ideas merely. They were ideas used in the sense that T. S. Eliot used the word when he said of Henry James that he "had a mind so fine no idea could violate it."

What I believe Eliot meant by the lilting phrase "a mind so fine no idea could violate it" is not that Henry James was uninterested in ideas, or was incapable of mastering them, but that he, James, felt that there were truths above the level of ideas, truths of the instincts, of the heart, of the soul, and these were the truths that James, once he had attained to his lit-erary mastery, attempted to plumb in his novels and stories.

Ideas, however resplendent and grand they may be, are, as we know, endlessly subject to revision, if not to utter destruction. Two of the grand idea systems of the past century and a half—that of Marxism and that of Freudianism—have by now gone by the boards; and the third, Darwin-ism, is currently under heavy fire. Come to think of it, there were prob-ably not eight but eight hundred reasons for the Renaissance, and 678 of these have by now doubtless been shown no longer to hold up.

Not that the literary and the ideational need be mutually exclusive in any-one's education. Combined in the mind of some thinkers the result can be most impressive. John Maynard Keynes was a regular reader of novels and poetry. So was Justice Holmes. Clifford Geertz, the leading anthropologist of his generation, made it his business to keep up with contemporary fiction, some of it fairly ghastly. Sigmund Freud claimed that much of what he knew he learned from the poets, though the world, in my view, would have been much better off had he taken a pass on Sophocles.

My friend Edward Shils, one of the great sociologists of the past half century, read Dickens, Balzac, Conrad, and Cather over and over; and there can little doubt that his having done so made him a better social scientist. I shall never forget Edward telling me one evening how much he admired Milton Friedman, George Stigler, and other of the free-market economists who were his colleagues at the University of Chicago. "They are highly intelligent," he said, "and subtle and penetrating and have intellectual courage. Yet with all that, Joseph, I fear that they are insufficiently impressed with the mysteries of life."

I F I THINK OF MY OWN EDUCATION as chiefly a literary one, it is not in the conventional sense that a literary education might have been construed a century or so ago. The beneficiary of such an education at that time would have been expected to know thoroughly the literary history of his own and at least another nation; he would be in possession of two or three if not all the Romance languages and the two main ancient ones; he would have a mastery of the rules if not the practice of prosody, and carry in his head yards and yards of poetry and long tracts of Shakespeare.

My own literary education bears no resemblance to this. Describing it quickly, I should call it slapdash, wildly uneven, and chiefly autodidactical. But, then, apart from those people trained as professional scholars or scientists, we are all finally autodidacts, making our way on our own as best we can, with our real teachers being the books we happen to read. Because of this, the best that any university can do is point its students in the right direction: let them know what the intellectual possibilities are and give them a taste of the best that has been thought and written in the past. In this regard, the University of Chicago of my student days may be said to have done its job.

But the reason I call my own education literary is that it is anchored in the belief that literature, largely though not exclusively imaginative literature, provides the best education for a man or woman in a free society. "It is the business of literature," wrote Desmond MacCarthy, "to turn facts into ideas." The method of literature, MacCarthy means, is induction: facts first, ideas afterwards. Scientists and social scientists claim to be operating by induction, but there are grounds for thinking that they do not, not really; that instead they are testing, hopefully, hunches, which they call hypotheses. But novelists and poets, if they are true to their craft, are not out to prove anything. If they tell their stories honestly and persuasively, straight and true, somehow all those little frogs of fact might just turn into a handsome prince of a beautiful idea.

Still, ideas are not really what literature is chiefly about. When you have identified and extracted the ideas from novels and poems, I'm not sure that you have a lot to show. In his *In Search of Lost Time*, Proust, scholars have revealed, was working under Bergsonian conceptions of time; Thomas Mann, in *The Magic Mountain*, was limning the flood of political ideas in the time of the rise of European Fascism. But when you have said these things, when you have extruded the ideas from these writers, what, really, do you have? Perhaps you would have done better to have read Henri Bergson directly, or an intellectual history of Europe between the wars, than either Proust or Mann. While novelists may have a plentitude of ideas, or deal with complex ideas in their work, it is rarely their ideas that are the most compelling things about these works.

Consider Theodore Dreiser, a glutton for ideas, almost all of them bad. Dreiser was a man who fell for Stalin and Hitler both, who coarsened the already crude Social Darwinism of his day, who believed in the heavy role of something called "chemisms" in determining human fate. This same Dreiser, born homely and poor, raised in a household dominated by religious superstition, was probably America's greatest novelist of the past century. This, I would say, was because he felt more deeply than anyone else what it was like to be an outsider and knew more about the heat of desire, of sheer human wanting—think of *Sister Carrie,* or think, even more, of *An American Tragedy*—than any man who ever wrote. If Dreiser's work had to live on its ideas, it would today be justifiably dead.

So it was not the search for ideas that was at the center of my literary education. The great vast majority of ideas, after all, are endlessly, infinitely mutable, subject to revision and rejection, not to speak of obliteration and eradication. And it is a good thing that many ideas have a relatively short shelf-life. Some because they are bad, even pernicious ideas: the Master Race, the class struggle, the Oedipus complex, and Socialism are four bad ideas with wretched consequences that come immediately to mind.

"To create a concept," wrote Ortega y Gasset, "is to leave reality behind." Ortega is saying that no concept, no mere idea, is sufficiently comprehensible to capture the reality of the phenomena it seeks to describe. Concepts do, true enough, serve the function of distracting our minds from the richness of the reality that generally manages to evade us. Give something a concept label—ah, attention deficit disorder, ah, mid-life crisis, ah, soccer moms, ah, the Invisible Hand of the Marketplace—ah, how soothing it all is! But it oughtn't to be. Invoke those concepts—and many others—and, *poof!*, reality leaves the room.

ONE OF THE INADEQUATELY RECOGNIZED FUNCTIONS of literature is to show how reality always eludes too firmly drawn ideas. Owing to the spread of so-called (always so-called) higher (higher than what, one wants increasingly to ask) education and the pervasiveness of the mass and online media, the world today is perhaps more concept- and idea-ridden than at any other time in history. One of the reasons for anger at the theory-ridden English departments of our day is that they sold out the richness of literature for a small number of crude ideas—gender, race, class, and the rest of it—and hence gave up their cultural birthright for a pot of message.

One of the most important functions of literature in the current day is to cultivate a healthy distrust of the ideas thrown up by journalism and social science. Novels and poems can be the antidote here. "The novel's spirit is the spirit of complexity," Milan Kundera writes. "The novelist says to the reader: things are not as simple as you think." When he is working well, the good novelist persuasively establishes that life is more surprising, bizarre, fascinating, complex, and rich than any shibboleth, concept, or theory used to explain it. A literary education establishes a strong taste for the endless variousness of life; it teaches how astonishing reality is—and how obdurate to even the most ingenious attempts to grasp its mechanics or explain any serious portion of it! "A man is more complicated than his thoughts," wrote Valéry, which, if you think about it, is happily so.

For the thirty years that I taught literature courses at Northwestern University, I preferred to think that I was a better teacher than I was a student. (I also came to believe that a better education is to be had through teaching than through listening to teachers—and if that ain't the sound of one hand clapping, then I don't know what is.) In this teaching, I made no attempt to turn my undergraduate students into imitation or apprentice scholars, but instead I wanted them to acquire, as best they were able, what a small number of great writers thought was useful knowledge in this mystery-laden life.

I wanted my students to come away from their reading learning, for example, from Charles Dickens the importance of friendship, loyalty, and kindness in a hard world; from Joseph Conrad the central place of fulfilling one's duty in a life dominated by spiritual solitude; from Willa Cather, the dignity that patient suffering and resignation can bring; from Tolstoy, the divinity that the most ordinary moments can provide—kissing a child in her bed goodnight, working in a field, greeting a son returned home from war; and from Henry James, I wanted them to learn that it is the obligation of every sentient human being to stay perpetually on the *qui vive* and become a man or woman on whom nothing is lost, and never to forget, as James puts in his novel *The Princess Casamassima*, that "the figures on the chessboard [are] still the passions and the jealousies and superstitions of man."

Literature operates neither by telescope nor microscope. "Impression is for the writer," noted Proust, "what experimentation is for the scientist." Impression is by its nature inexact, but it does in time give a point of view, a many-angled point of view. One of the lessons Proust's great novel teaches is how different a character, a situation, an event seems from different angles and perspectives, and even then how inexact our knowledge remains. The British historian Lewis Namier remarked that we study history so that we can learn how things didn't happen. That may seem a small profit, but it isn't, since so many people are regularly attempting to foist on us their own false version of how things did or do happen.

So from the study of literature we learn that life is sad, comic, heroic, vicious, dignified, ridiculous, and endlessly amusing—sometimes by turns, sometimes all at once—but never more grotesquely amusing than when a supposedly great thinker comes along to insist that he has discovered and nattily formulated the single key to its understanding. One of the reasons that most literary artists are contemptuous of Sigmund Freud—whose thought Vladimir Nabokov once characterized as no more than private parts covered up by Greek myths—is that his extreme determinism is felt to be immensely untrue to the rich complexity of life, with its twists and turns and manifold surprises.

I N 1887 MATTHEW ARNOLD wrote a review of a French translation of *Anna Karenina*. In this review, Arnold finds Tolstoy's novel, as we still do today, filled with "great sensitiveness, subtlety, and finesse, addressing itself with entire disinterestedness and simplicity to the representation of human life. The Russian novelist is thus master of a spell to which the secrets of human nature—both what is external and what is internal, gesture and manner no less than thought and feeling—willingly make themselves known."

Later in his review, Arnold, inevitably, compares Tolstoy's novel to *Madame Bovary*, another novel on the same subject and theme. *Madame Bovary*, Arnold writes, "is a work of *petrified feeling*; over it hangs an atmosphere of bitterness, irony, impotence; not a personage in the book to rejoice or console us; the springs of freshness and feeling are not there to create such personages." Flaubert, Arnold concludes, "pursues her [Emma Bovary] without pity or pause, as with malignity; he is harder upon her himself than any reader ever, I think, will be inclined to be."

Tolstoy, we now know, originally set out to crush Anna Karenina quite as thoroughly as Flaubert did Emma Bovary. But in mid-composition, discovering the richness of the character he created, he fell in love with her. This caused him radically to rework his novel, to soften Anna, to harden Alexi Alexandrovich Karenin, to make Count Vronsky more foolish than he originally intended. The major difference between Tolstoy and Flaubert is that Tolstoy worked from life, Flaubert from ideas—and in this instance, from a very poor idea, which was hatred of the bourgeoisie and of provincial life. Of the two men, Tolstoy had the larger heart, which gave him the greater appreciation of the complexity of human existence and stronger skepticism about the ability of coarse and blatant ideas to encompass it, including those of the Russian novelist who began this work.

I hope that I am not taken for the enemy of ideas generally. I am not. The separation of Church and State (with the details to be negotiated), the ends-and-means argument, the scientific method, $E=mc^2$, all of them are excellent, irreplaceable ideas. Plato's cave is a wonderfully provocative idea. Yet, for the person of literary education, all ideas, as Orwell felt ought to be the case with all saints, are guilty until proven innocent.

THE EFFECT OF A LITERARY EDUCATION is not to gainsay the usefulness of many ideas, but to understand their limitation. In the end, a literary education teaches the limitation of the intellect itself, at least when applied to the great questions, problems, issues, and mysteries of life. On this point, Marcel Proust wrote:

> Our intellect is not the most subtle, the most powerful, the most appropriate instrument for revealing the truth. It is life that, little by little, example by example, permits us to see that what is most important to our heart, or to our mind, is learned not by reasoning, but through other agencies. Then it is that the intellect, observing their superiority, abdicates its control to them upon reasoned grounds and agrees to become their collaborator and lackey.

A literary education teaches that human nature is best, if always incompletely, understood through the examination of individual cases, with nothing more stimulating than those cases that provide exceptions that prove no rule—the unique human personality, in other words. A literary education with its built-in skepticism about flimsy ideas and especially about large idea systems, is naturally against fanaticism. It provides an enhanced appreciation of the mysteries and complexities of life that reinforces the inestimable value of human liberty—liberty especially of the kind that leaves us free to pursue that reality from which we all live at a great distance and run the risk of dying without having known.

"First grub," said Bertolt Brecht, "then ethics." A bad idea, I would say. A better idea is, "First reality, then ideas." This in any case is what my own literary education has taught me.

Part Two

Memoir

Coming of Age in Chicago

(1969)

I HAVE ALWAYS DOUBTED that Chicago ever even faintly resembled the city of Carl Sandburg's poem, but I know for certain that by the time I was born there the city of the big shoulders had developed a serious slouch. The year was 1937, the event took place on the West Side. The neighborhood of my birth is the same one described in Meyer Levin's novel, *The Old Bunch*. The old bunch has long since departed, and blacks live there now. Today the place is a jungle into which, even in a car, one enters with trepidation and from which one exits with relief. Apparently it was at best never much more than a good place to flee from. Flee my family did, as part of a general Jewish migration across Chicago to the far North Side and thence, later, into the northern suburbs. This particular migration was conducted in moderately high style, topping, surely, our family's previous migrations: my grandfather's from Bialystok to Montreal to avoid conscription into the Czar's army; my father's from Montreal to Chicago at the age of seventeen, because if you were a smart Jewish kid in Canada even mildly on the make, you sensed that the United States was where the action—which is to say, the money—was. On our way to Chicago's North Side, I recall living briefly in a reasonably fashionable apartment hotel, then in an apartment on Sheridan Road off Lake Michigan, and then finally settling into a neighborhood called West Rogers Park. At the time, the *West* in West Rogers Park was no mere geographical distinction, for it denoted a full notch up on the status gauge over plain Rogers Park. It was in West Rogers Park, in a predominantly Jewish, wholly middle-class atmosphere that I grew up—without want, without fear, without, as we used to say around the neighborhood, sweat.

My friends and I were the sons of survivors, successes, in a modest sense of the word, even winners. Our fathers owned small businesses, were doctors or dentists, or shrewd, knowing lawyers. My own father began as a salesman. Too old for World War II, he stayed in Chicago during the war and made a bundle. A realist, he would tell you that you had to be very inept not to do well during those years. On one occasion, in less than an hour's time, a single sale brought him a $10,000 commission. He did so well, in fact, that the people he worked for couldn't stand it and attempted to cut his commissions. So not long after the war he left the firm and went into business for himself. It was shortly after this that we moved to West Rogers Park. As a child I remember that whenever I asked about our financial situation I was told that we were not wealthy but "comfortably off."

This was typical. In all financial and social matters conservative, my father played his cards not so much close to his chest as inside his shirt. During a stretch in the middle and late fifties, he began driving Cadillacs. He did so largely for business reasons. His customers were impressed with the outward signs of success, and if it helped business, he was ready to supply these signs. But he was always a bit uncomfortable about the ostentation of a Cadillac, and every night, returning from work, he would hide it in the garage. He had a partner in those years, who bought his clothes in New York—half-a-dozen pairs of shoes at a whack!—and who, in addition to driving a Cadillac himself, also kept a red Corvette convertible and wore a carefully manicured goatee. In later years, my father bought him out; and soon after, with obvious relief, he dropped the Cadillac and began driving an Oldsmobile.

We belonged to none of the town or country clubs open to Jews in Chicago, though the parents of a great many of my friends did. Insofar as I could see then, or can now, these clubs all operated on wholly plutocratic principles: if you had the cash, could pay your tab, were not too clearly involved with the Syndicate (though at some clubs this didn't hurt at all), and were a sufficient number of years removed from the West Side, membership was yours. The number-one subject in these clubs was money. Money, indeed, was the meaning of Chicago, what the city was all about. Unlike the East, Chicago's pretensions to an aristocracy or social elite were nonexistent. The city's long-established families, the Armours, the Swifts, the Wilsons, were, quite literally, butchers. Everywhere in the city money was the sole, the whole, measure of the man.

Often I was taken by a friend as a guest to one or another of these clubs. The Town Club, which then occupied the top floors of the Sheraton Hotel, in whose card-rooms men played gin, Hollywood-Oklahoma, for a dollar a point, games in which, without any trouble at all, on a bad night one could drop five or ten grand. The Covenant Club, where the big attraction was the food and the *shvitz*. Green Acres, the country club in Northbrook, in whose locker-room I can still recall four men, bald and fat and hairy-backed, swathed in towels, smoking cigars, nibbling at immense slices of blood-red watermelon, and playing gin, while elsewhere in the room Filipinos in white shirts and black trousers with a gold stripe down the sides hustled about shining members' shoes, arranging lockers, and greeting members freshly emergent from the showers with great puffy blue towels. Two other clubs—the Standard Club downtown and the country club in Lincolnwood, known as Bryn Mawr—were both then said to be controlled by German Jews and I had no connections in either.

My father would not have allowed himself to be caught dead in such clubs. I never found them anything but fascinating. Later I came to find certain virtues in my father's conservative style, but in my teen-age years it was the wheelers, the hustlers, the smart-money types, who made the strongest impression on me. The father of a friend of mine, for example, who was supposed to have bet $100,000 on a mid-week baseball game. He had to have been a very high roller to get the bookies to take on that kind of action, but in any event one drizzly Tuesday afternoon (as I have always imagined it), feeling lucky, or impatient, or bored with small victories, he called his book, placed the bet—and lost. A complicating factor was that he didn't have the money to pay off. Normally, this would entitle a man to a bullet in the head, his dead body stuffed into the trunk of an old car which, about two weeks later, would be discovered in the parking lot of some quiet neighborhood Lutheran church. However, it was in the middle of World War II and, as the story goes, the word had gone out not to make any hits on men in uniform. So my friend's father did the only sensible thing to do under the circumstances: he joined the Navy. In Navy bell-bottoms he walked into the office of the men to whom he owed the hundred grand. With a confident smile, he is supposed to have said: "I just dropped by to see if my debt to you gentlemen can't be negotiated." Here was a man I admired.

Yet one could be a certified Chicago hustler on a much smaller scale. Big time or small, it seemed almost everyone I knew or heard about in Chicago in those days was on the make, in on the take, with the show, dedicated not to be done in, to be—to put it flat out—the screwer rather than the screwed. There were cab drivers half of whose income derived from taking passengers to hookers' apartments; lawyers who founded whole careers on whiplash and other fake injury cases; doctors and dentists for whom medicine was strictly a sideline and whose prime interest was real estate; bailiffs, driver's-license-, elevator-, restaurant-, building-, and health-inspectors who tripled and quadrupled their regular salary through handouts, bribes, and other assorted *shmeers*; cops who specialized in making out and signing phony robbery insurance claims, fixed traffic tickets, collected personal and business debts in uniform, or, as happened in one noteworthy instance, actually burglarized homes.

To A CERTAIN EXTENT this went on in other American cities. But in Chicago it went on to a very great extent, and in fact most of the people I knew took a fierce kind of pride in the city's corruption. It was the badge of our sophistication, and we wore it early. As soon as I acquired my driver's license—I was fifteen at the time—a friend taught me to insert a five-dollar bill between it and the wallet-window in which I kept it; this way when a cop stopped me for a traffic violation and asked to see my license, the bribe would be at the ready. Watching the smiling, red-faced Irish cop slip the bill out of my wallet after stopping me for running a red light was a distinct thrill. Smooth! Along with the fin, an air of perfect understanding passed between us. It was a rite of passage successfully brought off, a Chicago Bar Mitzvah.

Not so much behind everything in Chicago but towering above it was the Syndicate. Or rather the idea of the Syndicate. Nobody really knew anything specific about it, yet nobody really doubted its existence. In Chicago the "Outfit" or the "Mob" or "the Boys," as people who liked to be thought very hip sometimes called the Syndicate, seemed quite different from what it has since been revealed to be in such places as New Jersey. From a distance, at any rate, it seemed no cozy Cosa Nostra, no hierarchically-arranged network of small-business-minded hoods, but a crunching corporation—smoothly and efficiently run, if still a little rough round the edges. Nor was it so exclusively Italian as it appeared to be in the East. In Chicago, Jews were heavily involved, mostly in administrative jobs, such as bookies or lawyers or fight promoters. West Rogers Park had its own Benya Kriks, men with names like Acey Feinman, Potsey Pearlstein, Hawkface Bernie Greenburg. Rumors were nagging, unverifiable, and delicious. I went with a girl in my junior year in high school, for example, whose father never worked. From the beginning of spring to the end of fall, he golfed. Winters he played gin at the Town Club. His brother, it was firmly established, had been a Capone lieutenant in the twenties. It was said that, as a legacy from those days, he, the younger brother, still collected a dollar a month on every juke box in the city of Chicago.

WHEN I LOOK BACK ON IT NOW, it all seems a bit like bad Damon Runyan, but it was very rich stuff at the time. The entire set-up was one I felt wonderfully comfortable in. Its guiding philosophy was "let Paris be gay," and its rules were uncommonly simple: go easy; don't make waves; why fight City Hall when for less than you might think you may be able to buy it?—and at all times and in all ways take particular care to distinguish yourself from the marks, the rubes, and the general lot of losers. In Chicago there were finally only two classes: winners and losers.

Self-regard had a lot to do with determining which of the two classes one fell into. The Fat Man was a case in point, a loser by most standards but his own and therefore not a loser at all. "Kid," the Fat Man once said to me, "who's got it better than me? Not many guys, that's for sure. I like my job, I eat good, I see all the movies I want, and I get it on the average of three times a week—plus once at home." That may not have been a true champion talking, but the man has to be counted a contender.

Fred Moscowitz, the Fat Man, made collections for my friend Philley Goldman's father's finance company. I first met him when I was sixteen, and for years afterward I thought of him as the first adult to take us seriously, to treat us, at a time when such treatment was terribly important, as grown-ups.

In order to lend his father a hand and, while at it, to learn the business, Philley Goldman began working on Saturdays with the Fat Man sometime during our sophomore year in high school. Philley brought great stories back from these Saturday outings. The Fat Man was a riot of good humor, a mine of information, a superior guide through certain inner chambers of the city. He took Philley to special restaurants (cheap but good), placed small bets for him through his various bookies, accompanied him to inexpensive hookers, and put him on to others whom he himself had visited during the week and who had some specialty he thought Philley might get a kick out of. Sometimes Philley and I would follow up on these tips. (Once Philley telephoned the Fat Man to thank him for a number which proved very satisfactory. "Hi Fred," Philley said, "just calling to thank you for that Doris number. Terrific! Really great! Everything you said she was, and more." A gravelly voice at the other end responded: "This is Mrs. Moscowitz.")

Philley arranged for me to accompany him and the Fat Man on their rounds one Saturday. It was just after seven o'clock in the morning when the Fat Man drove up to Philley's house in the company car, a powder-blue, 1950 Plymouth station wagon. He was bald, ruddy, had a warm rasp to his voice (a milder version of the late Andy Devine's), stood about 5' 10" and weighed in at well over 300 pounds. His skull apart, he seemed not to have a bone in his body. His specialized knowledge of the best cheap restaurants in Chicago had taken its toll, and one had only to see him eat once to realize that his tremendous heft was in no way connected with glandular trouble. In the driver's seat of the Plymouth he draped a bib-like rag—his *shmatte*, he called it—over the great hump of his stomach to prevent the rubbing of the steering wheel from wearing out his pants.

After Philley introduced us, I addressed him as Mr. Moscowitz, but he immediately told me to cut out that "Mr. Moscowitz crap" and call him Fred. So as not in any way to make me feel the outsider, he insisted we all three sit up front; and so we did, with Philley crammed in the middle and I wedged flush against the door. The Fat Man was the kind of driver who was so good you didn't particularly notice he was even at the wheel. When a car behind us honked and passed us on the left, however, he rolled down the window in time to yell at the passing driver, "Blow it out your duffelbag, farthead!" Heading toward the city's South Side for the first collections, the Fat Man provided a tour of Chicago's great bordellos. On Lake Shore Drive he pointed out one in an expensive high-rise which, according to him, had been one of the city's glories in the thirties. "Three bucks a trick is all it was," he said, "and they served cocktails. Lovely girls, too. Break their little hearts if you didn't dance with them a time or two beforehand."

In the back of the Plymouth the Fat Man kept a few old sheets, a blanket, and some loose rope. These were there in case he had to repossess some item on which the payments were hopelessly behind. Mr. Goldman had gone into the finance business only a few years before, and most of his business still came from furniture stores—"risky paper," it was called in the trade, but not at all unusual for a small company just starting out. Philley had told me earlier that a repossession was to be avoided at all costs, the reason being that the repossessed item usually turned out to be worthless. When a man saw that he couldn't keep up payments on his television set, or refrigerator, or bedroom suite, and was therefore going to lose it along with all the money he had thus far paid in on it, he almost invariably entered his own little criticism of the system by demolishing whatever it was that was about to be taken away. (The logic of this still seems to me impeccable.) So if you were in the finance business, you threatened, you cajoled, you negotiated, you allowed for every kind of slackness, you stood ready to be called Jew-bastard (whether, I suppose, you were in fact Jewish or not)—and despite all this, in many cases in the end someone like the Fat Man would have to drag the sheets, blanket, and rope out of the back of his car and haul a television console with a smashed picture window and cigarette burns all over the cabinet down three flights of stairs. Not a very clean business, but profits were high.

The plan for the day was to begin on the South Side, making the first collections in black neighborhoods, then work our way back north. For

the most part, the collections were fairly routine. The buildings in which
we made them were almost uniformly dilapidated, with only minor variations in decay. In one the mail boxes swung loose, sprung from their
hinges. In a number of others not very witty graffiti—"Henrys Mother
Sucks"—adorned the walls. Stairway carpets, where they existed, were
threadbare. Hallways stank of urine, vomit, cooking odors. Behind doors
dogs barked, men and women argued, babies cried. An occasional apartment still had a *mezuzah* nailed to its door-jamb, the remnant of previous occupants in these hand-me-down buildings.

The Fat Man knocked on the doors of his accounts with meaty authority. Our first call brought a young mulatto woman to the door in her
nightgown, a child at her breast. A few calls later a large black man who
looked to be in his mid-thirties shoved a five-dollar bill into the Fat Man's
hand and, without a word or a look at any of our faces, slammed the door.
Later in the morning an elderly woman who didn't have that week's payment came on overly friendly, asking, with what she must have thought
was great con, if we'd care to come in for a bite of breakfast. Some of
the Fat Man's accounts had their payments when they came to the door,
some went back into their apartments to get the money, some didn't have
their payments but assured the Fat Man they would get some money to
him the following week, and some didn't have the payment and chose to
make no excuses about it. The Fat Man, meanwhile, gave pretty much
what he got: he returned friendliness with friendliness, con with con,
surliness with surliness. After each call he made a check mark on a 5" x
7"pink card.

Since it took a lot out of the Fat Man to climb so many stairs, that
morning Philley and I handled the accounts who lived in third-floor
apartments, leaving the Fat Man to wait in the car. In one apartment five
men were sitting around watching a baseball game on a television set for
which we had come to collect a payment. The account, a flat-featured,
very black man in his forties named Leroy Green, had missed his last
two payments and he now informed Philley that he didn't have a payment this week either. He said so without any apparent anger or anxiety;
in fact, he never really took his eyes off the ball game. Nor did the other
men in the room look away from the game.

"Hell, Mr. Green," Philley said, "that's OK. Frankly, just between the two of us, I personally don't give a damn if you ever pay another penny on that set. My problem, though, is that I've got that prick of a boss on my back. That's a mean son-of-a-bitch, man, you better believe it."

I thought of Mr. Goldman, a tall, slightly stooped man, very gentle in manner, who had a sly sense of humor and kindly eyes.

"When I get back to the office today," Philley continued, "I know exactly what he's going to say. He's going to tell me, screw that Leroy Green. He misses one more payment, you pull the television set out of his apartment. Let him stare at the walls."

Green seemed unmoved, a little bored even. He wanted only to get back to his friends and the game. I vaguely wondered what restrained this roomful of black men from pitching the two of us out of the window. Green finally mumbled something about trying to have next week's payment; and as we were leaving, Philley, putting on the finishing touch, remarked on the high quality of the television set's reception, comparing it favorably with his own, a last indirect reminder of what a shame it would be to have it repossessed.

WE HAD LUNCH THAT DAY at a restaurant on the West Side called Little Jack's. Chopped liver, chicken soup with *kreplach*, rolls and rye bread and pickles and sour tomatoes. Philley and I each ordered a corned-beef sandwich, but the Fat Man told the waitress to make it two sandwiches each and better add a side of fries. For himself, he ate everything we did, only more; instead of the corned beef he had an entire flounder served with a small mountain of mixed vegetables and flanked by two baked potatoes. The house specialty at Little Jack's was cheese cake. After we had crammed down a huge wedge, the Fat Man asked, "How's about a second hunk, boys?" He was clearly disappointed when Philley and I each said no, we couldn't handle another piece. "Never know when you'll be back this way again," he said. "Fact is, you owe it to yourself to have a second piece," and then to keep his own books clear he ordered another for himself, which he washed down with his third bottle of soda.

After lunch the Fat Man parked the Plymouth in front of a one-story frame house on Carroll Avenue, the only residence on a block otherwise made up of small factories. He banged on the door, which at first opened only partially, held back by a chain lock. "Why, it's the fat boy himself," said a small yellowish woman in an apron, wrinkled and in her fifties, who stood in the doorway. "How you making it, tons of fun?"

"Just barely, Gert, just barely," the Fat Man said.

Philley and I followed him inside, past a small foyer into a cluttered room. The room had, among other things, a lunch counter and six rather beat-up high stools. Behind the counter was a double hot-plate and a shelf stocked with seven or eight cans of Campbell soups and a few packages of breakfast cereals. A menu listing three or four sandwiches along with a meat-loaf plate was scribbled on a cracked blackboard resting on the shelf. A man in a pair of Army surplus coveralls sat at the counter drinking a cup of coffee and watching cartoons on an old television set perched on a stand high in a corner behind the counter; he probably worked at one of the factories in the neighborhood.

"Can I fix you boys something to eat?" Gert asked.

"To tell the truth, Gert," the Fat Man said, "the boys here are a little more interested in what you got in the back."

The man at the counter was leaving, and Gert excused herself to take his money. After paying, he said: "Say, Gert, can you take care of this for me?" He slipped a traffic ticket out of his wallet.

"Sure can, honey. No big deal." Gert took the ticket, unfolded it, and put it in a cigar box with a number of others. "My man comes in to pick these up on Monday. Whatever it comes to, you pay me later." She followed the man to the door and locked it behind him.

"Now," she said, speaking to the Fat Man, "I believe you said something about these boys' interest in what's out back. How's about yourself today, fatso?"

"Shit, Gert," the Fat Man said, "you know I make it a rule never to pay for it." They both laughed.

In the next room two women in housedresses sat on a couch whose stuffing was coming out of the arms and back. One woman was short, on the chubby side, and light skinned. The other, who was filing her nails, was large and very dark. Neither was young or attractive. Philley left with the shorter woman, and I followed the other one into a small room off to the right. After we had settled on price and she had checked me for disease, she slipped off her housedress and eased herself onto the bed. I had just removed my windbreaker and kicked off my shoes when she said: "No need to take off that sweater or your socks, sugar." The whole business was over with very quickly.

P ROSTITUTES WERE NOTHING NEW TO US. My own first venture was at fifteen, which set no records for precocity. The woman's name was Leona. She was truly striking, biracial, what the sporting crowd in those days called a high yellow, the ex-wife of a fighter who, for a few brief moments in his life, was light-heavyweight champ of the world and who, while still not yet forty, was stabbed to death in the Sutherland Lounge on Chicago's South Side. The walls of Leona's apartment were painted black and Chinese red; the ceiling of her bedroom was mirrored. Professionally she executed a stunt called "around the world," which, combined with her good looks, brought her in a brisk business. She drove around the South Side in a new maroon Lincoln convertible. In her bathroom a burnt spoon, a needle, and a syringe lay on a shelf above the toilet.

The lush air of corruption surrounding women like Leona was always at least as enticing as the sex, which in fact tended to be quick and, to put it mildly, perfunctory. ("Wham, bam, thank you ma'am"—an old Chicago whoremonger's expression.) In running off to hookers as early as we did we sought, certainly at least as much as any kind of sexual relief, emulation. Whom were we emulating? Not our fathers, not any one person, not even any particular group of people, but rather what we loosely though confidently took to be a Chicago style of manhood. To go to hookers, to have a bookie, to know someone with proven Syndicate connections—this was to partake of the finest Chicago had to offer.

There was also the sheer fun of it. Trips of fifty or sixty miles to the cathouses of Braidwood or Kankakee, Illinois, were for us great communal events, and we went off on them the way I suppose other high-school kids went off to a state high-school basketball tournament. Five or six of us would pile into one of our father's cars for the big drive out. On the way we would laugh, sing, tease any novice who might be along—

"Whatever you do, Danny, don't let her get her legs outside of yours"—
and on the way back lie a little about the action with the girls, who usually had names like Rusty, or Bobby, or Pam. The highlight of these trips
came on the drive back. On a turn on the Outer Drive we passed a large
neon sign—since taken down—which blinked, "Dad's Old-Fashioned
Root Beer, Have You Had It Lately." A very big laugh line, this.

It was on one of these trips that I first got to know Jeremy Levy. He
was a year and a half older than I, an excellent athlete with an enviable
reputation as a gambler as well as a number of unusual sexual adventures
to his credit. One of the stories about Jeremy was set in Miami Beach.
While down there on vacation, this story went, an uncle and three of his
uncle's friends offered Jeremy a hundred dollars apiece if he would throw
himself in with two lesbians who were performing for private parties in
a suite at the Saxony Hotel. Jeremy collected the money. When I got to
know him better, I never asked him to authenticate the story. Yet I found
no reason to doubt its truth.

Jeremy's father was a millionaire. He had made his money over a very
few years in the home-improvements business—a hustler's operation,
borax all the way. It was a business so lucrative that many of his salesmen
were making (this was in the middle fifties) a thousand or twelve hundred
dollars a week. Jeremy's father, a sport, would fly back and forth between
two distant cities to attend all the games of the World Series. It was not at
all unusual for him to bet ten grand on a welterweight fight in, say, Phila-
delphia, fly out to watch it, and return to Chicago that same night. He
kept odd hours, and I never saw very much of him, but you didn't have to
to know that he was a man with no small talk. He was lean and tall, bald,
with a thin mustache, a hooked nose, and dark, cheerless eyes.

Jeremy looked more like his mother. He was small (around 5′5″), almost
dainty, fair, though with dark hair, and had clean straight features inclin-
ing slightly toward the delicate. Like his mother, he was good-looking in a
soft, toned-down way. With his mother's manner and looks and his father's
mind and heart, Jeremy was doubly dangerous. In the murky waters of Chicago corruption, he swam effortlessly. He was the only person I've ever seen
who looked absolutely at home in a whorehouse. Through his father's connections, he had tickets to everything: Bear games, Cub games, Blackhawk

games, all fights, musical comedies, a box at both tracks, memberships in both a town and a country club, free rein with charge accounts at stores and restaurants. His cash was unlimited. On one particular afternoon I saw him blow $400 at Arlington Race Track and then return that night to the trotters at Maywood and win $600. He had of course his own car—a red and white Olds convertible, the current year's model. Yet with all that his parents gave him, it never occurred to me to think of Jeremy as in any way spoiled, or as the son of a rich man. The reason was that I was sure that even if his parents had nothing to give him, Jeremy would still have gotten whatever he wanted. He was too intelligent, too single-minded in his desires, to be denied. In this world he was a guest, a taker, a winner born and bred, with a quiet though abiding love of putting it to his fellow man.

J EREMY'S FRIENDSHIP WITH ME, at least at its beginning, involved the purest calculation on his part. Not long before he had taken up with me, he began dating a girl in my year at school named Sharon Levenson. Sharon was one of the most popular girls in the school. There was about her a certain vulnerability, a quality of fragility, that evidently made all males want to protect her. My own feeling toward her at any rate was protective, and I recall feeling not at all good about learning that she was going out with Jeremy Levy.

Yet it was in connection with Sharon that Jeremy enlisted my friendship. With all his other action, Jeremy had not expended much effort on girls, certainly not on girls of Sharon Levenson's kind, and now that he had started dating Sharon he was setting up a full-court press to win over her and her entire family. My place in this campaign was to be fixed up with Sharon's younger sister, Roberta, who, Jeremy told me, had a crush on me. Not only did he arrange a date between Roberta and me, but he saw to it that on this first date he and Sharon doubled with us. His style with Sharon that evening was husbandly, with her sister and me almost fatherly. We saw Sarah Vaughan on stage at the Chicago Theater and afterward ate at Miller's Steak House in West Rogers Park, where Jeremy signed for the bill. We dropped the girls off at about one o'clock, and then took off to a poker game already in progress on Lake Shore Drive.

A word here on our attitude toward girls. Girls for us were of two kinds, nice and not-nice, and in either instance certainly never of primary importance. The nice girls, as a local hustler once remarked to me, you had to be a genius to lay. Besides, our criterion for a nice girl was not merely that she be sexually almost unapproachable, but that, should she be approachable, she should be sexually awkward. I remember a friend of those years once describing in fairly intricate detail what seemed to him a scene of special horror. It went something like this: it is your wedding night, and you are about to consummate your marriage to a girl you had all along thought good and pure and sweet and innocent. You kiss, she says oh darling, then disappears under the sheets to perpetrate something Byzantine on you. There it was: one's wife ought in all decency to be neither good at nor remotely interested in sex. Sex and the kind of girls one thought of marrying were separate subjects. Grand little mobster that I was, I once joined three friends at the apartment of a hillbilly hooker on the Near North Side before taking a "nice" girl to a dance.

Jeremy thought along the same lines as the rest of us on this subject. It would be making him out a harder number than he was to say that he planned his relationship with Sharon to turn out as it did. At the outset, I think he cared a great deal about her, and cared even more about the idea of her being his girl. Perhaps his campaign to win her over succeeded beyond his own expectations, for before long he took me into his confidence by telling me that he and Sharon had begun to sleep together. I felt no envy at this piece of news, but I would be lying if I said it didn't somehow pain me. And apparently Jeremy himself felt at first somewhat queasy about the whole business. He told me later that he went to his uncle, his father's younger brother, to ask his advice about it. The advice he got was that if he didn't screw this broad someone else would. The queasiness disappeared.

In its place appeared a firm determination to get the most out of what he had. Jeremy now played at being the husband with even greater intensity. He was always leaving Sharon his car. During the week he would take her out to the track, to the fights, to ballgames. Weekends there were musicals, nightclubs, movies. Sundays, while his parents were at their country club, he and Sharon spent all day at his house. A very different tone entered his accounts of their sexual adventures. Where earlier he seemed to be telling me what they had done together in order to signify her love for him, now his stories were told with a fiercely cynical pride, such as one of his father's salesmen might adopt to tell how he had sold screens and awnings to a family of Eskimos. I suspect I must not have been sufficiently enthusiastic about these tales of conquest, because now Jeremy began telling them to me with a certain persistence, filling me in on more details than I cared to hear. Jeremy now regarded her with the easy contempt with which in Chicago any loser is regarded. Perhaps she had been a disappointment to him. Sweet, pure, innocent Sharon—she was Jeremy's final proof that all the world was, if not corrupt, corruptible.

NOT QUITE FINAL, though, for Jeremy evidently felt this particular theorem still needed notarizing and, though I did not yet know it, I had been chosen to serve as notary public. We were watching a baseball game one Saturday afternoon on television in his parents' richly finished basement, when Jeremy suggested that I stay for dinner and after that watch Sharon and him make love. It would be very simple, as he saw it, practically no chance of being caught. I would wait in a closet behind the bar in the basement; he would bring Sharon down, ostensibly to watch television, though of course to do what they always wound up doing. Once they had gotten down to business, I could slip out of the closet to station myself behind the bar, from where, in a crouching position, I could watch the whole thing.

Jeremy began emptying out the closet to make room for me. I would of course have to be very quiet, he said, pitching out galoshes, raincoats, and odd sports equipment. He had clearly been planning this escapade for some time. I was not especially shocked or disgusted by what he proposed; the voyeur in me was even slightly attracted. But I decided finally to refuse to go along because I somehow sensed that my position in that closet would be much more compromising than Sharon's beneath Jeremy on the basement couch. When I told Jeremy I had other plans for the evening that I really couldn't get out of, he wasn't pleased.

In the fall Jeremy went away to the University of Florida. He called me when he came home for Thanksgiving holidays and I saw him once during

Christmas vacation, but before the year was out we had lost touch. In later years I would sometimes see him at a basketball game at Chicago Stadium or at the Amphitheater, but we no longer had much to say to each other. Every so often a friend would report that he had seen him. His father had in the meantime become involved in a scandal that held the front pages of the Chicago papers for better than a week. He was called before a number of Senate subcommittees, and at one point was sought simultaneously by both the FBI and the Syndicate. The scandal had broken Mr. Levy, and the last I heard he had lost his business and was reduced to managing an apartment building on Sheridan Road. The official line on Jeremy was that he was selling insurance. Then one day in a middle-of-the-paper story in the *Chicago Sun-Times*, one of those stories to which in Chicago there is invariably no follow-up, I read about a raid on a North Side bookie joint whose weekly handle was estimated at seventy-five grand. The police and for good measure the FBI were looking for the three men who ran it, one of whom was identified in the story as Jeremy Levy. About six weeks later a friend of mine, out for the day with his daughter at Lincoln Park Zoo, bumped into Jeremy, who was there with his young son. He was looking very well, my friend said, and claimed to be finally gaining a foothold in the insurance business.

I shall always be grateful to Jeremy, as I shall be to growing up in Chicago, for teaching me many valuable things and, valuably, teaching them to me early in life. Because of Chicago, that is, certain kinds of knowledge came quickly: that men are attracted to power in all its forms and much less respectful of its uses than of its attainment; that with only the slightest encouragement men are ready to give vent to extraordinary viciousness; that, finally, there is nothing very original about sin. These conclusions, so startling to others when they stumble upon them in their maturity, were the A-B-Cs of growing up in Chicago. If one were immersed deeply enough in the life of the city they were likely to seem the whole alphabet. But if, with a bit of luck, one was able to rise a few inches above Chicago without losing sight of its lessons, then what a different look the world takes on: how extraordinary goodness seems and how exhilarating to come upon a simple act of decency!

Memoirs of a Fraternity Man

(1971)

I NOT LONG AGO LEARNED that my college fraternity, Phi Epsilon Pi, has become defunct, its chapters all over America having closed their doors and locked them for good, and I found myself unexpectedly sad at the news. I say "unexpectedly" because, insofar as I have thought about them at all, I rather disliked fraternities in general and my own in particular I was sure I despised. Fourteen years ago, at the end of my freshman year at the University of Illinois, I moved out of Phi Ep (Psi Chapter) at the first opportunity and into an apartment. Not long afterward I was to leave the University of Illinois, at which point I lost all interest in fraternities. A few years ago, however, I happened to mention to a very perceptive woman that I had spent a year at the University of Illinois and belonged to a fraternity there. "Don't tell me which one," she said, "I'll bet I can guess. You were a Phi Ep, one of the elite effete." Appallingly correct! Appalling because of all the various views I have of myself—and their range is extravagant—that of a fraternity man is perhaps least prominent of all. Phi Epsilon Pi is now dead. Its song is over but the melody lingers on—apparently even in me.

The song itself began fifteen winters ago at Chicago's 12th Street Illinois Central Railway Station, where, as a mid-year graduate of a Chicago public high school, I was setting off to college. The decision to go "downstate," as the University of Illinois campus in the dismal twin-cities of Champaign and Urbana is still called, was an utterly conventional one. At that time of smaller college enrollments, the state university had to take anyone who had a high-school diploma, but in fact many people who finished well in the upper reaches of their high-school graduating classes went to the University of Illinois anyhow. For many of us, most of whose parents had not themselves gone to college, the University of Illinois was about as far as our horizons extended. Going to college was not then—though it was fast becoming—the automatic business it now is for the majority of the children of the middle class. It was a matter still in the realm of decision, and while I and almost all my friends chose to go, we did so with the greatest possible seriousness. To demonstrate that seriousness most of us chose the glummest of majors: accounting, marketing, economics. I myself could not go quite that far, but I was not above the need to establish my purposefulness, which I did by informing my relatives and parents' friends that I was going downstate to study something called "pre-law."

Implicit in the decision to go downstate to college was the decision to join a fraternity. To do otherwise was very nearly unthinkable. The University of Illinois was then one of the largest and most active "Greek" campuses in the country. Fraternities and sororities not merely abounded but gave the place its tone, coloration, and (finally) character. To choose not to join a fraternity, to live instead as an "independent," was, at the University of Illinois, to cut oneself off on almost every level: socially, academically, even gastronomically—to consign oneself to a life as lonely, colorless, and sterile as the single piece of bologna that went into the sandwiches served for lunch at the men's independent dorms.

There were, of course, a great many independents at the University of Illinois, though I suspect that in the vast majority of cases their independence was enforced by financial limitations, by social inadequacies, by simple discrimination against them on the part of fraternities and sororities. I was not myself independent by temperament nor did I have independence thrust upon me in any of these negative ways. My father, a successful businessman, had made clear that he would pay every cent involved in my education, and he was not about to boggle at the extra cost of a fraternity for his son. Having gone to an intensely social high school, one so divided off into scores of clubs, fraternities, and sororities as to make it almost a mini-University of Illinois, I suffered none of the social awkwardness, or inexperience, that might have kept me out of a college fraternity.

Still, not one to take chances, as the train pulled out of the 12th Street Station for Champaign, I was dressed for approval. Consider the outfit: a brown Harris tweed jacket, a maroon cashmere sweater, a careful rep tie over a white button-down oxford cloth shirt, Cambridge gray trousers with a small buckle in the back, and plain-toed cordovan shoes. The semester before a good friend of mine had been blackballed from a leading Jewish fraternity at the University of Michigan for, among other things, or so I thought, his rather individual style of dress, which included a penchant for white sweat socks and box-car loafers. My own socks were black and rode high up on the calf.

Virtually all fraternities were, of course, segregated by religion or social class, and within each group there were fairly rigid hierarchies of status. Phi Ep was one of the elite Jewish fraternities. Its scholastic rating was high, its record in intramural sports was excellent, and its showings in Stunt Show (the campus musical-comedy competition), Spring Carnival, and other university events were superior. But in larger part, the fraternity's status derived from the social background of its membership, or rather from that of a handful of its members. The collective identity of some fraternities might be based on a single member, usually an athlete. Around this time, for example, Sigma Chi seemed to be totally epitomized in the person of Hiles Stout, a football player from Peoria, Illinois. Stout *was* Sigma Chi: small-town, blond crew-cut, burly, something less than highly cerebral. Phi Ep was not so conveniently summed up in one person. But the typical member would have come from the Chicago area, probably either from one of the more prosperous Jewish suburbs to the north or Lake Shore Drive. He would be slender, well-turned-out—his principal source of haberdashery being Brooks Brothers—and with hair worn short and parted to one side, in the style then known as the "Princeton." While his father probably made his money working for someone else, or had a small business of his own, he himself would be headed for the professions—medicine, law, dentistry, or accountancy. There would be a self-assurance about him, a casualness that came from a sense of being at ease in the world. And the truth is, he really was at ease in the world; he knew where he wanted to go and he knew precisely how to get there.

The Phi Eps admired few things more than casualness, the difficult trick made to look easy, the conventional move stylishly executed. So, in those days, did I. Although I never seriously considered pledging any other fraternity, and although I was flattered by the hard rush they put on me, as a matter of form I showed some hesitation about accepting their pledge pin.

THERE WERE TWELVE OF US IN ALL in the pledge class that year and for the most part we were a fairly similar lot; or at any rate most of us dressed and talked roughly alike and seemed to share roughly similar values. Most of us, but not all. The twelfth member of the pledge class, Marv Schmidt, was another story. His clothes were wrong, his style was wrong, he really didn't, as the saying went, "quite fit in." Schmidt was an engineering student, and the reason, the sole reason, he was asked to pledge Phi Ep was that one of the members, an upper classman from a small town in Arkansas who also studied engineering, wanted an engineer for the pledge class and was able to prevail. But Schmidt excepted, we were the pick of the pack, the best there was, the most intensely sought after candidates for the Jewish fraternities to come downstate in February of 1955, and there was pride in that.

Once settled in, pledging was not as irksome as I feared it might be. Unlike most of the other fraternities on campus, the Phi Eps did not paddle their pledges—a sign of their superior civility? But at least one pledge was assigned to each table in the dining room and we were all instructed in a rigid set of table manners: knife placed across upper right portion of plate, blade turned in; all food both passed and received across the body, and so forth. Five nights a week we were herded back into the dining room at seven-thirty for study hours, which lasted till ten. Each morning two of us were assigned wake-call, which involved waking the members—gently, oh, ever so gently—for their morning classes. After lunch and often after classes we ran errands: picking up members' laundry or dropping it off, fetching a book from the library, buying a packet of envelopes, or picking up clothes from the dry cleaner's. Saturday mornings we did a general housecleaning.

Although pledges slept in a common dormitory on the top floor of the fraternity house, each of us was also assigned to a member's room, where we kept our clothes and books. I drew Sidney Straus. Sidney was the son of a multimillionaire, a self-made man who owned, along with other holdings, what was then the premiere hotel in Miami Beach and a controlling interest in one of Chicago's major banks. "I'm glad you're going to be my roommate," Sidney said when I arrived at his room with my books and suitcases. "I was worried I'd get that German kid, Schmitz, or whatever his goddamn name is." Sidney proved an amiable roommate, being, as it turned out, rarely there. A graduating senior, engaged and soon to be married, he seemed to spend most of his time aloft in airplanes, carrying out obscure, though clearly not petty, errands for his father's various businesses. Within less than ten years, he would be president of his father's bank in Chicago. From photographs that appeared from time to time in the Chicago press, he seemed not to age at all—at thirty-five, as at twenty-one, he still looked fifty-four. Short, pudgy, already nearly bald in his last year at college, it was as if the fates, in endowing Sidney so well financially, had exacted his youth in exchange.

But then nearly all the seniors among the Phi Eps seemed almost excessively mature. A kind of heavy seriousness, thick with sobriety, was the model not merely aspired to but generally achieved. The Phi Ep seniors *were* older men, and though only just past adolescence touched with the gift—curse?—of perpetual early middle age. Harold Goldberg, the president of Phi Ep at that time, had all the playfulness of a member of the President's Council of Economic Advisers. Dark and extremely earnest, he wore the same sweaters and washpants that everyone else did during the week, but never seemed quite convincing in them. It was only in a suit, and at that rather a severe business suit, that he looked at home and really comfortable.

Once I began living at the fraternity, it began to take on a different, more variegated, less idealized, look. A common fraternity phenomenon in those days was "the closet case," a member who had either been left as a legacy from some Phi Ep older brother or who simply represented a mistake in judgment, a lapse of discrimination. These unfortunates were asked not to show up at certain important occasions—rush weeks, big dances, exchanges with prestigious sororities. Phi Ep had no formal closet cases, though it did have a number of members whom it chose not to feature too prominently. These ranged from Bernie ("The Animal") Lefkovitz to Kenny Gaynor. I liked The Animal from the start: hairy, rough, he was what he was, with no airs about him. Kenny Gaynor was something else again—a fop of such extraordinary dimension, a character so clearly made of cardboard, that he would be unbelievable in the pages of a novel. Soon after I had unpacked my things in Sidney Straus's room, Kenny came by to inspect my ties, which hung on a rack against the door. "Not bad at all," he commented with gravity. "You should see Schmidt's." And here he made a face—a wrinkling of the nose, a puckering of the mouth—appropriate to the swallowing of some small vile animal. My own foulards, challis, reps, I should gauge, rated from him somewhere between a C+ and a B-.

PHI EP ALSO HAD A NUMBER OF MEMBERS who did not come from Chicago, and were known as the "out-of-towners." There were not many such members, at most they comprised perhaps 15 per cent of the total, and in general they tended to fall a cut below the Phi Eps who came from Chicago. They were from such places as Paragould (Arkansas), Minneapolis, and Memphis; from as far away as New York City and from as nearby as the Illinois towns of Springfield, Mattoon, and Peoria. The out-of-towners were thought of as having a special cachet for the fraternity; they made it seem somehow less parochial. Since no one knew very much about them, they seemed, most of them, bringing along rather extravagant pasts. The members from Paragould and Memphis, for example, were said to have been all-state football players in Arkansas and Tennessee. One member from New York—he was in the pledge class preceding mine—claimed to have been offered a bonus to pitch for a major-league baseball team as well as to have scored higher than anyone else in the history of certain Regents' exams. He was a liar of such magnitude, such purity, such transparency, that one had to strain really to dislike him. Although a pre-med student, he took great pains never to be caught studying, but would announce the highest grades nonethe-less. He would return from the simplest coffee date or movie with his face covered with lipstick in a kind of Jackson Pollock effect. Phi Ep in fact was loaded with pre-meds, and on the whole they were a dreary lot. The pressure of getting into medical school showed badly on all of them. Having to bend themselves to this single purpose so early in life, they quickly grew dull, and some of them mean.

So far as cultural interests were concerned, there was bridge and there was musical comedy, especially musical comedy. In those days a madness for musical comedy was common not merely in Phi Ep but in the Mid-west generally. I used to think it a Jewish phenomenon, but in fact it was more widespread, touching, at one time or another, almost every one of the middle class. Hard-eyed businessmen, Mafiosi, crushing moth-ers—all were enormous suckers for a musical. It was not unusual for the well-to-do in Chicago to take a week or two off for a trip to New York, and see nine or ten musical comedies in a row. Men in the used-car, finance, or steel business, men otherwise without the least grain of sentimentality, would sit there with their wives, eyes wide, jaws slack, entranced, as boys and girls traipsed across the stage shrieking "Pajama Game! Pajama Game!" Then they would see the same shows, or at least the more successful of them, again when their road companies came through Chicago, and comment on the relative merits of the two differ-ent casts. Then they would buy the albums, which they listened to over and over again.

Phi Ep's zeal for musical comedy was of a piece with all this. For our pledge dance, we did an elaborate revue called "New Faces of 58.50" which we worked on for about six weeks, honing our thin parodies of the origi-nal New Faces songs into bland perfection. But this was as nothing com-pared to the fraternity's effort for Stunt Show. For this production, Phi Ep teamed up with a sorority to compete against every other fraternity and sorority on campus for the best performance of a musical-comedy routine. Although the competition did not take place until late in the fall, rehearsals got started the previous summer. Once the school year began, those Phi Eps involved in the show would troop over to our part-ner sorority every night for further rehearsals. As the competition drew closer, weekends, too, were taken up with rehearsals. No matter which sorority was involved, Phi Ep invariably made the finals.

More was at stake, it soon became clear, than the Stunt Show competition itself. The hope was to win the damn thing so that the following year Phi Ep could have as its partner one of the great Wright Street sorority houses. Wright Street faced the campus, and lining it were the sororities of Kappa Alpha Theta, Pi Beta Phi, and Kappa Kappa Gamma, all of them prestigious and none of them Jewish. The plan at Phi Ep, though it was never worked out in a dank basement on a pool table under a bare light bulb, was to sing and dance its way into the heart of America, or—what was much the same thing—into the living room of the Theta house.

In case I make myself sound superior to all this, I should emphasize that I was as good and obedient a pledge as any of my pledge brothers and no less strenuously wished to become a member. It was with a longing eye that I looked upon the pins and paddles and beer mugs and other accoutrements decorated with the fraternity's crest and Greek letters (supplied by the Balfour Company, Inc., makers of fraternal jewelry and accessories). Like everyone else, I did as I was told and I submitted as meekly as everyone else to the humiliations to which a pledge was subjected.

One such humiliation that stands out is the time we pledges were awakened late at night and marched down from our dormitory to the living room by Al Sampson, a member from Arkansas who was known for his rich appetite for country ribaldry. We expected the worst. The worst, which we had all heard about, was something called with brutal simplicity "The Meat," a very rude exercise having to do with getting a raw piece of steak up and down a staircase while naked and without the use of one's hands. It was a stunt calculated to bring about solidarity throughout the pledge class by humiliating each of us in precise democratic measure.

After lining us up in the living room, Sampson, with a great show of anger, began with verbal abuse. We were a terrible pledge class, he shrieked, one of the worst ever to come through the house, and he, for one, was goddamn sick of us. We would shape the hell up, fast, or answer to him. He walked down the line, blasting each of us in turn. Then he put us through calisthenics: push-ups, sit-ups, deep knee bends. Next we were told to strip. We all did so, except for Billy Schwartz. The son of a

Chicago fight promoter, Billy, though small, was a tough kid; normally even-tempered, he had a notably low tolerance for taking insults. As the rest of us stood there, vulnerable in our nakedness, Billy announced that he didn't care what happened, he wasn't about to take his pajamas off. Sampson went red in the face. He said he was going to leave the room for ten minutes, during which time the rest of us had better convince our pledge brother to strip. If we failed to do so, he could promise us that our lives in Phi Ep would be made more miserable than any of us would care to contemplate. Ten minutes later Sampson returned to find us, Billy included, unanimously naked.

Part of being in Phi Ep, or for that matter in any fraternity, involved going along with the game—and this included members as well as pledges. Lenny Klein, an upper-classman, was large and lumbering. At twenty-one he had an old man's mind inside a middle-aged man's body. He was the son of a rich man who had extensive holdings in real estate in Chicago. Less conservative by choice than tired by temperament, he never made a move of any kind without first elaborately plotting it out. Yet even Klein, surely the least romantic of figures, when he became pinned—and to become "pinned" in those days meant one was engaged to be engaged— went through the traditional "pinning serenade" like everyone else in the fraternity. Standing in front of the Alpha Epsilon Phi sorority house across the street from Phi Ep, Klein stepped out before the rest of us, and in a voice more appropriate to the reading of a personal bankruptcy statement, sang about how Gibraltar might crumble and the Rockies might tumble but his love was here to stay.

As the semester wore on toward final week, pledging eased up, and everyone began concentrating on grades. One night we pledges were called into the regular Monday night fraternity meeting for a bull session in which each of us was told, singly, of our inadequacies, of how disappointingly we had turned out, of how far short we had fallen of the Phi Ep measure. The week before finals we went through our last ordained ritual of this period, singling out the member who had been hardest on us as pledges throughout the semester. One evening before dinner we grabbed our man, dragged him out behind the house, tied him up, and dumped pancake syrup, sand, and feathers on him, as the rest of the Phi

Eps looked on. Then came the week of final exams, after which we all, members and pledges, left the campus for the summer.

THE FALL RUSH at the start of the following semester was, of course, much more hectic than the winter one had been, and the traffic of potential pledges coming through Phi Ep was thick. The fraternity pretty much knew which incoming freshmen it wanted from Chicago, though it was still sitting in judgment on certain marginal types and kept on the lookout for out-of-town freshmen that no one had any line on. The rushees came in regular sessions: some remarkably confident and poised, others nervous in their eagerness to please. They were met by the Phi Eps in the foyer of the house, walked into the living room, shown through the upstairs floors. But all the while, it was they, not Phi Ep, who were on display.

The evenings of rush week were devoted to blackballing sessions— or "spot" meetings, as they were called, for the word "blackball" was never used. At these meetings it was decided who would be offered a bid to pledge and who would not. The meetings ran well into the night, sometimes breaking up at three or four in the morning. As might be imagined, some very fancy talk was involved, with everyone putting the finest possible point on everything he said. "I don't wish to reiterate what Mickey Schwartz just finished saying," a representative comment might run, "but it seems to me this kid is, on balance, hardly Phi Ep material." Which was of course just another way of saying what was apparent to all but could not be said straight out: that a rushee was too ugly, too garishly dressed, too aggressive, too shy, too broken out, too "Jewish," or too something else which put him beyond the Phi Ep pale. Kids were rejected for much the same reasons that I and almost everyone else who sat in on these meetings had rejected the other fraternities on campus to pledge Phi Ep. There was very little subtlety about the procedure—one either approximated the Phi Ep mold or fell hopelessly, irretrievably, short of it.

That rush week presented only one noteworthy incident, which involved the blackballing of a "legacy." This particular candidate wasn't, strictly speaking, in that category—technically, to be a legacy either one's father or older brother or brothers had to have been a member. His brother-in-law, however, was a Phi Ep who had graduated about three years before and some of the upper-classmen present at the meeting had known him. At one point, one of them telephoned the brother-in-law in Chicago, then returned to announce that he would be driving down that night—such was the urgency of the matter—to talk on behalf of the blackballed rushee, his wife's younger brother. The major claim against the candidate seemed to be an insufficiency of distinctly admirable qualities. The opposition would take the floor and ceaselessly reiterate, "I don't wish to reiterate, but this kid doesn't show me anything." Finally, sometime around three in the morning, the brother-in-law arrived. Dark, with a close-cropped haircut, and wearing a light blue cashmere sweater over a white button-down collar shirt, he was still vintage Phi Ep. After being introduced to the meeting at large, he spoke of his young brother-in-law's eagerness to be a Phi Ep. If he were not asked to pledge the fraternity, he said, he very probably would not remain downstate for more than a semester. He had chosen to come to school here precisely because of Phi Ep. He was exactly the sort of kid that Phi Ep could make a man of, which after all was one of the things the fraternity was about. Everything, in short, was brought up but the main point: the kid would be unthinkable if he were not a legacy; but, goddamn it, he *was* a legacy, at least almost! At the next vote, taken while his brother-in-law was out of the room, it was decided that the bid would be extended after all. Tradition had held, and we all shuffled off to bed.

A few weeks after the pledge class of '59 had been assembled and school had gotten underway, my own pledge class was awakened late one night and told that we were on "hell week." During the seven days that followed we got almost no sleep, we were made to wear a suit and tie to class, and were allowed out of our suits only to get into work clothes suitable for executing our hell-week project: building a restraining wall roughly three feet high and seventy or so feet long behind the fraternity house. When we were not either in class or working on the wall, we were locked into various rooms, sometimes separately, sometimes together, where we were left to study a small, maroon leather-bound book containing the fraternity's history. At odd hours throughout the week we were arbitrarily shifted about from room to room; we were shouted at, rather than talked to; members who had been friendly now froze us out. The week droned on, dreary and wearying.

EARLY SUNDAY MORNING, at the end of the week, our initiation was at hand. Phi Ep's ceremony was not, as I have since learned, as elaborate as that of other fraternities, or especially of some sororities, where incoming members were said to have been moved by the ritual to the point of tears. At Phi Ep we were brought down to the living room one-by-one, blindfolded. When the blindfold was removed, we found ourselves in a candlelit room with all the curtains drawn. There, as each of my pledge brothers would do, and as every member in that room had done before me, I was put through the litany of Phi Ep's history. I was asked to name its founding members, to recite its historic dates and events, to reel off the names of its various chapters round the country. At the end of it I was told that I had done execrably, and then instructed to enter the chapter room, a small room off the main one which generally served as the site of all-night bridge games. Before this moment it had been exclusively off-limits to pledges.

In this privileged sanctuary the officers of the fraternity awaited me. They asked if I thought I deserved to be initiated into Phi Ep. I mumbled that I did indeed so think. They asked what I thought I could contribute to the fraternity. I mumbled some clichés about continuing its tradition, augmenting its prestige on campus, and so on. Everyone in the small room then rose to shake my hand. There remained to instruct me in the Phi Ep handshake, in the use and meaning of the password, and finally to place the fraternity's pin on my shirt. Again there were handshakes all around. As I left the chapter room to return to the living room, I was met by applause and still more handshaking.

At lunch that day, after our entire class had been initiated, there was much singing and an air of high self-congratulation. The whole bizarre business had worked, another successful rite of passage had been brought off. Exhausted, I went to bed shortly after lunch, to sleep for seventeen straight hours. Before falling off I recall feeling confidently—more confidently than I shall probably ever feel again in my life—that I had arrived.

Postscript

ND YET—IT IS A VERY LONG STORY, to be told, perhaps, another time—sooner than I or anyone else would have dreamed, I was to depart, both from the University of Illinois and from Phi Ep. For more than a decade I would have nothing further to do with Phi Ep nor it with me. Then, on a visit to Champaign, I was suddenly overtaken by curiosity to see what had become of my old fraternity. I telephoned the University's Intra-fraternity Council to get the address of Phi Ep, for I had heard that the fraternity had moved out of its large white house on Third Street. A secretary gave me an address but the house to which she sent me was locked and quite empty. Phi Ep, it turned out, had ceased its formal existence the semester before. "It was a damn good house," a young man I met in the offices of the Intra-fraternity Council at the Student Union said. "In their last year, just before folding, they won intramural sports on campus." Phi Sigma Delta, another of the Jewish fraternities, had also folded, not just on the Illinois campus but all over the country. A third Jewish fraternity, Tau Epsilon Pi (TEP) still existed, but had fallen on evil days. I remembered the TEP house as a grand and richly furnished place; now it was distinctly shabby. The piano was banged up, the furniture needed reupholstering, the whole place could have used a paint job.

When Phi Ep dissolved, a few of its members had joined other fraternities, and two of them were now in the TEP house. One came down to meet me. He was in chambray shirt and Levis, and had mutton chop sideburns connected to a thick black mustache. Nonetheless, he was still a fraternity man, for on meeting me he clasped my hand in what must certainly have been the Phi Ep handshake. He invited me up to his room where the other former Phi Ep was waiting.

Our conversation there was given over almost wholly to their unhappiness. The school, they said, was an enormous drag these days. All they seemed to do was study—or else sit around and talk about their future. As the talk continued, one of the things that emerged was their reverence for me because of the fact that I was a Phi Ep in the good old days when the fraternity was strong and being a member of it meant something. To my own eyes everybody on that campus seemed strikingly unhappy, but it's possible that as fraternity men they were even more so. For they were, quite simply and quite astonishingly to anyone who could remember back to what fraternity men had been only a few years before, out of fashion, out of phase, and entirely out of joint.

My 1950s

(1993)

I want to live in a place again where I can walk down any street
without being afraid. I want to be able to take my daughter to a
park at any time of day or night in the summertime and remember
what I used to be able to do when I was a little kid.

HILLARY RODHAM CLINTON, *New York Times Magazine*

S OCIALISM, IT USED TO BE SAID, was a system in which the past
could not be predicted. Perhaps the same has by now become true
of capitalism. The fate of the past—all pasts—is to be regularly
twisted into different, sometimes quite grotesque, shapes by people with
their own, frequently sentimental, often ideological, reasons for doing so.

This is what seems to be going on in the revisions of the 1950s. The
decade is being judged in the light of the decade that followed, and, it
will hardly surprise anyone to learn, it is either found wanting or, at best,
seen to be merely preparing the ground for glories that came afterward.
In this new reading, what some of us fondly think of as the good old days
turn out, on inspection, to be the bad old days.

What is really at stake in getting the 1950s right is a proper judgment
of the 1960s. That key decade—it ran, strictly speaking, from the Berkeley Free Speech Movement in 1965 to the end of the Watergate scandal
in 1974—remains, culturally, politically, socially, the great Rorschach test
of our times. Say what you think of the sixties—loved them, hated them,
found them a mixed bag—and you say a very great deal about yourself. But
whether they are ultimately deemed a disastrous wrong turning, a road better not taken, or a necessary liberation is a matter of no small importance.

The decade—that historical decimal system by which we categorize contemporary history—is of course a perfectly arbitrary chunk of time. Decades also happen to be chronological units that gather clichés the way a blue serge suit gathers lint. Every decade must live in history under the weight of the clichés bestowed upon it.

Let us, class, review a few of these clichés. The twenties were the Jazz Age, with flappers and Prohibition-era drinking—a sense of excitement pervaded, a good time was had by all. The thirties ushered in radical politics and unending fears about money, otherwise known as the Depression mentality. The forties don't quite figure, having been half-lost to the century's largest war, which called for a strict rationing of clichés along with meat, butter, and gasoline. The sixties were all asizzle (ah, those sizzling sixties) with idealism, political activism, and daring experiments both sexual and pharmacological. The seventies were—thanks to Tom Wolfe, who so tagged them—the Me Decade, given over to excessive self-regard and heavy-breathing narcissism. But the seventies would come to seem positively Taoist in generous spirituality next to what the *clichémeisters* have laid on the eighties, the decade of unexampled greed and vicious disregard for one's fellow man: Reaganism is the code word here. Finally, although the clichés for the nineties have not yet been posted, not to worry, they will arrive as inevitably as baby boomers will get to Golden Pond, to drop in two further clichés.

I have delayed hauling out the clichés for the fifties chiefly because I am rather touchy about them. I was thirteen when the decade began and a newly married man of twenty-three when it ended. That decade had a good deal to do with forming me, and, though I hope I do not sound smug in saying so, I consider myself lucky in the time in which I was born.

A peculiar view to hold, some would no doubt say, about the age of Senator Joseph McCarthy, of Marlon Brando and James Dean and Elvis Presley, of Marilyn Monroe, Charles Van Doren's national television swindle, the great golfer named Dwight David Eisenhower, and, let us not forget, the hula hoop. Slip on a pair of blue suede shoes, pomade and comb your hair back in a duck's ass, put "You Ain't Nothin' But a Hound Dog" on the phonograph, and we can all dance to it.

TRUE ENOUGH, McCarthy, Brando, Dean, Elvis, Van Doren, Marilyn Monroe, Eisenhower, and the hula hoop all came to prominence in the fifties. But in what sense were they central to the quotidian lives of those of us who lived through the decade? David Halberstam, in his thick book, *The Fifties*, spends many pages on these figures and many more on others less widely known, from atomic scientists to discount retailers, in his attempt to capture the decade, both in its flavor and in its character. Yet in the end, for all his efforts, he has led us on not much more than a somewhat soured nostalgia tour. He has not caught life—at least not life as I knew it—in the fifties but instead those phenomena, such as the Beat Generation of writers, that earned heavy publicity during the decade. His book brings to mind nothing so much as the English critic F. R. Leavis's pointed remark about the self-promoting poet Edith Sitwell and her brothers being no part of the history of literature but only part of the history of publicity.

If Halberstam puts something like a full-court press on the fifties, wanting to cover everything from the *I Love Lucy* show to the U-2 spyplane incident, Calvin Trillin, the *New Yorker* and *Nation* writer, in a slender book titled *Remembering Denny*, concentrates his fire on an old friend, a man named Roger D. Hansen, a college classmate of whom great things were expected and whose life he takes to be in some way symbolic of the decade. Trillin was in the same class at Yale ('57) as Hansen, who went on to Oxford as a Rhodes scholar; who seemed so completely to epitomize the wholesome glamor of the fifties that his graduation was covered by the young Michael Arlen and the photographer Alfred Eisenstaedt for *Life* magazine; and who, a few years ago, ended by committing suicide. Trillin casts about for reasons for his friend's failure and sad end—his temperament, his worldly mistakes, his late-discovered homosexuality—and finally concludes that he was a victim of the crushing fifties combination of ambition and conformity, a combination forming a "rigid notion of success" that someone at the poor man's memorial service called "silly and presumptuous."

Trillin, I believe, is wrong both about his friend and about the fifties. He does not want to recognize how devastating the discovery of homosexuality might be in a man raised on the values of Yale—values not of the 1950s but described as long ago as 1920 by George Santayana as muscular

Christianity in the service of success. It cannot have been an easy thing for a man such as Hansen, whose friends thought he would surely end no lower than the United States Senate, to discover himself in his fifties in the *Satyricon* atmosphere of a contemporary gay bar. My guess is that neither Yale nor the fifties killed Roger D. Hansen, but rather a profound mortification which Calvin Trillin, committed to the rosy view of progressivistic liberalism, cannot hope to understand.

David Halberstam, like Calvin Trillin, is a man of impressive limitations. He is a man of neither wide nor deep culture but, in fact, of newspaper culture. As such he is attracted to the fad, the trend, the gross event, above all to the journalistic cliché that can always be extracted from these things. But unless one lives one's own life in public, such items are likely to touch one only peripherally. Searching Edmund Wilson's journals for the fifties, for example, one finds a paucity of references to the decade's presidential figures and candidates—Harry Truman, Dwight David Eisenhower, and Adlai Stevenson. Only in totalitarian or truly authoritarian countries do politics so dominate lives. Quite as much to the point, perhaps, there is no entry in David Halberstam's *The Fifties* for Edmund Wilson, whose writings were one of my own great personal discoveries in the fifties.

The standard view of the fifties, which is David Halberstam's, though he does not announce it straight out, is that it was a time when idealism slept, cruel discrimination was everywhere in force, mindless affluence was in the saddle, conformity reigned, and the cold war defiled everything. Such, such caused the absence of joys. People who grew up in the fifties have been called the silent generation, implying that these things turned them away from an interest in politics. The epithet "silent generation," clearly not meant as a compliment, was later set in concrete. But what it really means is that the fifties were not a good time for left-wing politics. Whether this is the same as not being good for the country is rather a different question.

Perhaps no one grew up more isolated from politics than I and my friends in middle-class Jewish Chicago in the 1950s. As was true of many another Jewish home, our family was ardent for Franklin Delano Roosevelt; that is, my father was, while my mother, a very intelligent woman, did not find politics even an interesting distraction. My father despised Colonel Robert McCormick, publisher of the *Chicago Tribune*, for his isolationist views during World War II, and would not allow his paper in our home. As a young boy, I thought this a shame, for the *Trib* carried *Dick Tracy* and generally had much better comics than the *Daily News* or the *Sun*. Yet so passionate was my father about McCormick that once, in a snowstorm, when a *Tribune* delivery-truck driver offered to help him with a flat tire, my father, normally a well-mannered man, told him to screw off.

Because of his ardor for FDR, I always assumed my father was a Democrat for life, which is the way I started out. Some years later I was more than a little surprised to learn that he had voted not once but twice for Eisenhower. My father thought Ike was good for business and he was right, for his own small business flourished in the 1950s. Not being an intellectual—not, in fact, having gone to college—my father was not much of a sucker for style, and hence Adlai Stevenson, whom he thought a good enough man, left him a little cold.

Politics, though, was rarely discussed in our home. *Look* magazine came into our apartment, and so did *Life*, which everyone in the fifties, children and grown-ups, devoured weekly; but not *Time*. The only way we qualified as mildly ahead of our day was through early ownership of a television set, a great mother of a mahogany Philco console, with something called a cobra-arm on the accompanying phonograph. I watched my share of television, especially sports, but I was never swept up in it as I had been earlier, in the forties, by radio shows, particularly the lineup of kids' programs on weekday afternoons and Saturday mornings.

At the close of a longish life, the British social historian R. H. Tawney claimed that the only progress he had noted was in the deportment of dogs. I suppose I could add that the chief progress in my lifetime has been in the manufacture of gym shoes. Not quite true, of course; but it is true that all the progress I have known has been technical: in medicine, in engineering, in calculation and computation and communication. Rich though they are, the rewards of technology do not bring happiness or wisdom.

Quite as much has been lost, not least the sense of progress itself. A belief in progress requires a setting of stability, and stability begins in the family. Growing up in the fifties, I had no friends whose parents had played the rough trick on them of divorcing. Only one acquaintance among the kids I went to school with was in revolt against his parents (later it occurred to me that they should more properly have been in revolt against him). We respected our parents, loved them, but found them, if I may now disrespectfully say so, rather beside the point—by which I mean that they did not have all that much to do with our daily lives.

Play was not yet organized. The endless cycle of lessons and special tutoring for middle-class children had not begun in furious earnest. Little League baseball had not yet been fully formed. Children were left pretty much on their own. Far from wanting our parents hanging around, we were pleased to cut loose from them. The father of one of my acquaintances used to come to all our softball games, and was contemptuously tagged by a Latinist among us as the Omnipresent.

Not only was there no pressure on me to go to a good university, but it would have been perfectly acceptable to my parents if I had chosen not to go to university at all. ("I think you have the makings of a good salesman," I recall my father saying to me. Since he was himself a good salesman, this was a compliment.) From the age of thirteen on—after Hebrew school—I made every decision about my education on my own: what foreign languages to study, what university to go to, what to study while there.

The relationship between parents and children in the fifties had not yet taken on the heavy therapeutic freight it bears today. The therapeutic had not yet triumphed, at least not in Chicago. (It was only when I moved to New York that I came to know anyone in psychoanalysis.) Our parents— certainly, my parents—had not yet reached the stage of culture where psychotherapy seemed a serious solution to anything. When, not long ago, my mother struggled through a lingering death from liver cancer, someone suggested that she might benefit from a support group made up of other people with terminal cancer. I should never for a moment have suggested such a thing to my mother, whose response I could have perfectly predicted. "Tell my troubles to strangers?" my mother would have said. "Why would I want to do that?" As a man of the 1950s, I have to report that I not only understand but quite agree with her.

WE OF THE FIFTIES WERE NOT REBELS, with or without a cause (a damn poor fifties movie, *Rebel Without A Cause*, by the way). To be a rebel, to be in revolt, implied being locked into youthfulness. Far from wishing to stay young, we who were young in the fifties were eager to grow up. Growing up meant growing into freedom, which was the name of our desire.

I am reminded here of the English poet Philip Larkin's saying that his religious sympathies first began to wane when he discovered that in the Christian version of heaven one would become as a little child again. Staying a child was not what Larkin, or my friends and I in the fifties, had in mind at all. Like Larkin, we wanted "money, keys, wallet, letters, books, long-playing records, drinks, the opposite sex, and other solaces of adulthood." Everything in the culture of the 1950s provoked one to grow up. ("Oh, grow up," sisters would say to troublesome younger brothers.) The ideal, in the movies and in life, was adulthood.

In the fifties, one was encouraged to be adult which didn't discourage one from believing in progress and hence in the future. Since the sixties, one has been encouraged to remain young for as long as possible, and yet not many people believe in progress and the future seems terrifying. This has all the makings of a paradox, until one realizes that the difference between the two cultural injunctions is that the first comports with biological reality and the second does not. Since one cannot really hope to stay young for long, the future brings with it nothing so inexorably as the prospect of growing old, which is to say, the prospect of certain defeat.

I do not want to make the fifties seem some altogether prelapsarian time, but the subsequent decades have tended to make them look good. Even what might otherwise seem their drawbacks have come to appear as advantages. Take sex. ("We didn't," I hear a well-timed Henny Youngman-like reply from the peanut gallery.) A man of my generation who is still single reminded me not long ago that when we were young we would go into a drugstore to buy a pack of cigarettes and shamefacedly ask to be slipped a packet of prophylactics, while today the procedure is exactly the reverse. Pornography was not so plentiful. Avant-gardists among us read Henry Miller in the green-colored paperbacks published by Olympia Press in Paris, which at nineteen seemed pretty thrilling stuff. Now pornography just seems part of the general plague of decadence.

As for the real thing, sex itself, in the fifties supply never came close to meeting demand, thus in one stroke confounding the Chicago School of Economics and frustrating almost all male adolescents. All boys wanted it and no nice girls provided it. If they did they were, *ipso facto*, no longer nice girls. A character in a Willie Morris novel, referring to his adolescence in the fifties, offers belated thanks to Frank Sinatra and Nat King Cole for making possible what little sex he was able to obtain in those years. I used to make the joke, perhaps no longer quite comprehensible today, that a number of my contemporaries, after all the amorous hours they logged at drive-in movies, would need a steering wheel and gear shift installed in their conjugal beds to make the transition from adolescence to married life.

Up-to-the-moment psychological thinking would no doubt say that all this repression could not have been other than distinctly unhealthy. The invention of the Pill, as everyone knows, allowed an easing-up of the rules in the sex game, though AIDS and other snakes in the field would soon bring players, badly shaken, back to the locker room. But even before AIDS, more sex did not seem to bring about more happiness, if happiness can be measured like the GNP. The institution whereby young people live together in trial marriages has not in any way lowered the divorce rate; quite, as it happens, the opposite. A strangely unsuccessful revolution, the sexual revolution, for in its aftermath there seems to be more rape, perversion, and other nightmarish sexual action afield than ever before. It is almost enough to bring back that line from a margarine commercial of a later decade: "It's not nice to fool mother nature."

A S FOR THE CLICHÉ ABOUT FIFTIES CONFORMITY, by choosing to go to the University of Chicago in the middle 1950s, I managed simultaneously to sidestep conformity and to acquire my first taste of bohemian culture. Highly exhilarating it was, too, for this was before the entire culture had gone bohemian. Bohemianism at the University of Chicago was artistic, even in some of its aspects social-scientific, at least insofar as being a social scientist meant distancing oneself from the society one was studying. But it was also distinctly apolitical. The energies of serious people did not then seem to go into politics.

True, a forlorn Marxist bookshop on 55th Street was hospitable to those who wished to pass an afternoon complaining about Wall Street and the bosses. I recall, too, a scraggly SANE nuclear-policy group passing out leaflets at a card table on the corner of University Avenue and 57th Street, and seeming particularly hopeless while doing so. (Apologies to Stanley Kubrick, creator of the movie *Dr. Strangelove, or How I Learned to Stop Worrying and Love the Bomb*, but, without ever loving it, somehow I never was able to begin worrying about the Bomb in the first place.) A man named Maynard Krueger, who ran for Vice President of the United States on the Socialist-party ticket and taught in the college in sandals worn over socks, was a mild political curiosity on the campus. But all this seemed slightly aberrant behavior. Politics, clearly, was not where the main action was.

Where the action seemed to be at the University of Chicago was in science, learning, and high culture, the last-named of which was immitigable, making allowance only for folk singing, the one bow in the direction of Midwestern prairie populism. As unembarrassed elitists—of an intellectual, not a social, kind—we at the University of Chicago were cognizant of Lonely Crowds, Organization Men, also Men in Gray Flannel Suits, and the other tags of the sociological literature bemoaning conformity in the fifties. For us, the point about conformity, clearly, was to avoid it, which, so long as one was a student at the University of Chicago, was, as we should say today, no problem. Merely going there conferred nonconformist status, which I, for one, as part of the then-small but rapidly gathering herd of independent minds of our time, was pleased to have.

The only kind of nonconformity worth attaining, or so it seemed to me, was available through a seriousness about culture. In the stumbling way of earnest young men from unbookish homes, I attempted to educate myself. Allen Ginsberg may have claimed to see the best minds of his generation "destroyed by madness/starving hysterical naked" and so forth, but it seemed to me that some of the best minds of the generations before mine had been devoted to literature, and I attempted to follow them. Unlike the case now, many of them were even located in literature departments: for example, Erich Auerbach, R. P. Blackmur, Lionel Trilling, Robert Penn Warren. Among novelists, Hemingway and Faulkner and John Dos Passos were still at work in the fifties. In poetry, so were T. S. Eliot and Robert Frost, Wallace Stevens and Marianne Moore, W. H. Auden and William Carlos Williams, not to speak of the ambition-crazed younger generation of poets then hitting their stride which included Robert Lowell, Randall Jarrell, John Berryman, and Elizabeth Bishop. Edmund Wilson still functioned outside the academy as the arbiter of literary culture generally.

None of these names appears in David Halberstam's book. Nor does the name of any serious American painter—even though it was during the 1950s that the center of contemporary art shifted from Paris to New York. Of serious music during the 1950s, not a word. Instead we have a lengthy treatise on Elvis Presley, whose music, in Halberstam's words, was "a sign of the political, economic, and social empowerment of the younger generation." Neither does the murderous conduct of Communist regimes during the 1950s get much space in his book. My own first clue to the evil of Communism was that Communist regimes not only would not tolerate writers and artists generally but had a distinct penchant for murdering them.

Two writers seemed particularly attractive to my generation, at least if I and the people I knew were any gauge. They were F. Scott Fitzgerald and J. D. Salinger. Fitzgerald had died in 1940, with none of his books in print and thinking himself a dismal failure, but by the fifties a revival of his works was well under way. Salinger was already famous for his quirkiness and the paucity of his literary production. Weaknesses and contradictions resided in both these writers, but they tended to be *our* weaknesses and contradictions, which perhaps made them seem all the more attractive.

Fitzgerald, who was greatly taken up with the rich, was filled with social snobberies; Salinger, dedicated to the sniffing-out of phoniness in contemporary life, sometimes lapsed into the precious. Yet both novelists were exceptional stylists—each made his own sweet music in prose— and in the fiction of each, style was put forth as the surest clue to determining a character's quality. A Fitzgerald hero was gracious, understood the refinements of personal relations, and had an enormous yearning and admiration for lives lived stylishly. A Salinger hero was marked by his superior awareness; even when mad, he saw not only more but more deeply than other people. The heroes of both writers were nonetheless relatively passive figures, not men of action. Style and awareness, their literary hallmarks, were the qualities that we of the generation of the fifties who considered ourselves thoughtful, whether readers of Fitzgerald and Salinger or not, tended to pride ourselves on.

F. Scott Fitzgerald's snobberies were all carried over, very much intact, into and straight through the fifties. American life, apart from the Army, was not only thoroughly segregated racially, but many neighborhoods were still "restricted" (to use the old euphemism for "no Jews allowed"). Even Catholics did not have a clear way, and the Irish were not home free, either, as John F. Kennedy would learn when he ran for the presidency in 1960. College fraternities and sororities, country clubs, corporations, large law firms, other social associations of various kinds were organized along lines of religious and (it went without saying) racial exclusion. Adverting to these old discriminations, I used occasionally to joke about not realizing that they now let Jews into the Book-of-the-Month Club.

To be black was the worst of all social bargains in the fifties. Finding a middle-class restaurant to take black friends to was not then an easy thing to arrange. Unrepentant bigots walked the land, North and South, without official disapproval from society at large. Apart from rare positions in law and medicine, the ministry and the military were the only two institutions through which blacks had a chance to attain middle-class respectability and professional advancement. Early in the decade even sports had not yet fully opened up to black talent.

Yet, despite the many and very real restraints on blacks in the decade, one has to ask why fifties' black writers (Ralph Ellison and the early James Baldwin) and black civil-rights leaders (Martin Luther King, Jr., Roy Wilkins, Whitney Young, Bayard Rustin) were so much more impressive than the black figures in culture and politics who came later, under much less constrained conditions. How account for the distance in seriousness between, say, Ralph Ellison and Maya Angelou, between Martin Luther King and Jesse Jackson? In music, too, where blacks dominated jazz, the accomplished Negro jazz musician of the fifties was an immensely impressive figure: talented, dignified, often witty in the elegantly understated way that has always been inseparable from my own idea of cool.

Legal discriminatory arrangements against blacks began to break up in the 1950s. This was the decade of *Brown v. Board of Education*, the Montgomery bus boycott, and the rise of the civil-rights leader as moral hero. For Jews, institutional acceptance also increased, in law firms, corporations, and especially in universities. Northwestern, where I taught for thirty years, still had a quota in the fifties on accepting Jewish students. Fewer than ten blocks from where our family lived when I was a boy was the restricted Edgewater Country Club where I caddied briefly; I cannot say that I spat each time I passed, but I was not displeased to see it go out of business in the 1960s.

As a boy, I was aware of social discrimination, but I took it as part of life. There was enough in my own Jewish ambit that was socially exclusionary, the distaste for intermarriage being but the most heavily italicized example. Jews also made lots of social distinctions, German Jews holding themselves above East European Jews and some East European Jews choosing to look down upon others. Anyway, being a Midwesterner, and not having tasted the rich snobberies of the Ivy League, I had no interest in becoming the first Jew to join the New York law firm of Sullivan & Cromwell or the West Side Tennis Club in Forest Hills or the Union League Club. Success on earth did not require attaining such dull heights.

ODD, BUT FOR ALL THAT WAS EXCLUSIONARY in American life, Americans seemed to get on better then than now. The fifties were still pre-ethnic America, at least to the extent that ethnicity was not featured as it began to be in the 1970s. One was still an American Italian or American Irish, rather than, as later, the other way around. In private, groups might call each other every kind of degrading name, but in public, life ran along pretty smoothly. The rise not so much of ethnicity as of public ethnic consciousness seems to have isolated people more than previously. The assertion of ethnic pride, which was fair enough, pretty quickly turned into slightly nasty ethnic chauvinism, which was not.

In the 1950s, there was, it seems to me, a better sense of belonging to the nation. With certain exceptions—the upper and the lower classes—one lived less exclusively among one's own social class. In part, this may have been owing to such things as the military draft, then still extant. My own two years in the US Army (1958–1960) I found boring and a great waste of time. In retrospect, they have come to look better and better. Among other things, being in the Army as an enlisted man lifted me out of my own social class, ethnic group, tight little island. It provided a chance, too, to see parts of the country I should not otherwise have known: in my case, Missouri, Texas, and Arkansas. Most important, though, it gave me—and I suspect many others who did their time in the Army—a sense of being part of the larger country, which is no longer so easily available.

People lived not only on better but on less fearful terms with their neighbors than now. In Chicago, we locked our doors, but many people who lived through the 1950s claim never to have done so. Crime there was, but much of it seemed, in those days, in the hands of professionals, where it ought to be. The epidemic of drug addiction had not set so many dangerous amateurs loose in the streets. Whole neighborhoods were not then surrendered to the violent young. Not that one walked fearlessly everywhere; I am old enough to remember having been frightened by white guys. But in the fifties, unlike in the past 25 years or so, city life did not seem so menacing; not so many areas seemed so obviously out of bounds; paranoia did not seem so clearly the better part of valor. The rhythm of middle-class life was closer to that yearned for in the piquant epigraph Mrs. Clinton has supplied for this essay—closer than one fears it will ever be again.

Of course there is the danger that the past only looks better because it is further away. But even allowing for that, I feel, to repeat, lucky to have come of age in the 1950s, a time of prosperity, tranquility, and extraordinary optimism about the future. Growing up during that time, one felt that one's life was going to be richer than that of one's parents—and not merely financially richer.

It is a measure of the psychological distance we have come since the fifties that one looks today upon one's children and grandchildren and feels, with sadness, that their lives, far from being better than one's own, are likely to be worse. The very real prospects of scarcity, perpetual animosity among social groups, radical slackening in educational and every other kind of standard—such are among only the larger disfiguring craters looming on the lunar landscape of the future. Even after the resounding defeat of Communism, which should have called forth jubilation for the freeing of millions of souls from the most crushing organized villainy in the history of the world, the feeling of decline and fall still hangs in the air.

Nearly everything that was most troublesome about life in the fifties—Communism abroad, racial segregation at home, domination by an often narrowly intolerant mainstream culture—has been eliminated, changed, or defeated, without life seeming qualitatively better. Might this be because so much that was good about that decade—its wide margins of optimism, its insistence on ambition being redeemable only by merit, its belief in every kind of progress—seems to have been lost in the social and political shuffle of the ensuing decades? Some may say that the past, like so much else about modern life, is not what it used to be. But those of us who lived through the fifties, who can answer affirmatively the perfectly sensible question of "Baron Münchhausen"—*vas you dere, Sharley?*—are under an obligation to remember them as they really were.

A Virtucrat Remembers

(1988)

Well, I hope you think a little better of the world.
We mustn't make up our minds too early in life.

HENRY JAMES, *The Princess Casamassima*

FAMOUS AMERICAN CORNERS, permit me to name a few: Hollywood and Vine, State and Madison, Broadway and 42nd Street, Haight and Ashbury. Shortly before beginning this essay, I happened to be in San Francisco, staying with someone who lives in the Haight-Ashbury district, and over a three-day visit walked past the corner of Haight and Ashbury and along the street and in the neighborhood known as "the Haight" perhaps twenty times. I never did so without a rich stew of emotion boiling within me. If San Francisco was the spiritual capital of that period in recent history we think of with chronological inexactitude as "the sixties," then nearby Berkeley was its Finland Station and Haight-Ashbury its Red Square. To alter my trope rather abruptly, if the sixties were your idea of a good time, the Haight was Ciro's, the Chez Paris, the Copacabana; it was, baby, where the good times rolled.

Although some small changes have been made on the Haight—a few new shops have gone in, a few head shops have gone out—and although rising real estate prices presage other changes in the near future, I found myself surprised how little the street seemed to change, how very "sixties" it all still appeared, at least outwardly. Block after block of shops sell handcrafted jewelry, gay and feminist books (such as the Anarchist Collective Bookstore), used clothing, berets, (putative) health food, aggressively uninteresting paintings—in short, as Zorba the Greek might say, the full catastrophe. The street's denizens are got up in sixties regalia: beards, long hair, dreary denim, backpacks, bedrolls, bandanas. Walking past the corner of Haight and Ashbury, I noted a man of perhaps my own middle years, red-eyed and in an advanced stage of scragglitude, who plunked his guitar and intoned, "Oh, ya drop dead in the street and they give ya a ticket for littering." A block or so farther on, I heard, behind me, one man say to another, "Whaddaya say we go up to Montana, get hold of some shit, and take it down to Mexico?"

On the Haight I felt like I was Rip Van Winkle in reverse—as if I fell asleep and awoke to find not that it was forty years later but twenty years earlier. Except of course it wasn't, and there was ample evidence to prove that it wasn't. The young, blond, longhaired, be-sandaled girls who seemed so much a part of the counterculture fantasy—a pipe of pot, a book of *Howl*, and thou—are now older, gray, still long-haired and be-sandaled women, looking much the worse for wear. The man who sang about dropping dead in the street, the chances are, may do just that. While many of these aging hippies sleep in Buena Vista Park, where they are not disturbed by San Francisco's highly tolerant police, others drop off on stoops before pastel-painted houses or in doorways. When they wake in the cool San Francisco morning, they are not a charming sight; they are, instead, a reminder of the good sense of Santayana's remark that "the state of nature presupposes a tropical climate."

As I walked along the Haight, I, who am perhaps about as square as one can get on this earth, felt no hostility directed at me. Yet I felt a good deal of my own hostility directed toward them, these sad and aging hippies, who seemed to be standing around awaiting a bus into the past. I felt about them a sense of revulsion, and loathing, and above all depression—the latter, especially, when I would notice a young adolescent who looked to me as if he might be a runaway come to the Haight to live the countercultural dream. Looking into the drug-besotted eyes of these people who are now pushing middle age, I thought, my God, the squalor, the waste, the horror! And I also felt, what good luck that the counter-cultural dream progressed no further than it did! Passing a clutch of these people, men and women, on the very corner of Haight and Ashbury, I muttered to myself, "What you do with your own life is your own business, but I'm awfully glad that, in the battle of competing visions, yours lost."

But did it? The pathetic creatures lingering on the Haight are but the lost remnant of a now dead movement, people who bought the whole package of inchoate philosophy, quarter-baked politics, and sappy transcendentalism that made up the intellectual content of the movement. And yet in diluted form much of the spirit of the sixties lives on; and in some quarters it seems not merely living on but very nearly prevailing, even if not in the preserved-in-amber form one finds it in on the Haight. I find this spirit alive and all too well in the universities, for example. Those professors now in their forties, and hence dominant as full professors, department chairmen, and deans, were all in their twenties in the late 1960s. Wherever they actually went to school, the true alma mater for most of them is the sixties, when they were graduate students. One sees the sixties influence not only in their dress and ubiquitous beards—theirs is surely the first generation of full professors to teach in jeans—but in their chumminess with students, their readiness to subvert tradition, their rush to align themselves with what they construe to be virtuous causes. The generation of the sixties was above all the generation of virtue. They set out to make America better. America, unfortunately or fortunately, was not as good as they and, in their view, still isn't.

Tell me what you think of the sixties and I shall tell you what your politics are. Tell me that you think the period both good and bad, with much to be said for and against it, and you are, whether you know it or not, a liberal. Tell me that you think the sixties a banner time in American life, a period of unparalleled idealism, a splendid opportunity sadly missed, and you are doubtless a radical, sentimental or otherwise. Tell me that you think the sixties a time of horrendous dislocation, a disaster nearly averted, a damn near thing, but a thing nonetheless for which we are still paying and shall continue to pay, and I shall tell you . . . well, I am not sure what you are precisely, but your views, friend, are close to mine and I am pleased to meet you.

Can there have been nothing good about the sixties, which, to become chronologically more exact about the period, I should date as beginning in 1965 with the Free Speech Movement at the University of California at Berkeley and closing with the resignation of Richard Nixon from the United States presidency after the revelations of Watergate in 1974? The role of student and left-wing protest in bringing about the withdrawal of US troops from Vietnam, of which the protesters of the day were so exaltedly proud, must now receive credit as well for what happened after American withdrawal, which includes leaving Vietnam in the grip of totalitarianism and permitting the massacre of millions in nearby Cambodia. Such progress as was made in the late fifties and early sixties in race relations—and it was serious progress at the state and institutional levels—was in many respects nullified by the surgent black consciousness movement, which claimed not only that Black is Beautiful but more than implied, corollarily, that white was mean, racist, and generally soulless, and put an end to the dream of an integrated society, where things remain today. During the sixties, too, the black plaint of oppression was picked up by women, by homosexuals, and by every other group that found it useful; if you weren't a member of a group that could claim a heritage of oppression—and almost everybody could set out such a claim—you were in bad shape psychologically. A society that felt itself so widely oppressed needed to discover a regular supply of oppressors, and here the nation's journalists came to the rescue, tirelessly pumping out fresh conspiracies, hidden plots, secret deals.

The investigative journalist, Seymour Bob Halberstein (as I tend to think of him), became one of the heroes of the sixties. College-educated, usually middle or upper middle class, secure and happy in his work, the investigative journalist, when successful, won fame and sometimes vast fortune from a society that he portrayed as corrupt, decayed, sick. A man well paid and highly honored by his society for telling it how rotten it was, the investigative journalist lived a contradiction, and it is fitting that he be one of the heroic figures of a period in American life in which, for a long stretch, it appeared that the law of contradictions itself had been rescinded. It was the sixties, let us not forget, that brought us those splendid contradictions, not to say oxymorons, known as "open marriage," "free and easy abortion," and "repressive toleration."

The sixties also brought us the initials SDS, JDL, and LSD, not to speak of such nonacronymous but plenty acrimonious organizations as the Black Panthers, the Weathermen, and The Fair Play for Cuba Committee. It was a time of vast national yearning, when youth was revered and everyone, including the young, seemed to forget that the chief problem of youth is that it doesn't last. Men left their wives, wives smoked their adolescent children's marijuana, and everyone spoke—tsk, tsk—of the sad misunderstanding between the young and the adult known as the generation gap. Standards were lowered in education, Norman Mailer and Andy Warhol became leading figures in literature and art. All kinds of essential responsibilities ceased to be people's "bag," and every kind of trivial irresponsibility became known as "doing one's thing." It wasn't quite a matter, in Yeats's famous formulation, of "Things fall apart; the center cannot hold"; it was more a matter of people taking joy in the prospect of things falling apart and nobody claiming even to represent the center. Really to hate it you had only to have been there.

I was, and did, but not at first, and not unequivocally.

Let me begin with the year 1968, in some ways the height of the madness, the year of the riots at the Democratic National Convention in Chicago, the closest in some ways that America has come to having a year like 1848 in Europe. That year Hubert Humphrey was running against Richard Nixon, whose portrait then had primacy of place in my personal American political rogues' gallery. As a down-the-line, pull-the-lever man of the left, I was not too keen on Humphrey either. Humphrey had an honorable record as a liberal on domestic matters, true enough, but on foreign policy, as vice president under Lyndon Johnson, he had become an administration spokesman for continued prosecution of the Vietnam War, which, again as a man of the left, I detested. Lyndon Johnson didn't leave those who worked for him much, especially in the way of dignity, and certainly this was true of poor Hubert Humphrey. Yet for me Hubert Humphrey had one powerful thing going for him in 1968—he was not Richard Nixon.

Around this time I attended, purely as a sightseer, a large rally in Grant Park in Chicago, a block or so away from the Conrad Hilton

Hotel, headquarters of the Democratic Party during the convention. I was there chiefly to see Genet, the French novelist, who, along with Norman Mailer and Terry Southern, was in Chicago to cover the convention for *Esquire* magazine. A compact little man with a bald head shaved on the sides, well ahead of the fashion of our day, Genet was most unimpressive on the platform, muttering a few revolutionary banalities. Norman Mailer, who also spoke that afternoon, adopting a Southern noncommissioned officer's accent for his platform appearance, had not even attained the level of unimpressiveness; he was merely ridiculous. The principal theme of most speakers was the crudity of Mayor Daley, the brutality of the Chicago cops, the racism of the United States. And then the police arrived, perhaps a hundred of them. They lined up in formation outside the crowd; they had gas masks and billy clubs. "Fuck the pigs," someone shouted, and then someone else threw a bottle into the police formation, and then another and yet another. That was the ball game. Gas masks were clamped on, tear gas canisters let loose, the police, cutting a swath with their clubs, marched through, dispersing the crowd, myself among it, choking with tear gas.

This little outing was my initial, firsthand hard evidence that an anti-war crowd was not necessarily an anti-violence crowd. Worse is better, said Lenin, and it was clear, at least to me, that most of the people who came to the protests connected with the 1968 Democratic Convention were interested in making things a whole lot worse—and as dramatically as possible. These same people knew they couldn't hope to bring off anything like the same spectacle at the Republican Convention. The Democratic was their party, disaffected though they might be from it at present. The Democrats, they felt (and acted on the feeling), owed them sympathy, had to put up with them, could not with a clear conscience put them down, whereas the Republicans owed them nothing. As the time of the election drew nearer, it occurred to me that a vote for Hubert Humphrey meant a vote for greater chaos. Left-wing though I was, I was not for chaos, I was not for tearing down the universities, I was not for the party of Allen Ginsberg and Abbie Hoffman and Paul Goodman and Joan Baez and the revolution-in-consciousness, polymorphously perverse, pot-minded, guitar-playing, commune-living culture of the radical left. Of this I was convinced. Yet to vote my convictions I would have to vote for Richard

Nixon, which, at that time, I could not do. But to every liberal dilemma there is a liberal solution, usually involving political cowardice. My solution, as I recall, was not to vote and hope that Hubert Humphrey lost.

I refer to myself as a liberal in the above paragraph, but I then thought of myself as a radical. "Radical" at that time seemed to me an honorific term—radical, as radicals used to be fond of pointing out, as in going to the root causes of any problem. Let pass that there was something terribly self-congratulatory about thinking oneself a deep thinker, for after all that is what "going to the root" implies. Although I had worked as a director of an anti-Poverty program in Little Rock, Arkansas, I did not think of myself in any serious sense a radical activist. I carried no placards; I took part in no demonstrations; I had not the least touch of what an acquaintance of mine, feeling a twinge of admiration for people who went to jail for political causes, once called "subpoena envy." No, in thinking myself a radical I chiefly thought of myself as a man of the left who thought things were radically wrong in the world and was not fearful of applying radical solutions to right them.

How did I come to hold the political views I then held? That is a question I have pondered, and ponder still. Our politics come from the air we breathe, from our background, our prejudices, our social class, our ethnic origins, our education. Except perhaps in rare instances—and mine is not one of them—we do not arrive at our politics through careful, or even careless, reasoning. "You cannot," wrote Swift, "reason a person out of something he has not been reasoned into." Few of us having been reasoned into our politics, few can be reasoned out of them. I know that I have never lost a political argument in my life, a statement that will seem rather less impressive when to it I add that I have never really won a political argument either. And I have engaged in lots of political arguments, especially since, having reached the age of fifty, which after a reasonably well-mannered life I have unofficially declared the age of tactlessness, I do not hesitate to make my own views known. But what I have found is that arguing a person out of his politics is akin to arguing him out of his religion. Swift was correct; it cannot be done.

This much about my youthful politics I can say with moderate certainty: I did not acquire them at home, at least not directly. Mine must have been one of the least overtly political households on record. In his best-selling book on the Jewish immigrants to America, *World of Our Fathers,* Irving Howe implies a strong connection between Jews and the labor movement and, beyond that, between Jews and socialist and utopian politics. This, though, was not the world of my father, nor of my father's father, both of whom were in business for themselves, the former very successfully, the latter rather dismally. I had an uncle, whom I never met, who died in the Spanish Civil War, but he appears to have been less a political character than an adventurer, one of those boys who ran away from home when he was fifteen to go to sea. Politics was never more than a passing subject at our table, never anything remotely like a consuming one. As an adolescent, none of my friends was the least bit interested in politics, though I believe we all thought of ourselves, somehow or other, as Democrats, and this chiefly because Jews were not then Republicans, or at least we knew no Jewish Republicans.

Yet being Jewish, even if one wasn't at all an observant Jew, was a subtle influence upon one's political consciousness. Looking back, I at any rate feel it has been on mine. In an interesting essay entitled "Jews in the Russian Revolutionary Movement," the late Leonard Schapiro notes that some Jews threw themselves into revolutionary politics owing to oppression, but that more did so in the belief that, with the coming of the revolution, they would be fully the equal of anyone in Russian society. Boy and man, I have never felt the least oppression in America owing to my Jewishness, but, as a child, in the 1940s, it was difficult not to know that there was a good deal of anti-Semitism in the United States, some of it quite open and some of it quite close to home. A country club less than a mile from where I lived did not permit Jews; many a nearby neighborhood was, to use the term of the day, "restricted"; and there were restaurants, hotels, resorts where Jews did not attempt entrance.

As a small boy, I recall once returning from the school playground and chanting before my father "Eenie, meenie, minnie, moe/Catch a nigger by the toe," and his flying into a rage. My father was not a man easily enraged, but this was during World War II, when Jews in vast numbers were being killed in Europe, which my father, cooled down now, explained to me, rounding off his explanation by adding that "our people" had a special responsibility not to use a word like "nigger," which was a word soaked in hate. Six or seven years old at the time, I remember taking his point, but also wondering what kind of world it was that would kill "our people." Out of the soil of such incidents does political consciousness take root and grow.

In my particular case, political consciousness grew very slowly indeed. Later, as a student at the University of Chicago, I met contemporaries, many of them from New York City, who had been reading the *Nation* and the *New Republic* since early in high school; some of their parents had become enmeshed in sectarian politics in the thirties, from which they never freed themselves, and about which, naturally enough, their children, from table talk alone, became fairly well informed. Politics was never part of the table talk in our home, unless there was a passing reference to some fresh piece of corruption at city hall, of which, in Chicago, there was never a paucity. Of politics in the larger sense—that is, of politics as an expression of views about how the world ought to be organized—there was no talk whatsoever. Had there been, I am not sure I should have been much interested in it. I seem to have been a fairly normal adolescent boy, which means that my head, filled with dreams of athletic glory and sex, had no room for a vision of the good life lived through politics.

Just as well, I have no doubt. If I had had political views at fifteen or sixteen—as so many people who grew up in the Depression did—I should have been an insufferable little prig. At twenty or so when I began to have such views, behind them were the standard set of proper liberal humanitarian principles. They were very moral and, worse, moralizing—and there was scarcely a politician about whom I could not have told you whether he was on the absolute right or the absolutely wrong side. Need I add that I, invariably, was on the absolutely right side?

Although I was not a good student, I did go to a good school, the University of Chicago, whose implicit political orientation was liberal, even if none of the professors I encountered there pushed a liberal political line. But one had to be rather thick not to know that, in the 1956 election between Dwight David Eisenhower and Adlai Stevenson, for the thinking man there could be no real choice. (Ike and Adlai were supposed to have a meeting before the election, the comedian Mort Sahl joked at the time, but they had to call it off because they couldn't find an interpreter for Ike.) Along with providing me with some of the appropriate language with which to talk about politics, the University of Chicago put into my head the desire to be that odd combination of scholar and philosopher—without the learning of the former or the depth of the latter—known as "an intellectual." Here was a fateful decision, for my politics and my life.

In those years—the late 1950s—the decision to be an intellect implied the decision to be something of an outsider. In the presidential elections of 1952 and 1956, for example, Adlai Stevenson was frequently referred to as an "egghead," the dysphemism for an intellectual (which, apart from his using language with some nicety, Stevenson really wasn't), and to be considered an intellectual was clearly a mark against him. To the larger society, to be an intellectual meant that there was something insubstantial, untrustworthy, possibly even slightly dangerous about one. As a liberal has been defined as a person whose interests aren't at stake at the moment, so an intellectual has been defined as a person whose only stake is in his ideas. Intellectuals have often felt that this only proved their disinterestedness and hence redounded to their greater glory; nonintellectuals have construed it to mean only that intellectuals have nothing to lose—and, as any sensible businessman will tell you, you want to be a bit wary about entering into a deal with someone who has nothing to lose.

Part of the pleasure for me of being an intellectual was in the position of permanent nonconformity it seemed to provide. (I had not then heard Harold Rosenberg's devastating phrase, "a herd of independent minds," which has on more than one occasion been pressed into service to describe the collective behavior of intellectuals.) In *The Secret Agent,* Joseph Conrad remarks that "the way of even the most justifiable revolutions is prepared by personal impulses disguised into creeds." I know that by the time I was in my late adolescence, the impulse of, or at any rate toward, nonconformity was already powerful in me. Mine was, I like to think, a nonconformity not of manner but of spirit. When I was in high school, for example, I was invited to join an exalted senior boys' honor club, but turned it down—the first boy, I believe, in the history of the school to do so. It was my manner that got me invited; it was my spirit that would not permit me to join. At various times in my life, something in me has caused me to turn my back on conventional success, to swim out of the mainstream, to want to make do without the world's more obvious rewards. As a self-appointed intellectual, I was able to achieve all this in one swoop, for in determining to live my life for intellectual things, I guaranteed forfeiture of a clearly tracked career, a normal middle-class existence, and anything resembling serious wealth.

As a self-appointed intellectual, I was also taking on a fairly heavy ideological cargo. My notion of what an intellectual was came in part through my sketchy undergraduate study of history—here I learned that Voltaire, that splendid troublemaker, was an intellectual—but in even larger part through reading the intellectual journals of the day, which I began to do in a passionate way in my last year in college. Chief among these journals were *Partisan Review, Commentary, Dissent,* and *Encounter* (in London). All, be it known, were strongly anti-communist; but, let it also be known, none at the time was pro-bourgeois or even mildly in favor of capitalism. These journals were edited by that species of the genus intellectual known as New York intellectuals (including *Encounter,* whose dominant co-editor was Irving Kristol). The New York intellectuals of the day seemed to me, viewed at a distance of 800 miles, brilliant and radical, and the two qualities appeared interwoven, each dependent upon the other. They were too clever (any longer) to be taken in by communism, and also too clever to let up on criticizing their own country. As David Riesman once put it, "Were not intellectuals of more use to this country when they had less use for it?" As such, intellectuals functioned, permanently, as a not particularly loyal opposition—or, to put it more precisely, as loyal principally to the idea of being in opposition.

The idea of being in permanent opposition suited both my temperament and my youthful recalcitrance. As a boost to my morale, I retained only the white squares in the checkered history of intellectuals in politics: the distrust they had often shown for empty authority, their yearning for equality, their hunger for social justice, their belief in the possibility of greater freedom of a kind that would perhaps one day bring nearer the prospect of an earthly paradise. I now also began to read history rather more selectively, with an eye out for intellectual heroism. Men who could make moot the question of which was more powerful, the pen or the sword, by possessing both, particularly impressed me: T. E. Lawrence, André Malraux, Leon Trotsky. I soon became fairly well read in not the workers' but the intellectuals' revolution of 1917 in Russia, for the Russian Revolution was nothing if not a revolution choreographed, orchestrated, and staged by intellectuals. Although I now believe (not entirely without evidence) that the Russian Revolution was one of the great catastrophes of world history, I nonetheless knew more about it than I did about the American Revolution, and probably even now know more Russian than American history; I can tell you a good deal more about the Decembrists, for example, than I can about the presidential administrations of Van Buren, Harrison, and Polk. Nor, my guess is, am I alone among intellectuals in this regard. The reason, I strongly suspect, is that intellectuals tend to become highly stimulated by revolution—by the actuality, the prospect, even the idea of it. In *Hope Against Hope*, Nadezhda Mandelstam noted; "My brother Evgeni Yakovlevich used to say that the decisive part in the subjugation of the intelligentsia was played not by terror and bribery (though God knows there was enough of both), but by the word 'Revolution,' which none of them could bear to give up."

By the time I graduated from college, at twenty-one, my politics were pretty well set for the next decade. I should describe these politics as highbrow liberalism. A student of literature, a devotee of Proust and Joyce and Kafka, I discovered a way to carry over my tastes in literature to politics by choosing British models: George Bernard Shaw's socialism, John Maynard Keynes's economics, E. M. Forster's "aristocracy of the sensitive, the considerate and the plucky." A continental modernist in literature, an English Fabian in politics, Brooks Brothers in dress, hey, daddy, they didn't make 'em much more sensitive, considerate, and plucky than I at twenty-one.

I don't wish to make too much fun of my younger self. For one thing, he can't fight back; for another, there is a lot about the kid that I really like. I think he was genuinely offended by the world's injustice. I think he would have done what he could to diminish it; and, in extenuation of the fact that he didn't do anything to do so, it must be added that nobody else had many bright ideas on the subject at the time either. But this much must be said against him: there was undeniably an element of snobbery in his youthful politics. Leftism was not so endemic among the educated classes then as now. The writers from whom he took many of his political notions—Lewis Mumford, Paul Goodman, C. Wright Mills—were still a minority taste. He considered himself a radical, true enough, but above and beyond that he thought of himself as a member of an even smaller band, an unashamed idealist. This put him, he felt, in a select company of the happy few—and the important thing always about the happy few is that, in politics and in culture, the fewer the better.

Why, though, didn't the snobbery inherent in my youthful politics as easily turn me rightward? Why was I not an admirer of the intellectuals around *L'Action française* or the cultural theories of T. S. Eliot? Why didn't I insert a first initial in front of my name (F. Joseph Epstein), carry a walking stick, deplore progress and modernization, and live in America as if I were in exile, as I have seen many a right-wing youth do in the 1980s? Too strong a sense of the absurd, I should say. Then there is the unblinkable fact that much of right-wing intellectual life had been besmirched by anti-Semitism. (So, as I would later learn, has been a good deal of left-wing intellectual life.) But the attraction of left over right was also to be found in snobbery of another kind—in this instance, moral snobbery.

The right is the side of the liver, as everyone knows, the left that of the heart. To be on the left, then, was to be on the side of the large-hearted, the good, and (though the odious term had not yet come into vogue) the "caring." Part of the appeal of being on the left is that it puts one among the implicitly virtuous, and to believe virtue is on one's side is no small thing in politics. (Just now a belief in its own superior virtue may be all that the left in America has remaining to it, but it is nonetheless a lot.) On the right, one can always accuse the fellow to the left of one of being unrealistic, which is nice. But on the left, one can always accuse the fellow to the right of one of being cold and callous, selfish and insensitive, which is better. I know that when on the left I always did, and I found it exhilarating.

My politics also fitted in nicely with my chosen vocation. I wanted to be a writer, not an easy thing to be, in America or any other country, for in writing, unlike many another line of work, there wasn't much room for mediocrity—at least not on the level of writing to which I aspired. If I failed, my politics would prop me up. Being an anti-capitalist, after all, how could I hope to succeed under a system I contemned? (In later years, I would appreciate the rich irony with which capitalism seemed to reward its enemies; I am thinking here of such best-selling left-wing novelists as E. L. Doctorow, Kurt Vonnegut, and Robert Coover.) Being an anti-capitalist and hence being able to blame capitalism—often known more simply as "the system"—for any failure I might encounter through my own lack of talent or absence of energy not only provided me with a fine fallback position, but permitted me to view anyone who labored at a workaday job in the system with a rather lofty contempt. Even if I didn't win, in other words, I couldn't lose.

Every idea has its psychological uses. The chief use of the political ideas I held when young was to make me feel quietly but confidently superior. Their other use was to furnish me with something I thought was a point of view but realize now was only a set of opinions. The problem with such opinions is that they can intercede between experience and feeling, coloring the one and blocking the other. I recall a particularly vivid instance of this when I was a soldier, an enlisted man, in basic training at Fort Leonard Wood, Missouri, in the late 1950s. Our company was returning from a 25-mile march undertaken with full 40-pound packs, steel helmets, and rifles. (I labored under the additional weight of the autumn number of *Partisan Review* in the pocket of my field jacket.) The day was clear, the weather crisp, we were within a mile of reaching our company area, our whippet-lean black sergeant, Mr. Andrew Atherton, was booming out cadence count, and, flush with pleasure at having survived a minor hardship and filled with camaraderie shared with the men in my platoon, I thought, God, this is fine!—when, wait a minute, I remembered that, as a socialist and a man of the left, I hated the military and all it stood for. And so I finished out the final mile of the march in a proper mood of cynical detachment.

Our opinions can exert a powerful tyranny over us, especially when we are simultaneously uncertain whence they derive yet nonetheless determined to live lives congruent with them. One of the advantages that the left has over any other political grouping in the struggle for the minds of the young is that it provides them with the most complete set of opinions. In my own youthful time, I held them all. One might imagine a free-association game called Left-Wing, in which one responds quickly to flash cards: BUSINESS—"A swindle." THE MIL-ITARY—"Barbarian institution." CONVENTIONAL PATRIO-TISM—"For Mencken's Booboisie." RELIGION—"Opiate of the people; also beside the point." RACISM—"Endemic in America." Then, too, the left provides a rich cast of conspirators and secret controllers of society: Wall Street, Madison Avenue, the CIA, the FBI, the mili-tary-industrial complex, and so on into the dark night. In the left-wing mind, people are regularly polluting, poisoning, pillaging, corrupting, carcinogenating. There are the utility boys, agribusiness, the pharma-ceutical companies, the lobbyists, and surely I don't have to mention the weapons manufacturers. It's a wonder that a reader of the *Nation* can get any sleep at all.

Even in my hardiest, most confident left-wing days, I never suffered the full political paranoia available on the left, but I was not above doing what I now think of as "an opinion check" as a means of judging not only acquaintances but writers and public figures. Where their opinions dif-fered from my own, which were the standard received liberal wisdom of the day, I found them wanting.

I do not mean to mock the importance of opinions. I have lost friends over opinions, as I suspect many an intellectual has, for opinion is the chief stock in trade of the intellectual. As Santayana says, "the person of the friend is distinguished and selected from all others because of excep-tionally acceptable ways of acting, thinking, and feeling about other things or persons." Yet in the realm of opinion conservatives have a natu-ral advantage over liberals. Conservatives may think what they believe; liberals may only think good thoughts (except of course about those who disagree with them). Conservatives can often surprise one with the large discrepancy between their opinions and their actions. I think here of H. L. Mencken, behind nearly every one of whose harsh opinions one can find a kindly action that contradicts it. Liberals, being under the burden of espousing lofty opinions, can only disappoint—and often do. With only a single exception, which I shall get to presently, I have never met a liberal who did anything serious to help any member of the working classes, apart from giving money to one or another cause (and the test of giving, I have always believed, is not how much one gives, but how much, after having given, one has left) or allowing one's cleaning woman to call one by one's first name. The truly large-hearted people whom I have either known or heard about—a middle-aged woman in Chicago who has given her life to looking after stray animals, Mother Teresa of Calcutta—seem to be above politics.

The one exception in my lifetime that I can think of is the behavior of certain young white men and women during the glory years of the civil rights movement. These were the years from the first sit-ins in the late 1950s through the passage of the Civil Rights Act of 1964, shortly after which whites were told by young blacks in the movement, in effect, to bug off. But these young men and women put their heads on the block for a cause; and a good cause it was, perhaps the last altogether morally clear cause in the politics of this nation: the removal from the books of a number of Southern states of certain indisputably unjust laws. To challenge these laws required courage, physical as well as moral courage, from blacks and whites alike; and if I underscore here the efforts of whites, I do so only because, in the highest sense, their contribution to the civil rights movement of those days was the more immediately disinterested.

I was living in the South during a part of this time, and, though never called to the test of physical courage, was greatly impressed by those who came through the test—and, in the case of some civil rights workers, came through it again and again. When lives are risked (and sometimes lost) in a good cause, it enhances—ennobles, even—the lives and the cause. Living in the South at that time was strange in many respects, not least among them that one's life revolved around a single political issue: race. How one felt about segregation-integration defined one. One's opinion on this subject not merely loomed large but eclipsed the moon and the sun. It was all and it was everything. Karl Jaspers used to claim that each of us is our situation personified. For nearly everyone living in the South, race was *the* situation, and it took over nearly everyone's life.

It was during these years, when I worked as the director of the anti-Poverty program in Little Rock, Arkansas, that the salad of illusions I now think of as my liberalism began first to show signs of wilting. Such a job demonstrated that social arrangements were not as malleable as one might have thought. Large infusions of federal money, such as the anti-Poverty program then offered, tended to excite the greed and corruption in everyone. To cite but a single instance, when in Little Rock a legal aid program was set up under the anti-Poverty program, the secret political hope was that the poor, now supplied with lawyers, would sue the city and the school district and other institutions that ostensibly had made life all the harder for them. Instead the poor tended to sue one another. Blacks, as all but a liberal of my kind would have recognized at the outset, were fully the equal of whites in self-interest, greed, and petty-mindedness. My unsentimental education was beginning to be under way at last.

There remained the thrill of virtue, which liberalism, like many a religion, holds out to its adherents and which I was myself not yet ready to relinquish. Even after the *coup de grâce* was delivered to the civil rights movement by the racist ranting of Stokely Carmichael, H. Rap Brown, the Black Panthers, and other of the madder brothers, I still did not want to renounce my belief in its righteousness. Or was it my own righteousness in which I did not wish to renounce my belief?

Shortly after the Free Speech Movement got under way at Berkeley in 1965, soon spreading to other universities around the country, violence began to be threatened more and more insistently. At first this violence was to be upon property and not upon people, but when the riots broke out in such cities as Newark, Los Angeles, (Watts), and Chicago, the line between property and people became more than a little blurry. Under the direction of Martin Luther King, Jr., the power and the glory of the civil rights movement derived in great part from its brilliant deployment of Gandhian nonviolent resistance, which lent the cause of civil rights in the South a splendid moral authority. I may have been a hypocrite, but I was not entirely a fool. I was not one of those people on the left who, to use their word, "empathized" with the rioters in black slums or with the students who took over buildings and destroyed university property, including in some instances professors' manuscripts. Thugs were thugs, violence violence, and when violence is approved, or even sympathetically understood, a social movement has taken a serious turn from which it cannot hope ever to re-turn.

As someone who wanted to continue to think himself a man of the left, much that was now going on in left-wing circles felt to me very wrong. It was clearly wrong, I felt, for professors beyond the draft age to encourage their students to burn their draft cards as a protest against the Vietnam War. It was wrong for a rather twerpy journalist named Andrew Kopkind, in the *New York Review of Books*, to instruct Martin Luther King, Jr., that "morality starts at the barrel of a gun." It was wrong for Lewis Mumford, in the pages of the *New Yorker*, to link Richard Nixon's name alongside those of Hitler and Stalin as among the moral monsters of the twentieth century—wrong for a writer who claimed a historical imagination to be so historically ignorant and wrong for a magazine as reputable as the *New Yorker* to let him get away with such ignorance. It was wrong, and comic into the bargain, that Mr. and Mrs. Leonard Bernstein would throw a fund-raising party for the Black Panthers, though fortunate that they were obtuse enough to invite Tom Wolfe to it. It was wrong, and not at all comic, that the radical left would at the first opportunity declare itself anti-Israel (wrong but scarcely surprising, given the guru Marx's opinion that the Jews were a kind of recurrent international disease produced from the intestines of bourgeois society). That such wretched excesses had long qualified as part of the tradition of the left any reader of Stendhal, Balzac, Henry James, and Conrad ought to have known. "Everything is eternal," as Santayana once remarked, "except our attention."

Yet one mustn't blame Christianity because of the quality of the Christians, or so at the time I continued to feel, substituting leftism and leftists for Christianity and Christians. In other words, there was nothing wrong with the left, I decided, it was only leftists I abhorred. Virtue, as the subtitle of the old melodramas often read, finds a way. True enough, this position of mine kept my sweet virtue intact, but this does not mean that, whatever my falsity on that front, I did not immensely despise what in the late sixties and early seventies was going on in the name of left-wing politics, and especially in what I think can properly be termed left-wing culture. Here of course I have in mind drugs, let-it-all-hang-out sex, and the general idealization of youth that infiltrated so much in the life of the country.

I might have felt differently about all this if I had been, say, five years younger—if, that is, in 1968 I had been twenty-six instead of thirty-one.

If I had been twenty-six, unmarried, without responsibilities, I might well have loved every moment of the vaunted sixties culture: puffin' on the good stuff, rappin' the nights away, making plenty of love, and no war whatsoever. But not my age but my having two stepsons in their teens made this impossible. To have teenage children in one's charge during those years gave a whole new sour perspective on the Age of Aquarius. One saw kids frying their brains kitchen-testing drugs; one saw all discipline break down in high schools, especially middle- and upper-middle-class schools; one saw that ultimate act of racism well under way, not asking the same standards of performance from black kids as one asked from whites (and then eventually lowering those asked from whites), all in the name of good-heartedness, liberal version. So much garbage in the air, if a slight euphemism will be allowed, and everybody rushing to turn on fans.

Had I been five or so years younger and unmarried, I should also have had to face the question of what to do about the draft. Had I been drafted, would I have served in the Army? Opposed to the Vietnam War though I was, I am confident that I would not have had the courage to declare myself a conscientious objector if it meant a certain prison term, with the prospect such a term held out such jailish delights as, say, homosexual rape. Would I have fled the country, jumped to Sweden or, more conveniently, to Canada, where I have relatives? Doubtful. More likely, I suspect, as with so many of the confreres of my social class, I should have saved my rosy middle-class bottom by hying off to one graduate school or another, where, unmolested, allowing the poor boys and the black boys to fight this nasty little war in my place, I could protest in peace if not quiet.

I must say that I am extremely grateful never to have had to make that choice. Had I chosen to avoid the draft through hiding out in graduate school, behind alma mater's skirts, I should my life long have been in doubt about the authenticity of my protest: was it the war in Vietnam I hated or the above-mentioned rosy middle-class bottom I loved? It has always seemed to me that the authenticity of the anti-war protest movement of the sixties generally has been in doubt, owing to the undeniable fact that, though the war slogged on to its horrendous conclusion, once the United States draft law was abrogated, all protest abated (so to speak) radically. I do not claim a pattern here, but in recent months

I have talked with two men, one a professor of English at a Southern university, the other an editor in Chicago, who each separately told me he had misgivings about not serving in Vietnam. One felt that that war was the central experience of his generation, and he had missed it; the other felt a plain bad conscience about letting the working class do all the fighting, and he regretted it.

Visited with no such complicating emotions, I was able to hate the Vietnam War with a cool and evenhanded contempt. When such figures as General Westmoreland, Robert McNamara, and (for reasons now lost to me) particularly Dean Rusk appeared upon my television screen, I felt the want of a brick. What, I now ask myself, made me so angry? There was of course the lying, there was the ineptitude, there was the sense of sheer waste. But every war offers such spectacles. No, I think I was offended by what I construed to be the immorality of this war. In its foreign policy, my country was not as moral as I should have liked—not to put too fine a point on it, it was not as moral as I.

I was never a pro-communist; I was never for a moment so deluded as such heavy American thinkers as Susan Sontag, Noam Chomsky, and Mary McCarthy, who believed in the gentle, peace-loving people of North Vietnam. Yet nowhere is it written, or so I then apparently believed, that one could not be anti-communist and anti-American both. I was in those days, I now see, a plague-on-both-your-houses man; and as generally is the case with such men, I had even more complaints about the house I happened to be living in, the United States. And yet why? Why did I wish my country to lose a war that we all know, and ought to have known, to have been a war against a tyrannous communist country that immediately proved its true nature after its victory? If someone had asked me this question then, I think I might have mumbled something about our betraying our ideals in this war. I now think that my anti-Americanism was a part of my believing myself to be a man of the left, and hence anti-military, and a part of my believing myself to be an intellectual, and hence someone whose first duty is to criticize his own country. I was locked into clichés and false traditions of my own choosing.

If you think these clichés and false traditions are not powerful, you are mistaken. Take, for example, the three great American political trials of this century: Sacco-Vanzetti, Hiss-Chambers, the Rosenberg case. As anyone who has even dipped a big toe in the oceanic literature of those trials knows, one could easily drown in their vast and choppy waters. Yet, being a man of the left, self-declared, I took it as axiomatic that Sacco and Vanzetti were innocent, that Hiss was framed, that the Rosenbergs, though probably guilty, should nevertheless not have been executed. I took all this to be so because I assumed that every political trial was essentially a rerun of the Dreyfus trial, with the government being in the wrong, the defendant a victim, the proceedings in some way rigged on the side of injustice. Some may argue that this is healthy intellectual skepticism; I would argue that it is automatic left-wing thinking—that, with its taste for conspiracies and its distaste for authority, it goes with the liberal-left territory. (For the record, I have since come to believe that Sacco and Vanzetti were probably guilty, that Hiss clearly was, and that the Rosenbergs absolutely were, though they still didn't deserve to be executed.)

Another left-wing axiom, this one involving a paradox, is the belief in progress joined with the refusal to admit that much has ever been made—or, where some progress has indisputably been made, the denial of its importance. This is conjoined with the liberal-left belief in the slippery slope, which holds that one false political step is not merely likely to send a society rolling down a hill, but more likely start an avalanche. One sees the slippery-slope argument brought into play in the contemporary university fairly frequently. When one suggests, for example, that professors ought not to be permitted to teach courses that provide sheer political propaganda—at my own university, for example, a famous left-wing journalist taught a course entitled "Reagan and the Crisis of the Modern Presidency"—one is warned of the slippery slope: start telling people what they cannot teach and pretty soon you will be telling them exactly what they can teach and pretty soon you will have a McCarthy-like atmosphere and . . . in short, you will have fallen down the slippery slope, with an avalanche of the Inquisition, fascism, McCarthyism, and Salem witch burning to follow.

For an interesting example of these axioms and assumptions at work, permit me to draw attention to an extremely well-written essay that appeared in the spring 1973 issue of *Dissent* under the title "The New Conservatives:

Intellectuals in Retreat." Close readers will note that the very title is a dead giveaway. Retreat? From what? From the spirit of Onward Left-Wing Soldier, it turns out. The gravamen of the essay is that a number of intellectuals—among them Irving Kristol, Daniel Patrick Moynihan, Norman Podhoretz, and Nathan Glazer—have left the political fray, chiefly through an uncritical acceptance of something that looks suspiciously like the status quo. A careful polemicist, the author of this essay begins by giving these intellectuals full credit for their devastating criticisms of radical excess, and joins them in their condemnation of the antinomian strain of that "congeries of personalities, organizations, and trends that went by the name of 'the Movement'" during the late sixties and early seventies. But haven't they, he now asks, gone too far in the other direction? His is of course a rhetorical question. Damn right they have gone too far in the other direction. They have come to accept such Tory notions as that the chief responsibility for reform may not fall upon the government; that personal reform may not be a task that government regulation can bring about at all; that the arrangements of society are immensely complex and ought not to be tinkered with until we have a reasonably sophisticated understanding of them; and that—unforgivably—we must recognize that in many areas of American life real progress has been made, and ought not to be gainsaid. Granting the subtlety and high intelligence of these new conservatives, our author nonetheless concludes that "the bitter sadness is that . . . [the new conservatism] may well end up a more genuine obstacle to the alleviation of social pain than the obtuse and retrograde conservatism of the privileged that preceded it."

Our author—"Hey," as the kids nowadays say, "you gotta love him!" Maybe, though, you don't, if only because it is evident that he sure loves himself. Note that sensitive phrasing—that "bitter sadness," that "social pain." Note, too, how neatly he has positioned himself politically. There he stands, triumphantly in the middle, the red hordes (sixties radicals and others) to his left, the Black Hundreds (conservatives old and new) to his right, a good man ready to continue to fight the good fight. One can almost hear him humming to himself as he completed writing this essay, "Give me one man, who's a stout-hearted man, and I'll give you. . . ." Perhaps I can hear him better than you because it was I who wrote that essay.

The only use that that essay has for me today is to delineate with some precision what my politics were in the spring of 1973. As a document in the history of my opinions, it shows me to be a still fairly young man (at thirty-six) who has quite had it with the anti-democratic, pro-counter-culture antics of the left of the day but someone who is not yet ready to eschew the label of left or with it the appearance of high public virtue necessary to the political type I myself once termed "the virtucrat." Not dramatically but gradually over the next four or so years this, too, would change. Far from wishing to retain a sentimental attachment to the left, I developed a strong antipathy to it—strong enough, at any rate, not to mind thinking of myself as anti-left. How did this happen? Somehow I have the feeling that my explaining it by saying that I got smarter is not going to be adequate. Too bad, because I think that is what happened.

I am well aware of the cliché that has it that as one becomes older, better established, perhaps achieves a modicum of success in the world, one becomes more conservative. Irving Kristol once remarked that he has come "to believe that an adult's 'normal' political instincts should be" conservative, which is a kindly way of formulating it. A less kindly way is to remark, as people on the left do, that as some people grow old they get hardening of the arteries, especially those that lead to the heart. I am not sure that growing older has all that much to do with political change. What I think does is the strength of the emotional investment one has had in certain political ideas in one's youth. Some people—some astonishingly successful people—can never shake these ideas; and some others—I think here of the current-day university—live in an environment where holding on to the ideas of one's youth ensures the security that, in a contentious atmosphere, only careful conformity can provide.

In my particular case, nothing dramatic—no falling star, no shaft of sunlight on the forest floor, no weekend spent staring at the ocean—caused me to shed what I now think the political illusions of earlier years. Instead, as illusions most often do, mine decayed and fell away, rather like baby teeth. Like baby teeth, too, some of these illusions needed to be nudged, even yanked a bit before they came out. Here reading joined with observation helped enormously. Coming upon Edward Shils's *The Intellectuals and the Powers and Other Essays* gave me a more rounded view of intellectuals than any I had had before—of their social origin, their multivarious functions, their propensity for mischief making, and also their grandeur. One illusion that Professor Shils's book knocked permanently out of my head was that intellectuals ought to consider themselves in permanent critical opposition to the society in which they live. I was especially lucky in living in the same city as Edward Shils, whom I met and who befriended me. I discovered that there were no seams between his writing and his life: what he wrote, he lived. Belief and action were for him utterly congruent, and this requires a consistency and courage that one rarely finds in the world, and even more rarely among people who think themselves intellectuals. Intrinsically, the categories of left and right had little to do with the intellectual vocation; the attempt to grasp the truth in something approximating its complexity, through learning, insight, and common sense, had everything to do with it. Such were among the lessons taught by Edward Shils, in his books and through the example of his life.

Around the time I met Edward Shils I also began, at the age of thirty-seven, a career as a university teacher. The year was 1974, and though the revolution of the sixties was officially over, it didn't always seem so on university campuses. It was Edward Shils who once described the sixties to me in the metaphor of an enormous wave that rolled over the country, then slowly rolled back, but not without leaving a vast amount of debris on the beach. The university, I now at first hand came to see, was the beach. Debris was everywhere. It was found in university teachers (obviously not all of them) casually sleeping with their students; it was in a curriculum that was increasingly organized less to educate students than to please them; it was there in the new teacher evaluations that students were encouraged to make; it was there perhaps above all in the newly organized consciousness-raising academic units known as Afro-American Studies and Women's Studies and Queer Theory.

And as the years went by, it would not get better. It would get worse, as the young graduate students and instructors of the sixties grew into associate and full professors. Marxism became a hot item, and scarcely any academic department in the humanities and social science (with the exception, interestingly, of economics) felt it could carry on without one or two Marxists. Open protest, it is true, was now for the most part passé, left to those small student groups who could work off their sixties envy by marching with a banner or building a shack in front of the administration building. But open protest isn't any longer needed; no need to carry placards outside the gates when the barbarians are already inside, boring—in my view, in all senses of the word—from within.

When I say "the barbarians," I mean a modest number of hard-core characters who actively proselytize students and teach a fairly straightforward Marxist menu featuring distaste for America, in peace and war; unstinting admiration for the struggles of the people of the Third World; hatred of capitalism; and that old favorite the class struggle, served with a generous side order of alienation. Nothing new about any of this. What is new is the general tolerance for this dreary fare. The tolerance is so great because the general spirit prevailing in the preponderance of contemporary universities is that of liberalism. But it is liberalism which has lost its moorings, and which stands chiefly for tolerance for activities well to its own left and is finally convinced only of its own virtue. When a liberal myself, I used to wonder why people so despised liberals. I used to think it was owing to the liberal's avoidance of extremes, of his desire always to occupy the middle ground. No longer a liberal, I no longer think liberalism is, in its contemporary incarnation, informed by balance and fairness; I think it is instead motivated by fear and self-righteousness. Midge Decter once remarked that we should do away with the word "liberal," which has lost its old character anyway, and simply substitute for it the word "left." There is something to that; I would only add that to catch the spirit of the new liberalism, we require the adjective "weak" before the noun "left."

Something that it is not easy to convince people who live outside the university but that is evident to anyone who lives within it is that in the United States there are two political cultures: the culture of the country, which has twice elected Ronald Reagan; and the culture of the university, in which, if an election were held today between Ronald Reagan and Louis Farrakhan, the outcome would not be all that easy to predict (the largest number of votes, my guess is, would be abstentions). It is this political culture, for the most part composed of the weak left, that makes possible the almost continuous inroads of Marxism, feminism, and other isms too numerous to mention. As a rather chaotic teacher at my own university once put it at the close of a memorandum proposing an honors seminar in "gender and literature," our school and, in particular, our department had shown itself woefully behind the times in not having more such courses. When I suggested that being behind the times in this regard might not be such a bad thing, I received looks that could only be described as strange. When I went on to say that I was concerned about the built-in political content of such a course, it was as if I had loudly belched at a small dinner party for the French ambassador. How gauche! But then in the contemporary university just about everything that is not *gauche* is gauche.

Not in every university, I hasten to add, but chiefly in those that think of themselves as the better universities. Thus, the faculty at Stanford makes plain that it is not eager to have the Reagan Library; thus, when Harvard is beset by left-wing demonstrations against speakers, it boldly steps in and cancels the speeches; thus, school after school proudly announced it was divesting itself of its South African holdings, all duly reported in the section of the *Chronicle of Higher Education* called "The Divestment Watch." There is a very heavy traffic in the universities caused by everyone rushing to get on the right side.

In my anger at what I think of as the weakness of the contemporary universities and its baleful effects on the life of the country, am I merely like Ambrose Bierce's conservative, "who is enamored of existing evils, as distinguished from the liberal who wishes to replace them with others"? In politics, is it enough to know what one doesn't like? Do not one's aversions and fears imply preferences and desires? On this score, after my early years of looking at the world from the left, I must say that today any revolutionary zeal I might once have felt is quite gone. Having come through what I have to conclude is something in the nature of a political deprogramming, I feel like Henry James's young hero Hyacinth Robinson, in *The Princess Casamassima*, of whom James writes, "What was supreme in his mind today was not the idea of how the society that surrounded him should be destroyed; it was much more the sense of the wonderful precious things it had produced, of the fabric of beauty and power it had raised."

Like Hyacinth, after dropping my leftism, I feel the world has become a more interesting place—and I mean the world as it is. I have no strong impulse to reform it, outside those pockets of alterable injustice and organized cruelty where change is necessary. I wish people were wiser and better—I wish I were wiser and better—but I know of no clear or certain way to bring this about. I no longer see life as requiring a crescendo of reform, in which every day and in every way my neighborhood, my city, my nation, the world gets better and better. I haven't the least hint how to bring this about, and I am not sure I would if I could. I only wish the world, my nation, my city, my neighborhood to be more habitable—less dangerous, less diseased, less dirty, less dreary. I do not want people to suffer, and I am willing to do all that I can to alleviate this suffering, but I am fairly certain that the old left-wing methods of bringing about this alleviation are less than worthless—they are often, as in the case of so many welfare programs, part of the problem. I do not expect the United States to behave itself with greater moral rectitude than any nation in the history of the world simply because it is the country in which I live and therefore must come up to my standards of rectitude. I expect it instead to act in a rough consensus of what its citizens judge to be its self-interest, protecting itself from its enemies, coming to the aid of its friends, ensuring its own continued prosperity and hence that of its people. In sum, I haven't a utopian notion in my head, and I do not expect to have another such notion this side of the grave.

Shedding my left-wing views has left me much happier without, so far as I can see, making anyone else in the world more miserable (except perhaps those who violently disagree with what I write). But then figures on the left—Marx, Bakunin, Bentham, Mill, Lenin, Trotsky, reformers or revolutionaries—are not a famously happy crew. Being on the left, they are not supposed to be happy, for surely the whole point of being on the left is that one is dissatisfied with the world as it is and ardently desires to change it. I do not mean to say that being leftist condemns one to being humorless. Not at all. But there is, not so very deep down, an element of serious and perhaps immitigable discontent with life, of discomfiture with the world as it is, that turns most people left to begin with and that must remain if they are to stay on the left.

As a writer, someone primarily interested in understanding and not changing the world, I found removing the furry blinders worn through my left-wing youth an immense aid. In my writing I no longer did opinion checks; I no longer sought out heroes and villains through the measure of whether a particular figure's views gibed with my own. Whereas once such men as Henry Ford and John D. Rockefeller would have been boobs and rotters to me, I now found them, not necessarily heroic, but extremely interesting. Cliché terms such as "the robber barons" no longer held any real meaning for me; nor could they for anyone who cared to investigate that fascinating and varied generation in the round and without the bandages of ideology that a committed left-wing writer such as, say, E. L. Doctorow prefers to wear. For myself, once the blinders of liberalism came off, the present became much more enticing than the future—the way the world is became a subject of greater fascination than the way it *ought* to be.

To say that one has shed one's leftist views, even to think oneself anti-left, does not necessarily mean—I know it doesn't in my case—that one has automatically acquired the reverse of these views. In striving not to be deluded, for example, I don't think one has to drop one's compassion; in some respects, I have come to believe, it can grow even greater. Nor need all idealism begin, as left-wing idealism does, in dissatisfaction. Not all idealism, corollarily, need be invested in hope, where it is almost certain to be disappointed and turn sour; there is also the idealism of the actual, those instances of actual courage, altruism, and goodness. Released from bondage to the whole earth catalogue of left-wing views, one can take up more modulated and realistic ones.

I have, for example, recently seen H. L. Mencken and Justice Holmes described as approving capitalist economics without approving capitalist culture. On the practical level, I understand this to mean that one is permitted to approve the system of rewards for initiative and hard work that is at the heart of capitalism and still despise, say, the Waldenbooks chain because it treats what it sells as no more than another commodity. Under socialism, I hear my younger self stepping in to say, there would be no Waldenbooks. True enough. Unfortunately, under socialism, thus far along, there hasn't been much culture either.

I no longer have to be *for* some hopelessly vague entity called the Third World, an entity that includes Bangladesh and Saudi Arabia. Instead I can attempt to distinguish among those Third World countries that are run by clowns, those run by butchers, and those genuinely struggling with horrendous problems. I no longer have to give a hustler such as Jesse Jackson special dispensation from criticism because he is a black man. (How fine it was to read, as I not long ago did in a biography of Martin Luther King, Jr., that King, too, greatly distrusted Jesse Jackson!) I can agree with George Orwell, who was of course staunchly anti-totalitarian, that all revolutions are failures but that they aren't all the same failure—but I can add, because unlike Orwell I do not consider myself a socialist, that they sure are beginning to look like damn near the same failure.

My political deprogramming has given me a fine new sense of intellectual freedom. The, impulse to criticism always came readily enough to me, but I see that formerly it only did so within the constraints of left-wing catechism. Now I feel fully free to criticize anything or anyone, from any side or angle. Better yet, I feel free *not* to criticize—not everywhere to find the connection between something I don't like and capitalism, to discover over and over again that my country is not finally good enough for me, or to blame something called "the system" for my own deficiencies of talent and character. Without such false, if not to say wholly imaginary, connections, discoveries, and accusations, the world seems a livelier, a brighter, an altogether more interesting place. At the age of fifty-seven, Henry James, unable to bear any longer the beard he had worn for several years, shaved it off, after which he wrote to his brother William that he felt "*forty* and clean and light." There are, I have come to realize, other ways to acquire that same feeling without having to shave off a beard.

A Toddlin' Town

(2009)

TIME WAS, if you told me your address in Chicago, I could tell your ethnic origins, make a reasonably accurate guess at your family's household income, know whether your parents ate in the kitchen or in the dining room and whether your father came to table in his undershirt. So balkanized was the Chicago of my youth—the 1940s and '50s—that each Chicago neighborhood (and there are by current count some 237 of them) was a village unto itself, with its fairly intensive ethnic ethos, its own mores and folkways. And one didn't often, except to go to work, and not always then, leave the neighborhood; no great need to, for churches, parks, restaurants, movie theaters, taverns, and everything was there, close at hand.

Chicago was then filled with European immigrants—Poles, Greeks, Czechs, Irish, Italians—and very Catholic. Priests in dog collars and nuns in full habit were part of the urban landscape of my boyhood, so much so that, until perhaps the age of 10 or 11, I thought Catholicism and Christianity coterminous. Blacks were chiefly locked away in their own neighborhoods on the city's South Side, though soon to take over west-side neighborhoods, and were, in Ralph Ellison's sense, largely invisible, encountered only doing servile jobs. No homeless people walked the streets panhandling. We had only bums, in those days confined to one of Chicago's two skid rows, one just south, the other west of the Loop.

That time, of course, isn't any longer. I now drive through neighborhoods I once knew to be drab working class and find them filled with charmingly refurbished houses lived in by young, college-educated married couples. Neighborhood taverns—the workingman's country clubs—are largely gone, sometimes replaced by franchise fast-food joints but just as often by coffee bars or small chichi restaurants. The grand Catholic churches, built by the tithing of immigrants, still stand, and the parks remain, but neighborhood life doesn't seem quite so centered in these institutions as once it did. In former days, if you asked a Chicagoan where he lived, he was likely to answer with the name of his parish (St. Nicholas of Tolentine) or the nearest park (Green Briar), where he grew up playing the 16-inch-ball version of softball played only in Chicago or in whose field house he later went to do business with his Democratic ward committeeman. Catholic culture, if not the religion itself, seems to have all but disappeared; people are not so recognizably Catholic as once they were or so dedicated to sending their kids to what used to be called parochial schools.

Black life, once segregated, is largely segregated still, but no longer so strictly. In the bad old days, few were the Chicago restaurants to which one could take a black friend or acquaintance without fear of rebuff. The Hispanic population has grown greatly, demographically, politically, in prominence generally. Devon Avenue, the great Jewish shopping street of West Rogers Park, the neighborhood of my own boyhood, is now dominated by Indians and Pakistanis; on Saturday nights, women in saris and boys in cricket sweaters walk the street.

The older Chicago was an industrial city: steel-producing, meat-packing, candy-manufacturing, a great hub for shipping agricultural produce, justifying, at least partly, the heavy clichés of Carl Sandburg's spurious poem. Streets were dotted with tool-and-die makers, quasi-residential neighborhoods zoned "light industrial," so that on one side of a street one might have octagonal-fronted bungalows with tidy lawns and a Mars Bars Candy factory on the other.

But now the great steel mills have mostly been closed, the stockyards are long gone, manufacturing has slowly but relentlessly been leaching away. No more is Chicago a rail center, nor does its location smack dab in the center of the country yield the advantages it once did. By all rights the city should by now be one of those sad cities, like Detroit, Cleveland, Indianapolis, once vibrant centers of thriving commerce that have, clearly, seen their best days. But, somehow, it isn't.

Dominic A. Pacyga's *Chicago: A Biography* provides a history of the city, one that concentrates on its ethnic, political, and commercial elements, leaving the more amorphous though no less interesting questions of urban culture to the side. Filled with information lucidly if not stylishly set out, it recounts the founding and sweeping changes in the city, since the days fur trappers and traders took it over from the Pottawatomie Indians. The Chicago Fire of 1871 (Mrs. O'Leary's cow and all that), the Haymarket Riot of 1884, the unending tussle between unions and capitalists, the development of the Loop, the advent of skyscrapers, the wild politicians (Bathhouse John Coughlin and Michael "Hinky-Dink" Kenna, later Paddy Bauler of "Chicago ain't ready for reform" fame), the mostly futile efforts of the great reformers (Jane Addams and George Pullman), Al Capone and the St. Valentine's Day Massacre, the birth of the Democratic Machine, the Daley dynasty, the dissonant note of race playing throughout the city's history, it's all here, all covered in a comprehensive and careful way and brought up to the moment of the regime of Mayor Richard M. Daley. Good and worthy book though *Chicago: A Biography* is, having read it one is far from clear that it conveys what it was like to grow up and live out one's days in the Second, the Windy, the Hog Butcher City.

I was born and grew up in Chicago and have spent all but six years— two in the Army, two in New York, two in Little Rock, Arkansas—of my adult life in the city or its immediate environs. New York has vastly more stimulus, Los Angeles better weather, San Francisco superior views. But never has it occurred to me to live anywhere other than in Chicago. Nor am I likely to desert it for the gentler climes some seek as they grow older: the entire state of Florida seems an elephant graveyard; Arizona a prison sentence served under dry heat and unrelenting sun; the Northwest a black hole from which, once entered, no one emerges.

For me that leaves Chicago, a taste for which, once acquired, never departs. I have the taste in a strong way. I can remember, on long marches in the (peacetime) Army, relieving the tedium by letting my mind play on fantasies of myself driving along Chicago's Outer Drive, a lush freeway that runs, north to south, across much of the city, along its dazzling lakeshore, in a red Oldsmobile convertible, various beautiful girls in the passenger seat beside me. When I drive it today, every exit on the Drive, as we call it in Chicago, denotes an event in my life. Foster Avenue: the Saddle and Cycle Club, where I was a ball boy for Billy Talbert, Ham Richardson, and two members of the Mexican Davis Cup team. Wilson Avenue: the Louis Weiss Memorial Hospital, scene of my mother's death. Irving Park: Waveland, where we played high-school softball and touch-tackle football on Sunday mornings. Belmont: the Tango Restaurant, where my wife and I had our wedding dinner. And so forth, exit after exit, ending for me at 57th Street, where as a boy I was delighted by the exhibits of the Rosenwald Museum of Science and Industry and as a young man I lived in quasi-bohemian squalor as a student at the University of Chicago and picked up the wrongful message that unless one was an artist, scientist, or statesman, one's life was a waste. The Outer Drive, which I travel often, provides a regular mobile replay of my life.

We are all the result of the never quite similar mixture of the influences of our family, our religion (or absence of religion), our time, and our geography. For me the geography is not a secondary influence. "I am an American, Chicago-born," wrote Saul Bellow at the very beginning of *The Adventures of Augie March*. I tend to reverse the formulation: I am a Chicagoan, American born, and would add, "and very Jewish in point of view." The two, Chicagoan and Jewish, seem to have reinforced each other in odd ways. But both are united, I believe, in being schools of realism.

To BE JEWISH IN CHICAGO is different from being Jewish in New York. So often has it been said that it has nearly reached the status of platitude, but New York is a very Jewish city. The spirit of the place is Jewish, in its knowingness, in the things it reverences, and in its irreverence, too. When in my mid-20s I lived in New York, I felt an immediate sense of relaxation, specifically relaxation as a Jew. A guard, long held up, dropped; I felt I had come to a place where everyone ate my kind of food, used my syntax, understood my irony-laced humor. I felt I had come home.

Being Jewish in Chicago has always carried with it a slight but genuine outsider status. New York has always attracted the talented and the ambitious, which gives the city its wired, hyper, neurotic quality. But the European ethnic groups that came to Chicago were largely peasant in social class—they came to the burgeoning industrial city in search of work; muscle, not talent, is what they brought. Their appreciation of human difference was not wide, their tolerance of one another not deep. People stayed with their own, in their village-neighborhoods, because it felt more comfortable that way. Interlopers were not welcome.

Segregation in the Chicago of my boyhood was not by race alone, especially for Jews. Jews lived among Jews, partly by choice but also partly, in many instances, because of restrictive real-estate covenants. At the University of Illinois, the fraternities and sororities were Jewish and non-Jewish, with no exceptions, no crossovers, that I knew about. When my half-Jewish high school played working-class schools—Amundsen, Schurz, Waller—a note of tension was added, and once, after a basketball game at Waller, thuggish kids beat up our team outside the school after the game, badly enough to send a few of them to the hospital. When friends and I attempted to pick up girls (with an impressively low success rate, let me add) at Riverview Park, a landlocked Coney Island in the middle of the city, we invariably introduced ourselves by fake, usually highly *goyische* names: my own favorite, as I recall, was Michael Enright. Gentiles, the thought behind this was, had a better chance at this game than did Jews.

Chicago is a city of facts: plain, hard, obdurate facts. Local arrangements within its borders are not subtle. Perhaps that is why the city's best-known novelists have been men known in the literary histories as realists: Frank Norris, Upton Sinclair, Theodore Dreiser, Nelson Algren. Saul Bellow's subject was always the clash between the intellectuals, the *luftmenschen*, and those realists, operators, hustlers, mobsters, who take the world as it is—and in his fiction, the intellectuals generally lose, and, some might say, deserve to.

My mother, a Chicago girl, born on the city's Jewish west side, who took the commercial course at Marshall High School, was a realist without a typewriter. When I was a boy, I recall our driving through various Chicago neighborhoods—Sauganash, Kenilworth on the North Shore—and my mother quietly remarking, "It's restricted, you know." She would say this with utter calm. Did she secretly despise the people who put together such anti-Jewish real-estate covenants? I am far from certain that she did. She had no aspirations to live in these neighborhoods—she preferred to live around Jews—and would in any case have found her neighbors there boring in the extreme.

My mother read the newspaper very selectively, very, one might say, Chicagoanly. She read only stories about crime and scandal. Politics, unless scandal was entailed, was beneath her notice. Nor was political scandal really news, at least not to her: it was all the same story, the political story, crooks and fools everywhere one turned. She understood from her years in Chicago that people in a position to steal were more likely than not to do so.

Once, while my father was in Louis Weiss Hospital for gall-bladder surgery, my mother and I were having coffee in the hospital cafeteria. Doctors were walking in and out of the cafeteria, dapperly dressed under their white and gray smocks, with their names sewn in cursive above the breast pocket. Watching all the doctors Zimmerman, Murphy, Farber, Ferguson, parade past, my mother, lifting her coffee cup, her little finger slightly crooked, smiled and quietly observed: "They're all thieves, you know." My mother had no snobbery and was a perfect judge of a good heart no matter its possessor's social class, having such a heart herself, and yet she was able to live a contented life of kindness and charitable giving alongside the cynicism that a life in Chicago had taught her.

My father, born a Canadian, from Montreal, came to Chicago when he was 17. Cynicism did not come as naturally to him as my mother's did to her. But it didn't take him many years living in Chicago to learn the score. "Chicago aldermen spend a quarter of a million dollars for a job that pays $20,000 a year," I recall him saying to me. "Something's wrong with the arithmetic here."

He did business at the Illinois State Fair every summer, and to smooth the way lest any bureaucrat give him a hard time, he had secured the services of a state senator—at what price I do not know—named Nicky

Napolitano. I remember, too, a customer of his, a tidy little man whose last name was Perry, telling my father on more than one occasion that if he ever found himself in a tight spot for money, the Boys would be glad to help out. The Boys, of course, were the Mob, or, as we called it in Chicago when I was growing up, the Syndicate (or sometimes the Outfit).

Organized crime, political and other corruptions, a slight feeling of menace that was also exciting, sexy even, these were some of the elements that made Chicago, as the Sinatra song had it, a toddlin' town. I knew a few boys whose fathers were bookies, and one whose father, after a success in the aluminum-awning business, went into the fight game, where he got tied up with the Boys, so that at one point both the Syndicate—in particular, a man by the name of Milwaukee Phil Alderisio—and the FBI were in pursuit of him. Fortunately, the FBI found him first.

To have distant connections with the Syndicate gave one a certain cachet in the Chicago of my youth. I had an uncle who was a successful bookmaker—our family has long been in publishing, I used to joke—who went out to Los Angeles and later owned a few points of the Riviera Hotel in Vegas. Sinatra, to place my uncle socially, was at his granddaughter's wedding.

As adolescents, many of us took our clues on manly behavior from these characters. In eighth grade, before ballroom dancing lessons, which were held on Saturdays in the field house at Indian Boundary Park, we met to play penny poker and smoke cigarettes on the sly. In high school, gambling was one of our central activities. We bet football parley cards and played lots of cards: poker, gin rummy, an automatically stakes-escalating game based on blackjack called Pot Luck. I can recall even now the desolating feeling, at 16, of losing at Pot Luck, between after school and dinner, $80, in those days a month's rent on a two-bedroom apartment in a middle-class neighborhood.

We also frequented—if that is the right word—cathouses. Some weekend nights we would drive the 60 or so miles to the brothels of Kankakee or Braidwood; other times we would go off with streetwalkers back to their sad rooms, heedless of the danger involved in such adventures. Sex was never what this whore-mongering was really about. It was about learning the city, its ins and outs, its licit but, even more, its illicit pleasures.

Inserting a five-dollar bill in the same window of your wallet as your driver's license, there to pay off any cop who stopped you for a traffic violation—the cops charged two dollars more than the ladies of Kanakee and Braidwood—was standard procedure. Getting into a cab to an all-night Pot Luck game at Dickie Levinson's apartment at 3800 N. Lake Shore Drive, or going with my two-years-older cousin Jack Libby, whose Uncle Pete I spotted one night coasting down Rush Street in his red Cadillac convertible with Patti Page in the passenger seat, to a poker game already in progress in one of the sheds of the old Fulton Street Market—such things, at the time of my late adolescence, seemed like living with the throttle all the way out.

BOXING WAS THE SPORT OF CHOICE in the Chicago of my early boyhood. My father bought me a pair of padded gloves and used to spar with me when I was 6 or 7 years old. He took me a few times to watch Golden Gloves fights. The great three-weight-class champion Barney Ross's sister Ida Kaplan lived across the courtyard in the same building we did on Sheridan Road. My father had two friends from Montreal, the Brothers Spunt, Danny and Sammy, who ran, on Dearborn Street in the Loop, the Ringside Gym, where Tony Zale and Johnny Bratton and other boxers of the day trained. (Joe Louis and Sugar Ray Robinson trained for Chicago fights in a gym on the South Side.) When I was 10 or 11, I would get on the El and visit the gym. Danny, the more congenial of the two brothers, gave me my pick of the 8 x 10 glossies of the great fighters of the day that he kept in a file cabinet in his office and would introduce me to some of the boxers as the next lightweight champion. Once he took me back to meet Tony Zale, who had just finished his workout and was sitting, leaning against his locker, in shorts and heavy leather exterior jock, breathing heavily. "Champ," Danny said, "I want you to meet the kid. Kid, meet the middleweight champion of the world." "Hi, Champ," I bleeped out. "Hi, kid," he said, and thus began and concluded my first encounter with celebrity.

Zale was a Pole from Gary, Indiana, on Chicago's southern border. Dick Butkus, the great Chicago Bears linebacker, is a Lithuanian from the South Side of Chicago, a graduate of Chicago Vocational High School. I remember a basketball player from Lane Technical High School named Wally Mruk, three years older than I, whose bulky hair-covered body could have been used to clinch any argument that holds we are descended from the apes. Chicago, in short, has long had a tradition of brutes: working-class, peasant-types, not likely to be caught with a copy of the poems of Percy Bysshe Shelley in their raincoat pockets.

Mike Ditka, the former coach of the Bears football team who is not a native Chicagoan but has come to be identified with the city, has a successful restaurant here called Ditka's. I've eaten there only once; it's a congenial-enough place, filled with beefy customers. For those whose taste runs to the synecdoche, one item on the menu, under appetizers, can stand in for all the rest: Pot Roast Nachos. Chicago is the city of the steak house, of deep-dish pizza, the Italian beef sandwich that requires three hands to manipulate and eleven small paper napkins to mop yourself up with afterward.

BEEFY, BRUTISH, BRAWNY—in Chicago, unlike in Los Angeles or San Francisco, if you're 40 or 50 pounds overweight, nobody notices—Chicago remains relatively content with the corruption of its politicians, to have survived the demise of its once impressive industrial base, and to have witnessed the end of capital M Mob rule, for the old Syndicate has lost its stake in gambling to online betting and legal casinos, its drug money to individual entrepreneurs, and its revenues from prostitution to the fact that nice girls now do for nothing what hookers used to do only for money. The city's denizens do retain something of their old cynicism, at least to judge by their amused rather than outraged reaction to the regular succession of Chicago-based governors of Illinois who seem to have used the post of state executive as a stepping stone to prison.

Chicago today is younger than I ever remember it—by which I mean that it is a fine place to be living in when in one's twenties, thirties, or forties. One senses this everywhere: whether driving down Rush Street on a summer evening and noting all the out-of-doors dining by the Gold Coast young; or shopping among the less-well-to-do crowds in Andersonville, once a German and Swedish working-class neighborhood now regenerated and gentrified by gays and lesbians; or the bleachers in Wrigley Field, where, in college, I used to sit and make bets on every pitch but that now resembles nothing so much as a singles bar.

New York critics write enthusiastically about the theater life in Chicago. Galleries have sprung up to the west of the Loop, near Harpo, the headquarters of Oprah's operation in the city and the site of what passes for the hipper restaurants. The city is no longer under the sad old literary curse of Nelson Algren and Studs Terkel, with their pretense that everyone in town was immoral except for them. At present there are no great Chicago writers; just men and women, most of them youngish, trying to get some writing done, and it feels a lot better. Only the crowds for the chamber music at the Chicago Symphony—dominated, as it sometimes seems, by German Jewish women tottering on walkers—seems irretrievably aged.

The city is no longer mine. The pleasures it offers are those of other generations, all younger than my own. My view of it today is chiefly spectatorial and archival. In the stories I write, and in my point of view generally, I am more and more the historian and embodiment of a city that used to be. While I recognize that the new Chicago is a vast improvement on the one I grew up in, I am nonetheless grateful for the chance to have grown up in the one I did. I miss the old Chicago, just as I miss the adventurous boy who was ready to take the stupidest of risks for the pure excitement of risk itself. That boy has long since been replaced by a rather bookish gray-haired gent who walks Chicago's streets still hoping to pass for not altogether out of it, but knowing, not so deep down as all that, that before too long, he will be.

Old Age and Other Laughs

(2012)

What shall I do with this absurdity—
O heart, O troubled heart—this caricature,
Decrepit age that has been tied to me
As to a dog's tail?

W. B. YEATS, "The Tower"

I RECENTLY BOUGHT SOMETHING called catastrophic health insurance for my college-student granddaughter—a policy that has a high deductible but is in place lest, God forfend, she needs to undergo a lengthy and expensive hospital stay. The insurance agent who sold it to me is a man named Jack Gross, whom I occasionally see walking around the streets of my neighborhood and who always greets me, often with a new joke. Being an insurance salesman and having me there in his office, Jack couldn't resist asking me if my wife and I have assisted-living insurance, a policy designed for older people that pays for caregivers (or minders, as the English, more precisely, call them), thus allowing those suffering from dementia or other devastating conditions to avoid nursing homes. Assisted-living insurance is very expensive, especially if one first acquires it in one's seventies, which my wife and I are.

"Thanks all the same, Jack, but we have no need for assisted-living insurance," I said. "We have pistols."

"Great," he replied, nicely on beat. "I just hope when the time comes to use them you are able to find them."

The problem with that amusing response is that it has an uncomfortably high truth content. Memory lapses, sometimes significant ones, but often quite as maddening trivial ones, are as everyone knows a standard part of the problem of getting old. Why the other day could I not recall the name of an old Expos and later Mets catcher (Gary Carter), or the hotel in San Francisco that my wife and I favor (The Huntington), or the actress I used to enjoy talking with occasionally when we were both on the Council of the National Endowment for the Arts (Celeste Holm)? Where are my glasses? Why have I come into this room? I opened the refrigerator door for . . . what, exactly?

The word *old*, I have been informed, is now politically incorrect. I recently read a book on the aging of the baby-boomer generation, *Never Say Die: The Myth and Marketing of the New Old Age* by Susan Jacoby, that introduced me to the words *wellderly* and *illderly*. Not very helpful. *Aging* isn't much help either, for newborn babies are, ipso facto, aging the moment they emerge from the womb. *Old, getting old, being old*—these are words I prefer, and in this essay I'm sticking with them.

The difficulty enters in deciding who qualifies as old. Unless brought badly down by serious illness, in the United States one isn't any longer considered old at 62 or 65, the ages Social Security allows a person to begin collecting what used to be considered old-age benefits. Some people, owing to a good ticket in the gene-pool lottery, or through being scrupulously careful about their health, begin to get old 10 or so years later than do others. But old we all get, that is if we are lucky enough not to have been crushed by disease, accident, or war, and taken out of the game early. Next only to death itself, old age is the most democratic institution going—nearly everyone gets to enjoy it.

Enjoy is not the word most people would use in connection with old age. Many fight off old age through cosmetic surgery, strict exercise and stringent diet regimens, pills beyond naming, hair plugs, penile implants, even monkey glands (the useless remedy attempted by W. Somerset Maugham and W. B. Yeats). More struggle against old age with the aid of one or another form of positive thinking: Keep your mind active, look on the bright side of things, remember life is a journey, you're only as old as you feel, and all that malarkey.

The first physical signs that one is getting old are those slight altera-tions in your body that remain permanent. Sometime in my late fifties, I lost the hair from my shins and calves, to which it has never returned. Not much later a few brown spots appeared on my forehead, never to depart. Capillaries burst, leaving parts of one's body—in my case, my ankles—nicely empurpled. Bruises take longer to disappear than when one was young, and the scars from some of them never quite do. Time is a methodical and cruel sculptor.

Conversations among friends take up new subjects. When young, my male friends and I talked a fair amount about sports and sex. Later, con-versation about food and movies came to loom large. Nostalgia—"the rust of memory," Robert Nisbet called it—began to set in around 60. Sleep is currently a hot topic, and by sleep I do not mean whom one is sleeping with, but instead how long one is able to sleep uninterruptedly.

The first time one cannot make love twice in one night, I have heard it said, is disappointing; the second time one cannot make love once in two nights can be the cause for despair. Viagra and other aids have helped solve this problem, but pharmacology has yet to come up with a pill to make one physically appealing. Few things sadder than to watch a man in his seventies, forgetting what he looks like, flirting with a waitress in her twenties. Women are not without their own problems in this realm. I once heard a woman roughly my age tell a female friend that her bra size was now 34" long.

Things once done easily, even blithely, suddenly require taking sec-ond thought. Coming down a staircase, I seek the banister. Walking on slightly uneven pavement, I remind myself to lift my feet. Don't drive too slowly, I say to myself. The safety bar in the shower is there for a reason. Put on sunscreen. Virtue consists of ordering a salad for lunch; disap-pointment, in eating it.

I used to consider myself a Jewish Scientist, like unto a Christian Sci-entist, if only in my avoidance of physicians. Proust says that to believe in modern medicine is insane, and that the only thing more insane is not to believe it. My body forced me out of the church of Jewish Science in my late fifties. When once I had a single doctor—a primary and in my case only physician—I now have what feels like a medical staff: a gastroenterologist, an ophthalmologist, a cardiologist, and a dermatologist. In the past 15 years I have been diagnosed (not always correctly) with Crohn's Disease, autoimmune hepatitis, Celiac Disease; have had a triple-bypass surgery (though not a heart attack), cataract surgery, and a detached retina; and finally a charming skin disease called—and best pronounced in a W. C. Fields accent—bullous pemphigoid. Such a rich buffet of health problems eats into one's former feelings of personal invincibility.

At 70, in fact, one awaits both shoes to drop: the tumor to form, the strange pain not to disappear, the aneurysm to show up on the CAT scan. Hypochondria, at this age, is the better part of valor, for as paranoids sometimes have real enemies, so do hypochondriacs sometimes drop dead. One awaits the results of "blood work" like a prisoner on death row awaits a governor's reprieve. Preventive medicine, with its various specialists and panoply of tests, in old age can be as exacting as an illness. Santayana, at 85, was told by his physician to lose 15 pounds. "He evidently wants me in perfect health," the philosopher remarked, "just in time for my death."

Fatal illnesses often strike older people without clear—make that *any*—reason. An acquaintance of mine who spent his life staying in shape—weight lifting, jogging, competing in triathlons, the works—recently died of lymphoma. Everyone knows of someone who never smoked getting lung cancer. Alzheimer's blasts the most active and well-stocked minds. Immune systems break down, causing major problems no one could have predicted; body parts wear out, not all of them replaceable. It's a minefield out there, with deadly darts falling from the sky.

Physical change is accompanied by mental change. Time begins to register differently. Did this or that incident happen 8 or was it 11 years ago? Years back I met a lost unseen uncle, then about my age now, and asked him how old his son was. "Thirty-seven," he said confidently. "He's 45," his wife corrected him. I ask an acquaintance if his daughter got into Stanford, and he tells me that she graduated two years ago from Yale Law School. The minutes, the hours, the days, weeks, and months seem to pass at roughly the same rate; it's only the decades that fly by.

Then there is the matter of repetition. Have I done this, said that, written the other before? Some things refuse to stick in the mind. Movies are high on the list. I seem to have arrived at the place in life where I can watch *The Pelican Brief* as if seeing it afresh every 18 months. One of the saddest things an old person can hear is a younger friend saying, "You already told me." Friends one's own age are more likely to say, "You may have told me, but I've forgotten, so tell me again."

One begins to notice that contemporaries have, in their garrulity, become bores. As there is no fool like an old fool, neither is there any bore quite as tiresome as an old bore. How close am I myself to having achieved accreditation in this line? In too many conversations, I note that I wait patiently to slot in one of my standard jokes or surefire (I think) anecdotes. Have I arrived at my anecdotage, the stage of mental decomposition that precedes full dotage? Do I break into too many other people's monologues? Have I become like the man who, returning from a party, when asked by his wife if he enjoyed himself, replies: "Yes, but if it wasn't for me, I would have been bored to death."

Crankishness, complaint division, sets in. How is it no man born after 1942 carries a handkerchief in his back pocket? Why is the membership of the entire US Senate so bloody undistinguished? Might it be because the vast majority of its members are younger than I? One of the reasons the old complain about the world, Santayana wrote, is that they cannot imagine a world being any good at all in which they will not be around to participate.

One of the standby subjects of the old is how much richer, less gruesome, altogether better life was when they were young. The problem is that, when old, things genuinely do seem this way, and, who knows, they may well have been. Forty years ago, in my own line of work, universities seemed more serious, intellectuals more impressive, culture more weighty. I do not allow myself to lecture the young on how much better life used to be. I only talk about the old days with contemporaries, which is to say, with fellow cranks.

With age, curiosity is curtailed, attention attenuated. This is especially so in the realm of advancing technology. I have friends my age who, even 10 or 15 years ago, could not make the jump to learning how to use computers. Even among those of us who love email and have come to rely heavily on Google and adore smart phones, the continual refinements on digital technology tend to swamp us. Do I really require Apple's new app that will allow me to replay the entire Russian Revolution on my phone and store all my photos in my navel?

In classical music concerts, my mind, like musical notes in a hall with poor acoustics, wanders all over the place, although the fact that the median age of the audience for classical music appears to be roughly 114 does make me feel refreshingly youthful. My stamina for museums and art galleries is now almost nonexistent. Less than halfway through a play, I ask myself why I have paid 85 dollars to listen to the lucubrations of a fellow even more stupid than I. Confronted with the prospect of travel, the effort seems greatly to outweigh the prospect of pleasure. More and more I feel like the poet Philip Larkin, who, when asked if he wished to visit China, answered yes, indeed, if he could return home that night.

I live within a block of two large retirement homes. The people who reside in them, most older than I, are part of my everyday mise-en-scène. Many are in good enough fettle: Straight and kempt and cheerful, they have made the decision that living on their own has, for one reason or another, become too lonely or otherwise burdensome. Others have funny walks, or are bent with osteoporosis; a few have slightly vacant looks in their eyes. An occasional resident, in a wheelchair pushed by a Filipina minder, is deep into dementia and is not so much out for a walk as for an airing. I have watched some of these people go from walking confidently to using a metal cane to requiring a walker to disappearing. Doubtless you have yourself already heard the ugly rumor that the mortality rate at present is at 100 percent.

Henry James said that when one reaches the age of 50, someone one knows seems to die every week. Now, with increased longevity, I suppose the appropriate age is 70 when one's personal casualty list begins to grow at a swift pace. Reading the obits has long been part of my morning regimen. (A good morning with the obits—a word that sounds like a breakfast cereal—is one where no one under 90 pegs out.) If it's not someone I know who dies every week, then someone dies who is a friend of a friend, or the editor or agent or publisher of an acquaintance. Friends go down with one or another of the vast array of cancers, heart attacks, ALS, Alzheimer's. The latter drag on alive, but one begins to speak of them in the past tense. Sometimes people one knows die in clusters of three or four or five, as if mown down by a machine gunner. If I am allowed to live on for a decent interval longer, the dolorous time may arrive when I have more dead than living friends and acquaintances.

For all that can be said on its behalf, *Losing It*, William Ian Miller's book on the subject of old age, is not a gift one wants to present to a friend or relative on his or her 80th birthday. Professor Miller is an historian of the medieval world, with a special interest in Icelandic sagas, who teaches in the law school at the University of Michigan. Years ago I read—and reviewed in the *New Yorker*—an earlier book of his called *The Anatomy of Disgust*. He has written other books on revenge, fraudulence, and humiliation, and obviously has a penchant for darkish subjects. Self-described as "halfway between an essayist and a historian," he writes well, with a slightly macabre sense of humor, with irony added, shoring up his arguments with rich historical comparisons and analogies.

Writing a book called *Losing It* puts one in danger straightaway of giving evidence that one has oneself begun to lose it. Professor Miller's premise is that he hasn't quite lost it but is well on his way to doing so. "It" stands for one's intelligence, wit, intellectual penetration, verbal agility, physical prowess, and strength, all the powers that one felt confident of when younger but feels slipping away with age. Miller's bête noire in this book is the school of positive psychologists who claim that old age is the time of our lives, those serene golden years, all wisdom and tea (also tee) times. Miller's own view is closer to that of a friend of mine who recently turned 90 and, to the question of what is the best thing about old age, answered: "It doesn't last long."

Professor Miller laces his book with autobiographical bits, touching on his own experience of growing old. He is Jewish, despite that suspicious middle name of Ian, born and brought up in Green Bay, Wisconsin. (*Losing It* contains several references to the Green Bay Packers.) He was 65 when he began writing this book, 66 at its completion, a tad too young perhaps to claim the complaining privileges of old age. As a university teacher, his being around students may aid in making him feel old; nothing adds years on a person more than being regularly around the young. Miller worries, in fact, that in his book he may have exaggerated his decrepitude. He is after all a man who continues to teach, works out on an exercise bike, has a mother still alive (at 90), drives a motor-cycle—not, clearly, everyone's idea of an *alte kocher*.

Intimations of mortality are what Miller has begun to feel, but, I should say, intimations merely. He speaks of memory lapses, of thinning hair, of no longer being quick in response, of his more attractive female students grasping that he is not really in sexual contention: "Oh, Professor Miller, he's such a cute old man," a colleague reported one such student saying of him. At the close of his book, he mentions a memory blackout he suffered—Transient Global Amnesia is its clinical name—before a Packers game. But where are his surgical scars? Where his white hair or baldness? He admits to taking Zoloft and Paxil, anti-depressant and anti-anxiety drugs, but so far as I know, he doesn't even have a plastic weekly calendar pill box, that badge of the older player.

Where *Losing It* is most valuable is in its author's recounting of stories of growing old in warrior societies (such as the Vikings, Norsemen, and Ice-landers) and religious communities. In warrior, or honor, societies, a good death is one in which one goes down in battle, preferably with one's ene-mies defeated, a ticket for Valhalla under the shield. In a religious, or at any rate a Christian community, martyrdom is the speediest way to heaven, there to dwell among the angels. In warrior societies one dies with a sword in hand, in religious communities with a Bible in one's bed and a priest by one's side. In secular societies, one is more likely to die with an IV on one's wrist and a tube up one's nose. The best death in a secular society is one in which one expires in sleep—in other words, a death, next to birth the major element in life, that one isn't even around to witness.

Professor Miller relishes retailing the problems of old age. He describes the shrinkage that takes place in the human brain. Dubious about old age bringing about wisdom, he holds that wisdom is rare at any age, and no more likely to be found among the old than in any other group. He even cites studies that conclude the old are stupider than the young, in rely-ing more on stereotypes and appearances to make judgments. He is quite properly skeptical about the official wise men and women of our day: "I still find the wise dead considerably wiser than those we hold to be mod-ern-day wise men and women, who, the more famous they are, the more likely they are to be charlatans."

No one gets Miller's heart racing more quickly than those who find the prospects of old age cheerful. A book called *Successful Aging* he describes as advocating "staying spunky, thinking positively, and then dropping dead quickly when thinking positively finally succumbs to reality." F. Scott Fitzgerald claimed that the sensible state for the older man was mild depression. Miller wouldn't disagree: "As a general rule," he writes, "critical intelligence—mental acuity—wars with happiness."

Miller takes after Stanford professor Laura Carstensen, whose optimism on the subject of being old drives him up and nearly over the nursing home wall. For Professor Carstensen everything in old age presents an opportunity for contentment. For her even "brain rot," according to Miller, has its upbeat side. When Carstensen reports a sense of well-being among the elderly respondents to a study she has done, Miller asks: "Did she interview any old Jews? She couldn't have, unless we have become more assimilated than I would ever have thought possible." The work of Professor Carstensen and her followers he characterizes as "suspect science" and the selling of "snake oil bearing the Stanford label."

Miller's own view of old age is that it is downhill all the way, a journey that leads ultimately back to a second infancy, replete with diapers, hairlessness, loss of locomotion—a ride from goo-goo to ga-ga. In old age Miller sees only diminishment, humiliation, the curtailment of pleasure. Old age, he writes, "made it hard for several of the deadly sins to operate," though here La Rochefoucauld beat him to the punch by more than three centuries, writing: "Old people like to give good advice as a consolation for the fact that they can no longer set bad examples."

Live long enough, Miller warns, and even an exemplary career can be done in during one's dotage. "You end up remembered," he writes, "for your doddering vacancy . . . for your former self is now redefined in light of your drooling present." Think of Bertrand Russell, a genius when young, a political fool in old age, hostage as he was at the end of his life to nutty left-wing movements.

When I began teaching at Northwestern University, the great figure there was Bergen Evans, the lexicographer who had earlier been the host of a television show on ABC called *Of Many Things*. His courses drew six or seven hundred students; his lexicographical works were best sellers. A student in one of my classes who was taking Bergen Evans's course in American usage told me that three times during the current quarter, Professor Evans took a letter out of his suit-jacket pocket, announced it arrived in the previous day's mail, and read it to the class—and all three times it was the same letter. Oops!

Finding nothing good to say about old age, Miller does not ease up, either, on life after death. "Death does not lock in a reputation," Miller writes. "What if 10 years after you die it turns out that your son is a serial killer, your daughter a positive psychologist [I say, that's a joke, son], your grandchildren drug addicts and in prison? You are not safe, your virtue, your life, will be reevaluated, and . . . there is no relaxing, no satisfaction in a life once thought well lived if you have spawned a line of losers." Not a speaker much in demand at Ann Arbor Rotary Club meetings, Professor Miller, I should guess.

Do I need here to confess that I rather like my current age? I of course recognize, pace Yeats, that this is "no country for old men"; none, after all, is. Yet old age confers, if not wisdom—I would never claim that for myself, especially if I had it—then a certain amused perspective. From the parapet of 75, I can see the trajectory and final shape of the careers of my contemporaries, including the insignificance of my own. With the sense old age gives of time passing quickly, I find myself more patient now than in earlier years; old age has helped, if not entirely to defeat, then at least to quiet the traditional Jewish disease of *schpilkosis*.

My age has released me from the need to be *au courant*, or even moderately with it. I am no longer responsible for knowing much about Madonna, Lady Gaga, and the young women who will inevitably follow them. With the grave yawning, surely I cannot be expected to read the 600-page novel about the assistant professor of English who discovers his father is a transvestite? The imminence of death may or may not concentrate the mind wonderfully, as Samuel Johnson had it, but it does provide a few clues about how to expend what remains of one's mental energy. My hope, contra Dylan Thomas, is to go gently into that good night.

At 75, I feel I am playing with house money—the rest of my life, as people used to say before the worry about cholesterol set in, is gravy. Lovely it would be to stay in the game for another 10 years or so, and I hope to be able to do so. But if before then some bright young oncologist or grave neurologist informs me that the time has come for me to cease flossing, I shall be mightily disappointed but scarcely shocked or even much surprised. On such an occasion I hope to retain the calm to count my blessings, which in my case have not been few. Among them will be that I have lived in freedom during a time of unprecedented prosperity, been allowed to do work of my own choosing that has been appreciated and decently rewarded, while never having been called upon to betray my friends or my ideals. Another blessing has been that thus far I have dodged the land mines, the flying darts, and the machine gunner, and arrived at old age.

Day, day, enu, as the Hebrew chant has it, *dayenu, dayenu.*

Part Three

The Culture

The Kindergarchy:
Every Child a Dauphin

(2008)

IN AMERICA we are currently living in a Kindergarchy, under rule by children. People who are raising, or have recently raised, or have even been around children a fair amount in recent years will, I think, immediately sense what I have in mind. Children have gone from background to foreground figures in domestic life, with more and more attention centered on them, their upbringing, their small accomplishments, their right relationship with parents and grandparents. For the past 30 years at least, we have been lavishing vast expense and anxiety on our children in ways that are unprecedented in American and in perhaps any other national life. Such has been the weight of all this concern about children that it has exercised a subtle but pervasive tyranny of its own. This is what I call Kindergarchy: dreary, boring, sadly misguided Kindergarchy.

With its full-court-press attention on children, the Kindergarchy is a radical departure from the ways parents and children viewed one another in earlier days. Ten or so years ago I began to notice that a large number of people born around the late 1930s and through the 1940s had, as I do, a brother or sister five or six years younger or older than they. So often was this the case that I began to wonder if there wasn't some pattern here that I had hitherto missed? Then it occurred to me that mothers in those days decided not to have a second child until their first child, at five or six, had gone off to school.

Born into the middle class in the Middle West, growing up I did not know any married woman who worked. So the mothers I am talking about here did not put a five- or six-year separation between the birth of their kids for economic reasons, or because it gave them more time to devote to their first-born children, or any other reason I can think of other than their own damn convenience. They did it because—insensitive, selfish, appalling really to contemplate—it was easier not to have two children under four years old to worry about at once; it made more sense to them not to have to deal with two or more needy greedy little children simultaneously. Let one go off to school, then we shall think of having another—much easier for everyone all around. Or so I believe thinking on the matter went.

Did this arrangement make sense for the children? Five or six years' age difference between siblings is probably not an ideal difference for the development of closeness between brothers and sisters. When my younger brother entered boyhood, at eight or nine, I was already in high school; when he was in high school, I was away at college; and when he was in college, I was a married man with a son of my own. No, a five- or six-year separation is doubtless not the best spacing between two kids growing up in the same household. If you had confronted my mother and father with this psychological datum, they might have said, "Interesting." But I doubt that they would have found it very interesting at all.

Let me quickly insert that I had the excellent luck of having good parents. Neither was in the least neurotic, both were fair to my brother and me, neither of us ever doubted the love of either of them. I can also say with no hesitation that my parents' two sons were never for a moment at the center of their lives. The action in their lives was elsewhere than in child raising.

In my father's case the action was at his business—"the place," as he sometimes called it. A small businessman, he came most alive when at work. Without hobbies or outside interests, he worked a five-and-a-half day week, and didn't in the least mind if he had an excuse to drop in for a few hours on occasional Sundays.

My mother, who was not in any way a trivial person as the following details might make her seem, played cards at least three afternoons a week. She kept up a fairly brisk social round. She was at home to provide us lunch when my brother and I were in grammar school, and she cooked substantial dinners, baked, and was a careful housekeeper. Later she took an interest in charities and paid for and helped organize occasional fundraising luncheons. When her children were grown, she went to work in her husband's business as a secretary-bookkeeper-credit-manager, at all of which she did a first-class job.

When I was a boy my parents might go off to New York or to Montreal (my father was born in Canada) for a week or so and leave my brother and me in the care of a woman in the neighborhood, a spinster named Charlotte Smucker—Mrs. Smucker to us—who was a professional child sitter. Sometimes an aunt, my mother's sister who had no children, would stay with us. We seldom went on vacation as a family. When I was eight years old, my parents sent me off for an eight-week summer camp session in Eagle River, Wisconsin, where I learned all the dirty words if not their precise meanings. None of these things made me unhappy or in any way dampened my spirits. I cannot recall ever thinking of myself as an unhappy kid.

My mother never read to me, and my father took me to no ballgames, though we did go to Golden Gloves fights a few times. When I began my modest athletic career, my parents never came to any of my games, and I should have been embarrassed had they done so. My parents never met any of my girlfriends in high school. No photographic or video record exists of my uneven progress through early life. My father never explained about the birds and the bees to me; his entire advice on sex, as I clearly remember, was, "You want to be careful."

I don't recall many stretches of boredom in my boyhood. Life was lived among friends on the block and, later, during games on the playground. Winter afternoons after school were filled up by "Jack Armstrong," "Captain Midnight," and other radio programs for kids. Boredom, really, wasn't an option. I recall only once telling my mother that I was bored. "Oh," she said, a furtive smile on her lips, "why don't you bang your head against the wall. That'll take your mind off your boredom." I never mentioned boredom again.

After the age of ten, I made every decision about my education on my own. The one I didn't make, at ten, was to go to Hebrew school in order to be bar mitzvahed; this was a decision made for me and was non-negotiable. But my parents felt no need to advise me on what foreign language to take in high school, where I ought to go to college—though my father paid every penny of my tuition and expenses—or what I ought to study once there. That I was a thoroughly mediocre student seemed not much to bother them. Neither of my parents had gone to college, and my father never finished high school, moving to the United States and going off on his own at 17, and so they did not put great value in doing well at school.

At roughly the age of 11, I had the run of the city of Chicago, taking buses, streetcars, or the El with friends to Wrigley Field, downtown, or to nearby neighborhoods for Saturday afternoon movies. Beginning at 15, the age when driver's licenses were then issued in Chicago, I had frequent use of my mother's cream-and-green Chevy Bel-Air, which greatly expanded my freedom. I don't recall either of my parents asking me where I had been, or with whom, even when I came in at early morning hours on the weekends.

When we were together, at family meals and at other times, we laughed a lot, my parents, my brother, and I, but we did not openly exhibit exuberant affection for one another. We did not hug, and I do not remember often kissing my mother or her kissing me. Neither my mother nor my father ever told me they loved me; nor did I tell them that I loved them. I always assumed their love, and, as later years would prove, when they came to my aid in small crises, I was not wrong to do so.

I did not seek my parents' approval. All I wished was to avoid their—and particularly my father's—disapproval, which would have cut into my freedom. Avoiding disapproval meant staying out of trouble, which for the most part I was able to do. Punishment would have meant losing the use of my mother's car, or having my allowance reduced, or being made to stay home on school or weekend nights, and I cannot remember any of these things ever happening, a testament less to my adolescent virtue than to the generous slack my parents cut me.

The older I become the more grateful I am to my parents for staying off my case. Yet they were not unusual in this. Most of the parents of my contemporaries acted much the same, which is why very little anger or animus on the part of my friends against their parents was in evidence. Some parents were more generous to their kids than others, a few mothers showed anxiety about their sons and daughters, but no parents that I knew of seemed oppressive enough to give cause for feelings of revolt on the part of their children. Free and almost wildly uncontrolled though it may seem today, my upbringing was quite normal for middle-class boys of my generation.

I don't for a moment mean to suggest that such an upbringing produced a superior generation of adults. What it produced was another group of people who later spent their lives going about the world's business, with no strong grudges against their parents or anger at such abstract enemies as The System. All I would claim is that to be free from so much parental supervision seemed a nice way to grow up, and it surely resulted in a lot less wear and tear on everyone all round.

Parents generally didn't feel under any obligation to put heavy pressure on their children. Nor, except in odd, neurotic cases, did they feel any need to micromanage their lives. My father once told me that he felt his responsibilities extended to caring for the physical well-being of my brother and me, paying for our education, teaching us right from wrong, and giving us some general idea about how a man ought to live, but that was pretty much it. Most fathers during this time, my guess is, must have felt the same.

A single generation later, I have to confess, I didn't—at least, not quite. I tried to bring up my two sons on the model on which I had been brought up, but I was unable to bring it off very successfully. My own confidence in my doing the right thing as a parent was considerably less than that of my own parents. I was always telling my two sons how much I loved them. I told them this so often that I should imagine they must have begun to doubt that I had any real feeling for them whatsoever.

The time was the 1960s and early 1970s. The culture was beginning to change radically. Lots of marriages were falling apart, my own among them. (After divorce, I had custody of my sons, who were then eight and six.) Drugs seemed to be everywhere. Crime was getting a lot more press. The rise of political hippyism followed by feminism, itself in part a reaction to the male dominance of the political movement of the Sixties, brought on a strong contempt for the middle class, and what was thought its stolid ways and left a wide swath for anyone who wished to make a jolly damn fool of him- or herself, which lots of people did. The business of therapy appeared to be picking up; more and more people seemed to be undergoing it, and its assumptions became more deeply ingrained in middle-class life.

One of the direct results of the 1960s was that the culture put a new premium on youthfulness; adulthood, as it had hitherto been perceived, was on the way out, beginning with clothes and ending with personal conduct. Everyone, even people with children and other adult responsibilities, wanted to continue to think of himself as still young, often well into his forties and fifties. One of the consequences of this was that one shied away from the old parental role of authority figure, dealing out rewards and punishments and passing on knowledge, somewhat distant, carefully rationing out intimacy, establishing one's solidity and strength. Suddenly parents wanted their children to think of them as, if not exactly contemporaries, then as friends, pals, fun people. Parents of my own parents' generation may have been more or less kind, generous, humorous, warm, but, however attractive, they never thought of themselves as their children's friends. When your son becomes a man (or your daughter a woman), make him (or her) your brother (or sister), an old Arab proverb has it. But it's probably a serious mistake to make a kid of 9 or 14 your brother or sister.

Childrearing became a highly self-conscious activity, in all of its facets. Husbands were now called in not merely to help out with childrearing but in actual childbirth. They went to Lamaze classes with their wives; there they were, not infrequently videocam in hand, in the delivery room cheerleading and rehearsing breathing exercises with their laboring wives. Pregnant women were advised not to smoke, not to drink, not to do a great many other things that generations of expectant mothers had always done, lest their children pay the price in ill-health, if not actual birth defects.

A child being the most dear of all possessions, instructions—maintenance manuals, really—for his or her early upbringing were everywhere. Pacific mobiles swayed gently over cribs, nursery rooms were designed with the kind of care devoted to the direct descendants of the Sun King—and why not, for every child suddenly became his or her own dauphin or dauphine. In the background the music of Mozart—so good, parents were told, for heightening the intelligence quotient—played on at just the right volume. Impossible to be too careful about these matters, when so much was at stake.

"Children are best seen not heard," was a maxim once in frequent use. "Speak only when spoken to," was another piece of advice regularly issued to children. Now kids are encouraged to come forth, as soon and as frequently as they wish, to demonstrate their brightness, cuteness, creativity. A few years ago, I found it noteworthy (and still memorable) that when on the phone with an editor I was dealing with—he was working at home at the time—he said to his daughter, "Faith, don't disturb Daddy right now. He's working." Most people today would have put one on hold or offered to call back later. Kids, after all, come first.

On visits to the homes of friends with small children, one finds their toys strewn everywhere, their drawings on the refrigerator, television sets turned to their shows. Parents in this context seem less than secondary, little more than indentured servants. Under the Kindergarchy, all arrangements are centered on children: their schooling, their lessons, their predilections, their care and feeding and general high maintenance—children are the name of the game.

No other generations of kids have been so curried and cultivated, so pampered and primed, though primed for what exactly is a bit unclear. Children are given a voice in lots of decisions formerly not up for their consideration. "If it's your child, not you, who gets to choose your weekend brunch spot," writes David Hochman in the magazine *Details*, "or if he's the one asking how the branzino is prepared, it's probably time to take a hard look at your own behavior."

Where once childrearing was an activity conducted largely by instinct and common sense, today it takes its lead from self-appointed experts whose thinking is informed by pop psychology. Here, for example, is a blogger calling herself Millennium Mom on the subject of punishment. On spanking, Millennium Mom's view—quoting from an article posted on the iVillage website—is that spanking may give children a clear message about the un-acceptability of their behavior and sometimes stops the behavior in the short run. However, in the long run, it teaches children that it is all right to hit, and that it is all right to be hit. Even children are confused by the irony of the statement, "This spanking will teach you not to hit your brother."

On the subject of "time-outs" —those enforced recesses when children are asked to go off to contemplate their bad behavior—Millennium Mom notes:

The problem with time-outs is that they take a child away from a valuable learning experience. A child who hits another child can begin to learn empathy from watching the other child's response to being hurt, and if he stays around, he may also be able to participate in helping the other child feel better.

Bountiful is your heart, Millennium Mom; it is only your insight into human nature that is troubling.

The relentless cultural enrichment of children under Kindergarchy is not an option; it will be seen to, whatever the toll in time or money. At a minimum, visits must be made to Disneyland, the Epcot Center, national parks, children's museums, youth concerts, every new movie designed for the children's market. Various lessons—ballet, tennis, guitar, more—must be contracted, with mom or dad driving the kids to them and picking them up afterwards. ("Parenting," that dreary neologism, has given the old role of parent the status of a job, and no part-time one, either.) Each child must have a vast arsenal of toys, with emphasis currently on the wireless. The appropriate CDs and DVDs need to be acquired, books and iPads, Kindles, and smartphones. "Mackenzie has read Harry Potter, all seven books, three times." How nice for Mackenzie! "Gideon adores books about mythology, and, did I tell you, he's learning French?" *Merveilleux*! A parent can report nothing more satisfying than that her child is an eager reader, years and years ahead of himself, and, though only nine, already reading at the post-doctoral level of comprehension.

The names Mackenzie and Gideon are a reminder of how important the naming of children has become under the Kindergarchy. No more Edward, Robert, David, when you can have Luc, Guthrie, and Colby; no more Jane, Barbara, Lois, when Lindsay, Courtney, and Kelsey are available. Sometimes, in the naming of children, there is a dip back to the deliberately out-of-date—Jake and Max, Emily and Becky—but such names are tainted by an historical falsity, in the same way that Balanchine said that every beard grown after those worn by men in his father's generation was a fake.

One reads occasional stories about the spoiled children of the rich, those little tyrants of private schools, who wear designer clothes and mock classmates who do not; or about the kids whose parents drop a couple hundred grand on their bar-mitzvahs or sweet 16 parties; or of affluent suburban high-school parking lots filled with their students' BMWs and Porsches. In a rich country, a fair amount of this kind of sad vulgarity figures to go on. But what I have in mind is something more endemic—a phenomenon that affects large stretches of the middle class: the phenomenon, heightened under Kindergarchy, of simply paying more attention to the upbringing of children than can possibly be good for them.

The craze of attentiveness hits its most passionate note with schooling, and schooling starts now younger and younger. When Lyndon Johnson began the War on Poverty in 1965, its most popular, perhaps because least controversial, program was Head Start, which provided the children of the poor with preschooling, so that they would catch up with the children of the middle class by the time all began kindergarten at the age of five. But the middle class soon set in motion a head start program of its own, sending its children to nursery and preschools as early as is physiologically possible. Where one's child goes to school, how well he does in school, which schools give him the best shot at even better schools later on—these are all matters of the most intense concern.

Under Kindergarchy, no effort on behalf of one's children's schooling is too extensive, no expense too great, no sacrifice in time and energy on the part of parents too exacting. In a scandal of a few years ago, a New York stock-market analyst named Jack Grubman arranged some complicated stock shenanigans to get to a member of the board of the coveted

92nd Street Y Nursery School in Manhattan, whom he hoped would smooth the way for his twin children to get into this school, which he felt would in turn pave the way into the better New York private elementary schools and high schools, and thence obviously to the very Valhalla of the Ivy League itself. The Grubman story shows how much parents feel is riding on their kids' schooling and how far some are willing to go to get what they think is the best for them.

The pressure on the children upon whom all this attention is lavished is not slight. At New Trier, the upper-middle-class suburban high school on Chicago's North Shore, children load up their backpacks with SAT study guides to get as close to being toll free—present parlance for scoring two 800s on the SATs—as possible, carry lacrosse sticks and tennis racquets wherever they go, hoke up their sad little résumés to make themselves look like miniature Dr. Albert Schweitzers in search of lepers to whose aid they might come, and generally plow away at what they call Preparation H, shorthand for preparing to apply to Harvard.

Every high school now has its battery of counselors: guidance, psychological, college. A larger and larger segment of the student population seems to bring its own psychological tics and jiggeroos to school with them: ADHD, dyslexia and other learning disabilities, various degrees of depression requiring regimens of pills and therapy sessions. Some of these defects and disabilities are the result of parents' having their children at a later age. Might others be that the children are so intensely watched over and tested that more and more defects and disabilities show up, some among them possibly imaginary?

School is the pressure point. More and more teachers in grade and high schools complain not about the children they are asked to teach, but about the endless contact with children's parents. Parents are *in situ*, on the scene, unstintingly on the job. "How come Corey only got a B in physics? He's always been so wonderful in science." "Why isn't Lettice a better speller? Her father won the state spelling bee in Iowa." One wonders how many teachers have been driven out of the profession by parents' bombarding them with emails, phone calls, and requests for meetings?

As my sons were growing up, I began to notice parents taking a great deal of interest in their education, much more so than previous generations of middle-class parents had done. Everyone wanted his or her kids to get into one of the better-regarded colleges, and a lot more than education seemed to be riding on it. A son at Princeton, a daughter at Yale, such things seemed a validation of one's own virtue as a good parent, and hence, somehow, as a superior human being. Much snobbery was entailed, of course; having a child at Harvard being obviously thought more impressive than one at a nearby community college, but more than snobbery alone was involved. Payback time, getting into a good college is the child's return on his parents' immense psychological investment in him.

These much loved children eventually do, at staggering expense (but who's complaining?), go off to college. First, of course, there are the *de rigueur* pre-college visits, where parents load up the car during junior year of high school to tour all the colleges that are within the child's range of possibility. ("Thaddeus hated Tufts, loved Reed.") Then, the applications completed, the acceptances garnered, the decision made, one last trip: carting the kid off to the school of choice, with a carload of his clothes and appliances, with stereos, computers, television, DVD-player, PlayStation, cell phone, credit card. There he will learn from teachers raised not so very differently than he that it is precisely people like his parents—that would be you, Mom and Dad—who have made life hell for the wretched people of Africa, Bangladesh, and underdogs everywhere round the world. Which may not be the payback most contemporary parents quite envisioned.

How did earlier generations of parents seem able to manage raising children while putting in so much less time, avoiding so much *Sturm und Drang*? People raising children today will tell you that the world is a more frightening place now than it was 50 years ago. Much more crime out there, drugs are easily obtained, sex offenders are everywhere, lots of children turn up missing, as the back of your milk cartons will inform you. The spirit of therapy having triumphed, we now see more clearly than heretofore how fragile the young human personality is, how easily it can be smashed by mistreatment or mismanagement or want of affection. Add to all this that the options for children are much greater today; a child can go in any number of ways in education and in life, and all these need to be thoroughly investigated.

Failure today seems a much more dismal prospect; 50 or so years ago, if one didn't, for example, get into what was thought a good school, life didn't seem permanently dim, if not effectively over. America seemed to offer more then than now in the way of second chances. Today everything seems so much riskier, so much more appears to be at stake.

Why shouldn't parents do all in their power to make their children's lives less bumpy, more concentrated and carefully planned, thereby increasing their prospects for a happier, more satisfying life? No reason at all, really, except that trying to do so often comes to seem so joyless and the children who emerge from such ultra-careful upbringing so often turn out far from the perfect specimens their parents had imagined.

As a teacher at Northwestern University, I found the students in my classes in no serious way I could discern much improved for all the intensity of home and classroom attention most of them received under the Kindergarchy. A very small number, those who had somehow found passion for books and the life of the mind, were remarkable, a number proportionally probably little different than in any generation of students; the rest were like students everywhere and at all times: just wanting to get the damn thing called their education over with and get on with life with the best start possible.

The most impressive students I had over my 30 years of university teaching were those I encountered when I first began, in the early 1970s, who almost all turned out to have been put through Catholic schools, during a time when priests and nuns still taught and Catholic education hadn't become indistinguishable from secular education. Many of these kids resented what they felt was the excessive constraint, with an element of fear added, of their education. Most failed to realize that it was this very constraint—and maybe a touch of the fear, too—that forced them to learn Latin, to acquire and understand grammar, to pick up the rudiments of arguing well, that had made them as smart as they were.

So often in my literature classes students told me what they "felt" about a novel, or a particular character in a novel. I tried, ever so gently, to tell them that no one cared what they felt; the trick was to discover not one's feelings but what the author had put into the book, its moral weight and its resultant power. In essay courses, many of these same students turned in papers upon which I wished to—but did not—write: "D-, Too much love in the home." I knew where they came by their sense of their own deep significance and that this sense was utterly false to any conceivable reality. Despite what their parents had been telling them from the very outset of their lives, they were not significant. Significance has to be earned, and it is earned only through achievement. Besides, one of the first things that people who really are significant seem to know is that, in the grander scheme, they are themselves really quite insignificant.

Growing up with only minimal attention sharpened this sense of one's insignificance. One's fierce little opinions were all very well, but without the substance of accomplishment behind them, they meant nothing. Not long after I had graduated from the University of Chicago, at a family dinner, an aggressively confident cousin of my father's asked what I planned to do with my life. I mentioned, rather diffidently, that I hoped one day to be a writer. "You ought to try to get something in the *Reader's Digest*," he replied, in a challenging way. The *Reader's Digest* was not what I had in mind; in those days publishing in the *New Yorker*, in my young highbrow's view, would have meant selling out. Naturally, I wanted to tell this man how stupid his notion of literary success was and that he should stick to his own damn business (which was the hardware business), and to bugger off, thank you very much. I knew, though, that I daren't do so; I was untried, untested, still a kid (even though one of 22), without authority. Instead I nodded, as if I thought publishing in the *Reader's Digest* an interesting notion, and returned to my roast beef.

Had that incident occurred today, had I been raised under the Kindergarchy, I no doubt would have lectured him on his ignorance, put him properly in place, my approving parents ("Wonderful how young Joseph always speaks his mind!") looking on. I say this based on the fact that I note today many of the young, in late high-school or college years, suffer no shyness in putting forth their own opinions, observations, and usually less than penetrating insights. So many I have encountered also greatly overestimate their charm. But, then, why shouldn't they; their parents have for years been telling them how tremendously charming they are.

Every generation must have its journalistic label, and the most recent generation to depart school to enter the larger world are now called "the millenniums," after the fact of their coming into their maturity in the 21st century. Newspapers stories are beginning to report that, on the job, these people, raised under the Kindergarchy, don't tolerate criticism well, and need lots of praise to buck them up and get them through the day. A friend of mine, who works for a financial consulting firm, tells me that the brightest of the young men and women going into financial work he meets are almost all interested in hedge funds—they want big scores, 20 or so million before they reach 30. They didn't have to wait long for their toys or attention or anything else as children, so why should they wait for the world's prizes as adults?

The consequences of so many years of endlessly attentive childrearing in young people can also be witnessed in many among them who act as if certain that they are deserving of the interest of the rest of us; they come off as very knowing. Lots of their conversation turns out to be chiefly about themselves, and much of it feels as if it is formulated to impress some dean of admissions with how very extraordinary they are. Despite all the effort that has been put into shaping these kids, things, somehow, don't seem quite to have worked out. Who would have thought that so much love in the home would result in such far from lovable children? But then, come to think of it, apart from their parents, who would have thought otherwise?

Well, in the words of Vladimir Ilyich Lenin, who had no children, what is to be done? Not very much, I suspect. When such seismic shifts in the culture as that represented by the rise of Kindergarchy take hold, there isn't much anyone can do but wait for things to work themselves out. My own hope is that the absurdity of current arrangements will in time be felt, and people will gradually realize the foolishness of continuing to lavish so much painstaking attention on their children. When that time comes, children will be allowed to relax, no longer under threat of suffocation by love from their parents, and grow up more on their own. Only then will parents once again be able to live their own lives, free to concentrate on their work, life's adult pleasures, and those responsibilities that fall well outside the prison of the permanent kindergarten they have themselves erected and have been forced to live in as hostages.

Prozac, with Knife

(2000)

I MAGINE TYLER AND KELLY TUCKER—as I like to think of them—
on the first night of their honeymoon, in a glow of happy confidence
that sets a mood for postcoital intimacies. Tyler opens by confessing
to his bride that his thick hair is the result, partly, of hair plugs, implanted
three years before he met her. Kelly admits in turn that her high cheek-
bones, which Tyler has so often remarked upon, are the consequence of
silicone injections. He allows that, at age sixteen, he rid himself, through
surgery, of the aquiline Tucker nose. She confides that her once weak chin
has been augmented, her front teeth are capped, and six of her back teeth
are implants. Finally he shares the news of his penile enlargement. Her
breasts, she whispers back, have likewise been enlarged, her thighs and bottom reduced through liposuction. In a swoon of candor they embrace—
though Tyler, a former fat boy, has still to divulge his tummy tuck.

"Beauty fades," says the character played by Albert Brooks in *I'll Do
Anything*, bemoaning his weakness for knock-out young women. Then
he adds, "but it fades so slowly." Not slowly enough, apparently, for the
Americans, Europeans, Latin Americans, and Israelis who have been
going in for plastic surgery in continually larger numbers. The statistics
on these procedures—also known as cosmetic surgery, less frequently
as aesthetic surgery—show them to comprise a flourishing business. In

Making the Body Beautiful Sander L. Gilman, a professor at the University of Chicago, reports that from 1981 to 1984, the number of such surgeries in the United States rose from 296,000 to 477,700. By 1995, 825,000 operations were being performed on the face alone—quite apart from procedures to lift the skin of the upper arm; breast work (implantations, reductions, removal of earlier, faulty implants); buttock and thigh lifts; tummy tucks; liposuctions of various sorts; calf and other implants; foreskin reconstitutions; penile enlargements and implantations; and— the ultimate surgical alteration—sex-change operations.

Plastic surgery—from the Greek *plastikos*, meaning "fit for molding"— has, we learn from Gilman, a long history. The 7th-century Alexandrian physician Paulus of Aegina thought that the growth of breasts in men was something to be dealt with surgically. Later, surgery was called upon to camouflage wounds incurred in dueling or warfare, or to hide the depredations of advanced syphilis on facial bones, particularly the loss of cartilage in the nose. Surgeons also did their best through the centuries to undo nature's dirty tricks—repairing cleft palates, constructing missing body parts, reducing hideously outsized organs and appendages. But it was during and after World War I, when physicians worked to reconstruct faces destroyed in combat, that plastic surgery obtained its best press. This may also have been the last time it was not bogged down in the swamps of controversy.

The first of these controversies had to do with whether plastic surgery strictly qualifies as medicine, especially when its intentions are purely cosmetic. If the patient seeks the treatment, decides what is needed, and then is the chief judge of its success, is this really medicine? Plastic surgeons themselves used to worry over such questions, and in the first decades of the 20th century many refused to take on cases that they deemed trivial or requests for reasons that went no deeper than vanity.

But help was at hand by the 1920s with the widespread publicity given to the psychiatrist Alfred Adler's notion of the inferiority complex. The important word here is "complex," implying that feelings of inferiority are unnatural, an aberration, needing to be altered, cured, or . . . cut away. (The alternative, of convincing individuals that they really are inferior, and hence relieving them of the burden of carrying around a complex, has apparently never been tried.) Thus, cosmetic surgeons soon found themselves able to say that they were not only performing surgery but supplying therapy. With a cut here, a bob there, they combined the work of a sawbones with that of a shrink, turning a sad person—a person with too large a nose, a weak chin, big ears, a squint—into a happy person. In effect, they were supplying Prozac, but with a knife.

Leaving aside scandals over the possible consequences of silicone breast implants, physicians doing cosmetic surgery probably feel rather better about their work today than ever before. Cosmetic surgery is even creeping into other branches of medicine: dermatologists, for example, have begun doing skin peels, collagen injections, and liposuctions. A physician I see told me recently that if he had his medical career to plan over again, he would be a cosmetic surgeon. The work requires artistry, it makes most clients quite happy, and it is profitable: an eastside Manhattan facelift from a swank practitioner might run, with all the extras—consultation fee, nursing, anesthesia, recovery hotel—somewhere near $20,000.

The profit most often comes in the form of cash on the barrelhead. Since insurance companies reimburse only that portion of the surgery that is truly reconstructive or directly related to health, much of the usual bureaucratic-financial headache connected with the practice of medicine is eliminated. Fees are paid up front, which does away with bill collecting and also prevents unsatisfied customers from withholding payment (though a few have returned to murder their surgeons, causing many nowadays to screen for potential maniacs). As for patients who go to law to complain about the quality of the surgery they have received, juries tend to be most unsympathetic, viewing them as members of two vaguely but genuinely despised groups: the pathetically vain and the antipathetically wealthy.

VANITY ASIDE, what is cosmetic surgery really about? In my high school in Chicago—this is going back more than 50 years—a small but not negligible number of girls had already begun to have their noses done. "Done" invariably meant shortened, often made retroussé, or slightly upturned. Different surgeons conferred different looks: I seem to remember something called a Becker nose being popular in Chicago; in New York during those same years, Long Island girls went to a cosmetic surgeon named Howard Diamond to acquire a Diamond. A few among these girls claimed they needed to have an operation because a "deviated septum" was giving them trouble breathing. Most, of course, simply disliked the shape of their noses sufficiently to undergo the pain and general unpleasantness—they would show up at school with blackened eyes and vast quantities of tape across the middle of their faces—required to change it.

The younger sister of a close friend of mine in those days had a distinctly non-Beckerian nose. Like her mother's, it was slightly aquiline and with flared nostrils—clearly, as the old anti-Semites had it, one of the chosen noses. She also had an attractive shyness, a slight holding-back of herself that I found winning but that may well have been traceable in part to her unhappiness with her looks. At fifteen, she had her nose fixed. The operation was an almost unqualified success, definitively solving the problem of both aquilinity and—as writers on the subject call it—nostrility. Now altered by the knife, my friend's sister descended into the great adolescent female herd of the merely cute, losing, so far as I could determine, all distinctiveness whatsoever. Yet, I have no doubt, she was happier.

What this suggests is that cosmetic surgery is "about" the specific form of happiness that can accompany passing: becoming invisible by melting into the mass. Not that passing is necessarily the same thing as hiding out altogether. My friend's sister, for example, certainly did not want to de-Judaize herself—her name was Jewish, she went on to marry a Jewish man and bring up her children as Jews. She only wanted a face that more closely conformed to the then-prevailing American standard of beauty. In the 1960s, the ideal American nose was said to belong to Jacqueline Bouvier Kennedy Onassis. Study of that famous appendage—small, short, just slightly upturned—reveals no oddity or distinction of any kind. And that is just the point: it was a nose that gave no clues to origin, no hostages to ethnic identity.

Passing can take many forms. Some people wish to escape or elide their ethnic or even racial heritage: Asian girls, for example, who want western eyes. Others (John Dillinger is the famous example here) may wish to avoid detection by the cops. Some wish to add to their erotic cargo, which is what breast implants are about. Others—these days, they are the majority—wish to seem younger than they are. And some, as with Michael Jackson's estimated 40 operations, may not be quite sure what they are after but are confident that, in one way or another, cosmetic surgery will alter their lives for the better.

And it may well do so. Most studies report that handsome or beautiful men and women tend to do better in the job market and also—golly, Mom, wouldya believe it?—tend more easily to find partners for sex. Beauty is a quality, noted Montaigne in the 16th century, "that gives power and advantage"; to Aristotle, it was "a greater recommendation than any letter of introduction." True, in certain circles beauty can come under suspicion: I once heard two great scholars—the historian Arnaldo Momigliano and the social scientist Edward Shils—discuss in perfect earnestness how a graduate student's handsomeness seemed to suggest an incapacity for serious scholarship. Still, given the choice, most of us would undoubtedly prefer to come into the world beautiful, and most of us are also likely to have at least one unbeautiful physical quality that we feel may have held us back from the greater triumphs that were surely meant to be ours. Are not such flaws more costly to us than the price of eliminating them through cosmetic surgery?

Not that most people who enter into such surgery do so wholly without trepidation. A piece of flesh, after all, is hardly a piece of cake, and the literature is strewn if not with corpses then with post-operatively misshapen or malfunctioning body parts. There are women whose skin becomes stretched so tight from facelifts that they cannot close their eyes at night, or from whose faces the makeup slides off. There are women with silicone inserted in their cheeks in the hope of attaining the look of Audrey Hepburn who, when the silicone falls, end up looking more like Alvin the chipmunk. There are the noses that emerge snouty, the lips that curl or fall to one side, the scarring, the infections, the long-term slippage that, over time, needs to be redone, the occasional death.

Consider lipoplasty, better known as liposuction and employed to bring about what were once called "contour improvements" by vacuuming or sucking out fat from the face and neck, abdomen and flanks, thighs, hips, knees, calves. Because licensing laws are unclear in some states, and nonexistent in others, incompetent practitioners—not to say outright quacks—can never be ruled out. But even under good conditions, and in good hands, serious screw-ups can occur. In *The Unofficial Guide to Cosmetic Surgery*, E. Bingo Wyer notes that "In all forms of lipoplasty, . . . too great a loss of fat can result in a rumpled or unbalanced appearance, which can be difficult to correct." She then adds a brief but horrific list of possible side effects, including pain, bleeding, temporary numbness, excessive fluid buildup, clots that block the flow of blood, infection, shock. In *Lift*, an account of her own "brow lift, nose nip, secondary facelift, and lip peel," the journalist Joan Kron mentions matter-of-factly the post-operative removal of "fifteen or twenty annoying metal staples used to close the incision in the back of my head." A routine matter, this—and yet, one cannot help thinking, maybe it isn't merely not nice but not too smart to try to fool Mother Nature.

BUT PEOPLE DO CONTINUE TO TRY. For one thing, new techniques keep being invented and put into practice. For another, fashions change. Rhinoplasty (nose jobs) has dropped off in recent years—although some people, no longer shamed by their ethnicity, are going *back* to their cosmetic surgeons to have their old bumps or beakishness returned. The notion of "passing" has itself passed from the wish to seem normal, or invisible, or WASPish, to the wish, mainly, to seem young. Facelifts, along with eye- and brow-lifts and various skin peels (collagen and Botox injections, dermabrasion, laser resurfacing), currently lead all other forms of cosmetic surgery.

And what is wrong with the wish to remain youthful-looking? Medical technology has given us a great gift, one that enables us to fight off, for as long as possible, nature's slow, inexorable onslaught, to cheat that great sculptor Time. If we want to make ourselves seem younger and therefore (by our own lights) happier, and can afford the cost, why not?

One answer is that heredity and time—or, if one prefers, the heavens and fate—deal us a much more interesting hand than doctors can ever hope to do. Think, in all its immense variety, of the nose: from Gogol's long sharp proboscis to Tolstoy's potato nose to W. C. Fields's empurpled lighthouse nose to Jimmy Durante's two-pound cucumber nose to Igor

Stravinsky's isosceles-triangle nose to Bob Hope's ski-jump nose to Bar-
bra Streisand's grand depressed-tip, sloping-septum nose. Interesting
faces, oddly beautiful faces, are not created by surgeons, no matter how
skillful, but by the years, working in conjunction with character. Who
would have wished to subject the rhino-hide face of the older W. H.
Auden to a face-lift, or to change in any way the countenance of the novelist Marguerite Yourcenar, with its strong lines, shadows, dark nostrils,
sagging eyelids, and more than a hint of a mustache?

Novelists have long depended on the relation of physiognomy to
character; Balzac speaks with pity of people who have not yet learned
to read moral character in a face. And if beauty, as the cliché has it, is
in the eye of the beholder, here is the twenty-six-year-old Henry James,
the subtlest of beholders, writing home to his father after meeting the
English novelist George Eliot:

> To begin with she is magnificently ugly—deliciously hideous.
> She has a low forehead, a dull gray eye, a vast pendulous nose,
> a huge mouth, full of uneven teeth and a chin and jaw-bone
> *qui n'en finnissent pas*. . . . Now in this vast ugliness resides
> a most powerful beauty which, in a very few minutes, steals
> forth and charms the mind, so that you end as I ended, in
> falling in love with her. Yes behold me literally in love with
> this great horse-faced blue-stocking. I don't know in what
> the charm lies, but it is thoroughly potent.

This suggests a philosophical question for cosmetic surgeons: does a
change in one's body bring about a corresponding change in one's moral
character? And if so, can we be sure it is for the better? In his introduction to a 1937 book titled *New Faces, New Futures: Rebuilding Character
with Plastic Surgery*, Alfred Adler answered in the affirmative: after such
surgery, "the personality relaxes into naturalness and character is trans-
formed." One may be permitted to doubt this. Even, it turns out, radical
feminists do. Fifty years after Adler, a writer in *Ms.* confessed, "Before the
operation I rationalized how I wanted my face-lift so my exterior would
match my interior. . . . I realize now I was lying to myself. I just wanted to
look younger and prettier."

I am not sure that George Orwell was correct when he claimed that at fifty a man gets the face he deserves, but at sixty and beyond, I can attest, he tends to get reconciled to it. I look in the mirror and consider my ample, stick-out ears; my mottled complexion, with a beard that confers a five o'clock shadow sometime past noon; the impressive bags—two-suiters—under my eyes, which go so nicely with the sag that has shown up in my right eyelid; the slightly off-center circumflexes that my eyebrows have begun to form; the strong downward lines running from alongside the bridge of my nose to the top of my upper lip; the fairly recent addition of two further lines, running from the corners of my lower lip down to my jaw, giving my mouth the look of a ventriloquist's dummy and a not-so-gentle hint of pervasive depression. A face, clearly, begging for the knife. Yet, just as clearly, it is not going to get it: for I have grown accustomed to this face, a poor thing but mine own.

From both limited personal acquaintance and photographs in various books on the subject, I have noticed that cosmetic surgeons are not themselves a notably handsome bunch; yet most do not seem to have done anything about it. Why not, when the remedy is so obviously and easily and literally at hand? An old joke about psychoanalysts is that, after conferences in Vienna, they get drunk together and sing, "I want a girl/just like the girl/that married dear old dad." Can it be that cosmetic surgeons begin each day by crooning into their mirrors: "But don't change a hair for me/Not if you care for me/Stay, little Valentine, stay"? I would like to think so, at least for a few happily cynical souls among them.

You May Be Beautiful, but You Gonna Die Some Day

(2011)

You may be beautiful,
But you gonna die someday,
So how's about a little lovin'
Before you pass away.

OLD BLUES SONG

W E ARE ALL BORN with a serious and unalterable birth-defect: we grow old—at least the lucky among us do—and then we die. Some attribute this to the decisive side-effect of the poor judgment Eve showed in the Garden of Eden; some to the breakdown in the plot of evolution, which appears to have creaked to a halt before finishing the job and rendering human beings both perfect and immortal. Whichever the case, we are left with the blasted defect, which causes the appalling inconveniences of aging that end only with death.

Aided by careful diet, nearly constant exercise, serene thoughts, and relentless medical discovery, there are those who wish to deny death. They are counting on longevity without surcease. These people and their optimistic thinking are the targets of Susan Jacoby's book *Never Say Die*.

Ms. Jacoby wrote the book at sixty-five years old, and thus at the older end of the generation known as boomers, who, she feels, are especially loath to admit to growing older, let alone to dying. Not a generation, the boomers, to heed Homer, who advised, "Best not to be born, or to die young"; or for that matter Xenophon's Socrates, who submits to death tranquilly because he thinks it preferable to old age, which Trotsky called "the most unexpected thing of all that happens to man."

Boomers and other death-deniers find succor in all that heartening health news—and every television station and newspaper now has a health editor purveying it—that reports hopeful new cures for old diseases and successful longevity experiments on mice and other critters. They gobble up stories in the *New York Times* and elsewhere of a ninety-year-old woman tossing javelins, Elliott Carter still composing music at 100, and other elderly folks who, after putting down half a carafe of red wine, enjoy a good smoke and perhaps a robust bonk. Death they've heard of, but don't quite believe in, not really, at least not for themselves. For them "old" is a psychologically, if not politically, incorrect word, and one expunged from their vocabulary.

In her book, Ms. Jacoby serves as a reality instructor. Bad news flows from her as profanity from a rap group. And bad news is what she has for all who believe that, because longevity has doubled since the middle of the nineteenth century—this owing chiefly to improved sanitary and environmental conditions—there is no good reason for its not continuing to ascend upward, ever upward. She reports, for example, that of all who attain the stately age of eighty-five fully half will have that stateliness snuffed out by Alzheimer's; and, more wretched news, there is also a strong chance they will end up in a nursing home with some other dread medical affliction.

In Ms. Jacoby you have to imagine a modern-day Cassandra but one ticked to the max. She notes that whenever she hears or reads the phrase "'defying old age,' it fills me with rage." In her book she wishes to underscore "the prevalence of chronic, degenerative, irreversible diseases in advanced old age [that] ought to give pause to those promoting the belief that a long life, if one does everything possible to take care of oneself, is likely to be a healthy, self-sufficient life."

As a contributor on old-age health matters to the *AARP Bulletin* and other magazines and newspapers, Ms. Jacoby now feels that in the past she often idealized aging. "One of the reasons I am writing this book," she avers, "is that I came to feel, especially as I saw the real, not-for-prime-time struggles of much older friends, that I was presenting a half-truth that amounted to a lie."

Never Say Die is an attack on self-help health efforts and on the belief that medical technology, like the cavalry in a John Wayne movie, will ride to the rescue. Ms. Jacoby goes after physicians and scientists who overpromise, showing up the corruption of those who hope to grow rich through one or another kind of commercial Ponce de Leon pill. She fancies those scientists with a taste for facing unpleasant facts: "mice are not men," one such says, crushing the hope from all those rodential experiments that promise far longer life in the not-too-distant future. She blasts all media reporting and commercials that make the solutions to aging problems seem only a pharmacy call away.

Ms. Jacoby has a chapter on Alzheimer's that will take the curl out of your hair, if you are still young enough to have much remaining. First thing to know is that any cure for this cruel disease, feared only less than cancer, is not near. Exercise, of the body or mind, is no guarantee against it. Nor is inheritance a factor in acquiring it, at least in the case of late onset of the disease. In other words, Alzheimer's is a poisoned dart, raining down, hitting arbitrary targets, for which there is no real protection. She is no more encouraging about stem-cell research, which she is very much for, but wants her readers to understand that the best scientific thought on the subject has the main benefits of such research at least two generations away.

A longtime feminist, Ms. Jacoby expresses anger at her sister feminists for ignoring the plight of aging for women, especially women living alone. A majority of women will outlive their husbands—two-thirds of those over eighty-five in America are women—but with diminished finances and in terrible loneliness. "Old age," she writes, "is primarily a women's issue." She also underscores—no surprise here—that aging is even more difficult for the poor, of either gender.

Ms. Jacoby makes no effort to hide or even subdue her politics, which, as you will have already gathered, are liberal, standard left-wing. Brought up a Catholic, she long ago shed any belief in God or the supernatural. This makes it easier for her to be a strong advocate of physician-assisted suicide for those among the elderly who have no further interest in living.

After dismally setting out all the agonizing problems of aging, her chief solution for those that might admit of solution is increased taxation that will make possible greater government care. The European model of health care is the name of her desire. Her greater desire, though, is social justice.

Ms. Jacoby's barely suppressed rage is aimed chiefly at social injustice of the kind that exacerbates the already difficult problems of aging. She intends, she tells us, "to die angry," and there is little doubt that she is going to achieve her intention, for the social justice of which Ms. Jacoby dreams is likely to come about roughly two weeks after Armageddon, but not before.

The note of anger in *Never Say Die,* valorous though it may seem to its author, can be off-putting to readers. By including autobiographical bits in her book—she had a lover suffer Alzheimer's, a grandmother and mother forced by old age into retirement and nursing homes—Ms. Jacoby's attempts to establish her sensitivity to the problem of aging in particular and her virtue in general. But this doesn't suffice to obliterate the scolding tone of her book. She set out to write an exposé and, because of this tone, ended up with something closer to a tirade. One reads hundreds of the long and dense paragraphs of her book knowing that no relief in the form of wit or other leavening will relieve Ms. Jacoby's relentless hammer blows of anger and scorn.

So complete is her attack that she is not prepared to allow the one possible reward of old age, which is the potential for acquiring wisdom through experience. Depression rather than wisdom, she holds, is more likely to be the lot of the old. True, if one is stupid when young or foolish in middle-age there is no good reason that wisdom, like Social Security and Medicare, will arrive promptly at sixty-five. Still, one likes to think that the acquisition of considered experience may sometimes bring dispassion, disinterest, and thoughtful perspective of the kind that passes for wisdom.

"There is about as much proof of the wisdom of old age as there is of the medical efficacy of holy water from Lourdes," Ms. Jacoby writes. And: "The old-age wisdom canon is essentially a defense against the knowledge of the terrible fates that lies ahead for many of us before we actually die." At this point, in the margin of my copy of *Never Say Die* I scribbled, "Keep the laughs coming, kid."

One departs Ms. Jacoby's book with the impression that the only protection against the depredations and sheer bloody horrors of old age are lots of money or a benevolent government watching out for one. But the experience of aging is richer, more complex, more subtle and philosophical, I fear, than Susan Jacoby, with her feminist's depth and journalist's breadth, can hope to fathom.

Cicero, who had the required depth and breadth, would strongly have disagreed with much in *Never Say Die*. A reading of his brilliant essay, "On Aging," composed in the form of a dialogue—a work that goes unmentioned by Ms. Jacoby—is the best antidote to her book.

"Cicero," Montaigne wrote, "gives one an appetite for old age." And so he does. Of course old age, bringing with it diminished strength and appetites, cannot do some of things youth can; of course old age makes one more prone to illness and disease—parts, after all, do wear out; of course old age puts one closer to death. But weighed besides these, Cicero contends, are the opportunities old age brings for "the study and practice of decent, enlightened living," accompanied by a calm that youth, and even middle-age, do not allow.

For all the diminishments of old age Cicero sets out their accompanying consolations. "Great deeds are not done by strength or speed or physique: they are the products of thought, and character, and judgment," Cicero argues. "And far from diminishing, such qualities actually increase with age." The lust of youth, he contends, is not merely overrated but the seat of much outrage and indecent behavior. "When its campaigns of sex, ambition, rivalry, quarrelling, and all other passions are ended, the human spirit returns to live within itself—and is well off." He adds that "the satisfactions of the mind are greater than all the rest."

As for the attribution of such faults among the old as their being morose, ill-tempered, avaricious, and difficult to please, Cicero claims, rightly, that "these are faults of character, not of age." Ms. Jacoby argues that "anyone who has outlived his or her passions has lived too long." Cicero, less stringently, holds that "as long as man is able to live up to his obligations and fulfill them . . . he is entitled to live on." I would split the difference and say that the criteria for continuing to live are that one finds life amusing and that there are people in the world who need one.

Unlike Ms. Jacoby, with her penchant for physician-assisted suicide, Cicero agrees with Pythagoras that we mustn't "desert life's sentry-post till God, our commander, has given word." He was of course aware of the arbitrary nature of death, which can strike at any age: "what nature gives us is a place to dwell in temporarily, not to make one's own."

Death, Cicero knew, is an old joke that comes to each of us afresh; and he also knew that old-age is the straight man who prepares us, always inadequately, for the punch line. He was himself murdered at sixty-three, by order of his enemy Mark Antony, his head severed, the hands that had composed attacks against Antony cut off and nailed alongside his head and placed on display on the Rostra of the Roman Forum. Cicero was wise enough to know that even wisdom itself is no protection against the forces of nature or the malevolence of men.

Whose Country 'Tis of Thee?

(2011)

A FRIEND'S SON, 27-years old, has recently departed for Brazil, where, if things work out, he plans to spend the rest of his life. I have never met the young man, but from what I know about him, he is solid, congenial, gifted with good looks. He lived in Brazil for a year or so, working as a teacher of English, before making the decision to move there permanently. He bears not the least animus, or even the mildest of complaints, against the United States. He just happens to believe that life in Brazil is likely to be better for him than anything he expects to find in America.

The young, like the rich, are different from the rest of us. For one thing, today they stay young a lot longer. My friend's son is unmarried, unclear about what will be his life's work, free at 27 in ways that young men of my generation were not quite free at 17. At his age, I had four sons (two of them step-sons), a clear idea of what I wanted in life (to be a good writer), and not the least doubt about spending all my days (apart from occasional travel) in the United States. Having responsibility for four children at 27 may have been overdoing it, but most men and women of my generation felt as I did. We longed to get going in life, a life we assumed would be lived in the country of our birth, which, as good luck had it, was the freest, richest, most splendid country in the world.

I wrote to my friend to ask if his son was ready to give up his American citizenship. Being an American, it occurred to me, probably doesn't carry the same weight with his son's generation as it did and does with his and mine. My friend wrote back that somehow or other our country lost his son and the rest of his generation. "All I can think of, and it's misty as can be," he wrote, "is that over the years, almost imperceptibly, the collective sensibility of the country has changed . . . . It's almost as if . . . some moment of ripeness passed. Somehow we have become unworthy of the country's ideals. . . . But I don't think my son and his friends even think about such things at all."

What has happened to change things, if changed they truly are? Is the country different? What has brought about this difference in point of view among the young? Is the lessening of national loyalties strictly American or instead a global phenomenon? Why would one want not to remain a citizen of the United States, when vast numbers of people continue to risk everything to take up life here, legally as well as illegally?

What So Proudly We Hail, an anthology of American stories, speeches, and songs, is a book that indirectly yet pertinently addresses itself to such questions. The book's three editors are people of intellectual accomplishment and high seriousness: Amy and Leon Kass are in the pantheon of great teachers at the University of Chicago, and Diana Schaub is a well-regarded political scientist. In their introduction, they do not say straight out but rather suggest that the United States has a patriotism problem. Patriotism may, in Dr. Johnson's famous mot, "be the last refuge of a scoundrel," but respectable patriotism is also the first requisite for a healthy nation. Their book is a high-grade, gentle, but firm goad to the kind of patriotism a country intent on greatness needs.

The editors have thought long about the American virtues, and they realize the dangers into which such virtues, exaggerated or even slightly distorted, can lapse. "The love of gain, encouraged by our polity," they write in their introduction, "can produce a materialism that deadens the souls of its citizens and keeps them from thinking about life in other than economic and self-interested terms." They note that "our tolerance, and even encouragement, of ethnic and religious pluralism is a great national strength, but it also poses a challenge for creating a deep national bond and spirit."

Behind *What So Proudly We Hail* is the concern that America is slipping, that the country is no longer producing the sort of character in its citizens required to sustain the qualities conducive to the kind of honorable conduct that has made the nation great. "What, in the American Republic," the editors ask, "will keep liberty from producing scoff-laws and libertines? What will keep the pursuit of gain from destroying generosity and charity? What will keep free speech civil, religious freedom tolerant, and the love of progress grateful for blessings received? What will enable a rights-loving nation to produce citizens who will choose gladly to do their duty—to their offspring, their neighbor, their community, their nation?"

No indoctrination into the American creed is attempted. The larger goal has been "to foster a deeper sense of American identity and contribute to forming the character needed for robust American citizenship and public life." The editors hope instead that this character "can be fostered by looking into the multi-angled mirrors our finest authors provide, and by discovering in our reflections the richness and worth of American identity, character, and citizenship."

To this end, *What So Proudly We Hail* includes elevating speeches and documents and bits of autobiography among the selections in the book, but short stories predominate. Before each selection, the editors set out the reasons for its presence and close with questions to which the selection gives rise. The selections themselves are subtle and serious. Yet can one acquire the qualities of good citizenship and mature patriotism through reading alone? A book of the quality of *What So Proudly We Hail* can doubtless reinforce and deepen citizenship and patriotism, but can it inspire them? In a famous maxim about writers, Madame de La Fayette wrote: "We give advice, we do not inspire conduct."

The time and place in which a person is born has a lot to do with the kind of patriot he or she turns out to be. Born in 1937, I entered consciousness with World War II as the background, context, and dominant fact of life. Food and gasoline were rationed, air-raid drills were part of grammar-school days, newspapers and tinfoil were collected for what was known as "the war effort," stamps were bought and pasted into books until they amounted to the $25 needed to purchase a war bond. In school we pledged allegiance every morning "to the Flag of the United States of America, and to the Republic for which it stands, one nation, indivisible, with liberty and justice for all." My father, himself too old to go to war, routinely picked up men in uniform—servicemen, they were called—hitchhiking or at bus stops, in our 1942 pale green Dodge, and entered into easy conservation with them. It was the patriotic thing to do.

The movies of those years seemed preponderantly war films, from sweet comedies such as *See Here, Private Hargrove* to action flicks such as *First Yank in Tokyo*. John Wayne, Spencer Tracy, Clark Gable, John Lund, Robert Walker, John Hodiak, Robert Taylor, in leather flight jackets and 50-mission-crush officer's caps, reinforced one's sense of the heroism of our boys fighting the Axis on two fronts. In the neighborhood, up to the age of 10 or so, war games were as popular as baseball. If one lost in a choose-up, one had to play the part of a Nazi ("*Achtung, Schweinhundt Amerikanisch*") or a Japanese soldier ("Die, Yankee dog!"), which meant that sooner or later one was machine-gunned or hand-grenaded and had to stage a slow and dramatic death.

This was a time when being patriotic didn't require a second thought—it came with the territory, was automatic. America was in a righteous war against true barbarians; we had come to the aid of heroic England to save the world from vicious Nazism and, into the bargain, to rescue the Jewish people whom, still unconfirmed rumor had it, Adolf Hitler was systematically murdering.

"My country 'tis of thee, sweet land of liberty, of thee I sing. . . ." One sang this song, and the National Anthem, and "America the Beautiful," and all other patriotic songs with one's hat off and one's right hand over one's heart, in full throat and with complete sincerity. World War II was perhaps the last time in the United States that patriotism was instinctual, uninflected with the least dubiety or irony.

The Cold War, though the stakes were no less high, was too abstract to evoke patriotism in the same way. It would be the putative cause of my being drafted at 22 and spending two years between 1958 and 1960 in the US Army, all of it in the unenchanted lands of Missouri, Texas, and Arkansas. I was by this time a subscriber to *Partisan Review*, *Dissent*, *Commentary*, and *Encounter* in England, and hence a liberal tending toward radicalism in my general political views. Yet I don't recall feeling the least resentment about donating two years of my life as an enlisted man in the US Army. Conscription was part of the price of being a male in America. Case closed.

While boredom is the reigning emotion in military life, there were compensating factors, among them gaining a broader view of my country through living in the same barracks with men I might otherwise never have met: Chester Cooke, a Christian Scientist from Kansas; Jack Langer, an American Indian from Idaho; Johnson Gates, a Negro from Detroit; Bobby Flowers, an Appalachian from Kentucky; and many more.

My first doubts about America, incurred at the University of Chicago in the late 1950s, were not political but cultural. The most impressive teachers I encountered there were Europeans, refugees who were, as was then said, Hitler's gift to America. What they had to say, in classrooms or in lecture halls, seemed denser, deeper, in every way richer than the offerings of their American counterparts, who beside them appeared rather bush league. At the University of Chicago I first began to sense that America was perhaps a cultural backwater.

In the 1950s, Europe had the better bricks—villas, castles, museums, ruins—and the greater artists and writers. In France, Sartre and Camus, Mauriac and Malraux were still at work, as was Pablo Picasso. English intellectual life—with such figures as Bertrand Russell and Isaiah Berlin and Hugh Trevor-Roper on the scene—seemed so much richer than ours. Evelyn Waugh was then a working novelist, and if E. M. Forster was not, he was still a presence, thought to be a classic, living out his days in adulation in rooms at King's College, Cambridge. True, W. H. Auden had emigrated from England to live in New York. But T. S. Eliot had long before departed the United States for England. (Was there in this trade a player to be named later that we never received?)

Eliot left America for much the same reasons that Henry James had nearly half a century earlier: America, as James wrote, failed to provide "the denser, richer, warmer European spectacle" so much more fertile for the creation of sophisticated literary art. Gertrude Stein, Edith Wharton, Ernest Hemingway, and F. Scott Fitzgerald all found life in Europe more congenial to the artistic sensibility. Artists who could afford to live there tended to do so for as long as possible. To qualify as cultured meant one had to acquire the culture of Europe, and at firsthand. Without it one was a bit callow, underdeveloped—not to put too fine a point on it, a yokel. Had I been a young man with a trust fund behind him, who knows, I might be in Paris yet today, putting the finishing touches on my first volume of negligible verse.

I had, then, a slight cultural but not yet a political grudge against America. The cultural, though, can roll easily enough over to the political. Viewing the country through literary lenses, I came to see it as made up of two parts Sinclair Lewis's Babbitts and Main Street conformists and one part H. L. Mencken's Booboisie. America was essentially a middle-class country, and much of American writing was devoted to despising the supposedly drab middle class, which was deemed a frightful drag on the imagination and spirit. Let pass that I was myself entirely a child—and a quite happy one—of the middle class, and that later I came to understand that without a solid middle class no large country in the modern world can hope to function successfully.

As someone who considered himself an intellectual, and aspired to be a writer, I didn't really see a smooth entry for myself in American life. This nagging concern melded nicely with instruction I acquired when young from reading such professional intellectuals as Dwight Macdonald and Irving Howe, who held that it was the first axiom in the Euclidean geometry of the intellectual to be always critical of one's own country.

Plenty, certainly, there was to be critical about in the United States. The country was still entirely segregated in the South and far from hospitable to Negroes in the North. Anti-Semitism, in the form of university and professional-school quotas and real-estate restrictions, was still in official force. John Kenneth Galbraith and Michael Harrington published popular books on the wide disparities of income in the country.

Conventional politics—that between the two major parties, "Tweedledum and Tweedledumber," as Dwight Macdonald called them—offered little in the way of hope. Adlai Stevenson, who was thought to be an intellectual of sorts, was soundly defeated by Dwight David Eisenhower in two presidential elections. During these campaigns, "egghead," standing for intellectual, came into use as a term of unmitigated opprobrium. I recall not voting in 1960, my first presidential election, that between Richard Nixon and John F. Kennedy, because I didn't see much to choose between the two men. (For what it's worth, I still don't, and I wouldn't vote for either man if he were running today.)

I began to think of myself as a radical. A radical, Daniel Bell liked to say, went to the root of the matter; radical was, in other words, a self-congratulatory badge, standing for deep thinker. In politics, I wasn't deep, and I'm not sure I came anywhere near qualifying as a thinker, but I did honor the intellectual's responsibility to keep a critical eye on my own country, to cut it as little slack as possible, to judge all its actions as guilty until proven innocent.

Sidney Hook and Arthur Koestler prevented me from ever being in thrall to Marxism. Their writings showed what a justification for torture and murder the Russians and Chinese had made of that meager body of ideas. I did, though, keep a soft spot in my heart for socialism; owing to a strong strain of Anglophilia, I was more attracted to it in its Fabian than European or American forms. That George Orwell, whom I much admired and who went to his death believing in socialism, called himself a socialist was an added inducement.

I never bothered to formulate a clear idea about how society ought to be organized. Even today I hold no strict theory of government. I believe with Churchill that democracy is the best of all bad forms of government; and while I think the same of capitalism (the best of all bad forms of economic arrangements), I do not believe, with Milton Friedman & Co., that untethered capitalism is the obvious and only answer to all economic questions.

In criticizing my own country, my argument used to be that the United States could be so much better than it was. This line continues on among radicals to this day. Todd Gitlin, in a recent eulogy of the old SDS leader Carl Oglesby published in the *New Republic*, wrote: "No one I ever met loved America so much as to feel such anguish at what it was becoming." *Plus ça change....*

Yet, despite all my canned opinions, my views, somehow, never lapsed into anti-Americanism. I never felt, as did Edmund Wilson, that between the Soviet Union and the United States there wasn't all that much to choose. I always knew that there was plenty to choose between the two. The United States at its worst—the McCarthy Era, resulting in hundreds of people losing their jobs—was never to be compared with the Soviet Union, in whose gulags millions perished during the long span of Stalinist and post-Stalin rule.

The anti-American strain grew stronger in American life as the 1960s got well underway. Some Englishmen might hate Tories, some Frenchmen hate Socialists, all Italians hate Silvio Berlusconi, but no Englishmen were anti-English, no Frenchmen anti-French, no Italians anti-Italian. Only Americans, or a select cohort among them, had allowed themselves the privilege of despising their own country. From my days working as an editor at *Encyclopedia Britannica*, I remember a co-worker, who, after I had done him the most trivial favor—lighting his cigarette, providing him with a paperclip—would say, "Thanks. You're a great American." The joke here was that there are no great Americans, that the possibility for greatness in America was risible.

Not many of those who embraced anti-Americanism bothered, I suspect, to understand to what it was they were opposed. They might speak of an American plutocracy, or the country's imperialist project, or its inherent bigotry, but, proud though they were (and remain) to consider themselves anti-American, they never bothered to define Americanism. Here is a good definition of it from Theodore Roosevelt, in a letter written in 1917:

> Americanism means many things. It means equality of rights and therefore equality of duty and of obligation. It means service to our common country. It means loyalty to one flag, to our flag, the flag of all of us. It means on the part of each of us respect for the rights of the rest of us. It means that all of us guarantee the rights of each of us. It means free education, genuinely representative government, freedom of speech and thought, equality before the law for all men, genuine political and religious freedom, and the democratizing of industry so as to give at least a measurable quality of opportunity for all, and so as to place before us, as our ideal in all industries where this ideal is possible of attainment, the system

of cooperative ownership and management, in order that the tool-users may, so far as possible, become the tool-owners. Everything is un-American that tends either to government by a plutocracy or government by a mob. To divide along the lines of section or cast or creed is un-American. All privileges based on wealth, and all enmity to honest men merely because they are wealthy, are un-American—both of them equally so. Americanism means the virtues of courage, honor, justice, truth, sincerity, and hardihood—the virtues that made America.

I would add only the element of optimism prevalent in American life, a disposition toward happiness and the possibilities of improvement that the 18th-century founders of the nation are believed to have acquired from the French Enlightenment.

As the 1960s proceeded, I continued to think myself a liberal and man of the left, yet I loathed nearly everything about the period except for the 1964 Civil Rights Act. Those years turned me around in my politics and in my view of America. Because of the unstinting barrage of criticism that rained down on the country from its young and from its putatively educated classes, I began to feel that America could get along nicely without my criticisms. The country needed defending not only from outside enemies, but also from its enemies within. I once heard the essayist Midge Decter, at a conference on the family, say (I quote from memory): "Family, let's face it, can be a great pain in the neck. I've just about had it with the family. But when I see who's attacking the family, I've decided to defend the damn thing." I began to feel precisely the same way about the United States.

Not that I ever consciously announced, even to myself, that I would now defend my country. Self-dramatization of this kind is not available to me. Such defense as I could provide would of course come from my writing, prose being the only weapon in my small arsenal, and I choose to deploy it in the realms of literature and the social and university scenes.

So much American fiction during these years was anti-American in spirit. The literary 1960s began with Joseph Heller's *Catch-22* (1961). Published before the Vietnam War got underway in earnest, it was the

great commercial and critical success it became chiefly because it anticipated the anti-war spirit of the times that arrived with the Vietnam War.
The anti-American bandwagon was crowded with writers. On its capacious open-air deck sat Norman Mailer, Robert Lowell, Kurt Vonnegut,
Robert Coover, E. L. Doctorow, Elizabeth Hardwick, Robert Stone, all
the so-called Beat Generation writers, the many contributors to the *New
York Review of Books*, and several others.

In an utterance to which many American writers would have subscribed,
Norman Mailer announced: "I used to hate America for what it was doing
to us. Now I hate all of us for what we are doing to America." Another
novelist, Stanley Elkin, who wasn't all that political, remarked that Disneyland reminded him "of Dachau and Auschwitz. They put you in these little electric carts and trundle you around." During the Vietnam War, Mary
McCarthy and Susan Sontag wrote books making plain their desire that
the United States be defeated and humiliated. Sontag would later write,
in the *New Yorker*, that America got pretty much what it deserved on 9/11.

Later, in the 1980s, at Northwestern University (at which I was then
teaching), a radical professor staged a shout-down of a non-Marxist Nicaraguan speaker at the university, claiming that the speaker had no First
Amendment or any other kind of rights; he deserved instead, because
of his views, she said, to die. When the professor was "censured" for this
action and these remarks, more than 90 of her colleagues in the liberal
arts signed a petition in protest against the censure. That an American
university that doesn't stand up for free speech cannot have any honorable standing at all clearly never occurred to them.

As a university teacher, which I had become in the early 1970s, I saw
how the anti-Americanism of a handful of American intellectuals had
spread to become the common property of vast numbers of mediocre
academics, who found ways to incorporate it in their teaching of literature, history, sociology, and political science. From mediocre university
teachers it passed along to uncritical students, spreading and spreading
further and further, until anti-Americanism became a standard ingredi-
ent in college education in the humanities and social sciences.

"A stranger, freshly arrived from another planet," I recently wrote in
a review of a book called *The Cambridge History of the American Novel*,

"if offered as his introduction to the United States only this book would come away with a picture of a country founded on violence and expropriation, stoked through its history by every kind of prejudice and class domination, populated chiefly by one or another kind of victim, with time out only for the mental sloth and apathy brought on by life lived in the suburbs and the characterless glut of American late capitalism."

Place this next to the opening paragraph of "The Perpetuation of Our Political Institutions," Abraham Lincoln's address to the Young Men's Lyceum of Springfield, Illinois, reprinted in *What So Proudly We Hail*:

> We find ourselves in the peaceful possession of the fairest portion of the earth, as regards extent of territory, fertility of soil, and salubrity of climate. We find ourselves under the government of a system of political institutions, conducing more essentially to the ends of civil and religious liberty, than any of which the history of former times tell us. We, when mounting the stage of existence, found ourselves the legal inheritors of these fundamental blessings. We toiled not in the acquirement or establishment of them—they are a legacy bequeathed us, by a once hardy, brave, and patriotic, but now lamented and departed race of ancestors. Theirs was the task (and nobly they performed it) to possess themselves, and through themselves, us, of this goodly land; and to uprear upon its hill and its valleys, a political edifice of liberty and equal rights; 'tis ours only, to transmit there, the former, unprofaned by the foot of an invader; the latter, undecayed by the lapse of time, and untorn by usurpation—to the latest generation that fate shall permit the world to know. This task of gratitude to our fathers, justice to ourselves, duty to posterity, and love for our species in general, all imperatively require us faithfully to perform.

Oddly, the anti-American strain in American life had been deepening just at the time that the United States seemed, in nearly every realm, to be improving. In the visual arts, no longer Paris but America, more specifically New York, had since the early 1960s become the center of the arts universe. The great European conductors led American symphonic orchestras. American writers attracted much more attention than did European writers. Americans won a preponderance of scientific Nobel prizes, and Asian students arrived here in large numbers to take advantage of American scientific education. In the arts and sciences, the United States was where the action was, and, it is fair to say, where it remains.

Meanwhile, Europe seemed to be winding down, if not devolving. England was now a second-line power, no longer Winston Churchill's but Mick Jagger's country. France, not noted for its character since the reign of Louis XIV, has become more Muslimized, consequently more tainted by anti-Semitism, and less reliable than ever. Even after the fall of Communism, Russia would still be dominated by thugs, its chief leader today a former KGB man. Japan, after its brief economic rise in the 1980s, saw its financial surge short-circuited, and with it its pretensions to grandeur. America, artistically, scientifically, politically, was, as the Marxists liked to say, hegemonic.

Sometime in the 1980s, I began to realize that I was living in not only the most powerful but the most interesting country in the world. And also the most generous. America, dispensing vast sums of aid, was always top of the list of donors to humanitarian causes. None of the legions of George W. Bush haters seemed able to reconcile their distaste for the man with the large sums that the Bush administration gave to Africa to slow its AIDS plague, and so they chose not to recognize it.

More recently, I watched a television news anchor, Scott Pelley of CBS, ask Secretary of State Hillary Clinton if allocating money for the starving Somali women and children, driven out of their country by war and drought, made sense at a time when the United States was under the lash of such heavy financial burdens of its own. "We can't not do it," Mrs. Clinton said, as best I recall, "and still remain America."

Tolerance in the United States has widened. And yet anti-Americans cling to the claim that America is still a racist country. That the country has a biracial president, elected by a serious majority, has not lessened this claim. My sense is that most Americans want African-Americans to rise, to pull out of the doldrums that have kept so many of them down for far too long, and to cease to listen to Jesse Jackson, Al Sharpton, and others who preach, to their own profit, the gospel of relentless victimhood. Acceptance has been greatly extended, too, to homosexuality, to once exotic ethnic and religious groups, and to the extended ambitions of women.

At the same time, one feels a national slippage. The current sluggishness of the economy has added greatly to this feeling, even though the economic slump is worldwide. More than economics is entailed. We have a president, whom I wouldn't deign to call unpatriotic, but who seems uninterested in having the United States play a leading role in the world and is instead content with the country's being one strong voice among a chorus of reasonable nations, which might be a splendid ideal if nations were ever reasonable.

All this, alas, plays nicely into the standard anti-American view—the view, that is, of those who find comfort in thinking the worst of their country. Ten books like *What So Proudly We Hail* will not change this view. You cannot reason people out of something they weren't reasoned into, the philosophers tell us. One must leave them as they are, shimmering in the superiority of their dark view that in being born Americans they were given a frightfully raw deal, while trying to win over the young who do not have locked-in views.

Not long after I learned of my friend's son's plan to live permanently in Brazil, a young woman from Romania who cleans our apartment every two weeks, came to me with a request. Mike, her recent husband, also a Romanian émigré, was applying for citizenship, and together they asked me if I would agree to sponsor him.

Sponsoring an immigrant for citizenship involves filling in a few papers and sending them, along with one's own past year's income tax form, to the immigration office. Sponsorship also means that if Mike falls on bad times within the next two years I would, technically, be financially responsible for him.

I did so gladly, because I know how hard Michelle, an attractive woman in her twenties who has bought a car and an apartment since acquiring her own United States citizenship, works, and I have found her husband to be no less industrious. Michelle's English is excellent, Mike's is trailing behind hers only by a bit. (He was trained in Romania as a computer specialist but needs to learn all the American systems to earn his living at the trade for which he was educated.) On their holidays, they visit California or hike Yellowstone Park. They have family in Romania, a country on hard economic times, to whom they send money.

When Michelle thanked me in the most earnest way for standing in as a sponsor for her husband, I told her I felt it a privilege to do so. "America," I found myself saying, "needs people like you." Shortly before their wedding, I gave Michelle and Mike a bottle of good wine. When Mike attains American citizenship, I plan to give them a copy of *What So Proudly We Hail*.

Stand-Up Guys

(2003)

I N SEVENTEENTH-CENTURY ENGLAND, writes Adam Nicolson in
God's Secretaries, his book about the making of the King James Bible,
"renaissance" was not a word that was known or used. "Renaissance"
is not a word I would have thought of, in the late 1950s and early 1960s, to
describe the comedians I saw on television and, occasionally, in nightclubs,
but it is the word Gerald Nachman uses throughout *Seriously Funny*. As
he chronicles the efflorescence of comedy during this period, one begins
to believe he does not use it imprecisely: A genuine rebirth was underway.
For myself, I'm pleased to learn that I have lived through at least one renaissance before pegging out.

I have, for as long as I can recall, been amazed by stand-up comics—
chiefly by their courage, though effrontery may be closer to the exact word.
They stand there alone (though some have had companions: Costello had
Abbott, Allen had Burns, May had Nichols) and propose to make an audience of strangers forget their personal troubles, not to mention the world's
endless supply of suffering, and laugh. The announcing of it beforehand
is where the nerve comes in. Wit, says Paul Valéry, entails defying anticipation. Professional comics, humorists, by their very presence, begin by
establishing an anticipation—you will laugh at what I am about to say or
do—and then set out not to defy but to fulfill it. That is why, as a writer,

you never want to be known as a humorist; the only thing worse, in my opinion, is to be known as a national treasure.

Before the comedy renaissance, most comedians in America were known through radio, and a few through the movies. They did rather standard things: developed a set comic persona (Jack Benny's cheapness, Bob Hope's wiseguy patter), or, if in duos, ignorant figure (Lou Costello, Gracie Allen) played off commonsensical straightman (Bud Abbott, George Burns). An occasional wildly talented comedian—Danny Kaye comes to mind—could do both physical and verbal humor and toss in a few songs at no extra charge. Jackie Gleason, through great acting skill, could be poignant as a permanent underdog with pretensions to mastery over his world, as in his Ralph Kramden character on the television program *The Honeymooners*.

But about all this comedy there was a safeness. You could turn on *The Ed Sullivan Show*," or Milton Berle's *Texaco Star Theater*, or *The Jackie Gleason Show*," and a number of others and not worry about having your politics, religion, little snobberies in the least ruffled. The great god Show Biz set strict boundaries, with lines that could only be crossed on pain of ending one's career.

Then, poof and shazam, everything changed. Late one night—I wish I could recall the year—I was watching *The Tonight Show*, then run by a lachrymose man named Jack Paar, who introduced the comedian Mort Sahl. Seated upon the guest's couch, Sahl proceeded to report that he had just had a disarming letter from the NAACP, informing him that, liberal and man of the left though he was, he, Sahl, had no Negro (as the word then was) in his act. With an expression of chagrin Sahl allowed that this was so, but then, bucked up now, he added that he had hired a brilliant young Negro comedian and incorporated him smoothly into his act. Pause: allow two beats. Then Sahl, looking down at his wristwatch, announced, with a gritting of teeth, a slight shake of the head, "He should have been here by now."

THE TELEVISION AUDIENCE IN NEW YORK didn't know what to do with this complicated but superior joke. Is Sahl, a man of the left, playing off the old stereotype about blacks being tardy, also known as CPT (Colored People's Time)? Or is he skewering those who believe in the stereotype? Rather different, this kind of humor, than watching Milton Berle get hit in the face with a huge powder puff.

The argument of *Seriously Funny* is that the 1950s laid the groundwork for the loosening up of American culture that took place in the notorious 1960s, with comedians often serving as, in Gerald Nachman's phrase, "cultural harbingers":

> [Mort] Sahl of a new political cynicism; Lenny Bruce, of the sexual, pharmaceutical, and linguistic revolution (and of the anything-goes nature of comedy itself); Dick Gregory, of racial unrest; . . . Mike Nichols & Elaine May and Woody Allen, of self-analytical angst and a rearrangement of male-female relations; Stan Freberg and Bob Newhart, of the encroaching, pervasive manipulation by the advertising and public relations culture; Mel Brooks, of the Yiddishization of American comedy; Sid Caesar, of a new awareness of the satirical possibilities of TV; . . . Tom Lehrer, of the inane, hypocritical (and in Jean Shepherd's case, melancholy) nature of hallowed Americana and Nostalgia; and in the instances of Allan Sherman and the Smothers Brothers, of its overly revered folk songs and folklore; Steve Allen, of the late-night talk show as a force in Comedy and of the reliance on wit over verbal pratfalls; Shelley Berman, of a generation of obsessively self-confessional humor; Jonathan Winters, of the possibilities of free-form improvisational comedy and of a sardonically updated view of Midwestern archetypes; and Ernie Kovacs, of surreal visual effects and the unbound vistas of video.

Nachman provides chronicles of the careers of all these comedians, along with those of Phyllis Diller, Bill Cosby, Godfrey Cambridge, Vaughn Meader, Will Jordan, Bob & Ray, David Frye, and Joan Rivers. Much interesting information crops up along the way: Stan Freberg, for example, we learn is not Jewish, though Tom Lehrer (who wrote the song "I'm Spending Hanukkah in Santa Monica") is. He reminds us of George Jessel and Joe E. Lewis, the unfunny comedians the country had agreed to laugh at; he might have added Eddie Cantor and Danny Thomas to the list. Nachman makes the crucial distinction between the flat-out joke and the comic insight: The latter is set in a context and brings plausibility to the unpredictable. His prose is sometimes rather more juiced up than one would like: He refers to "comic-kazis" and "all-out girl-illa warfare," calls too many comedians "larger than life," and others "icons," and still others, yes, "national treasures." But he has written so solid and informative a book that these venial sins can be forgiven. Nachman's is a book that entailed much in the way of reading and interviewing; and though its subject may seem light, the stuff of trivial pursuits, its importance is genuine.

JUST AS WE WOULD KNOW A GREAT DEAL LESS about fifth-century BCE Athens without Aristophanes' comedies, so the stand-up comics who began to appear in the 1950s provide much insight into what followed them in the culturally revolutionary years in America of the late 1960s and beyond. Nachman announces that his aim in his accounts of the satirical comedians—I myself think "radical" comedians more precise, for the best were radical in their time—is to "show not just their genius but to catch glimpses of their demons, damaged souls, and desperate drive." He does all this, but I think that, without setting out to do it, his book does something more: It suggests that what certain comedians are able to joke about today can presage what will become reality a few years, possibly decades, later. These comics, out there trying to make a living, were, probably unbeknownst to themselves, an advance guard.

Think upon it: Mort Sahl's political iconoclasm, Lenny Bruce's sexual and pharmacological liberationism, Mel Brooks's deliberate tastelessness—all are, in Trollope's phrase, "the way we live now." For better and worse, they helped pave the way. A man who until then had been a great military hero was nicely reduced in stature when Mort Sahl mocked Eisenhower's limited verbal agility by saying—as I once heard him say at a now defunct Chicago nightclub called Mister Kelly's—that a meeting between Ike and Adlai Stevenson had to be cancelled because the interpreter failed to show up. The one time I saw Lenny Bruce, the weekend after the John F. Kennedy assassination, he claimed that the reaction of Vaughan Meader, a John F. Kennedy impersonator, to the news of the president's assassination was:

"What! 50,000 T-shirts down the crapper." After the initial shock, hearing Bruce one realized that of course he was on target—no political event, no matter how shattering, finally gets in the way of business as usual—and the result is a gain, however small, in perspective.

The comedians who are the subject of *Seriously Funny* had a distinct advantage over those operating today: censorship. For example, the ignominious Joe Kennedy, father of JFK, tried to stop Sahl from making jokes about his son. The man known as the founding father, in reaction to jokes about his son the president, told Sahl's agent, "I don't care how you do it, but get that Jew to shut his f—ing mouth," and suddenly it became tougher for Sahl to get club dates. Owing to Tom Lehrer's mocking song "The Vatican Rag," most radio stations round the country refused to play his other songs. Because of his insistence on using language judged obscene, Lenny Bruce lost his New York cabaret license and was embroiled—"broiling" seems the right metaphor here—in endless legal tangles in New York and Chicago.

DOSTOYEVSKY, himself operating under the censorship of the tsar, once said that anyone who couldn't find a way to get around the censors didn't really deserve to. Yet in the bad/good old days, censorship could give cachet to a comic. A stern bourgeoisie still existed to épaté. Now, when anything goes, one could have open-heart sex on the Comedy channel during prime time and no one would much care. Nachman makes the point that comedy doesn't, somehow, seem to have the weight now that it did then. Stand-up comedy has become more manic, an exercise, as he puts it, in "attitude," the word that "defined 1980s and 1990s comedians like Dennis Miller, Garry Shandling, Roseanne Barr, and David Letterman" —I'd throw in Robin Williams and Eddie Murphy—and, he adds, "cynicism replaced humor."

Nachman thinks of the comedians he has written about as heroic. I doubt that many, Lenny Bruce distinctly apart, thought of themselves that way. Most were trying to make a living. Their lives, true enough, tended not to be immensely happy ones. "I don't think being funny is anyone's first choice," Woody Allen has said. *Seriously Funny* is loaded with remarks of similar lugubriousness. The secret he and Elaine May share, Mike Nichols reports, "is that neither of us like people very much—they have no reality for us." "Childhood seems good in retrospect," said Jean Shepherd, who used to do comic vignettes over the radio about his growing up in Hammond, Indiana, "because we were not yet aware of the basic truth: that we're all losers, that we're all destined to die." Shelley Berman, who for a brief period in the late 1950s was a household name, says that "the future is a breaker of promises." I don't hear any laughs out there. C'mon folks, these are the jokes.

An optimistic comedian is oxymoronic, if not nonsequitorial. Depression, aggression, and monomania, with an occasional touch of alcoholism for added piquancy, are more like the order of the day for successful stand-up comics. Sid Caesar, who was perhaps the only comic genius to appear regularly on television, went into psychotherapy in later years, conquered his drinking problem, lost a lot of weight—and promptly ceased to be even mildly amusing. "Tragedy is if I cut my finger," said Mel Brooks. "Comedy is if you walk into an open sewer and die." And that, as the man said, is entertainment.

N OT ALL OF GERALD NACHMAN'S ROSTER OF STAND-UPS were, to use the French phrase, *messugah*. Bob Newhart, Steve Allen, Bob & Ray, Bill Cosby—all Gentiles—appear to have been less mad, much calmer. The calmest of all, though, is Tom Lehrer, who seems to have got the most out of a small talent for writing musical burlesques based on other people's songs. An academic mathematician, he worked fewer than seven years, giving only 109 performances and retiring from show business at twenty-nine, but made, one assumes, a good deal of money on recordings ("The Remains of Tom Lehrer," three CDs and a book of his lyrics, has recently been released by Warner Archives), and then returned to a light teaching load at the University of California at Santa Cruz. He claims to be a lazy man with a short attention span, whose inspiration for further songs dried up. "I just stopped getting funny ideas," he told Nachman. He also claims—the line is by now rather well known—that "political satire became obsolete when Henry Kissinger was awarded the Nobel Peace Prize." He is not the only comedian to complain about the toll that political correctness has taken on freewheeling comedy: "When I was in college there were certain words you couldn't say in front of a girl. Now you can say them, but you can't say girl."

A LONG WITH THE SMOTHERS BROTHERS, who took many shots at the way the Vietnam War was run, Tom Lehrer was one of the few comedians of the era who went after what were then thought conventional right-wing targets: the Catholic Church, the segregated South, and nuclear weapons (and, especially, German nuclear scientists). The other comedians really feasted on liberalism, no matter how liberal their own culture. Nichols & May, with their brilliant skits on psychoanalysis and highbrow culture heavily worn, were really mocking liberals. So, too, was Lenny Bruce, insofar as he abused his audience, which he often did, for liberals took a certain pride in feeling themselves hip when listening to him rattle on in filthy language about the joys of drugs. ("I'm going to piss on you," Bruce told an audience in Sydney, Australia.) Mort Sahl, though an equal-opportunity abuser of politicians, has gotten in some of his best shots against those on the left. He said Gary Hart was JFK "without the batteries"; and of Jesse Jackson he declared, "Jesse's a man of the cloth—cashmere." Sahl may have the best working definition yet of a liberal: "Liberals are people who do the right things for the wrong reasons so that they can feel good for ten minutes."

The individual careers of the stand-up comedians of the 1950s and early 1960s have not been long lived. Some have been as brief as four years (that was the duration of Nichols & May, the sublimely funny team who split up in 1961). *The Smothers Brothers Show* was on television for only three years. Many seem to have had five or six solid years of fame and high pay, and then, for one reason or another, crashed and burned, with the exception of those lucky enough to score with a television sitcom (Bob Newhart is the notable example here), or veer off into movies and theater (Mel Brooks, Woody Allen). Some go on to collect more honorary degrees than laughs (Bill Cosby). Some keep flailing away, operating where and when they can, their old magic dissipated into grossness, no longer even faintly amusing (Joan Rivers).

Stand-up comedy has never been easy. A comedian of another generation, Jerry Seinfeld, compares it to working in your underwear, so exposed is one alone on the stage with only one's wit for protection. Steve Martin claims that eventually it wears one down. Nor is there much available in what the low-grade psychologists call "support systems." Fellow comedians are likely to be your toughest critics (as journalists, novelists, poets, playwrights are of their own fellow workers). *Seriously Funny* is riddled with one comedian putting down another; and there is a great deal of talk among them of having their material stolen by comrades. "All the stuff in 'Annie Hall' is really me," according to Mort Sahl. Shelley Berman hints that Bob Newhart may have lifted his use of the one-sided telephone conversation. Johnny Carson is thought to have glommed Jonathan Winters's character Maude Frickert for his character Aunt Blabby. Of an impressionist named Will Jordan, whose distinction resides in his having done the first successful impression of Ed Sullivan, Nachman writes, "Larceny, both grand and petty, is the central theme of Jordan's life."

Most of the comedians in *Seriously Funny* feel that something has happened to the country to make it less appreciative of comedy of any subtlety. A grossness seems to have set in, perhaps owing to the fact that obscene language and the subject of sex are now standard fare. Political correctness has foreshortened possible subject matter. In the early 1950s, at the Compass Players, the precursor of Second City, I recall seeing Mike Nichols improvising a very swish businessman in a skit called "Executive Sweet." Tom Lehrer told Nachman that "you can't say anything now that won't offend an audience. It would be nice to just let 'em have it—feminists and anti-feminists and affirmative action and bleeding hearts and kneejerk liberals, and not be embarrassed about it." But, apparently, nobody is ready to do it.

THE MOST CONSISTENT COMPLAINT, though, is about the growing obtuseness of the audience. In an earlier time, comedians blithely fired away. Imogene Coca, Sid Caesar's co-star, said that on their television show "it never occurred to anyone to talk down to the audience. We just automatically assumed that people understood what we were doing." Tom Lehrer complains that "people don't know enough today. Who would get a Schopenhauer reference?" Shelley Berman adds that "what's happening now is that there is no life [in comedy shows and routines] after teenage. Not everyone can laugh at going to the toilet or diddling with oneself or whatever seems to amuse today—catching your penis in a zipper, which of course is so brand-new." Television, which was once the great entrée for stand-up comics, is so no longer. "TV," Woody Allen notes, "is idiot stuff, designed by idiots for idiots."

A few weeks ago someone lent me a videotape entitled *The Best of Danny Kaye*. Most of the material came from Kaye's television show of the early 1960s. Along with being a swell dancer and an amusing singer— Kenneth Tynan said he had perhaps the best diction of anyone in show business—Kaye was a skit comedian. The skits on this tape assumed that his viewers knew something about Sigmund Freud and psychoanalysis, classical composers, ballet, and French history—and Danny Kaye was never thought an especially cerebral comedian.

Why are producers of mass entertainment less willing to be richly allusive today when a greater number of Americans have participated in higher education now than then? The Internet and cable television are sometimes said to constitute a knowledge explosion. Why comedy, like learning, must be pitched to the lowest, not the highest, level, is far from clear, except for the belief that the cruder the presentation the larger the audience the safer the investment. Someone recently told me that when he performs today, early in his act Mort Sahl tells three jokes at three different levels of sophistication, and pitches the rest of his act on the basis of the audience's reaction to those three jokes: smart, passable, hopeless.

Every good joke, it has been said, requires three people: the person who tells it, the person who gets it, and the person who doesn't. It would be a great pity if everyone today is much too worried about those laggards, those dullish third persons. Catering to them can only kill the joyfulness of comedians *shpritzing* away at full sail, not particularly caring if everyone in the audience can keep up with them.

My memory of watching some of the superior comedians whose careers are chronicled in Gerald Nachman's book is that of being utterly charmed by witty invention. Connecting the bright-colored dots they strewed upon the air, one felt one was seeing things in a fresh and riveting and, somehow, useful way. Swept up in wave upon wave of laughter, one was utterly captured and yet didn't want to be released. Something like the reverse of a catharsis was at work: not pity and terror but exultation and delight were the reigning emotions. Above all, one didn't want the comedian to leave the stage, ever. Sad to have to describe this experience in the past tense, but there are, alas, too many reasons to believe that we may never know it again.

You Could Die Laughing: Are Jewish Jokes a Humorous Subject?

(2013)

"Two Jews, each with a parrot on his shoulder, are in front of a synagogue," Hyman Ginsburg begins to tell his friend Irv Schwartz, when the latter interrupts.

"Hy, old pal, don't you have any jokes that aren't about Jews?"

Ginsburg replies that of course he does, and begins again: "Two samurai meet on a dark night on the outskirts of Kyoto. The next day is Yom Kippur . . ."

WHAT IS IT ABOUT JEWS AND JOKES, and what, especially, is it about Jewish jokes? The most put-upon people in the history of the world, Jews, and they're telling jokes: endless jokes, ironic jokes, silly jokes; jokes about czars and commissars, rabbis and mohels, widows and wives and mothers-in-law and matchmakers; and some jokes which, if told by Gentiles, might result in strong letters from the Anti-Defamation League.

What happens when a Jew with an erection runs into a wall? Answer: He breaks his nose. One of the small perks of being Jewish is having the right to tell such anti-Semitic jokes.

Walking along the beach, Goldstein finds a bottle, picks it up, and—surprise! surprise!—a genie emerges. The genie instructs Goldstein that he will grant him one wish, and one wish only. Goldstein says he wishes for world peace. The genie tells him he gets that wish a lot, but it is impossible to fulfill, so, if he doesn't mind, please try another wish.

In that case, Goldstein says, he would like more respect from his wife, who maybe would spend less time and money on shopping and prepare a decent home-cooked meal for him every once in a while and possibly make some attempt to satisfy his sexual desires. The genie pauses, then says, "Goldstein, tell me what, exactly, it is you mean by world peace."

If I change the name in that joke to O'Connor or Pilsudski or Anderson, the joke dies. Why? Because it is based on certain stereotypical assumptions about Jews: about henpecked Jewish husbands, demanding Jewish wives, and even about liberal Jewish politics. Are these stereotypes true? Only, I should say, in that they tend to be less true (or so we are given to believe) of Irishmen or Italians or Poles.

Two Gentile jokes:

> A Gentile goes into a men's clothing store, where he sees an elegant suede jacket. "How much is that jacket?" he asks the clerk. When the clerk tells him $1,200, the Gentile says, "I'll take it."

> At the last minute, a Gentile calls his mother to announce that, owing to pressure at work, he will be two hours late for the family Thanksgiving dinner. "Of course," his mother says, "I understand."

Put Jews in both of those situations and you have the working premise for at least 50 possible jokes. Jews are rich material for jokes because they are so idiosyncratic, so argumentative, hair-splitting, self-deprecating, hopelessly commonsensical, often neurotic, and amusingly goofy. Not all Jews are, of course, but enough of them to have kept a vast number of Jewish comedians in business for decades.

Jewish history begins on a joke, of sorts. The Jews are designated God's Chosen People—chosen, it turns out, for endless tests and nearly relentless torment. ("How odd of God to choose the Jews," wrote the English journalist William Norman Ewer, to which some unknown wag, in attempting to come up with a reason, wrote: "Because the *goyim* annoy him.") Any Jew with his wits about him must assume that God Himself loves a joke—silly, practical, cruel—and it too often seems His favorite butt or target is the Jews.

Still, Jews themselves keep joking. Too bad we've all missed out on what must have been some terrific one-liners during the 40-year exodus from Egypt to the Promised Land.

Ruth R. Wisse claims that "Jewish humor obviously derives from Jewish civilization, but Jews became known for their humor only starting with the Enlightenment." A professor of Yiddish and comparative literature at Harvard, Wisse argues that "Jewish humor erupts at moments of epistemological and political crisis, and intensifies when Jews need new ways of responding to pressure." In *No Joke*, she demonstrates how this works, and successfully shows that "Jews joke differently in different languages and under different political conditions."

Wisse chronicles the humor of the European ghetto and *shtetl*, Talmudic humor, the humor of converts away from Judaism, humor during the Holocaust and in the Soviet Union, humor in Israel, and, above all, humor after the emigration of Jews to North America. Her book, as she writes,

> explores Jewish humor at the point that it becomes a modern phenomenon. . . . The ensuing rifts between the religious and agnostics, elites and masses, and especially warring impulses of loyalty and restiveness within individual Jews and their communities generates the humor that is the book's subject.

Retellling many good jokes along the way, Wisse makes a number of provocative connections about Jewish humor and the fate of the Jews in the modern world. A serious scholar, she is also an intellectual much engaged in contemporary political life, and she has a political point to make about Jewish humor that she only emphasizes in her final chapter.

"You can have too much even of *kreplach*," says a character in an Isaac Bashevis Singer story. Wisse wonders if, perhaps, Jews can have too much even of humor, and many perfectly formulated sentences in *No Joke* both bring to mind and explain classic Jewish jokes: "Jewish humor at its best interprets the incongruities of the Jewish condition," suggesting, for example, the joke about the meat shipment from Odessa. . . .

On a laceratingly cold and relentlessly snowy morning in Moscow, Soviet citizens are lined up for five blocks awaiting a shipment of meat from Odessa. After an hour, a loudspeaker announces that the shipment is rather smaller than expected, so all Jews are asked to leave the line. An hour later, there is an announcement that the meat shipment has been further curtailed, so anyone who is not a member of the Communist party must leave the line. Two hours later, there is a further announcement that a large quantity of the meat in the shipment turns out to have been spoiled, so everyone is asked to leave the line except members of the Politburo. Three hours after that, the snow falling continuously all this time, there is an announcement that the meat shipment from Odessa has been cancelled.

"Those Jews," says one member of the Politburo to another as they shuffle off toward home, "they always have it easy."

The Soviet Union, that great and useless bump in world history, in its wretched 69 years left in its wake nothing but suffering and organized murder and a dozen or so good jokes, perhaps half of them Jewish. "Jewish experience was never as contorted as under Soviet rule," Wisse writes.

The Holocaust, which she also combs for its dark jokes, surely the ultimate gallows humor, is finally tragic beyond joking. She does bring out the terrifying one-liner, said by Jews in the midst of Hitler's slaughter: "God forbid that this war should last as long as we are able to endure it." Her gloss on this sentence reads: "I take this expression as an acme of Jewish humor and recognition of its fatal potential."

Jewish jokes elide into literature, with Sholem Aleichem certainly the most beloved, and perhaps also the greatest, of Yiddish writers. Aleichem's comedy—turned into kitsch with the musical *Fiddler on the Roof*, where most people come in contact with it—is, Wisse notes, often "called 'laughter through tears,' [but] is more accurately understood as laughter through fears." The fears were those of a people arbitrarily awarded pariah status, living under Russian and Polish despots and among brutish peasants.

In *The Protocols of the Elders of Zion* (1903), powerless Eastern European Jews were accused of plotting to take over the world through their (nonexistent) international connections, they were libeled about using the blood of Gentile children to make matzos, and they met with murderous pogroms staged by Cossacks and drunken peasants—sometimes as official government policy. One of the reasons so many Eastern-European Jewish families are unable to trace their lineage far back is that so many of the memories of their forefathers were thought best forgotten.

Wisse explains scholarly rabbinical and Talmudic jokes. She sets out a nice array of comic curses used by Eastern-European Jewish women: "May you grow so rich that your widow's second husband never has to work for a living," is one example. "May you lose all your teeth but the one that torments you" is another. Wisse's own mother, an emigré from Romania, was a dab hand at curses and at twisting proverbs into cynical yet sound advice, and Wisse supplies samples of her work in this line. Wisse suggests that Jewish women, provided less education than men, "developed more freewheeling oral aggression."

In America, meanwhile, with Jews settling into affluence, Jewish wives have been the target of enough jokes to warrant establishing a special branch of the Anti-Defamation League. What does a Jewish wife make for dinner? Answer: Reservations. "A thief stole my wife's purse with all her credit cards," Rodney Dangerfield (born Jacob Rodney Cohen) used to remark, "but I'm not going after him. He's spending less than she does." What does a French wife say when making love? "*Oui, oui, oui!*" What does an Italian wife say? "*Mamma mia, mamma mia!*" What does a Jewish wife say? "Harry, isn't it time we had the ceiling painted?"

One could go on, and I think I shall. Ira Silverberg, walking up the stairs of a nearby bordello, discovers his father coming down the stairs, and, in dismay, asks him what he is doing there. "For three dollars," his father says, "why should I bother your mother?"

Jewish humor in America became professionalized. From the 1920s through the 1970s, stand-up, radio, and television comedians were preponderantly Jewish. Wisse estimates that, by 1975, three-quarters of professional comedians in the United States were Jewish, many of them using mainly Jewish material. She recounts the rise of the Jewish stand-up comic from his origins in the Borscht Belt, as the conglomeration of resort hotels in the Catskill Mountains was called, where such young comics as Milton Berle, Jerry Lewis, Red Buttons, Mel Brooks, and Lenny Bruce worked as waiters, busboys, and lifeguards during the day, and entertained at night.

Initially, these Jewish comedians specialized in recounting Jewish failings to a largely Jewish audience. But some of the more successful Jewish comedians did not mine Jewish material. One thinks here of Danny Kaye (David Daniel Kaminsky), Sid Caesar (Isaac Sidney Caesar), and Jack Benny (Benjamin Kubelsky), none of whom featured his Jewishness, thus increasing the size of his audience.

Jack Benny, perhaps the most beloved comedian of them all, had at the center of his act his miserliness. ("Your money or your life," a robber demands of him. After a lengthy pause, Benny replies, "I'm thinking.") But so un-Jewish did Jack Benny come off that no one, so far as I know, thought, anti-Semitically, to chalk his extreme parsimony up to his Jewishness.

As the years passed, and Jews began to feel more secure in America, many Jewish comedians became more aggressive. Don Rickles and Jack E. Leonard did insult comedy, attacking their own audiences. Some went after other ethnic groups. One night in San Francisco I heard a second-line, obviously Jewish comedian named Bobby Slayton—why did so many Jewish comics call themselves Bobby or Jackie?—say that in high school he took Spanish as his required language: "I figured the Puerto Ricans can learn it, how tough could it be?"

Philip Roth's *Portnoy's Complaint* (1969) is a work that Lenny Bruce, had he the literary skill, might have written himself. Wisse characterizes Roth's novel as the literary equivalent of stand-up humor: Like even the most superior stand-up, it does not have to be heard—or, in this instance, read—more than once. In its day, though, *Portnoy's Complaint* came with a shock value not since repeated. Most shocked of all were the Jews who were not of Roth's generation: The great scholar Gershom Scholem wrote that anti-Semites could not have done the Jews greater harm than Roth's novel. "*Portnoy's Complaint*," Wisse writes, "warns that the cure, laughter, may be worse than the disease. A strategy for survival may have become a recipe for defeat."

Roth is only one among the comic Jewish writers considered here. Wisse also discusses Sholem Aleichem, Israel Zangwill, Leo Rosten, S. Y. Agnon, Isaac Babel, Saul Bellow, and Howard Jacobson. She also takes up Israeli humor. Life in Israel, a country in perennial peril, might seem too serious to allot a place for humor. But the unfunny Israeli, Wisse reports, himself became a target for humor. The confident Zionist became another such target. Humor in Israel, there is—but it has a dark cast, with jokes playing off the Auschwitz generation and Arab bombings. "Political and social satire, censored or self-censored while Jews lived under hostile regimes," she writes, "acquired a thousand new targets once Jews began running a country of their own."

Wisse touches on Mel Brooks's musical *The Producers* in her chapter on Holocaust humor, but neglects to mention that Brooks's specialty as a comedian has always been bad taste in its Jewish variant (though Brooks's specialty has been to make bad taste amusing, even winning). Interviewed some years ago by Mike Wallace, Brooks averted Wallace's first earnest question by asking him what he had paid for his wristwatch. Before Wallace could formulate his second question, Brooks, feeling the lapel of Wallace's sports jacket, asked him how much such a jacket cost.

Larry David has taken Jewish bad taste a step further, playing on his television series *Curb Your Enthusiasm* (2000–2011) the Jewish boor, the small-advantage man with a flawless gift for always saying the wrong thing.

Of the current generation of Jewish comedians, the only one Wisse considers is Sarah Silverman. Silverman's act is to play the faux-naïf while attacking political correctness. In one of her bits, a niece tells Silverman that she learned in school that, during the Holocaust, 60 million Jews were killed. Silverman corrects the girl, saying that the true number is not 60 but 6 million—adding, "60 million [would be] unforgivable."

Much of Jewish humor in America over the past few decades has been about assimilation. With the increase of intermarriage between Jews and Gentiles, and the lessening of overt anti-Semitism, the fear among Jews who value both their religion and their ethnicity is that Jewishness and Judaism are in danger of dwindling and, ultimately, disappearing.

One such assimilation joke is about the rabbi who has mice in his synagogue; to rid himself of them, he sets out on the *bima*, or altar, a large wheel of Chilton cheese. "Nearly 80 mice appeared," the rabbi reports, "so I bar mitzvahed them all, and they never returned." (The joke here is about American Jewish children who never return to the synagogue once they have completed their bar mitzvah at age 13.)

Another such joke is about a nouveau riche Jew who has recently acquired a Porsche. He drives it to the home of a nearby Orthodox rabbi, who he asks to say a *brocha*, or blessing, over it. The rabbi refuses, because he doesn't know what a Porsche is. So the man takes his car to a Reform rabbi, who also refuses—because he doesn't know what a *brocha* is.

Is all this—is Jewish humor generally—good for the Jews? Wisse is not so sure. She begins her final chapter with an epigraph from the English comic novelist Howard Jacobson: "This is not the place to examine why I, a Jew, feel more threatened by those who would wipe out ethnic jokes than by those who unthinkingly make them. But it may be the place simply to record that I do." Although scarcely without humor herself— she tells too many good jokes here ever to be accused of that—Wisse nonetheless finds that the general recourse on the part of Jews to humor in the face of serious adversity may be overdone.

Humor was no help to German writers and artists when up against Hitler. Wisse is confident that there are limitations to the Jewish response of humor when Jews today face murderous, humorless terrorists in the Middle East or the cowardly politicians of Europe seeking the votes of their increasingly Muslim electorates. She isn't asking Jews to stop joking; yet, more than humor, she knows, is required to fend off the strong anti-Semitic fervor that finds its initial target in Israel. If Jews truly consider humor to have restorative powers, she argues, they ought to encourage others to laugh at themselves as well. Let Muslims take up joking about Muhammad, Arabs satirize jihad, British elites mock their glib liberalism, and anti-Semites spoof their politics of blame.

Wisse is undoubtedly correct about this. But it is less than certain that any argument, no matter how cogent, is likely to squelch, or even reduce, the habit of Jewish joke-telling. The jokiness of Jews as a people is imperishable—a reflex of millennial duration—and can be found in odd places. To cite a personal example: Not long before reading *No Joke*, I learned that the solemn and serious Rabbi Benjamin Birnbaum of Ner Tamid Synagogue in Chicago, the man under whom I was bar mitzvahed, was the first cousin of the comedian George Burns.

What the Jews in a hostile world must do, Ruth Wisse argues, is back up the jokes with military and political power. To ring a slight change on the line of the heroes in the old Westerns and detective movies, they have to have behind them the might to be able to tell their enemies, "Smile when you hear me say that."

Duh, Bor-ing

(2011)

Somewhere I have read that boredom
is the torment of hell that Dante forgot.

ALBERT SPEER, *Spandau: The Secret Diaries*

UNREQUITED LOVE, as Lorenz Hart instructed us, is a bore, but then so are a great many other things: old friends gone somewhat dotty from whom it is too late to disengage, the important social-science-based book of the month, 95 percent of the items on the evening news, discussions about the Internet, arguments against the existence of God, people who overestimate their charm, all talk about wine, *New York Times* editorials, lengthy lists (like this one), and, not least, oneself.

Some people claim never to have been bored. They lie. One cannot be human without at some time or other having known boredom. Even animals know boredom, we are told, though they are deprived of the ability to complain directly about it. Some of us are more afflicted with boredom than others. Psychologists make the distinction between ordinary and pathological boredom; the latter doesn't cause serious mental problems but is associated with them. Another distinction is that between situational boredom and existential boredom. Situational boredom is caused by the temporary tedium everyone at one time or another encounters: the dull sermon, the longueur-laden novel, the pompous gent extolling his prowess at the used-tire business. Existential boredom is thought to be the result of existence itself, caused by modern culture and therefore inescapable. Boredom even has some class standing, and was once felt to be an aristocratic attribute. Ennui, it has been said, is the reigning emotion of the dandy.

When bored, time slows drastically, the world seems logy and without promise, and reality itself can grow shadowy and vague. Truman Capote once described the novels of James Baldwin as "balls-achingly boring," which conveys something of the agony of boredom yet is inaccurate— not about Baldwin's novels, which are no stroll around the Louvre, but about the effect of boredom itself. Boredom is never so clearly localized. The vagueness of boredom, its vaporousness and its torpor, is part of its mild but genuine torment.

Boredom is often less pervasive in simpler cultures. One hears little of boredom among the pygmies or the Trobriand Islanders, whose energies are taken up with the problems of mere existence. Ironically, it can be most pervasive where a great deal of stimulation is available. Boredom can also apparently be aided by overstimulation, or so we are all learning through the current generation of children, who, despite their vast arsenal of electronic toys, their many hours spent before screens of one kind or another, more often than any previous generation register cries of boredom. Rare is the contemporary parent or grandparent who has not heard these kids, when presented with a project for relief of their boredom—go outside, read a book—reply, with a heavy accent on each syllable, "Bor-ing."

My own experience of boredom has been intermittent, never chronic. As a boy of six or seven, I recall one day reporting to my mother that I was bored. A highly intelligent woman of even temperament, she calmly replied: "Really? May I suggest that you knock your head against the wall. It'll take your mind off your boredom." I never again told my mother that I was bored.

For true boredom, few things top life in a peacetime army. For the first eight weeks there, life consists of being screamed at while being put to tedious tasks: KP, guard duty, barracks cleanup, calisthenics, endless drilling. After those first two months, the screaming lets up but the tedium of the tasks continues. In my case, these included marching off in helmet liner and fatigues to learn to touch-type to the strains of "The Colonel

Bogey March" from *The Bridge Over the River Kwai*; later writing up cultural news (of which there wasn't any) at Fort Hood, Texas; in the evening, walking the streets of the nearby town of Kileen, where the entertainment on offer was a beer drunk, a hamburger, a tattoo, or an auto loan; and, later, typing up physical exams in an old bank building used as a recruiting station in downtown Little Rock, Arkansas. Was I bored? Yes, out of my gourd. But, then, so heavy is boredom in peacetime armies that, from the Roman Empire on, relief from it has often been a serious enticement on its own to war.

But, ah, the sweetness, the luxuriousness of boredom when the details of quotidian life threaten to plough one under through sheer aggravation, or real troubles (medical, familial, financial) are visited upon one, and supply, as Tacitus has it, "ample proof that the gods are indifferent to our tranquility but eager for our punishment." Except that most people cannot stand even gentle boredom for long.

"I have discovered that all evil comes from this," wrote Pascal, "man's being unable to sit still in a room." Failing precisely this test, that of the ability to sit quietly alone in a room, brought about *acedia*, a Greek word meaning "apathy," or "indifference," among hermit monks in North Africa in the fourth century CE.

I come to this historical tidbit through reading *Boredom, A Lively History* (Yale University Press, 224 pages) by Peter Toohey, who teaches classics at Calgary University. His book and *A Philosophy of Boredom* (Reaktion Books, 124 pages) by Lars Svendsen are the two best contemporary works on the subject. Noteworthy that men living, respectively, in western Canada and Norway should be attracted to the subject of boredom; obviously their geography and occupations as academics qualify them eminently for the subject. A teacher, as I myself discovered after three chalk-filled decades, is someone who never says anything once—or, for that matter, never says anything a mere 9 or 10 times.

The radical difference between Toohey and Svendsen is that the former thinks boredom has its uses, while the latter is confident that boredom is *the* major spiritual problem of our day. "Is modern life," Svendsen asks, "first and foremost an attempt to escape boredom?" He believes it is, and also believes, I surmise, that this escape cannot be achieved. He holds that boredom is not merely an individual but a social, a cultural, finally a philosophical problem. He quotes Jean Baudrillard, the French philosopher, saying that the traditional philosophical problem used to be "why is there anything at all rather than nothing?" but that today the real question is "why is there just nothing, rather than something?" With Svendsen, we arrive at the exposition of existential boredom.

Svendsen remarks on the difficulty of portraying boredom in literature. (In *The Pale King*, the unfinished novel that David Foster Wallace left at his desk after suicide at the age of 46, Wallace set out to explore all the facets of boredom, which, if reviewers are to be believed, he was, alas, unable to bring off.) Toohey would not quite agree and includes in the literature of boredom Ivan Goncharov's great novel *Oblomov*, whose first 100 pages are about the inability of its title character to get out of bed and get dressed and do something, anything. But *Oblomov* is less about boredom than about sloth.

The difference is a reminder that boredom presents a semantic problem. One must discriminate and make distinctions when trying to define it. Ennui, apathy, depression, accidie, melancholia, *mal de vivre*—these are all aspects of boredom, but they do not quite define it. Perhaps the most serious distinction that needs to be made is that between boredom and depression. Toohey is correct when he argues that chronic boredom can bring about agitation, anger, and depression, but that boredom and depression are not the same. Boredom is chiefly an emotion of a secondary kind, like shame, guilt, envy, admiration, embarrassment, contempt, and others. Depression is a mental illness, and much more serious.

"Suicide," Toohey claims, "has no clear relationship with boredom," while it can have everything to do with depression. Perhaps. An exception is the actor George Sanders, who in 1972, at the age of 65, checked into a hotel near Barcelona and was found dead two days later, having taken five bottles of Nembutal. He left behind a suicide note that read:

> Dear World, I am leaving because I am bored. I feel I have lived long enough. I am leaving you with your worries in this sweet cesspool. Good luck.

If boredom isn't easily defined—"a bestial and indefinable affliction," Dostoyevsky called it—it can be described. A "psychological Sahara," the Russian poet Joseph Brodsky called it. If one wants to experience it directly, I know no more efficient way than reading Martin Heidegger on the subject, specifically the sections on boredom in *The Fundamental Concepts of Metaphysics, World, Finitude, Solitude*. Boredom, for Heidegger, is valuable in that it rubs clear the slate of our mind and is, as Svendsen has it, "a privileged fundamental mood because it leads us directly into the very problem of time and being." Boredom, in this reading, readies the mind for profound vision. I could attempt to explain how, in Heidegger, this comes about, but your eyes, in reading it, would soon take on the glaze of a franchise donut. Besides, I don't believe it.

Neither does Toohey, who is excellent on drawing the line of the existentialist tradition of boredom that runs from the acedia of the early monks through Heidegger and Jean-Paul Sartre to the present day. Toohey holds that existentialist boredom is neither an emotion nor a feeling but a concept, one "constructed from a union of boredom, chronic boredom, depression, a sense of superfluity, frustration, surfeit, disgust, indifference, apathy, and feelings of entrapment." As such, existential boredom has become a philosophical sickness, not part of the human condition at all, but available exclusively to intellectuals given to moodiness and dark views.

The most notable novel in the existentialist boredom tradition is Sartre's *Nausea* (1938), whose main character, Antoine Roquentin, lives in a condition of overpowering indifference that Sartre calls "contingency," in which the universe is uncaring and one's existence is without necessity. After reading the philosophers taken up with the problems of being and existence, I cheer myself up by recalling the anecdote about the student in one of his philosophy courses at CCNY who asked Morris Raphael Cohen to prove that he, the student, existed. "Ah," replied Cohen in his Yiddish-accented English, "who's eskin'?"

In France, boredom is given a philosophical tincture; in England, an aristocratic one: Lord Byron, having seen and done it all, is the perfect type of the bored English aristocrat. George Santayana, travelling on a student fellowship from Harvard, made the discovery that the Germans had no conception of boredom whatsoever, which explains their tolerance for the *Ring* cycle and the novels of Hermann Broch, and for so many other lengthy productions in German high culture. In Italy, boredom can take on the coloration and tone of amusing decadence, an emotion perfectly embodied in several movies by Marcello Mastroianni.

Alberto Moravia's novel *Boredom* (1960) plays the subject for darkish laughs. A man in his thirties, a failed painter with a rich mother, hounded by boredom all his days, takes up with a young painter's model. He has regular and uncomplicated sex with her, but off the couch she bores him blue, until she begins cheating on him with another man, which arouses his interest in her. Preferring not to be interested, he concludes that his only solution is to marry her and give her a large number of children; once she is his wife and he can insure her fidelity, he can lapse back into comfortable boredom. "In this lack of all roots and responsibilities," he thinks, "in this utter void created by boredom, marriage, for me, was something dead and meaningless, and in this way it would at least serve some purpose." To "divorce, Italian style" Moravia adds "marriage, Italian style," though in the novel the painter does not finally marry the young woman.

Moravia's novel is also a reminder that perhaps as many marriages fail out of boredom as out of anything else. "Of all the primary relations," Robert Nisbet writes in *Prejudices, A Philosophical Dictionary*, "marriage is probably the most fertile in its yield of boredom, to a wife perhaps more than to a husband if only because prior to recent times, her opportunities to forestall or relieve boredom were fewer." In Nisbet's view, the changing nature of marriage, from an institution with an economic foundation designed primarily for procreation to one that has become an almost "purely personal relationship," has rendered it all the more susceptible to the incursions of boredom. Nisbet speculates that, had God permitted Adam and Eve to remain in the Garden of Eden, their marriage, too, might have foundered on boredom.

Sameness and repetition are among the chief causes of boredom. If they haunt marriages, they are even more powerfully at work in the realm of vocation. Once work went beyond the artisanal state, where farmers and craftsman had a personal hand in their productions, once the assembly line and its white-collar equivalent, the large bureaucratic office, came into being, work, owing to its repetitious nature, became one of the chief sources of boredom in the modern world.

Views on boredom and work alter with changing economic conditions. For my father's generation, arriving at maturity with the onset of the Depression, the notion of "interesting" in connection with work didn't come into play. Making a good living did. Unless the work was utterly degrading, my father could not understand leaving one job for another at a lesser salary. How different from today when a friend in California recently told me that he thought he might cease hiring young college graduates for jobs in his financial firm. "Their minds aren't in it," he said. "They all want to write screenplays."

One can also tell a great deal about a person by what bores him. Certainly this is so in my own case. After perhaps an hour of driving along the coast between Portland, Oregon, and Vancouver, British Columbia, encountering one dazzling landscape after another, I thought enough was enough; Mae West was wrong, you can get too much of a good thing; and I longed for the sight of a delicatessen stocked with febrile Jews.

Tolerance for boredom differs vastly from person to person. Some might argue that a strong intolerance for boredom suggests, with its need for constant action, impressive ambition. Others longing to be always in play, have, as the old saying goes, ants in their pants, or, to use the good Yiddish word, *schpilkes*.

No one longs to be bored, but, if I am a useful example, as one grows older, one often finds oneself more patient with boredom. Pressureless, dull patches in life—bring them on. I recently read two very well-written but extremely boring novels by Barbara Pym—*A Glassful of Blessings* and *A Few Green Leaves*. She is a writer I much admire, and I found myself quietly amused by how little happens in these novels. *A Few Green Leaves* contains the following sentence: "'It is an art all too seldom met with,' Adam declared, 'the correct slicing of cucumber.'"

Toohey suggests that boredom is good for us. We should, he feels, be less put off by it. For one thing, boredom can function as a warning sign, as angina warns of heart attack and gout of stroke, telling those who suffer unduly from it that they need to change their lives. For another, "boredom intensifies self-perception," by which I gather he means that it allows time for introspection of a kind not available to those who live in a state of continuous agitation and excitement. Boredom can also in itself function as a stimulant; boredom with old arguments and ideas can, in this view, presumably lead to freshened thought and creativity.

In the last chapter of *Boredom, A Lively History*, Toohey veers into a discussion of what brain science has to tell us about boredom. I almost wrote a "compulsory discussion," for with-it-ness now calls for checking in with what the neuroscientists have to say about your subject, whatever it might be. What they have to say is usually speculative, generally turns out to be based on studies of mice or chimps, and is never very persuasive. Boredom, neuroscientists believe, is thought to be experienced in the part of the brain called the "insula," where other secondary emotions are experienced, and which a neurologist named Arthur D. Craig calls the region of the brain that stands at "a crossroad of time and desire."

Having said this, one hasn't said much. Brain studies, critics of them argue, are still roughly at the stage that physiology was before William Harvey in the 17th century discovered the circulatory system. Boredom is after all part of consciousness, and about consciousness the neurologists still have much less to tell us than do the poets and the philosophers.

Boredom, like Parkinson's and Alzheimer's at a much higher level of seriousness, is a disease with no known cure, but Professor Toohey feels the need to supply possible ameliorations, or palliatives, for it. Among these are aerobic exercise (good, some say, for the restoration of brain cells), music (Mozart, it has been discovered, calms agitated elephants in captivity), and social activity (along with crossword puzzles, a recipe for aging well from Toohey's Aunt Madge). Even Toohey has to admit that these sound "corny," which they do. Worse, they sound boring. He does not dwell on those more expensive and dangerous palliatives for boredom: alcoholism, drug addiction, adultery, divorce, skydiving, bungee-jumping, and psychotherapy.

Isaac Bashevis Singer once told an interviewer that the purpose of art was to eliminate boredom, at least temporarily, for he held that boredom was the natural condition of men and women. Not artists alone but vast industries have long been at work to eliminate boredom permanently. Think of 24-hour-a-day cable television. Think of Steve Jobs, one of the current heroes of contemporary culture, who may be a genius, and just possibly an evil genius. With his ever more sophisticated iPhones and iPads, he is aiding people to distract themselves from boredom and allowing them to live nearly full-time in a world of games and information and communication with no time out for thought.

In 1989 Joseph Brodsky gave a commencement address at Dartmouth College on the subject of boredom that has a higher truth quotient than any such address I have ever heard (or, for that matter, have myself given). Brodsky told the 1,100 Dartmouth graduates that, although they may have had some splendid samples of boredom supplied by their teachers, these would be as nothing compared with what awaits them in the years ahead. Neither originality nor inventiveness on their part will suffice to defeat the endless repetition that life will serve up to them, as it has served up to us all. Evading boredom, he pointed out, is a full-time job, entailing endless change—of jobs, geography, wives and lovers, interests—and in the end a self-defeating one. Brodksy therefore advises: "When hit by boredom, go for it. Let yourself be crushed by it; submerge, hit bottom."

The lesson boredom teaches, according to Brodsky, is that of one's own insignificance, an insignificance brought about by one's own finitude. We are all here a short while, and then—*poof!*—gone and, sooner or later, usually sooner, forgotten. Boredom "puts your existence into perspective, the net result of which is precision and humility." Brodsky advised the students to try "to stay passionate," for passion, whatever its object, is the closest thing to a remedy for boredom. But about one's insignificance boredom does not deceive. Brodsky, who served 18 months of hard labor in the Soviet Union and had to have known what true boredom is, closes by telling the students that "if you find this gloomy, you don't know what gloom is."

"Boredom," as Peter Toohey writes, "is a normal, useful, and incredibly common part of human experience." Boredom is also part of the human condition, always has been, and, if we are lucky, always will be.

Live with it.

Nostalgie de le Boeuf

(2010)

EVERY JEW OF A CERTAIN AGE has his own Jewish-waiter story. When I was 6, I was taken by my parents to a Romanian Jewish restaurant in Chicago called Joe Stein's. After my mother had ordered for our family, I piped up to ask our waiter, an older man with a strong Eastern European accent, if he had any soda pop. "Ve got pop," he said, mild contempt in his voice. "What kinds?" I asked. What sort of a world is it, his doleful look suggested, in which a serious man has to answer the trivial questions of an ignorant and impertinent child. "Ve got red," he said, his pencil poised over his order pad while looking away, "and ve got brown."

The delicatessen for many years functioned as the tavern of the American Jew. Among Jews, food, not booze, stimulated schmooze. Every Jewish neighborhood had a deli, a place to go to talk and relax in an atmosphere of familiarity centered on Jewish food, some many more than one. In the neighborhoods in which I grew up, the deli was, quite as much as the synagogue, a social center. People didn't eat in restaurants as much then as now, but when one did, one sought not exotic but familiar food, which the deli provided. Chicken, mushroom-barley, cabbage, the same soups one's mother and grandmother made were on offer there; beef brisket—spiced, pickled, and brined into corned beef and pastrami and served on rye or onion rolls—was the main attraction; chopped liver, pickles, and pickled tomatoes were also available. So-called healthy eating had not yet been invented. Cholesterol had not entered the English lexicon. Snakes had not yet been loosed in the Garden of Gastronomic Eden.

People tend to think of the Jewish deli as primarily a New York institution; and it is true that the archetypical Jewish delis—Katz's and the 2nd Ave. Deli foremost among them—were New York establishments. Today the still extant Carnegie and Stage delis have become largely tourist attractions, a part, so to say, of old but no longer quite vibrant New York, deli museums, serving monstrous sandwiches at appalling prices.

Fifty or so years ago, five different delis were in business within a mile of my parents' apartment; also an emporium called K-Rations, the K standing for *kreplach*, *kishke*, *kugels*, *knishes*, and other Jewish specialties. As an adolescent, my own favorite deli was a modest place, with 10 or 11 tables on Western Avenue, near Devon, called Friedman's. Open round the clock, with one of its owners always on the premises, Friedman's was a meeting place after dates or a card game. At any hour one could find friends there. In the background was the buzz of older men, bedizened with pinky rings, talking about deals they had cut or bets they had won. At one in the morning, my friends and I might tuck into a bowl of chicken *kreplach* soup, a corned-beef sandwich, and a Pepsi, maybe a couple of cups of coffee, a slice of cheesecake, possibly pick up a bit of halvah on the way out, a full fourth meal of the day, eating and arguing, before turning in for a perfect night's sleep. Youth is not always entirely wasted on the young.

If there were five delis in the neighborhood of my boyhood in Chicago, there are today probably not more than five genuine delis in the entire city of Chicago, including its vast suburbs. And only one of these that I know of has something of the taste of old-line deli food and its old-shoe, unpretentious atmosphere.

Haute is certainly what no one would choose to call Eastern European cuisine, which has supplied the basis for deli food. Jewish food generally is that of a poor but never peasant people. Nor has elegant presentation been part of its attraction; plain if often highly seasoned fare it always was, but for those of us brought up on it, it has a richness if not subtlety of flavor that is matchless. Familiarity, it turns out, breeds content.

I sometimes lunch in a nearby Irish restaurant where one of the items on the menu is Boston Corned Beef and Cabbage. When I inquired of the owner, what the need for the word *Boston* was, he replied that in Ireland, in the old days, very few people were able to afford beef, and so corned beef and cabbage was largely an American invention, à la chop suey. Something similar is true of the original food of Eastern European Jews, who could not have had all that much beef in their diet. Goose was the chief meat of the *shtetl*. The main trio of Jewish deli meat—pastrami, corned beef, and tongue—were dishes of Jewish immigrants rather than of indigenous origin.

As it is, none of these three meats is, in the nontechnical sense, choice. Pastrami, whose derivation is Romanian, comes from the flesh around the navel of the cow and has to be butchered with great care and then seasoned and soaked and steamed with all the subtlety that culinary chemistry can devise to make it edible and, with talent and a magic touch, delectable. Tongue, with its perhaps too "tactile values" (to cite Bernard Berenson's phrase), is not everyone's idea of a fine feed. Salami, which hung behind most deli counters, was also a staple in Jewish homes; we always had one hanging on a nail from the inside of our pantry door, from which, as a boy, I would not infrequently slice off a generous hunk, a Jewish version, I suppose, of the modern power energy bar. Corned beef was something my mother would occasionally bring in from one of the local delis. Deli was a variant of home cooking, many of its dishes prepared on the premises from the recipes of the family matriarchs (and matriarchs alone—my father, to take one entirely representative example, was as at home in the kitchen as Diaghilev might have been on the range).

The best Jewish delis have always been family-run. And therein lies the problem. The work is grueling, the customers who retain a taste for Jewish deli food diminishing, and the competition from other kinds of food advancing. The time, it would seem, has come to talk of the death of the Jewish deli—not quite up there, to be sure, with the death of politics and the death of culture, but for some of us, more than a touch sad and significant nonetheless.

The Death of the Deli was originally to be the title of David Sax's new book, *Save the Deli* a chronicle of the past, a report on the present, and a prognostication for the future of the Jewish deli. An unapologetic lover of Jewish delis and their provender, Sax has written not a threnody merely but a search for what distinguishes the authentic in Jewish deli food, what conditions are necessary for the survival of the deli, and why delis are currently on the endangered Jewish institution list. Filled with arcane information, written with verve and charm, *Save the Deli* is amateur sociology at its best, which means that it is superior to 95 percent of professional sociology.

David Sax comes by his extreme taste for Jewish delicatessen through his father's family. His grandfather, he claims, died straightaway upon eating a fat-laden smoked-meat sandwich at Schwartz's Hebrew Delicatessen in Montreal shortly after emerging from the hospital where he was being treated for angina. Sax never met his grandfather, "but his legacy has slowly pickled my soul with a craving for salt, garlic, and secret spices," he writes. "It is the continuation of a flavor-bound tradition that worships fatty sandwiches in brightly lit temples of abusive service and clanging dishware."

Save the Deli is Sax's account of his three-year journey across North America and Europe in search of an answer to the question of whether the Jewish deli has a future. Sax served a one-night apprenticeship hand-carving pastrami sandwiches at Katz's Delicatessen on the Lower East Side, visited and talked and ate with the owners of most significant delis in many of the major cities of America, stopping along his schmaltz-filled way to discover Jewish delis in Boulder (in Colorado), Austin (in Texas), Salt Lake City (in Utah), and elsewhere. His investigations included the Jewish-deli scenes in England, Belgium, and France, and even led to Krakow, a once great Jewish city the number of whose "Jewish residents have been reduced to the lunch crowd at Katz's."

A riddle: Know how to make a vegetarian faint? Answer: Have him read almost any chapter of *Save the Deli*. Sax's mere definition of *gribenes*, bits of chicken skin deep-fried in fat, also known as Jewish popcorn, ought to do the trick; and if it doesn't, the description of *p'tcha*, which is jellied calf's foot—"Garlic Jell-O," a waitress at the 2nd Ave. Deli calls it—should finish him off. Fat, a word of pure revulsion in contemporary life, is what gives much of Jewish-deli food its flavor, and is for Sax, who approves its use, relishes its taste, ardently describes its delights, purely approbative. Of the experience of eating *kishke*, an animal membrane stuffed with *matzo* meal and *schmaltz* now less and less found on deli menus because of the difficulty of its preparation, Sax writes: "The finely ground beads of *matzo* meal soaked up the velvet *schmaltz* and left a smoky sweetness in my mouth." Of eating stuffed goose neck in Poland, he notes that "the outer layers of crisp, oily skin gave way to a creamy membrane of sweet fat, which bathed the smooth, earthy liver in an undercurrent of richness that was almost unfathomable." This is a book, in other words, that requires a surgeon general's warning on its dust jacket.

Sax has himself decided to take a pass on healthy eating, not alone for this book but, one gathers, for life, however shortened his own may be. Friends have lectured him to eat less dangerously. "If my arteries succumb to the fat and salt," he writes, "I owe them all a posthumous apology." Meanwhile, he is mildly contemptuous of these friends' own diets, with their penchant for "whole wheat bagels and tofu cream cheese." They don't eat Jewish, but Israeli, hummus and chopped salads, which is essentially Arab food. (Israel is the one place where Jewish deli has not caught on.) "Today," he writes of his contemporaries among the Jews in Toronto, "it is a safe bet that on most nights of the week the food of Tuscany will feed far more of the Jewish households of Toronto than that of nineteenth-century Polish Galicia. At Jewish weddings and bar mitzvahs you'll find more sushi than salami."

Save the Deli is filled with rich bits of ethnic information. When Sax interviews Mel Brooks in Los Angeles—the city where he found Jewish delis flourishing more than in any other—on the subject of delis, Brooks tells him that "delis seem to be happy places. I've never seen anybody weeping at a deli." Sax reports that in every deli he visited across the country, immigrants were doing the actual cooking, Mexicans most of all. An aggressive deli owner in Austin, Texas, serves a Cheesecake Shake, which he lists on his menu as "heart attack in a glass." A cardiologist (of all professions!) named Ron Huberman attempted to open a deli in Rogers, Arkansas, near the headquarters of Walmart, but the place soon went under. The few delis left in the devastated city of Detroit are sustained by a black clientele. So, too, in Kansas City. "Blacks don't mind eating cholesterol," a deli owner in Kansas City told Sax. "If you've grown up eating barbeque, pastrami is a drop in the bucket. They'll come up the counter and say, 'Man, lay that fat on my corned beef sandwich.'"

A number of sensible general points are scattered throughout the book. Hand-carved sandwiches are always superior to machine-sliced ones, assuming skill on the part of the carver. "The decline of the deli has been foreshadowed by the meteoric rise of the bagel," most of which, apart from taking attention away from traditional deli dishes, aren't, as Sax rightly avers, all that good. Sax presents as his golden rule that "the larger the menu, the worse the traditional deli food"; and anyone who has been presented by one of the new deli-restaurant menus, taller than Torah scrolls and lengthier than Leviticus, will agree. Delis cannot be successfully franchised—successfully, that is, from the standpoint of the quality of their food—and none ever has been; the owner must be on the premises, worrying.

Sax displays a nice balance of anger at people who are contributing to the ruin of the deli and admiration for those who are making a gallant stand to preserve it in its largely traditional character. The former include those who have tried to corporatize, which generally means franchise, delis around the country, and those who have diluted their menus with multicultural and fusion dishes, serving wraps and salads and worse. (The only leaves that ever saw the inside of the traditional deli were those of a dab of iceberg lettuce used as beds for gefilte fish and those to support the outer architecture of spicy stuffed cabbage.) The tradition of the Jewish deli, in Sax's investigation, is not yet dead, and he ardently searches for signs of its living on. One such is Zingerman's in Ann Arbor, which seems to be run on Whole Earth Catalog principles of enlightened employment while serving the kind of solid Jewish deli that passes Sax's standard of culinary integrity. Another is Jimmy and Drew's 25th Street Deli in Boulder, Colorado, where they produce homemade *schmaltz* and two kinds of smoked lox and in their own kitchen make, from scratch, "*latkes*, chopped liver, noodle and onion *kugels*, several types of *knishes*, *gefilte* fish, herring in cream, stuffed cabbage polonaise, and of course *matzo* ball soup."

The hope-filled reopening of the great 2nd Ave. Deli, now on a side street near Third Avenue in New York's Murray Hill—the original, at the corner of 10th Street, was shuttered for a time following the murder of its owner—is the event on which *Save the Deli* closes. Yet, hope against hope, the evidence Sax lines up for the ultimate demise of the Jewish deli seems overwhelming. Here are some of the main items militating against a happy future for Jewish delis in America:

Although many connect the Jewish deli above all with New York, where it got its start and throve longer and more impressively than anywhere else, real estate and food prices in New York can be crushing and have in fact squashed many a New York deli in recent decades. If a deli owner does not own the building in which his restaurant operates, he may as well forget about it. Glatt-kosher delis are faced with the additional expense of having to have inspectors, on full salary, on the premises. These financial pressures have caused New York long ago to have lost in preeminence as the world's, or even the country's, deli capital.

The Jewish deli, as Sax underscores again and again, is a family business, but the sons and daughters into the third generation seem increasingly to have lost the energy for the long hours and would rather become lawyers or commodity traders or do root canal than give pleasure to a demanding yet diminishing clientele.

Healthy eating has been an enormous bomb lobbed into the future of the Jewish deli, making the mere eating of a corned-beef or pastrami sandwich into a guilty pleasure. Such is the diet and health consciousness of women of the current generation, as opposed to those earlier generations, that most delis have now become the gastronomical equivalent of cigar dens, frequented overwhelmingly by men. One can easily imagine the day that laws will be passed attempting to close down even these as health hazards.

A Chicago restaurant entrepreneur named Rich Melman, whose father was in the deli business, has opened every kind of restaurant in Chicago but told Sax that "I don't know if I could make money in today's world running the type of delicatessen I'd like to run." He doesn't mention it, nor does Sax anywhere in his book, but I wonder if the natural antipathy between Jewish delicatessen and alcohol doesn't have a good deal to do with it. The markup on alcohol is often the making of a restaurant, but no one goes to a deli to drink. The notion of a pastrami on rye with a nice Chablis (promiscuous but ultimately responsible) is comical, and even a corned-beef sandwich and a beer feels somehow wrong. Pop, seltzer, *grepsvasser*, is what is required.

Perhaps the most devastating point David Sax makes against the future of the Jewish deli is that the original source of Jewish cookery is gone. Jokey writer though he is, the one old joke Sax does not make about Jewish deli is that these restaurants, with their high-cholesterol offerings, killed more Jews than Hitler. In fact, Hitler, by slaughtering the Jews of Eastern Europe, closed off all further traffic between the old and new worlds of Jewish cooking. China will continue to send immigrants to North America to replenish Chinese cookery; the same is true of Greek and other ethnic cuisines. "In America," Sax writes, "every other immigrant group will always have a source for their authentic flavors. But not so the Jews, who are cooking from the fading memories of a time and place that no longer exists. No more Jews are coming from Poland to New York to open up a delicatessen." A tradition, in other words, may have come to the end of its line. "This, above all else," David Sax writes, "was the reason the deli was dying."

And yet, does the end of the traditional Jewish deli portend anything more than the loss of large quantities of cholesterol and vast numbers of calories? I believe it does. The loss of the Jewish deli, if it is to come about, will be yet another crack in the edifice of American Jewish identity, which grows more and more fragile under increased intermarriage and the secularization of Jewish life generally. No longer to be able to eat Jewish, not every day but when the mood is upon one, will be a genuine subtraction for those who find comfort in enjoying the food of their ancestors as well as for future generations who will not even know what they have missed.

The American Jewish deli, along with offering unique food of extraordinary flavor, also represented a distinctive style: urban, ironic, humorous, paradoxical, intimately Jewish. Culture, it turns out, can also be acquired at the end of a fork. In ways never dreamed of by modern nutritionists, it is just possible that, in the end, we really are what we eat.

The Symphony of a Lifetime

(2010)

I HAVE TAKEN TO SAYING that my wife and I are at the grandparent stage of life. I don't before now recall using the metaphor "stage" to describe any other segment or portion of my life. The notion of stages of life has been around for a long while, of course, and doesn't look to be going away.

The popular journalist Gail Sheehy wrote a book called *Passages*, but her passages are little different than stages. The psychoanalyst Erik Erikson was in his day best known for his "stages of development," in which human beings, properly developed, are able to grasp more and more complex realms of experience. In *On Death and Dying*, Elisabeth Kubler-Ross even spoke of the five stages of grief (denial, anger, bargaining, depression and resignation). Difficult, it seems, to get away from that metaphor of the stage.

"Yes," I say, "my wife and I are at the grandparent stage," and then pause and ask the person to whom I've just said it if he or she knows that the reason grandparents and grandchildren get on so well is that they share a common enemy. All the world, like the man said, is a stage.

Infancy, childhood, youth, the long stretch of adulthood, ending (if one is lucky) with mild decrepitude and (if one is really lucky) easeful death—such are the traditional stages of life on which most of us would agree. Some people cut it a lot finer. For some, marrying is a major stage of life, with having children no less—perhaps more—major still. Some click off stages of their lives by decades: 30, 40, 50, each turning into a great psychodrama of life slipping past, usually too quickly. For some the death of one's parents marks a sobering stage of life; it puts one, after all, next in line for entrance into the room where someone awaits with a garrote, which Pascal famously describes as *la condition humaine.*

Everyone, surely, will have his or her own demarcations for important stages in his or her life. Some may seem quite trivial. Getting a driver's license at 15, the legal age in the Chicago in which I grew up, was a big item for me and my friends, for having the use of a father's car gave us freedom to explore the grand city outside our neighborhood. I grew up a frustrated athlete—frustrated, that is to say, by abilities that came nowhere near matching my fantasies of athletic glory, especially in basketball. In this connection I can recall, sometime in my early thirties, walking under a glass backboard and newly netted hoop, and not ever bothering to look up to imagine myself making some acrobatic lay-up. Ah, I thought, all basketball fantasies are officially gone, finished, kaput—I have entered a new stage of life.

A crucial element in this matter of stages of life can be how important the question of being, staying or at least seeming youthful is to a person. I was spared this by being born in 1937, a time when not staying young but growing up into adulthood as quickly as possible seemed the ideal.

S TAYING YOUNG AS A WAY OF LIFE kicked in in a serious way in the late 1960s, when, you will recall the cliché, no one over 30 was to be trusted. Many who grew up under this rigid requirement have stayed at the game of remaining young, some would say with all too naturally diminishing returns: consider only all those men now in their sixties and beyond with their sad, dirty gray ponytails.

For those for whom youthfulness is all, perhaps there are only two stages to life: young and not young, with the latter being a kind of death unto itself. One thing for certain, in the consideration of stages, taking on biology is a no-win proposition. In a recent short story of mine called "The Love Song of A. Jerome Minkoff," a man named Maury Gordon, who is 85, is told that he has pancreatic cancer: "When you get to my age," Maury said [to his doctor], "you're just waiting to hear that your time is up. All this crap about 60 being the new 40, 70 being the new 50, well, I have some friends who've reached 90, and let me tell you, Doc, 90 looks to me like the new 112."

"Married, single," an old joke goes, "neither is a solution." I don't happen to believe that, being happily married to a superior woman, but it does point up the paradox offered by the question of when one enters various of life's stages. My generation, wishing to grow up quickly, tended to marry young and have children early. I had two sons by the time I was 25. Is it better to have children young, when one's energy is greater but one's attentions are often fixed on attempting to make good on one's ambitions? Or is it better to have children when one is older, when one's ambitions have tended to have had their run, but one's energy is less, though one can pay proper attention to the chaotic miracle that is the early life of one's children? Neither, once again, is a solution.

A solution implies a problem, and whether or not one has viewed one's life as a problem will have much to do with how one views the stages of one's life. Saddest of all—next, of course, only to early death— is to arrive at the close of one's life and see all that has gone before as a series of wrong roads taken, opportunities missed, courage wanted. Shouldn't have gone into this line of work . . . Shouldn't have married so late . . . Shouldn't of, shouldn't of, shouldn't of . . . In another short story of mine, this one called "The Philosopher and the Check-Out Girl," the main character, a retired academic, claims to be suffering, fatally, from what he calls "a late-life crisis, the one that occurs when, in the face of approaching death, a person realizes that his regrets greatly outweigh his achievements and there isn't enough time left to do anything about them."

LUCKIEST AMONG US are those who feel they've had a good run, and can look back and feel that even their mistakes made sense. I have had serious setbacks and have known profound sadness, yet I hope that I do not sound nauseatingly smug when I say that I think of myself as such a lucky person. My personal regrets, such as they are, reside in the small-change department. I wish I had learned how to play piano, if only so that I could play for myself the enchanting melodies of Maurice Ravel. I wish I had learned ancient Greek, so that I could read in their own language many of the writers I love.

My life has never been about money-making, but I nonetheless wish I had been able to accumulate enough money early in life so as not to have to think about it, a condition at which I am clearly not likely to arrive. I even, first time round, married the wrong woman, yet this (one would think) grave mistake resulted in talented and thoughtful children and grandchildren.

Much of my good luck has had to do with when and where I was born. I have lived my life through decades of unexampled prosperity in the richest country in the world. Although I served two years in the Army, the year of my birth put me in the fortunate position of not being called up to fight in any wars: I was too young for Korea and too old for Vietnam. Any man—and now women, too—who fought in a war, who was actually fired upon, would have to count the experience as among the crucial stages in his life, as, surely, did those who fought in World War II or in Vietnam, and soon the same will be true of those who fought in Iraq and Afghanistan.

I was also lucky going through my adolescence in the early years of the 1950s, when there were plenty of ways to get into trouble but at least the deadly alternative of drugs was mostly absent. Of all the stages of my life— and I've yet to figure out how many there have been apart from the conventional one I mentioned earlier—my four years in a public high school in Chicago have been the most unrelievedly happy ones. These were years in which I enjoyed neither athletic glory nor the least hint of academic distinction. I came to school each day not for learning but for laughter: riotous, raucous, unremitting laughter among friends. I still see some of these friends, and now, more than 50 years later, we continue to wring pleasure out of the old jokes, incidents, anecdotes of those charming days.

Once again the luck of history was on my side. Owing to the Depression, my generation had one of the lowest populations attending colleges, which took off the enormous—I would even say hideous—pressure that now haunts the young who want to get into the colleges of their choice. In my day, the University of Illinois had to take any student who graduated from a high school within the state, even if he finished last in his class. It was, in effect and in fact, open enrollment. I finished just above the bottom quarter of my graduating class, went to Illinois, and after a year there transferred to the University of Chicago, then, unlike now, not so difficult to get into, though fairly tough to get out of. Luck of the draw.

Not all stages of life are marked by chronology, biology or culture. How one recounts the stages of one's life has a good deal to do with the time in which one was young, adult, old. Some generations, of course, have been marked by a single historical event: the Depression, World War II, the Sixties. Then there are the stages of one's career: an old joke invoked the five stages of Joseph Epstein (supply your own name here): 1. Who is Joseph Epstein? 2. This is a job, clearly, for Joseph Epstein. 3. We ought to get someone like Joseph Epstein for this job. 4. This job calls for a younger Joseph Epstein, and 5. Who is Joseph Epstein?

Politics can mark yet another set of stages in the lives of men and women who take them seriously. The standard cliché on this subject is that when young one is liberal-leftish, turning more conservative ("Mugged by reality," in Irving Kristol's famous phrase) with the passing years. But many people retain their youthful politics all their lives. For a notable example, William Hazlitt, the great English essayist, never gave up in his belief in the glories of the French Revolution and later in Napoleon, upon whom he wasted his later years writing a wretched book.

For some, politics are much more important than for others; for most of us, politics tend to take a diminishing importance the older we get. I feel this in my own life, quite content to assume that all politicians of both parties are frauds and swine, unless proven otherwise. For the old-line American radicals of the 1920s and '30s, key stages in their lives would include when they joined the American Communist Party and when they left it.

FROM THIS ROUGH SKETCH, one gets at least a glimpse of the complexity of the notion of stages in a person's life. One also gets a sense of the subtle tyranny of stage-thinking. Recall that still active cliché of masculine life, the midlife crisis. The way the midlife crisis is supposed to have worked is that a married man, sometime in his early forties through late forties, decides that the conventional (by which is generally meant middle-class) married life does not fulfill him; what does is a much younger woman than he (and his wife), preferably one seated in a newly purchased red convertible with him at the wheel. And so in a fine triumph of random desire, not to say idiocy, over good sense, he gives up family and everything else he has worked for to begin this new fantasy life.

The problem with the cliché of the midlife crisis is that it apparently has had immense attraction, for to this day a disproportionately large number of American couples end their marriages when the man is in his early to mid-40s. Which is what I mean by the tyranny that thinking about our lives in stages can have upon us.

The midlife crisis, I'm pleased to report, seemed to float right by me. I hadn't the time, the money, the leisure or (sad truth to tell) the attractiveness to women to bring the operation off. I have even enjoyed going beyond midlife and understanding that I have passed the stage of being of sexual interest to anyone except my wife. I find myself from time to time, in fact, telling a young check-out clerk or saleswoman that she has beautiful eyes or lovely hands, and they seem to understand that I am not, in the phrase of the day, hitting on them but taking up the prerogative of an older gent to pay simple homage to female beauty.

A midlife crisis would not have done for me. I have never been one to believe he can make dramatic shifts in his own life, upsetting all the standard stages and plans. I have instead believed in living the prosaic life, going at things day by day, and hoping to evade such unexpected thunderbolts as serious illness, economic disaster and early death, my own or that of those dearest to me. Not everyone shares this general view. Although I was a wild young boy, somewhere along the way I chose to live the quiet life, and I have not regretted it.

Some years ago I read a brilliant essay called "Prosaics," by Gary Saul Morson, a teacher of Russian literature at Northwestern University, in which he showed how Tolstoy believed in the prosaic life and Dostoyevsky in the dramatic.

Things happen to Tolstoy's characters—they go to war, have vastly disruptive love affairs, suffer unexpected deaths—but they are most interesting in their ordinariness: a strong case in point is Natasha's family, the Rostovs, in *War and Peace*. Her brother and father and mother, with their rich but normal passions, appetites and family loves, are people who gain moral stature through an endless series of small acts.

In Dostoyevsky, on the other hand, nothing is ordinary: passions turn into obsessions; gambling addicts and epileptics are at the center of things; men are beating horses to death on the Nevsky Prospect; poverty has wrenched people's lives into little hells on earth. The question isn't really who—Tolstoy or Dostoyevsky—is the greater novelist, for both are great, but which shows life as it is more truly is.

As Professor Morson puts it: "Dostoyevsky believed that lives are decided at critical moments, and he therefore described the world as driven by sudden eruptions from the unconscious. By contrast, Tolstoy insisted that although we may imagine our lives are decided at important and intense moments of choice, in fact our choices are shaped by the whole climate of our minds, which themselves result from countless small decisions at ordinary moments." At some point in life, I think, one has to decide if one is, in one's belief in the shape of his or her life, a Dostoyevskian or a Tolstoyian.

I N THE END, OF COURSE, it is the final stage of life that is of the greatest interest. Learning to die well, it has been said many times, is the true point of philosophy. Yet what a blessing it is that we do not know the precise or even rough date of our death. It says a great deal about the paradox of life itself that this is no doubt the most important piece of information about our lives and yet we are probably better off without being in possession of it.

On this subject of the final stage of life, the philosopher George Santayana, who lived to the age of 89, thought it made good sense to assume, unless told otherwise by a physician, that one always had another 10 years to live. The wisest man I have known, Edward Shils, who died at 85, used to continue to buy kitchen gadgets and plateware and such things in his early eighties; it gave him, he once told me, "a sense of futurity," the feeling that the game was not yet over, however actuarial thinking might insist otherwise.

The tough question is whether one is oneself in the final stage of his or her own life. I have just turned 73, and part of me would like to think that I have yet another stage to play through: older I indubitably am but surely not elderly. Yet lots of evidence suggests this might be wishful thinking. Henry James said that when he reached the age of 50, someone he knew died every week. I find the same was true for me at the age of 70: if it is not someone I know closely or even personally (the editor of a friend, for example, or the former wife of one's publisher), the body count, as I read the morning *New York Times* obituary section piles up. Then at a certain age—for me it kicked in around 60—one begins to notice the ages of the dead, and how many of the newly dead are of one's own generation. Not always the best way, perhaps, to begin one's day, with this gentle reminder of one's own mortality, but once begun difficult to stop.

Santayana, who was very smart on the subject of the end of life, remarked that one of the reasons older people often grow grumpy about the world is that they, with the presentiment of their own death, can't see what good it can be without them in it. One hopes of course to fight off this grumpiness; one hopes not to purvey fantasies about the purity of life when one was young as opposed to life now with all its corruptions.

In the last stage of life, even with the cheeriest outlook, it isn't easy to keep thoughts of death at bay. Consider, though, the advice of the Greek philosopher Epicurus (341-270 BCE), who lent his name to the school of Epicureanism but who was, in my reading of him, the world's first shrink. Epicureanism is generally understood to be about indulging fleshly pleasures, especially those of food and drink, but it is, I think, more correctly understood as the search for serenity.

Epicurus, who met with friends (disciples, really) in his garden in Athens, devised a program to rid the world of anxiety. His method, like most methods of personal reform, had set steps, in this case four such steps. Here they are:

- **Step One:** Do not believe in God, or in the gods. They most likely do not exist, and even if they did, it is preposterous to believe that they could possibly care, that they are watching over you and keeping a strict accounting of your behavior.

- **Step Two**: Don't worry about death. Death, be assured, is oblivion, a condition not different from your life before you were born: an utter blank. Forget about heaven, forget about hell; neither exists—after death there is only the Big O (oblivion) and the Big N (nullity), nothing, nada, zilch. Get your mind off it.

- **Step Three**: Forget, as best you are able, about pain. Pain is either brief, and will therefore soon enough diminish and be gone; or, if it doesn't disappear, if it lingers and intensifies, death cannot be far away, and so your worries are over here, too, for death, as we know, also presents no problem, being nothing more than eternal dark, dreamless sleep.

- **Step Four**: Do not waste your time attempting to acquire exactious luxuries, whose pleasures are sure to be incommensurate with the effort required to gain them. From this it follows that ambition generally—for things, money, fame, power—should also be foresworn. The effort required to obtain them is too great; the game isn't worth the candle.

To summarize: forget about God, death, pain and acquisition, and your worries are over. There you have it, Epicurus' Four-Step Program to eliminate anxiety and attain serenity. I've not kitchen-tested it myself, but my guess is that, if one could bring it off, this program really would work.

But the real question is, even if it did work, would such utter detachment from life, from its large questions and daily dramas, constitute a life rich and complex enough to be worth living? Many people would say yes. I am myself not among them.

Part Four

The Arts

What To Do About the Arts

(1995)

"Art for everyone": anyone regarding that as possible is unaware
how "everyone" is constituted and how art is constituted. So here,
in the end, art and success will yet again have to part company.

ARNOLD SCHOENBERG

OBODY WITH A SERIOUS or even a mild interest in the arts
likes to think he has lived his mature life through a bad or
even mediocre period of artistic creation. Yet a strong argument can be made that ours has been an especially bleak time for the arts.

One of the quickest ways of determining this is to attempt to name
either discrete masterpieces or impressive bodies of work that have
been written, painted, or composed over the past, say, 30 years. Inexhaustible lists do not leap to mind. Not only is one hard-pressed to
name recent masterpieces, but one's sense of anticipation for the future
is less than keen. In looking back over the past two or three decades,
what chiefly comes to mind are fizzled literary careers, outrageous exhi-
bitions and inflated (in all senses of the word) reputations in the visual
arts, and a sad if largely tolerant boredom with most contemporary
musical composition.

People who look to art for spiritual sustenance have been dipping into
capital—they have, that is, been living almost exclusively off the past. In
literature, less and less do the works created since the great American
efflorescence earlier in the century seem likely to endure. (One thinks of

1925, that *annus mirabilis* for the American novel, which saw the publication of F. Scott Fitzgerald's *The Great Gatsby*, Theodore Dreiser's
An American Tragedy, John Dos Passos's *Manhattan Transfer*, Sinclair
Lewis's *Arrowsmith*, and Willa Cather's *The Professor's House*.) In visual
art, the line is drawn—if not for everyone—at Abstract Expressionism,
after which no powerful school or movement seems to have arisen, and
so many reputations seem, as the English critic F. R. Leavis remarked
in another connection, to have more to do with the history of publicity than with the history of art. In serious music, *performing* artists continue to emerge, but the music they perform is almost exclusively that
of past centuries; the greatest appetite of all remains for the works created between J. S. Bach (1685–1750) and Maurice Ravel (1875–1937).
True, dance, under such geniuses as George Balanchine and Martha Graham, has had a fine contemporary run. But no one, I think, would argue
against the proposition that the only works of art capable of stirring anything like extensive excitement in the nation just now are movies, which,
given their general quality, is far from good news.

In explanation, and partially in defense, of this situation it has been
suggested that we are living in a time when sensibility has been fundamentally altered; and, it is sometimes also argued, advancing technology—the computer, the video—only figures to alter it further. The artistic result of this putative shift in sensibility goes under the banner of
post-modernism. Although the word means different things to different
people, generally post-modernism in the arts includes the following: a
belief that a large statement, in everything from poetry to architecture,
is probably no longer persuasive; a self-reflexiveness, a playfulness, and
a strong reliance on irony which the advocates of post-modernism find
a refreshing and fair exchange for spirituality in art; and a contempt for
criticism traditionally understood as the activity of making discriminations, distinctions, and, especially, value judgments.

At the same time that some argue for a change in sensibility, suggesting in turn the need for a change in the nature of art, others feel that if
art is not to lose its standing entirely, more than ever it needs to give
itself directly to social and political purposes. We have driven around
this block before, of course, most notably in the 1930s when novelists

and poets, painters, and even musicians were scolded for insufficient engagement in the political struggles of the day. These criticisms were then directed by Communists and fellow-travelers; today they are made under the aegis of an ideology that finds its chief outlets in environmentalism, sexual liberation, a lingering anti-capitalism, and an inchoate but determined multiculturalism.

The paramount enemy for such people, then as now, is disinterested art that attempts to transcend political and other sorts of human division. This is art of the kind that Marcel Proust had in mind when he wrote that it "gives us access to higher spiritual reality resembling the otherworldly metaphysical speculations of philosophy and religion." This is art that, among its other effects, seeks to broaden horizons, to deepen understanding, and to enhance consciousness as well as to convey the ultimately unexplainable but very real exaltation that is integral to heightened aesthetic pleasure.

By such measures, most contemporary art has fallen down badly on the job. Art still functions to confer social status on what today one might call the educated classes, as witness the large crowds that attend certain museum shows and operas and concerts given by performers who have been declared superstars. But high art (except the political kind) has more and more been relegated to a minority interest and is under attack for doing what it has always done best. Much of high Western art is now even judged, *mirabile dictu*, to be politically less than correct.

S OME OF THIS MIGHT HAVE BEEN PREDICTED—and, in fact, it was. More than 40 years ago, in an essay entitled "The Plight of Our Culture," the late Clement Greenberg wrote that "high culture has lost much of its old implicit authority." In that essay, Greenberg ran through those brutal simplicities—as he rightly called them—known as highbrow, middlebrow, and lowbrow.

Highbrow art, from Homer through Rembrandt to Schoenberg, had always made the greatest demands on its audience—and those demands, it had always been understood, resulted in the highest rewards, both philosophical and aesthetic. In its modern forms, highbrow art, wrote Greenberg, tended to be synonymous with avant-garde art, which made even stricter demands. Avant-garde art was often about itself, and the avant-garde artist, turning inward, was interested above all in solutions to the problems his particular art presented: problems of surface and perspective in painting, of tonality and dissonance in music, of language and depth psychology in literature.

Because of this it had become more and more difficult to admire a modern artist's work apart from his technique. As Greenberg had put it in an earlier essay, as the avant-garde became highly specialized, so "its best artists [became] artists' artists, its best poets, poets' poets," and this, not surprisingly, had "estranged a great many of those who were capable formerly of enjoying and appreciating ambitious art and literature, but who are now unwilling or unable to acquire an initiation into these craft secrets."

Lowbrow art presented no difficulties of definition: it was mass art, produced for and aimed at the lowest common denominator, and promising nothing more than entertainment. But then there was middlebrow art, where the problems, for Greenberg and others, arose. Middlebrow art promised both to entertain and to educate, and attempted to pass itself off as highbrow by its appearance of seriousness. Yet the middlebrow was not finally serious; it was instead merely earnest, which was not at all the same thing. Middlebrow art was always teaching, if not preaching. (In our own time, it has been chiefly preaching political lessons.) And middlebrow art was responsible for deploying one of the most self-serving myths of our age, the myth of the artist as a permanent rebel against society.

Writing in a special issue of the British magazine *Horizon* in 1947, Greenberg called for a frankly highbrow elite that would help bring about an art characterized by "balance, largeness, precision, enlightenment." We have had, he wrote, "enough of the wild artist." What we need now are

> men of the world not too much amazed by experience, not too much at a loss in the face of current events, not at all overpowered by their own feelings, men to some extent aware of what has been felt elsewhere since the beginning of recorded history.

NEARLY A HALF-CENTURY LATER, all one can say of Clement Greenberg's aspirations for art is that none of them has come into being, whereas most of his worst fears have. Middlebrow art is taken so much for highbrow in our day that the very category of highbrow is in doubt. My own personal, shorthand definition of a middlebrow is anyone who takes either Woody Allen or Spike Lee seriously as an artist. And most of the supposedly educated portion of the country, it will not have gone without notice, does.

One of the consequences of the debasement of art is that fewer and fewer people are able to make the important distinctions which high art itself requires for its proper appreciation. An institution that has played a large role in bringing this situation about is the university. Formerly free from the tyranny of the contemporary—the tyranny, that is, of being up to the moment—the university now takes great pride in being a center for the creation of contemporary art. Over the past three or four decades, the university has become something akin to a continuing WPA program by furnishing an ever-larger number of artists—chiefly writers but painters and musicians, too—with jobs.

This might not be so bad, but, with all these artists on hand, the university now also provides a fairly strong diet of contemporary fare in its curriculum. Once, it was not thought necessary to teach the works of contemporary writers, painters, and composers; if a student was a reasonably cultivated person, or had the desire to be such a person, he could learn about such things on his own. No more. Some artists even teach themselves.

Although many universities continue to offer traditional subjects in the arts, the university has, at the same time, caved in to the demand for courses that fit the politics of a large number of the people who teach there: feminism, Marxism, Lacanism, the new historicism, deconstructionism, semiotics—"the six branches of the School of Resentment," as the literary critic Harold Bloom has called them. In the contemporary university literature and painting are often put through the meat grinder of race, class, and gender. This is well-known. What is perhaps less well-known is the odd way it has skewed the arts themselves.

To give an example of how the skewing works, the week before President Clinton's inauguration I was called by the (London) *Daily Telegraph* for my opinion of the poet Maya Angelou, who had been chosen to read a poem at the inaugural. I told the reporter that I had no opinion of Maya Angelou, for I had read only a few of her poems and thought these of no great literary interest. Ah, he wondered, did I know anyone who might have an opinion that would be interesting to English readers? I conceded that I knew of no one who read her. When asked how that might be, I responded that what the reporter had to understand was that in the United States just now there were a number of authors who were not actually for reading but only for teaching, of whom Angelou, who herself teaches, lectures for vast fees, and probably has more honorary degrees than James Joyce had outstanding debts, is decidedly one.

By teaching so many contemporary writers and simultaneously laying itself open to the political aspirations of multiculturalism, the university has had a serious hand in helping to discard the idea of standards, which is absolutely essential to high art. The politics of many university teachers have played a key role in this, with the result that today we no longer have in force the only distinction in the arts that really matters—that between the good and the bad, the well-made and the shoddy. Once one starts playing this particular game, the essential, the only really relevant, fact becomes not the quality of an artist's work but which category it fits into: black composers, women painters, gay/lesbian poets, and the rest of the multicultural mélange.

All but a handful of people who currently work in the arts—writers, painters, musicians, arts administrators, and patrons—seem to go along with this program. Multiculturalization has for many seemed a way out of the wrenching dilemma of wishing to seem as democratic as possible while knowing in one's heart that serious art is nothing if not thoroughly meritocratic and, in the best sense, finally and irremediably elitist.

"In art the ideal critical ethic is ruthlessness," wrote the music critic Ernest Newman. "The practice of art should not be made easier for the weaklings; it should be made harder, so that only the best types survive." Such notions are troubling to people of tender liberal conscience. The arts are now somehow construed to carry the message that they are themselves a means to progress, and progress implies encouraging the downtrodden; clearly, the last thing such people want to be caught acknowledging is that the arts are not—at least not necessarily—for everyone.

THE MISGUIDED BELIEF that art is one of the forms that progress takes is connected with the notion that the avant-garde itself is a kind of movement, or party, for progress—an appealing notion for people who wish the arts to do things they were never meant primarily to do: to fight censorship, to give groups pride in what is called their "identity," to increase the awareness of AIDS, to fight inequities of every kind. As Clausewitz said that war was diplomacy carried on by other means, so art is seen as social justice and political enlightenment carried on by other means.

The avant-garde of an earlier time, beginning in the 1890s and proceeding through the early decades of the 20th century—the "banquet years" of French painting, music, and writing—was (again) an avant-garde of technique. It was impelled by a spirit of experimentation; it attempted to provide fundamentally new ways of seeing, hearing, and understanding: post-impressionism, atonal music, stream of consciousness, and free verse were names given to some of these experiments. Whether or not one admires the results, the utter seriousness as well as the aesthetic purity of the enterprise cannot be mistaken.

The practitioners of what must now somewhat oxymoronically be called the old avant-garde were true revolutionaries. They wished to— and often did—change the way we intuit and understand and feel about the world around us. They *truly* altered sensibility. For a complex of reasons, their revolution has been halted. While new experiments in style and technique continue, the avant-garde has largely turned away from technique and toward content.

Obscenity, homoerotic exhibitionism, sadomasochism, political rage— these have been the hallmarks of the advanced art of our day. In a way never intended either by Matisse, whose early paintings so upset the Parisian audience, or by Stravinsky, whose *The Rite of Spring* caused its audience to bust up chairs in the hall in which it was performed, the avant-garde artists of our day are knocking themselves out to be outrageous. An avant-garde magazine puts a woman's vagina on its cover and runs the tag line, "Read My Lips"; child pornography, if set out "tastefully," is not thought beyond the bounds of respectability; neither is a production of *Tannhäuser* with the title character as a TV evangelist and Venus as a hooker. If the political revolutionaries of an earlier day cried, "Burn, baby, burn!," the artistic revolutionaries of ours exclaim, "Squirm, baby, squirm!"

The targets for such art, it ought to be clear, are middle-class respectability, the family, organized religion, and finally high culture itself. The aesthetic standard by which this art asks to be judged is the degree to which it succeeds in hitting its targets. As a panel for the National Endowment for the Arts (NEA) once put it, a work that is "challenging and disturbing . . . precisely . . . shows us that it is worthy of consideration." The more outrageous the art, the more worthy of notice and protection.

Consider by contrast how T. S. Eliot, a great avant-garde poet himself, saw the role of the artist:

> The artist is the only genuine and profound revolutionist, in the following sense. The world always has, and always will, tend to substitute appearance for reality. The artist, being always alone, being heterodox when everyone else is orthodox, is the perpetual upsetter of conventional values, the restorer of the real. . . . His function is to bring back humanity to the real.

Yet the contemporary, putatively avant-garde artist is neither alone nor heterodox. He is today almost invariably part of a larger group—a feminist, a gay liberationist, or a spokesman for an ethnic or racial group—and his thought, far from being heterodox, is, within both his own group and what is called the "artistic community," more rigidly conformist than a Big Ten sorority. He is published in the fashionable magazines, exhibited by the toniest galleries, awarded Pulitzers and other prizes, given federal grants, and generally rewarded and revered.

The politicizing of art, setting it on the side of all the politically-correct causes, has rendered it more acceptable even as it has become less artistic. A commercially successful painter named David Salle, a man with a good feel for the ideological winds, was quoted in the *New Yorker* apropos the politics of contemporary artists:

> Because in art-politics to be homosexual is, *a priori*, more correct than to be heterosexual. Because to be an artist is to be an outsider, and to be a gay artist is to be a double outsider. That's

the correct condition. If you're a straight artist, it's not clear that your outsiderness is legitimate. I know this is totally absurd, that I'm making it sound totally absurd. But the fact is that in our culture it does fall primarily to gays and blacks to make something interesting. Almost everything from the straight white culture is less interesting, and has been for a long time.

How could we possibly get into a condition in which what David Salle says, absurd as it assuredly is, can nonetheless be taken as axiomatic truth? We did it by accepting the quite false notion of the artist as an outsider and extending it to the point where the farther "outside" one represents oneself as being, and the more victimized, the greater one's standing as an artist.

I first came across the name of the dancer Bill T. Jones in an article in the *New York Times Magazine*, where he was described as the "HIV-positive son of migrant workers," which, in current *New York Times*-speak, means a man beyond any possible criticism. Jones and what he represents have come in for some trenchant comment in, of all places, the *New Yorker*, a magazine where earlier he had been the subject of a fawning profile. Arlene Croce, the magazine's distinguished dance critic, wrote a powerful piece demurring from the general celebration and entering the opinion that "the cultivation of victimhood by institutions devoted to the care of art is a menace to all art forms, particularly performing-art forms."

Croce's article, "Discussing the Undiscussable," takes up the question of how the art of victimhood—so depressing, so manipulative, so intimidating, and ultimately so uncriticizable—has risen to such a high place in contemporary culture. She understands that some of its appeal is a combination of false empathy and real snobbery on the part of its audience: "There's no doubt that the public likes to see victims, if only to patronize them with applause." But she makes the larger—and, I think, valid—point that the behavior of government, specifically through the National Endowment for the Arts (NEA), has had a great deal to do with the situation she deplores.

IN 1984 I WAS APPOINTED A MEMBER of the National Council of the National Endowment for the Arts, a body on which I sat for six years. One of the most impressive moments I can recall from my years on the Council was when the director of the music program mentioned that a particular orchestra had had its grant reduced by something like $20,000 because of some "spotty playing in the cello section." I was much taken with how the NEA music panelists were able to pin down this fault, by the professionalism with which they went about the task of judgment. It seemed to me the way things ought to operate.

But outside certain select programs at the NEA, they seldom did. By the end of my term, every member on the Council had been appointed under either the Reagan or the Bush administrations—and yet, despite this, the reigning spirit in the room, as among the staff of the Endowment generally, was preponderantly liberal-Left. Time and again, when arguments about standards and quality came up against what was taken to be democratic fairness and sensitivity to minorities, the latter inevitably won the day.

How could it be otherwise? Given our debased standards, how could one hope to make the hard professional judgments about modern painting or sculpture or literature, let alone mixed-media works? The chief problem with "the peer-panel system," as it was reverently called at the NEA—a system in which artists were asked to sit in judgment of other artists in their field—was that the sort of people who served on these panels were the same sort of people who applied for and received grants themselves. Like was giving money to like.

I could not help noticing, too, the special obligation which the people who worked at the NEA felt toward what passed for avant-garde or "cutting-edge" art. The cutting edge, almost invariably, was anti-capitalist, anti-middle-class, anti-American, the whole-earth catalogue of current antinomianism. What was new was that the artists who wanted to seem cutting edge also wanted the government they despised to pay for the scissors.

Most people at the NEA and on its Council thought this a perfectly workable arrangement. If someone ever suggested that a grant application had all the earmarks of something too obviously political as well as boring beyond excruciation, the air would crackle with potential accusations of censorship and Cassandra-like warnings about slippery slopes heading into McCarthyism.

Those NEA grants that issued in obscenity and horror—Karen Finley smearing her nakedness with chocolate, Robert Mapplethorpe's photographs of men with plumbing and other appurtenances up their rectums, a man spreading his HIV-positive blood on paper towels and then sending them skimming over an audience—gave the Endowment its most serious problems in the press and on Capitol Hill. Yet the NEA's defenders were correct in saying that these comprise only a minuscule proportion of the Endowment's total grants. What they do not say—possibly because they are themselves unaware of it—is how mediocre have been so many of the artists who have received NEA grants.

Mediocrity, the question of what may be called quality control, was rarely discussed during my time at the NEA. It could not be. Most NEA panelists believed in encouraging the putatively disadvantaged more than they believed in art itself, and this made them prey to the grim logic of affirmative action. (Even the panels themselves were put together on an affirmative-action basis.) Add to this the assumption at the NEA that artists themselves were yet another downtrodden minority group, as "entitled" to their grants as other supposed victims. And then toss in plain old-fashioned politics in the form of Congressmen and members of the Council who wanted to make sure that, say, Florida and Colorado got their share of grants. What we had was a fine recipe for spreading artistic mediocrity across the country.

Viewed from the middle distance of a seat on the NEA Council, the grants to individual artists seemed small potatoes. Most were for less than $20,000—an award which generally encouraged self-congratulation and the continued production of unnecessary art. What drained the spectacle of triviality was that the money was not "ours" to give away. No one felt too badly about this, for the NEA budget, generally hovering around $170 million, was, as government spending went, just above the level of walking-around money. Still, the spectacle was more than a little depressing.

THE QUESTION OF WHAT IS NOW TO BE DONE about the arts and arts policy in America is not one that admits of easy or persuasive answers. It is made all the more complicated once one concedes how hard it is to explain what, in any society, actually encourages the production of great art.

Traditions help immensely. In 18th- and 19th-century Vienna, the pressure of strong musical traditions along with a system of monarchical patronage played a part in fostering the magnificent music of that era. The splendid efflorescence of painting in 19th- and early-20th-century France can also be partially understood through the role played by French artistic traditions—and the reactions of artists to and against certain of those traditions. But how does one explain Russian literature in the 19th century, except to say that in Pushkin, Gogol, Dostoyevsky, Turgenev, Tolstoy, and Chekhov, God chose to create six geniuses who happened to share a geography and a language?

Since genius can never be predicted, one looks to institutions that might encourage art to set out in directions likely to be more rewarding than those of the past few decades. What, today, might such institutions be?

The first that comes to mind is criticism. Critics of the arts have traditionally functioned as gatekeepers, deciding what meets the mark and passes through and what does not and is therefore excluded. Some critics have also taken a much more active hand, preparing the ground for the acceptance of new and difficult art through explication and the main force of their authority. One thinks of Edmund Wilson who in *Axel's Castle* (1931) did just this for modernist literature, and, two decades later, of Clement Greenberg who did something similar for Abstract Expressionism.

Critics of this power are not on the scene today. Nor are there important movements in the arts that require such skills. Today our critics commonly function as doormen—or, more precisely, as cheerleaders. Their job often consists in justifying the trivial, vaunting the vapid. Yet they seem quite happy in their work.

In part this derives from the fact that, like so many of our artists, many of our critics too are not merely university-trained but university-employed. As such they participate in the culture that has dominated academic life over the past few decades: they tend to disbelieve in the possibility of dis-interested art; they condone the new multiculturalism and are willing to lower standards to make way for it; they are dubious about judgments of value; and they understand that "criticism" of the work of minority-group members, feminists, or homosexuals must be restricted to praise.

Criticism, then, is not an institution that can be counted on to help revive the arts of our age or in any serious way to arrest their decline—at least not for now. There are a few serious critics on the scene, but the best they can do is continue to remark that the emperor has very few clothes, and wears them badly.

Private foundations, on which many people in the arts depend, are also less than likely to help, for they, too, are hostage to the notion that art ought to be socially useful—that it is most relevant and vibrant when in the service of "social justice." The Lila Wallace-Reader's Digest Fund is fairly typical in this regard. Consider its program for resident theaters. According to the Fund, money for such theaters should be used

> to expand their marketing efforts, mount new plays, broaden
> the ethnic make-up of their management, experiment with
> color-blind casting, increase community-outreach activity,
> and sponsor a variety of other programs designed to inte-
> grate the theaters into their communities.

Other major foundations—Rockefeller, Ford, MacArthur—are not dif-ferently disposed. All are committed to art for almost anything but art's sake.

THAT LEAVES THE INSTITUTIONAL LINCHPIN of the arts in the United States, the National Endowment. Supporters of the NEA, those who like the system as it now is, talk a good deal about the economic soundness of federal support for the arts. They trot out the numbers show-ing that governments in Canada and Europe spent much more on the arts than we do. The arts create jobs and bring in taxes. The arts, the argument goes, are good for the economy. So shut up, and eat your arts.

Not only have other nations throughout history supported the arts, NEA publicists maintain, but future generations will judge us by the extent to which we support the arts as "the finest expression of the human condition." (Ah, Mapplethorpe! Ah, humanity!) When, they remind us, Congress established the NEA in 1965, it noted:

> An advanced civilization must not limit its efforts to science and technology alone but must give full value and support to the other great branches of scholarly and cultural activity in order to achieve a better understanding of the past, a better analysis of the present, and a better view of the future.

The arts, therefore, are not only good for the economy, they serve the purposes of moral uplift. So shut up and eat your arts.

To hear its advocates tell it, the NEA enriches community life, stimulates local economies, supports the promising young, makes culture available to the masses, works with "at-risk" youth, satisfies a deep demand for art among the American people—the NEA is in fact good for everything but growing hair. The arts are good for the city, good for the country, good for everyone. So shut up and eat your arts.

But—aside from all these magnificent side-effects—what, exactly, do the arts do? Here we return to the same old litany. Paul Goldberger, the architecture critic, answered the question by writing that "what art strives to do . . . is not to coddle but to challenge." In other words, painters who mock your religion, playwrights who blame you for not doing enough for AIDS, poets who exalt much that you despise, opera composers who make plain that your politics are vicious—all this is by definition art, and, whether you like it or not, it is good for you. So go eat your arts out.

The NEA might have been spared much anguish if someone truly knowledgeable had been in a position of leadership. But in its 30-year history, it has never had a chairman with anything approaching an understanding of the arts. The specialty of Nancy Hanks, the first chairman, was charming Congressmen to support the agency it had founded in 1965. Her successor, Livingston Biddle, was a platitudinarian, who liked to expatiate on his slogan that "the arts mean excellence"; one need only listen to him for two minutes to cease believing in art and excellence both. Biddle was followed by Frank Hodsoll, an intelligent and capable civil servant who, when it came to the arts, was clearly learning on the job. Over the years the people in the job did not improve.

One wonders what it might be like to have someone in a position of leadership who knows what the point of the arts is. But who of any standing would want to take on the job? In the current political climate, he would find himself locked between radical artists shouting censorship and conservative Congressmen crying obscenity. His or her efforts could only come to grief.

THAT THE FUTURE of the National Endowment for the Arts is in peril ought not to be surprising. What people at the NEA and those who accept grants from it have never seemed to realize is that they are sponsoring and producing *official* art, just as surely as the academic painters in France or the socialist-realist novelists in the Soviet Union produced official art. That our official art is against the society that sponsors it does not make it any the less official. But given the obscenity and the mediocrity and the politicization of so much of this art, government sponsorship of it has come to seem intolerable, and there is now talk of closing down the Endowment.

Should that be done? Any serious scrutiny of the NEA must begin with the stipulation that politically motivated art ought not to be underwritten by taxpayer money. (The argument that all art is ultimately political is greatly exaggerated; it is a question of degree, and everyone knows it.) Nor for their part should artists upon receiving a grant be asked to accept any condition that will inhibit them, such as not offending any segment of the population. Since these criteria cannot be satisfied in the case of grants to individual artists, and especially those on the "cutting edge," my own sense is that it would better if all such grants were eliminated: better for the country and, though they are likely to hate it, better, finally, for artists.

In one of his essays the eminent cultural historian Jacques Barzun makes a distinction between "public art" and all other kinds. Individual artists, he believes, should fend for themselves, as artists have always done; I agree with him. But then there is public art, by which Barzun means museums, opera houses, orchestras, theaters, and dance troupes. "If as a nation," he writes, "we hold that high art is a public need, these institutions deserve support on the same footing as police departments and weather bureaus."

William F. Buckley, Jr. has supplied a corroborating argument derived, for conservatives, from the most impressive of all possible sources. It was Adam Smith who, in Buckley's words, "counseled that free societies are obliged to contribute state funds only for the maintenance of justice, for the common defense, and for the preservation of monuments." It is only a small stretch, Buckley suggests, to claim that a great many artistic works qualify as monuments.

I agree with that, too—but only in theory. In a different political-cultural climate—less confrontational and litigious—one could easily imagine a place for a federal presence in the arts. The government could contribute to preserving art: it could help to maintain the costs of museums in financial difficulty and ease the financial strain entailed in the performance and exhibition of established and often difficult art that does not figure to have a wide following. Some valuable art cannot realistically hope to survive in the marketplace, ever, and some of the good things the NEA historically helped to do are not likely to be done by private philanthropy—bringing in art from abroad, underwriting costly exhibition catalogues, helping small but serious local musical and dance groups get under way. There are other things, too, that the federal government would perhaps be in the best position to accomplish, if the political climate were not so deliberately abrasive.

Proponents of the NEA point to the fact that most West European governments do support the arts, without great tumult, for the perfectly legitimate reason that they feel a responsibility to their national cultural heritage and to culture generally. But there would not have been a great tumult in the United States, either, if the NEA's advocates, artists' lobbying groups, and artists themselves had not felt the need to justify the mediocre, the political, and the obscene. These justifications have even extended to the argument that *not* to receive an NEA grant is to be the victim of censorship. When Karen Finley and other performance artists were denied an NEA grant in 1990, they took their case to the courts on this basis, and won. As long as such things go on the federal government would do better to remain outside the arts altogether.

When the abolition of the NEA is discussed, many people talk about turning the task over to the states. But the effect of this would most likely be to enlarge state bureaucracies, and art selected for support on the state level is likely to be even more mediocre, and no less political, than that selected on the federal level. The prospect of "devolution" is thus not one that ought to fill anyone with optimism.

It does, however, seem doubtful that, if government divorces itself from the arts, private philanthropy will pick up the whole tab. People who run large artistic institutions—museums, symphony orchestras— seem to agree that the new generations of the wealthy have shown themselves less generous than their forebears: the philanthropic impulse is not, evidently, a genetic one.

This is unfortunate. Although money has its limitations in the arts, there is no question that it also has its distinct uses. In my own time on the NEA Council I sensed that if an art was weak, there was nothing that the injection of money—which was finally all the NEA or any federal program had to offer—could do to strengthen it. If, on other hand, an art was strong, as dance was in the middle 1980s, money could help in small but real ways to support it in its vibrancy. Many dancers, for example, work a 26-week season, or less, and hence are unemployed half the year; and, in a profession that almost guarantees injury, few dance companies are able to offer health insurance. Although nothing was done to rectify either of these situations during even the palmiest days at the NEA, the answer in both instances was fairly simple—money.

Other things that seem eminently justifiable are also not likely to be picked up by private philanthropy. The NEA has sent dance and theatrical and musical groups into rural and backwater parts of the country, so that people, and especially the young, could have an opportunity to see live performance, which, even in a television age, has its own magic. Arts education in the lower grades, which has been gradually yet seriously slipping in recent decades, is something that needs attending to. Private philanthropy is unlikely to step in here, too.

All that having been said, it still remains the case that if the Endowment were shut down, the arts would probably for the most part not be drastically affected. In some instances, fresh patrons would step forward to fill the financial gaps; in others, cutbacks in production and exhibition schedules would have to be made; in a minor number of cases, smaller institutions—literary magazines, design projects, local music groups—might go under. But much as the NEA and its advocates would like everyone to think otherwise, the presence of the Endowment is not crucial to the artistic life of this country. This may be a good time to lie low and have no arts policy whatsoever. After all, we had an artistic life—a much richer and more distinguished one—before we had an NEA.

Thanks in part to the NEA, we are now in an age of artistic surfeit. To provide only a single depressing statistic, I read somewhere that there are currently 26,000 registered poets in the United States. Where, it will be asked, do they register? With the Associated Writing Programs, I gather, which are chiefly made up of teachers of writing, who are even now busy producing still more poets, who will go on to teach yet more poets, who will . . . so that in twenty years' time we will have 52,000 registered poets. Degas, more than a century ago, remarked: "We must discourage the arts." Sometimes that doesn't seem a bad idea.

Who Killed Poetry?

(1988)

There are certain things in which mediocrity is intolerable:
poetry, music, painting, public eloquence.

Jean de La Bruyère

I AM NOT ABOUT TO SAY OF POETRY, as Marianne Moore once did, that "I, too, dislike it," for not only has reading poetry brought me instruction and delight but I was taught to exalt it. Or, more precisely, I was taught that poetry was itself an exalted thing. No literary genre was closer to the divine than poetry; in no other craft could a writer soar as he could in a poem. When a novelist or a dramatist wrote with the flame of the highest inspiration, his work was said to be "touched by poetry"—as in the phrase "touched by God." "The right reader of a good poem," said Robert Frost, "can tell the moment it strikes him that he has taken an immortal wound—that he will never get over it." Such quasi-religious language to describe poetry was not unusual; not so long ago, it was fairly common. "The function of poetry," wrote Robert Graves, "is religious invocation of the Muse; its use is the experience of mixed exaltation and horror that her presence excites."

Both these quotations and several others in the same spirit are to be found at the back of Oscar Williams's *A Little Treasury of Modern Poetry* (revised edition), a small stout volume that has something of the look and heft of a missal or other religious tome. Even Delmore Schwartz, not a man noted for heightened rhetoric or empty ecstasy, referred to the poet as "a kind of priest." To those for whom literature, and culture generally, came increasingly to stand in as a substitute for religion, poetry—and modern poetry specifically—was High Church.

The copyright date on my edition of Oscar Williams's anthology is 1950, and it was during the 1950s that poetry last had this religious aura. Many of the high priests of the cult—T. S. Eliot and Wallace Stevens, Robert Frost and William Carlos Williams, E. E. Cummings and W. H. Auden—were still alive and still writing, even if the best of their work was already behind them. The audience for poetry was then less than vast; it had diminished greatly since the age of Browning and Tennyson. In part this was owing to the increased difficulty of poetry, of which T. S. Eliot, in 1921, had remarked: "It appears likely that poets in our civilization, as it exists, at present, must be *difficult*." Eliot's justification for this difficulty—and it has never seemed quite persuasive—is that poetry must be as complex as the civilization it describes, with the modern poet becoming "more comprehensive, more allusive, more indirect." All this served to make the modern poet more exclusive as well, which, for those of us who adored (a word chosen with care) modern poetry, was quite all right. Modern poetry, with the advance of modernism, had become an art for the happy few, and the happy few, it must be said, are rarely happier than when they are even fewer.

But such snobbish considerations aside, the generations of poets between W. B. Yeats (1865–1939) and W. H. Auden (1907–1973) produced an impressive body of poetry—of the kind that, in Frost's phrase, really does make "an immortal wound"; once read, it never is quite forgotten. Nor were all of these poets imposingly difficult: Yeats isn't, nor is Robert Frost. The most difficult poems of all, the *Cantos* of Ezra Pound, seem over the years to have slipped outside the canon of great modern poetry and to be thought instead the interesting fragments of a great cultural impresario— the Diaghilev of modernist poetry—who finally flipped, betraying both his country and himself. These poets did not, except occasionally, teach. Occupationally, they ranged from physician (William Carlos Williams) to editor (Marianne Moore) to insurance executive (Wallace Stevens); in personal style, from traditionally formal (T. S. Eliot) to bohemian (E. E. Cummings) to suicidally desperate (Hart Crane). No one would ever think to describe them as academic.

They were, however, the first living poets to be given the full academic treatment. Their works were dissected in classrooms, the intellectual quarterlies ran solemn essays about them even while continuing to run their poems, book-length critical studies about them began to be written and continue to be written even now. Their fame was neither of the general nor of the wealth-producing kind that Ernest Hemingway and William Faulkner knew—though T. S. Eliot was an international celebrity—but within the circumambience of the university they were revered. No body of critical writing produced during this period was more efficacious than that of T. S. Eliot, whose essays could affect the reputation—"the place in the canon," as academics put it—of writers born three hundred years earlier. In the view of F. R. Leavis, Eliot, along with Samuel Johnson, Coleridge, and Matthew Arnold, is one of the four great English literary critics, yet without the authority lent his criticism by his poetry, it is plain that Eliot's critical power would have been nowhere near so influential.

But the clearest evidence of the reverence in which these poets were held is found in the way they were worshipped by the generation of poets, or at least those in America, who followed them. Randall Jarrell, Robert Lowell, John Berryman, Delmore Schwartz not only wrote some of the most brilliant essays on their immediate poetic forebears, but in their lives they tended to be obsessed with them. The young Robert Lowell set up a tent on the lawn of the home of Allen Tate, to learn at the feet of one of his masters. Delmore Schwartz viewed T. S. Eliot as a culture hero, pure though not so simple, and his letters and conversation were filled with references to Eliot. Randall Jarrell, after writing about Wallace Stevens's latter-day weaknesses, capped his criticism with the thought that Stevens was "one of the true poets of our century, someone whom the world will keep on reading just as it keeps on listening to Vivaldi or Scarlatti, looking at Tiepolo or Poussin."

Jarrell, Lowell, Berryman, Schwartz, as anyone who has read much about them cannot mistake, were all immensely ambitious men. Had their ambitions been applied to business or politics or perhaps anything other than careers in poetry—and all four were the most careful caretakers of their careers—they might not have ended as sadly as they did:

in repeated mental breakdown, alcoholism, early death, and suicide. I believe poetry was implicated in their disastrous lives in that they had set out to forge brilliant careers like those of their predecessors and knew that, for a complex of reasons, they could not make it. Jarrell wrote an essay entitled "The Obscurity of the Poet," which he claimed had to be surmounted if civilization were to carry on, and another entitled "The Taste of the Age," which he found trashy. Delmore Schwartz wrote essays on "The Isolation of Modern Poetry," "The Vocation of the Poet," "Views of a Second Violinist, Some Answers to Questions about Writing Poetry," and "The Present State of Poetry," a state that he thought, to put it gently, uninspiring. The main modernist poets had written with assurance in their bones, as if they knew their worth and knew that posterity would one day know it, too. But the poets who came after them were less sure; they knew something had gone wrong. And they were right. It had.

B EFORE I ATTEMPT to get at what I believe has happened, perhaps I ought to describe what I think is the situation of contemporary poetry. Pressed to formulate this situation in a single sentence, I should write: contemporary poetry in the United States flourishes in a vacuum. Today there are more than 250 universities with creative-writing programs, and all of these have a poetry component, which means that they not only train aspiring poets but hire men and women who have published poetry to teach them. Many of these men and women go from being students in one writing program to being teachers in another— without, you might say, their feet, metrical or anatomical, having touched the floor. Many colleges and universities that do not have formal writing programs nonetheless hire poets to teach a creative-writing course or two; and the course in writing poetry has also become a staple of the community-college and adult-education menu. None of this puts poets up there in wealth with the Helmsleys and the Trumps, but it has made it possible for a large number of poets—and more than 6,300 poets and other writers are listed in the most recent edition of the *Directory of American Poets and Fiction Writers*—to earn their living in work closely connected with their craft. Such work, thirty or so years ago, was available only to a small handful of poets, and these of the highest stature.

Robert Frost, when in his eighties and a great draw on the poetry-read-
ing circuit, thought it a good thing that poets had become teachers "in a
thousand, two thousand colleges," and added that colleges and universities gave poets "the best audiences poetry ever had in this world." Writing
in 1985, in an essay entitled "The Poetry Reading: Public Performance/
Private Act," the poet Donald Hall noted: "In the past thirty years, the
poetry reading, which used to be rare, has become the chief form of publication for American poets. Annually, hundreds of thousands of listeners
hear tens of thousands of readings." The great majority of these take place
on college campuses, but many others are given at such cultural centers as
the 92nd Street Y in New York, the Poetry Center at the Art Institute in
Chicago, the International Poetry Forum in Pittsburgh, not to mention
various churches, synagogues, bars, art galleries, bookstores, and other
public forums. Donald Hall reminds us that such poets as Vachel Lindsay,
Carl Sandburg, and Robert Frost were giving readings in the 20s and 30s,
but it was Dylan Thomas, in the late 40s and early 50s, who by providing quite beautiful performances and the added attraction of outrageous
behavior really put poetry reading on the cultural map.

Poetry readings can draw anywhere from a pathetic handful of bedraggled students to a tony audience of several hundred. The fame of the poet
is decisive. Fame, too, determines fees. Donald Hall, in 1985, claimed that
a standard good fee for a reading was $1,000, though most poets, I sus-
pect, accept a good deal less, while others—Allen Ginsberg, Adrienne
Rich, John Ashbery—can command more. James Dickey claimed to have
received as much as $4,500 for a reading. Sometimes two or three nearby
colleges will invite a poet to read at each of their institutions, and the
poet will pick up two or three fees while the colleges share the cost of a
single airplane ticket. Intramurally, there are arguments about whether
readings are corrupting to poets. Some claim that reading too frequently
can make a poet tend to compose simpler, jokier poems that can be readily understood by an audience, whereas complex poems—imagine hearing Wallace Stevens's "Le Monocle de Mon Oncle" without ever having
read it—do not, so to say, play well at readings. Yet readings have helped
many poets who do not have, or want, teaching jobs to keep going financially. Readings, too, are often the only payment in the coin of the realm

of the ego that they ever receive, for the printed work of poets, sometimes including poets who have been at it a long while, often gets hardly any response at all in the way of reviews or even letters from readers.

No one keeps very precise records on such matters, but the general sense is that more poetry is currently being published than ever before. Poets are not being all that widely published by the major trade houses of New York and Boston, though almost all of them do publish some contemporary poets. Many university presses have begun to issue books of poetry, and some have been doing so for years. What have come to be called the "small presses" also publish a fairly large amount of poetry. Some of these—David R. Godine of Boston, for example, or North Point Press of Berkeley—aren't as small as all that, but others, which carry such names as Dragon Gate or Aralia Press, truly are. The best general answer to the question of how well these books of poetry sell is probably "not very." It used to be said that the only serious poet in America who was ever able to live off the sale of his work was Robert Frost, but according to Donald Hall, even Frost was able to do so only toward the end of his life.

Yet there is no shortage of outlets for poetry. The *New Yorker* publishes it, most of the literary monthlies and quarterlies do; *Poetry*, founded by Harriet Monroe in 1912, rolls along, and, with a $100 million benefaction from Ruth Lilly, of the Lilly Pharmaceutical Company, now does so in rather princely fashion. And beyond such publications are the many little magazines that print vast quantities of poetry. The circulation of these magazines is often not in the thousands but in the hundreds. Almost all of them would go under without subsidies. So numerous are the little magazines that there exists an organization—an "umbrella organization," in the bureaucratic phrase—called The Coordinating Council for Literary Magazines. It, too, is heavily subsidized, in good part by the National Endowment for the Arts. Sometimes it seems as if there isn't a poem written in this nation that isn't subsidized or underwritten by a grant either from a foundation or the government or a teaching salary or a fellowship of one kind or another.

And so, as the disc jockeys say, the beat goes on. The pretense is that nothing is wrong, that business is proceeding pretty much as usual. There are today, for example, prizes galore: Pulitzers and Lamonts and National Book

Critics Circle and Yale Younger Poets and Rome Fellowships of the American Academy and Institute of Arts & Letters and Guggenheims and National Endowment for the Arts Fellowships and Library of Congress Consultantships and the Lilly Prize and now a national poet laureate and even—how he, most ambitious of poets, would have wryly smiled at the news—a Delmore Schwartz Memorial Award. Poets regularly parade as spokesmen and spokeswomen for their ethnic group or race or political tendency. Some few poets—Robert Penn Warren, perhaps Richard Wilbur is soon to arrive at this position—have more medals than Baron von Richthofen.

No shortage, then, of honors, emoluments, publication possibilities, opportunities to garner public adulation. In such ways may contemporary poetry be said to be flourishing.

B UT WHAT OF THE VACUUM? I should say that it consists generally of this: that however much contemporary poetry may be honored, it is, outside a very small circle, scarcely read. Contemporary poetry is no longer a part of the regular intellectual diet. People of general intellectual interests who feel that they ought to read or at least know about works on modern society or recent history or novels that attempt to convey something about the way we live now, no longer feel the same compunction about contemporary poetry. The crowds in London once stood on their toes to see Tennyson pass; today a figure like Tennyson probably would not write poetry and might not even read it. Poetry has been shifted—has shifted itself?—off center stage. Literarily, poetry no longer seems in any way where the action is. It begins to seem, in fact, a sideline activity, a little as chiropractic or acupuncture is to mainstream medicine—odd, strange, but with a small cult of followers who swear by it.

One might counter that poetry was in a similar state when the modernist poets set out on their ambitious artistic adventure. They published their work in magazines read only by hundreds; their names were not known by most members of the educated classes; their following, such as it was, had a cultish character. But beyond this nothing else seems comparable. Propelling the modernist poets was a vision, and among some of them a program—a belief that the nature of life had changed fundamentally and that artists now had to change accordingly. Free verse, fragmented syntax, radical disjunctions, slangy diction, the use of subjects before then thought poetically impossible—these were among the techniques and methods employed by the modernist poets. New, too, was their attitude toward the reader, whom they, perhaps first among any writers in history, chose in a radical way to disregard. They weren't out to *épater*. If what they wrote was uncompromisingly difficult, they did not see this as their problem. They wrote as they wrote; as for their difficulty, the question was whether or not, in Henry James's phrase, theirs was "the difficulty that inspired." By that phrase I take James to have meant difficulty of a kind that inspires one to surmount it because one senses the reward to be eminently worthy of the struggle. Somehow, through the quality of their writing, the authority of the sacrifices they made for their art, the aura of adult seriousness conveyed in both work and life, the modernist poets won through. Theirs was the difficulty, ours the inspiration.

Whereas one tended to think of the modernist poet as an artist—even if he worked in a bank in London, or at an insurance company in Hartford, or in a physician's office in Rutherford, New Jersey—one tends to think of the contemporary poet as a professional: a poetry professional. Like a true professional, he is rather insulated within the world of his fellow-professionals. The great majority of poets today live in an atmosphere almost entirely academic, but it is academic with a difference: not the world of science and scholarship but that of the creative-writing program and the writing workshop. (Everything that has gone wrong with the world since World War II, Kingsley Amis once noted, can be summed up in the word "workshop.") The poets who have come out of this atmosphere are oddly positioned both in academic life and in the world at large; they are neither wholly academics nor wholly artists. They publish chiefly in journals sheltered by universities, they fly around the country giving readings and workshops at other colleges and universities. They live in jeans yet carry a curriculum vitae. I have seen scores of such curricula, and they tend to run along the following lines:

> James Silken [a name I have made up] published his first book of poems, *Stoned Jupiter*, with the University Presses of Florida. His second book, *The Parched Garden*, will be published early next year by Black Bear Press. A chapbook,

Apaches and Parsley, was brought out by Wainscotting Books in 1983. His poems and reviews have appeared in such journals as *Poetry Northwest, New Letters, The Arizona Review, TriQuarterly*, and *Worcester Review*. He has given readings at Iowa State University, the University of Michigan, Drake University, and Bread Loaf. Next summer he will be a fellow at the Oregon Center for the Creative Arts. A native of Tennessee, he now lives in Tempe, where he directs the writing program at Arizona State University.

Well, it's a living.

In 1941 Delmore Schwartz, in an essay originally published in *Kenyon Review* and entitled "The Isolation of Modern Poetry," wrote that "It is not a simple matter of the poet lacking an audience, for that is an effect, rather than a cause, of the character of modern poetry." The character that Schwartz then had in mind was its difficulty (in the Henry James sense). In *Partisan Review*, in 1949, Schwartz added, "Anyone who wants to understand modern poetry can do so by working about half as hard as he must to learn a language, or acquire any new skill, or learn to play bridge well." But in fact, with an occasional exception (the obscurity of much of the poetry of John Ashbery comes to mind), contemporary poetry has not grown more but less difficult, and the audience still isn't there.

I F **Delmore Schwartz** blamed the obscurity of modern poetry on its difficulty, Randall Jarrell, in a lecture at Harvard called "The Obscurity of the Poet," blamed the national culture. "The poet," said Jarrell, "lives in a world whose newspapers and magazines and books and motion pictures and radio stations and television stations have destroyed, in a great many people, even the capacity for understanding real poetry, real art of any kind." In more recent years, poets have taken this a step further to blame America for an anti-intellectual and anti-artistic strain in our national life. "Pushkin could count on railway workers to know his poems," John Berryman told Eileen Simpson, his first wife. "*Think of it*! Who reads poetry in America?" Poetry, it is elsewhere claimed, is ill-taught in grammar and high schools. The neglect of poetry by major trade publishers is sometimes blamed. Capitalism generally comes in for its share of lumps, sometimes for encouraging supermarket bookselling techniques, sometimes for holding up the wrong models: What kind of country is it in which Lee Iacocca is better known than A. R. Ammons? Everything, in short, is blamed but the drinking water.

Some poets, attempting to swallow the hand that feeds them, even blame the university, arguing that, through the emergence of so many creative-writing programs, poets have created their own, largely inbred audience that simultaneously requires a great deal in the way of care and feeding and asks little of them, the poets, in the way of literary ambition. ("Within five years," wrote Greg Kuzma, a poet and teacher of poetry, "there will be a creative-writing program available for anyone in America within safe driving distance of his home.") Creative-writing programs, this argument runs, are not only producing more people who think of themselves as poets than this or any other country needs, but, through the encouraging, the somewhat therapeutic, atmosphere of the work-shop, are generally lowering the high standard of work which is poetry's only serious claim on anyone's attention.

From a higher, more historical point of view, there are those who claim that the game was up for poetry with the advent of romanticism, which retained great themes for poetry but saw them through a filter of the self—whereas now, this argument holds, the great themes are gone and all that remains to poetry is a pallid subjectivity. "With the development of romantic theory in the 18th, 19th, and 20th centuries," the critic Yvor Winters wrote, "there has been an increasing tendency to suppress the rational in poetry and as far as it may be to isolate the emotional." A grave mistake this, at least for those who tended to view poetry as a vehicle for truth and a repository as useful as any ever invented for ideas and insights. Christopher Clausen, author of an excellent little book entitled *The Place of Poetry, Two Centuries of an Art in Crisis*, underscores this point when he writes: "Since the rise of science to intellectual preeminence, poets have been less able either to show equal claim with scientists to clarify the problems Western civilization has (perhaps wrongly) seen as most important, or to incorporate and epitomize the conclusions of their rivals."

Romanticism, science; even modernism itself has been put in the dock, for draining the joyousness out of poetry or, with the introduction of free verse, depriving poetry of the delights of meter and rhyme. Philip Larkin, for one, laid the blame for the broken connection between poets and readers on what he called "the aberration of modernism, that blighted all the arts." He meant in particular the modernist tendency to deify the artistic vocation, to separate it from any obligation on the part of a writer to instruct or entertain an audience. In a three-page essay entitled "The Pleasure Principle," Larkin wrote that "at bottom poetry, like all art, is inextricably bound up with giving pleasure, and if a poet loses his pleasure-seeking audience he has lost the only audience worth having, for which the dutiful mob that signs on every September is no substitute."

To screw things yet one notch higher, there are those who believe that the decline of poetry in our day is an inevitable accompaniment of the disintegration of language generally. Wendell Berry, a poet and essayist, writes: "My impression is that we have seen, for perhaps 150 years, a gradual increase in language that is either meaningless or destructive of meaning. And I believe that this increasing unreliability of language parallels the increasing disintegration, over the same period, of persons and communities"—and, one gathers, by extension, of the power of poetry to recover much of value from the wreckage. At a slightly lower level of generality, others believe that the use poetry has traditionally made of rhythm and meter, of image and metaphor, to bring its readers to a condition of susceptibility to the emotion and thought it wishes to convey simply no longer finds an adequate response in any but a minuscule handful of trained readers. It is as if an old human skill, like following a trail or scenting game, had atrophied and died. Still others appeal to the mysteries of history. Might we not just be going through a bad patch in the history of poetry, as the country did between, say, 1870, when Emily Dickinson and Walt Whitman were still at the height of their powers, and 1910, when the modernist poets exploded upon the scene?

NO DOUBT ROMANTICISM, MODERNISM, and other literary ideas and ideological movements have all had their effect in landing poetry in the position it finds itself in today. Institutional, linguistic, historical factors have also doubtless exerted their influence in pushing poetry into the dark corner it now inhabits. Yet nearly every explanation of the situation of poetry in our time—attempting to account for its isolation, its seeming irrelevance to the general culture, the depressing sense that this once most elevated of human activities is now rather second-rate—seems to let the poets themselves off the hook. There may be something to Walt Whitman's remark that "to have great poets, there must be great audiences too," but, as Delmore Schwartz once rejoined, "To have great poetry it is necessary to have great poets. . . ."

Not that anyone has been claiming that ours is a great age of poetry. Literary forms, or genres, after all, have their own, odd, often indecipherable rises and falls. English drama never again reached the heights attained in the Elizabethan Age. Who could have predicted the great burgeoning brilliance of the novel in mid-19th-century Russia? It may well be that sixty or seventy years ago, in our Eliots and Yeatses and Stevenses and Hardys and Frosts, we had our Donnes and Marvells and are now living through our Wallaces and Lovelaces. Another view, one straightforwardly formulated by Karl Shapiro, holds that there is precious little poetic talent around even at the best of times. As Shapiro notes:

> I have for a long time come to the conclusion that at any one time the production of true works of art is even rarer than we think. I even devised a rule-of-thumb dogma which I call the B-S-K theory of poetry: Byron, Shelley, and Keats. According to this dogma, there can only be three poets at any one time. In periods of resplendent renaissance, the number increases slightly but not much, perhaps up to half a dozen. Around the points of these stars, there are a certain number of satellites, and so on. Actually, this is a historically realistic way of looking at art.

But even if there were any B's or S's or K's about nowadays, it is not certain we would know who they were. Poetry is published in such plenitude that last year the *Los Angeles Times* announced it would no longer review books of poems, on the grounds that it was impossible to tell which were important. The same, by extension, applies to poets. There is nothing resembling a consensus on who might be the important poets of our day. Richard Wilbur is everywhere taken for eminent, and everyone for whom poetry matters reveres him for his craftsmanship, yet Wilbur does not seem to stir passionate advocacy in his readers, except when held up as a model of the literary decorum that has been lost to poetry in its confessional, sexier, Visigothic aspects. Seamus Heaney, the Irish poet, is generally written about as if he were a major figure, yet his poetry, too, has failed to break out of the tight, claustral little circle of professionals. Doubtless the most famous poet in America was Allen Ginsberg, but poetry isn't really what he was famous for: politics and a talent for the outrageous and a small genius for publicity are the three cornerstones on which his fame rests. John Ashbery is also publicly honored and written about with critical reverence; yet, though he is not himself an academic, his poetry—about which he has said, "Poetry does not have subject matter because it is the subject. We are the subject matter of poetry, not vice versa"—is perfect for academic treatment, being allusive, desultory, and nicely self-deconstructive, which also means that it is most unlikely to hold any interest outside the academy.

I not long ago had occasion to hear two poets read and talk about their craft. Both were men, both in their thirties, both had regular teaching jobs at large universities, both had published two books and had their share of grants and awards. One of the two was a Hawaiian of Japanese ancestry, the other was middle-class Jewish. Both were zealous about poetry, which they took to be insufficiently appreciated in an essentially philistine country. The first poet viewed himself as a spokesman for his people, the truth of whose past he saw it as his task to keep alive in his own poetry. The second poet did not announce himself as a spokesman for the Jews, but he came across in the style one thinks of as tough but sensitive, the champion of a beleaguered art. His father, he disclosed, is a salesman, and it had been no easy thing to get him to understand his son's need to be a poet. (A salesman, evidently, can die deaths unknown even to Arthur Miller.) In their discussions after they read, both poets were full of quotations from Pound and Eliot and Kant and Rilke, giving off a strong whiff of the classroom.

As for the works themselves, the first read a lengthy poem about a visit to a strip of land in Hawaii that had once been the site of the cemetery where his grandfather was buried but which had since been plowed up by a developer. His was a poem, in short, about victimization, with a bit of anti-capitalism thrown in at no extra charge. The second read a poem entitled "Proustian" about the brief happy moments when, as a child, his grandmother fed him cookies and milk and he had no knowledge of time, and another poem about a visit to his former high-school football coach, who had always preached the powers of the body, but was now sadly powerless in a body racked by cancer. A poem, the New Critics held, cannot be paraphrased, but in paraphrasing—summarizing, really—these poems I do not think I am doing them a grave injustice. I bring them up only because they seemed so characteristic, so much like a great deal of contemporary poetry: slightly political, heavily preening, and not distinguished enough in language or subtlety of thought to be memorable.

I S IT ALL UP WITH POETRY, THEN? As early as the 1940s, Edmund Wilson wrote an essay carrying the questioning title, "Is Verse a Dying Technique?" Wilson's answer was, essentially, yes, it is. Prose, in Wilson's view, had overwhelmed poetry. By Flaubert's time, he notes, "the Dantes present their vision in terms of prose dramas or fiction rather than epics in verse." Wilson mentions Flaubert because he is the first novelist to lavish the kind of care on his prose that poets did on their verse; James Joyce would be another. Yeats was the last great poet to write convincingly in iambic pentameters, which, Wilson noted, "no longer [have] any relation whatever to the tempo and language of our lives." Antiquated forms can only render an antiquated point of view, and "you cannot deal with contemporary events in an idiom which was already growing trite in Tennyson's and Arnold's day. . . ."

Wilson does allow that our lyric poets may be compared with any who have ever written, but he adds: "We have had no imaginations of the stature of Shakespeare or Dante who have done their major work in verse." Edgar Allan Poe had anticipated much of this a century earlier. In "The Poetic Principle," his essay of 1848, Poe wrote: "If, at any time, any very long poems *were* popular in reality—which I doubt—it is at least clear that no very long poem will ever be popular again." We shall continue to read Homer, Dante, Shakespeare, Milton, perhaps Byron and Browning, to cherish and derive great pleasure from them, but with the understanding that what they did—specifically telling magnificent stories in poetic form—can never be done again.

Not that writers haven't tried. Philip Toynbee published a novel in verse in the 1960s. Clive James has written lengthy travesties of contemporary London literary life in heroic couplets. A novel entitled *The Golden Gate*, composed in a Pushkinian rhyme scheme by a young writer named Vikram Seth, appeared in 1986 to much acclaim. But it was acclaim of the odd kind that Samuel Johnson felt was owed to women preachers and dogs walking on their hind legs: "You are surprised to find it done at all." So swept away were readers by the sheer freakiness of Vikram Seth's accomplishment that they overlooked its rather clichéd Berkeleyan (California not Bishop) message about making love not war.

Poets have not altogether given up on telling stories. Some of Robert Frost's best poems are narratives. Although fragmented and disjunctive, even "The Waste Land" tells a story; so, too, in a very different way, does Wallace Stevens's "Sunday Morning." In *Life Studies* (1957), Robert Lowell conveyed portions of his autobiography in verse. Among contemporary poets, Herbert Morris, in finely controlled blank verse, has written dramatic monologues and accounts of his childhood that are essentially narrative in character and quite successfully so. But for the vast most part contemporary poetry has gone off in the direction of the lyric. In practice, this means a shortish poem, usually fewer than forty lines, generally describing an incident or event or phenomenon of nature or work of art or relationship or emotion, in more or less distinguished language, the description often, though not always, yielding a slightly oblique insight.

SAMUEL JOHNSON, who said of *Paradise Lost* that "None ever wished it longer than it is," said in the same essay on Milton that "All that short compositions can commonly attain is neatness and elegance." There are various reasons why so many contemporary poems are, in Johnson's phrase, "short compositions," and not the least among them is that most magazines do not provide space for long poems. They choose not to do so on the assumption, probably correct, that few even quite serious readers wish to read a poem that runs ten or more pages. (Let us not speak of the talent that it takes to sustain an extended poetic performance.) But in taking up the lyric as its chief form, contemporary poetry has seriously delimited itself. It thereby gives away much that has always made literature an activity of primary significance; it gives away the power to tell stories, to report on how people live and have lived, to struggle for those larger truths about life the discovery of which is the final justification for reading. Thus has poetry in our day become, in the words of the poet and critic Brad Leithauser, "a sadly peripheral art form."

Even here on the periphery, though, it would help to be able to make a few distinctions. Although it hardly guarantees the production of great poets, a start might be made by deciding who are the greatly overrated ones. This is not likely to happen soon. Contemporary poetry, in the cumbersome new usage of the academic literary criticism of the moment, has been "privileged"—that is, in our day it has been given a special dispensation, set apart, released from the burden of undergoing tough criticism. Helen Vendler, the most talented critic of contemporary poetry now at work, almost exclusively writes elucidary appreciations; one can only infer which poets Professor Vendler doesn't care for by her neglecting to write about them. Randall Jarrell, the most talented critic of contemporary poetry in his day, felt no such compunction; he kissed and slapped with equal exuberance. But then poetry in Jarrell's time may not have seemed as sickly as it does now. Now, for so many poets, critics, editors, small-press publishers, creative-writing programs, the chief thing seems to be keeping the patient alive.

Yet if survival is genuinely at stake, it won't do to ignore symptoms. For an account of symptoms, of what is wrong with so much contemporary poetry, one does well to consider an extraordinary essay by Witold Gombrowicz, the Polish novelist who died in Paris in exile in 1969. The essay is entitled, straight out, "Against Poets." In his second paragraph Gombrowicz states, if not his case against contemporary poetry, his condition when reading it:

> The thesis of the following essay, that almost no one likes
> poems and that the world of verse is a fiction and a false
> hood, will seem, I assume, as bold as it is frivolous. Yet here
> I stand before you and declare that I don't like poems at all

and that they even bore me. Maybe you will say I am an impoverished ignoramus. Yet I have labored in art for a long time and its language is not completely alien to me. Nor can you use your favorite argument against me, claiming that I do not possess a poetic sensibility, because I do possess it and to a great degree. When poetry appears to me not in poems but mixed with other, more prosaic, elements, for example, in Shakespeare's dramas, in the prose of Pascal and Dostoyevsky, or simply as a very ordinary sunset, I tremble as do other mortals. Why does rhythm and rhyme put me to sleep, why does the language of poets seem to me to be the least interesting language conceivable, why is this Beauty so unattractive to me and why is it that I don't know anything worse as style, anything more ridiculous than the manner in which poets speak about themselves and their poetry?

When Gombrowicz gets down to his bill of particular complaint, it turns out that he is put off by the professionalization of poetry—"today one is a Poet, the way one is an engineer or a doctor"—which has robbed poetry of its spontaneity, made poetry itself seem artificial, and rendered the poet a less than complete human being. Poetry has been surrounded by altogether too much piety, so that poets have begun to think themselves priestly in their exclusivity. Poets tend to keep the company of other poets, which not only fortifies them in "their ostrich politics in relation to reality," but protects them from seeing their own weaknesses. Poets create chiefly for other poets—for people like themselves, which, in Gombrowicz's view, is another weakness. Here, he notes, "I am not demanding that they write 'in a way comprehensible to everyone.'" He merely wishes that they would not so insistently pose as artists and neglect the fact that beyond their enclosed private world exist other, quite as interesting worlds. He mentions the way poets honor and praise and generally suck up to one another, writing about their fellow poets in a "bombastic gibberish so naive and childish that it is difficult to believe that the people wielding the pen did not feel the ridiculousness of this publicism." But enough.

If Gombrowicz's condition seems slightly self-exacerbated, his case more than slightly exaggerated, nevertheless anyone who has followed contemporary poetry will have shared some of his irritation with it and will recognize a general truth to his charges. No world I have ever peered in upon can seem simultaneously so smug and so hopeless as that of the world of contemporary poets, especially in its creative-writing program phase. All too often contemporary poets comport themselves as if they were self-appointed to E. M. Forster's little aristocracy of "the sensitive, the considerate, and the plucky." ("When what they really are," a wag I know has said, "is the insensate, the outrageous, and the lucky.") The last thing they wish to hear is that they are producing something not many people outside the classroom want; and instead they act as if those who do not appreciate what they do are, on the face of it, spiritually crippled.

But among serious poets, and people serious about poetry, there is a stabbing recognition that something has happened. It is as if poetry has lost its weight, and hence its reality, and hence its value. Speaking for myself, there have been contemporary poets I have much admired—to mention only two, L. E. Sissman and Philip Larkin—but none has been able to plant language in my head the way that poets of an earlier generation could: "The salmon-falls, the mackerel-crowded seas"; "Complacencies of the peignoir, and late/Coffee and oranges in a sunny chair"; "But I have promises to keep/And miles to go before I sleep"; "In the room the women come and go/Talking of Michelangelo"; "All in green went my love riding"; "Like a patient etherized upon a table"; "a low dishonest decade"; "Something there is that doesn't love a wall"; "imaginary gardens with real toads in them."

Where did all that elegant, potent, lovely language go; or, more precisely, where went the power to create such language? Perhaps, like W. B. Yeats in Auden's poem, it "disappeared in the dead of winter."

To return to Marianne Moore, whence we set out:

> I, too, dislike it.
> Reading it, however, with a perfect contempt
> for it, one discovers in
> it, after all, a place for the genuine.

And more than the genuine, I should say, though just now the entire enterprise of poetic creation seems threatened by having been taken out of the world, chilled in the classroom, and vastly overproduced by men and women who are licensed to write it by degree if not necessarily by talent or spirit. Wallace Stevens once described poetry as "a pheasant disappearing in the brush." One gets a darting glint of it every once in a while in the work of the better contemporary poets, but to pretend that this meaty and delectable bird freely walks the land isn't going to get him out of hiding, not soon, and maybe not ever.

Culture and Capitalism

(1993)

I HAPPENED THE OTHER DAY to be listening, while in my car, to a tape of a 1940s *Fibber McGee & Molly* radio show. During this particular episode, the McGees were visited by their sweet but milquetoasty neighbor, Mr. Wimple. When asked what he was up to, Mr. Wimple allowed that he was just now doing some writing. Molly McGee, ever commonsensical and intellectually inquisitive, then asked why a certain kind of poetry was called *free verse*. "Gosh, Molly," replied Mr. Wimple, "did you ever try to sell any?"

Mr. Wimple was on to something. Free verse—also, one might add, constrained verse—is still not easy to sell in America, or, for all I know, elsewhere in the world. Let me mention a few other cultural items that are not exactly flying off the shelves. Among them would be modern dance, verse drama, much chamber music, highbrow and experimental fiction, opera by contemporary American composers, contemporary musical composition generally. Should such art, under the capitalist system that now rules almost unrivaled round the world, be forced to make its way on its own, as do other products and commodities, its demise would not be in serious question. It would, almost all of it, be gone.

A strict capitalist, the economic equivalent of a fundamentalist in religion, might argue that the inability of art forms to survive in the marketplace is the best indication that they probably do not deserve to survive. Best, our fundamentalist capitalist might conclude, to let sleeping arts, like sleeping dogs, lie. The way we know they are sleeping, the way we know they are (in the market sense) dogs, is that people will no longer pay for them in sufficient numbers and thus make their continued creation worth the while of artists. The market rules; and through the market the people, as in the gladiatorial arena of Rome, register thumbs up or thumbs down.

Fortunately, despite capitalist theorizing, this is rarely the way the most successful practicing capitalists have traditionally behaved. In the United States, there was the generation of astonishingly successful businessmen who are known to political history as the Robber Barons but who ought to be known to cultural history as the Great Benefactors. These men left a vast heritage, off which many subsequent generations have lived, of universities, visual-arts institutions, symphony orchestras, natural-history museums, planetaria, and a great deal else that continues to supply much of the richness of urban cultural life.

Why did the Morgans, Rockefellers, Fricks, Guggenheims, and the rest—many of them less than refined in the level of their own personal culture—provide so handsomely for the public out of their profits, and in an age before it was prudent, from a tax standpoint, to do so? Sheer guilt is one answer frequently given. But since these men lived before all public actions were strained through the cheesecloth of public relations, guilt has always seemed to me a dubious explanation. The only explanation I find persuasive is a most unFreudian one: whatever their own cultural limitations, these men and their families felt the urge to express their public responsibility through culture, and—weighing in whatever measure of egotism you like—it gave them pleasure to do so.

Historically, from the great merchant princes of Italy to the good burghers of Holland to the business tycoons of the United States, culture has clearly done relatively well under capitalism. Yet there has always been a strong sense, felt among artists and those who have tended to make a religion of art, that capitalism is their enemy. For all who have felt this way—and, with varying degrees of intensity, their ranks would include the vast majority of intellectuals—until recently the hope remained socialism: presumably a more sensitive and creative form of socialism than any the world has hitherto known, but socialism nonetheless. In Oscar Wilde's *The Soul of Man Under Socialism*, the soul in question is plainly that of the artist, for that is what Wildean socialism promises: under socialism the arts will flourish—and why not?, since all will be arranged to provide maximum freedom for the artist.

The fall of Communism, and the almost thorough discrediting of socialist schemes that has gone along with it, has put these dreams in mothballs for a long while. Whatever else socialism—in its malevolent as well as its relatively benevolent forms—was notable for, it was never the production of impressive art. No one can accuse the Soviet leaders of not taking artists seriously: they murdered them. And nobody despised socialism more earnestly than those great Russian artists—Vladimir Nabokov, George Balanchine, Aleksandr Solzhenitsyn—who saw it up close in its menacing Soviet version. But even under unmurderous forms of socialism—under the limited socialism of England, for example—the arts cannot be said greatly to have flourished. Such forms of socialism have often produced, if not the plain dreariness of Soviet socialist realism, then jeremiads about the drabness of life in the welfare state.

Socialism, then, no longer provides a realistic alternative, except perhaps among the very dreamy. Just now, capitalism, for all its indelicacies, its inefficiencies, even its injustices, reigns supreme. My title, "Culture and Capitalism," might as easily be Culture and Oxygen—which is another way of saying that capitalism is the atmosphere in which culture must now survive.

NOT THAT THE OXYGEN-LIKE NECESSITY OF CAPITALISM is likely to sway the minds of those artists who have aligned themselves with anti-capitalism. One of the strongest of our cultural traditions is that of the artist deliberately setting out to outrage the comfortable classes: *épater le bourgeois* and all that. This tradition began in earnest in the middle of the 19th century in France with Baudelaire and with Flaubert, whose icy contempt for the bourgeois—his own class—dominates *Madame Bovary*. Those with a taste for *épaté*-ing soon enough extended their targets from Flaubert's provincial shopkeepers and minor officials to include all who were content under the economic system known as capitalism.

Even before this, however, under the pre-capitalist system of aristocratic patronage, making a good living in the arts was never easy, sometimes even for truly superior and prolific artists. Mozart, admittedly an improvident man, was always under great pressure to produce. Given the vast musical treasure that resulted in so brief a life, I would say this was a damn good thing. Still, as Mozart's letters reveal, patronage brought its own difficulties. Everyone recalls Samuel Johnson's famous response of February 7, 1755, to Lord Chesterfield for his too-long-delayed patronage of Johnson's long and lonely work on his *Dictionary*: "The notice which you have been pleased to take of my Labours, had it been early, had been kind; but it has been delayed till I am indifferent and cannot enjoy it, till I am solitary and cannot impart it, till I am known and do not want it." Fifty or so years later, when the young Thomas Carlyle set out on a career of authorship, he knew that "the road to subsistence, I do not mention fame, in that direction is not very clear." Nor, some 175 years later, is it any clearer. Until success arrives—and its attendance record often rivals that of Samuel Beckett's *Godot*—work in the arts remains precarious.

Lucky, I have always thought, are parents whose children do not choose careers in the arts. They are lucky for two reasons: first, the chances of success are inevitably small; and, second, once a young person is infected with true passion for an art, no other of the world's work ever seems quite as enticing. In his brilliant story, "The Alien Corn," Somerset Maugham describes a young man passionately intent on a career as a concert pianist. After arduous training, it is made persuasively plain to him that musically he can never expect to transcend the mediocre. Soon after he realizes this, the young man repairs to the stables on his family's estate, where he shoots himself. The devastating thing about this story is that, in reading it, Maugham makes you feel he was probably right to do so.

The way of the artist is hard, and that of the would-be, or failed, artist impossible. To become more specific, performing musicians are perhaps the most fortunate in that, even though the competition they face is unrelenting, at least they know fairly early in life whether they have genuine talent. Writers often do not know this till they are forty. (Joseph Conrad published *Almayer's Folly*, his first novel, when he was thirty-eight.) As for visual art, the more it has veered away from the representational and into the abstract and the conceptual, the less sure, I suspect, most young artists must feel about the quality of their own talent. But whatever one's art, setting out, even under the best of conditions, is a great gamble. One is betting on one's talent; on one's determination to stay the course; on the hope that, even with talent and determination, one will eventually be recognized. The state lottery, at times, seems a safer bet.

A FEW YEARS AGO the (London) *Times Literary Supplement* published an essay on the effort of Lord Esher during World War II to save English artists as a previous generation—including Rupert Brooke, Wilfred Owen, Isaac Rosenberg, to name only poets—had not been saved in World War I. Esher met with other well-placed Englishmen to draw up a list, but complications, as one might expect, arose immediately. Ought all arts to be included: architecture, for example, and city planning? Performing as well as creative artists? And if artists were to be saved, what about scientists? Committees of experts were formed and asked to submit names from their own realms of expertise. In the end, the scheme was rejected by the government, on the quite sensible grounds that it was inherently unfair to the rest of the population to allow such advantages even to the authentically talented.

Of course, the scheme's greatest flaw was that it could do nothing to save the new generation of artists, then in their twenties, who had not yet had time to prove themselves. Here we come to the greatest single stumbling block in all socialist, governmental, or other plans to save or encourage or guide the arts: the almost complete unpredictability of youthful talent. As an occasional university teacher of would-be writers, I fairly regularly encounter young men and women who have what looks to me like that dazzling magical property, true talent. Many of them certainly have vastly more ability at deploying words than I had at their age. Yet, over two decades of observation, I have had to conclude that most among them, however much they think they want to be literary artists, apparently do not want it badly enough. They find themselves choosing other roads, devoting themselves to family, moneymaking, neuroses, and other of life's responsibilities, entanglements, entertainments, and sand traps. In part, I think of them as possessing, to quote Carlyle again, "a high endowment with an insufficient will." Desire—hot-breathed, unreasonable desire—is missing in them.

The novelist Eudora Welty, in her autobiography, remarks that genuine talent cannot be discouraged, which may or may not be true. What seems to me more true is that it probably cannot be all that much encouraged, either. If you are a young artist, your teachers can assure you that you are greatly gifted; and the more acute among them, if you happen to find them in time, can suggest how you might get the most out of those gifts. Prizes can be awarded to you, thus reinforcing your own belief in your quality; heavy doors can be opened early in your career, thus saving much mental wear and tear in attempting to beat them down on your own. Yet if sometimes adversity crushes an artist, sometimes it brings out the best in him. Because so much in this realm is ambiguous and unpredictable, written in the stars, it is not easy to set out general principles for the care and training of artists, with the exception perhaps of young dancers or performing musicians. Which is a roundabout way of saying that, so long as artists are neither gymnasts nor uncollectivized farms, planning in the arts, as under socialism, was probably never a very good idea in the first place.

I USED TO BROOD A FAIR AMOUNT ABOUT THESE MATTERS while sitting in a large yellow stuffy room at the old Post Office Building in Washington, DC during the six years that I served on the National Council of the National Endowment for the Arts (NEA). The National Council did not make grants, though it had the power—perhaps not often enough exercised—of vetoing them. The Endowment itself has had an annual budget of about $170-million—a mere drop in the bombsight, as proponents of the arts like to claim, in comparison to the immensely greater sums spent on defense and highway programs, but a substantial sum nevertheless.

With so many grants being made, it has not been difficult to find offensive ones, as the press and a vast portion of Americans did in Andres Serrano's photograph of a crucifix in a bottle filled with urine or in Robert Mapplethorpe's sadomasochistic photographs. Among the NEA grants I encountered, I personally found myself more impressed with the extremely absurd than with the deliberately offensive ones; after all, as a good bourgeois, I have been taking a pretty good *épaté*-ing right along, and short perhaps of human sacrifice, the time has passed for being shocked by any of it.

What I mean by the absurd included, for example, a program to bring art into prisons. "Even to death row?" I asked the NEA staff member who had presented the proposal. "You mean to say that you are going to teach art and music appreciation on death row?" The affirmative answer tendered by this hopelessly caring person suggested that my inquiry was extremely insensitive, not to say impertinent.

I also remember a grant application that would bring art to patients with terminal cancer, which I thought not only absurd but at least as obscene as Mapplethorpe's precisely aimed toilet plungers and bull-whips. People dying of cancer have enough to think about without having to contend with the kind of art they are likely to be proffered under the auspices of the NEA. If you sat in that yellow room in Washington long enough, listening to art discussed as if it were religion, medicine, and social reform all rolled into one, you began to become skeptical about encouraging the arts.

But I also thought a good deal in those days about how little *could* be done—by the federal government, by the sheer force of money—to encourage individual artists, which is where all art ultimately begins and ends. I concluded that if the federal government had to put its thick-fingered hands on the arts, it should do so through what are known as challenge grants to encourage greater private philanthropy in local communities and by making grants to carefully selected institutions. I found myself impressed, too, by grants that bring costly-to-produce art—ballet, say, or orchestral music—to small communities that cannot otherwise afford it. I was less and less impressed with the idea of giving money—even though generally it was not more than $20,000—to poets, painters, and composers to knock off for half a year and produce more of the same kind of stuff they were already producing at perhaps too great a clip.

Yet even if those grants to artists had been ten times larger, would the artists concerned have changed their views of capitalism or of their society? Not very likely. For yet another of our cultural traditions holds that the artist is disenfranchised from birth, a citizen only of his own imagination—the original, and perennial, man without a country. Such alienation somehow comes naturally to all but the best artists; and the poorer the artist, I sometimes think, the more naturally it comes.

This stems from the feeling of so many artists that their genius is unappreciated, and it does not help that many people who seem to be not the least bit interested in the arts flourish economically. What kind of a country is it, after all, that will pay a real-estate lawyer $2.6 million a year, while a poet gets $45 for a perfect sestina? If you ever have a couple of hours to spare, ask the poet and he will tell you in some detail what kind of country he thinks it is.

IN CHOOSING A CAREER—a life, really—in the arts, one is presumably ready to give up much that is worldly. Socrates believed that people were divided into three categories: those who wished for pleasure; those who wished for honor, fame, and social success; and those who wished for truth and wisdom. Artists, if not in Socrates' time then surely in our own, are supposed to fall into the last category. But like everyone else, they want the delights available to all three.

Not only do they want these things, they also want to go on *épaté*-ing the rest of us while gathering them in. The view of the avant-garde and its supporters has been that artists must have maximum freedom to do what they want, and deserve to have this freedom underwritten by their government. All must be allowed them because they are artists, and art, like Ovaltine, is good for you. Yet how much stronger their position would be if they risked the marketplace, and did not fall back on public money. Once they accept that money, they are compromised, their claims to absolute freedom greatly diminished. An artist who takes the taxpayers' money to attack the cherished beliefs of taxpayers and then pleads his rights as an artist to do so is pretty much in the position of the young man who murders his parents and then throws himself on the mercy of the court because he is an orphan.

A deep ambivalence if not hypocrisy runs through the contemporary artist's view of capitalism. At the same time that artists tend to be wary of capitalism, many of them realize that a substantial commercial success has set the final seal on some of the most admired artists of our time. In a capitalist society, in fact, one probably feels one has truly arrived as an artist only when one has had a large-public kind of success, which includes recognition as well as financial reward. I do not for a moment say that a commercial and popular success is in any way equivalent to a true artistic success; I do say that, in a capitalist society, the absence of such a success tends to leave a lingering doubt.

These matters would be much simpler if we could conclude that whatever achieves a commercial success under capitalism is, *ipso facto*, inferior cultural goods. Yet the examples of Balanchine, Picasso, Stravinsky, and others in the realm of high and serious art, suggests that even this is not exactly so. Both Picasso and Stravinsky were themselves fairly potent capitalists in their own right. Picasso marketed himself with true genius; and Stravinsky used to prefer to conduct his own works whenever possible so that he would not have to split fees.

Capitalism, it seems to me, shares many qualities with the avant-garde. Neither, in its purest form, is a notable respecter of tradition. Both capitalism and the avant-garde honor, and continually strive to produce, the freshly made. Each is always on the lookout for new opportunities: capitalism for profit, the avant-garde for new forms—many of them, of late, designed not merely to offend but to outrage. Yet when it comes to innovation, capitalism has proved much the more creative force, illustrating Paul Valéry's penetrating remark that "everything changes but the avant-garde."

And herein hangs a sad tale. Because the avant-garde has for some while seemed exhausted, unable to devise any impressively radical changes in technique that look to have enduring value, it has turned to politics, not least to the politics of sexual liberation. No one in the nation would today be offended by NEA grants to artists who wished to compose music without notes, or to use perspective in visual art as it has never been used before, or to revolutionize English prose style. But such projects, the projects of an older avant-garde, hold almost no interest for the contemporary avant-garde. Its interest lies elsewhere; it lies, specifically, in attacking mainstream American life. Its politics are usually coarse in the extreme. Expressing contempt for Ronald Reagan, for example, counts as an avant-garde activity. It is in large part because the avant-garde has turned so directly political that, at least in the realm of federal funding, it has become so controversial.

I MYSELF HAVE A GENUINE yet not uncritical admiration for capital-ism. While I think capitalism can build character—it encourages hard work, planning, savings, competition, honorable dealings—it has never been known for its niceties of discrimination. Left to its own devices, unfettered capitalism, given half a chance, is likely to chew up the coun-tryside: to erect hideous buildings, to mar natural beauty in the name of profit, to interrupt the peace to sell goods.

In Chicago, we have a superior FM radio station, WFMT, that plays classical music 24 hours a day. It has a relentlessly highbrow tone: over its airwaves, foreign languages are pronounced perfectly; serious music, early and modern along with the canonical works of the 18th and 19th centuries, is played without stint or abridgment; operas are presented in their entirety, often in live "simulcast" productions. The station, which is the radio equivalent of cable television, claims an audience of half-a-million listeners. Its expenses cannot be low, and it survives on revenues from commercials and donations from listeners.

For many years WFMT ran only commercials read by its announcers, in the most culturally earnest and modulated of voices. Then, feeling the economic crunch, the station began to run "canned" commercials. As I am no enemy of capitalism, neither, I hope, am I an aesthetic prig, but I have to report that I found these commercials repellent in the extreme. I can take—have come to expect—endless beer, car, and even hemorrhoid-prep-aration commercials interrupting television sports events or movies. These are necessary evils, and I, for one, understand their necessity more than I believe in their evil. But after listening to, say, Schubert piano impromptus or a group of Reynaldo Hahn songs, it is not easy to have to attend to jin-gles about the friendly skies of United or a too-clever-by-half spiel for the new Lexus. Listeners began first to complain and then to organize. I shall not recount the full struggle here, but in the end the listeners won. The canned commercials were outlawed, the general musical seriousness of the station maintained. All this was made possible chiefly through financial contributions from devoted listeners, for whom the price of high culture had thereby gone up.

The price of high culture, I would guess, is going to go up a good bit more all around. The star system among concert performers has driven up ticket prices for an Itzhak Perlman or Yo-Yo Ma concert or an appearance by Luciano Pavarotti or Placido Domingo in an opera, while also draining off interest in first-class musical performers who do not have "superstar" standing. The prospect grows less and less likely that a person of upper-middle-class income will be able to own an original work of art by even a moderately well-known painter or sculptor.

Of course, some art, and some of the very best art, is simply unmarketable because it is, in the nature of the case, small-public art. One is reminded of the time that Edith Wharton arrived at Rye in the south of England to pick up Henry James in one of her splendid Panhard automobiles. The car, she told James, had been purchased from the royalties earned by her last novel. Not one to let an opportunity for ironic response pass, James is reported to have pointed to a nearby wheelbarrow, which he claimed he had purchased from the royalties of *his* last novel, and then added that he planned to have it painted with the royalties from his next.

James once remarked that he liked gold, and plenty of it, but, despite occasional high expectations—for such novels as *The Bostonians* and *The Princess Casamassima* and then later for the New York edition of his fiction—he never came close to earning much more of it than made possible his bachelor upkeep, and even this, toward the end, became a stretch. I would argue that this situation was not the fault of Henry James (who did not, thank goodness, know how to lower his artistic sights), or of his publishers, or of the economic system (capitalism) under which he wrote. If blame need be assigned, the fault is God's for not making more readers intellectually fit to read Henry James.

W E KNOW THAT UNDER THE CRUSHING POLITICAL POWER of the Communist party in the Soviet Union and its satellites, artists could only create (badly) in support of the regime or create (bravely and at great personal price) against it. Few had the good fortune to create precisely as they might have liked. Capitalism, though tough on artists when they are young—it is tough on everyone when young, except those lucky enough to have inheritances—leaves them the widest margins to create as they wish. Sometimes capitalism seems arbitrary in those artists it chooses to reward, conferring a large success on difficult work, or, with a heavy-handed irony, seeming kindest to those who show the most contempt for it. But this much may be said for capitalism: operating under it, artists know that finally they are in business for themselves—a condition, one would have thought, to which every good artist aspires.

The high aspirations of the artist, and the high valuation he puts on himself, remind me that I once told a joke to a conservative economist about an airplane in grave difficulty whose pilot has to ask one of the passengers to leave in order to lighten the load, thus making it possible to land the plane safely. The pilot explains, over the public-address system, that he and the crew are going to ask that person to leave who is of the least use to society. The punch line runs: "At which point, a used-car dealer and a disc jockey get up in the middle of the aisle and begin fighting." Complete silence was the response from the economist, who finally said: "I would have liked that joke better if the punch line was, 'At which point a psychotherapist and the curator of a museum of contemporary art get up in the middle of the aisle and begin fighting.'" His punch line may be not only funnier but truer.

"I believe in the salvation of humanity through art," wrote the composer and music critic Cecil Gray in his autobiography. I guess that I, finally, do not. I love art; apart from family and friends, nothing in life is so important to me; and I am grateful to have been able to arrange my life so that I can spend a greater part of it than most people indulging myself in the splendors and delights of others' artistic production. But however necessary to some of us art remains, it is well to remember that, in the larger perspective, art is a luxury—the luxury of luxuries—and one that is only earned by societies that, in the fundamental sense of the phrase, first take care of business.

Educated by Novels

(1989)

O N MORE THAN ONE OCCASION in recent years, usually in conversation with quite intelligent people who report to me that they have stopped reading fiction, I have found myself claiming to have been educated by novels. An interesting phrase; but what does it actually mean? Were I to tot up all the books I have read in thirty or so years as an adult, novels might or might not outnumber other kinds—history, philosophy, social science, belles-lettres, but, more than those others taken together, novels, I feel, have been the most decisive in forming my character. They have been decisive in giving me a method or style of thinking, a general point of view, and a goodly portion of such understanding as I may have of the world.

I want to get at how this has come about, but first I should note that novelists have themselves been among the first to warn that reading too much fiction can be a dangerous thing. Don Quixote, Cervantes's poor noodle of a knight with the doleful countenance, is driven nearly mad by the fantastical novels he reads. In more than one of her books, Jane Austen's characters have their views distorted, and hence their good sense thwarted, by reading too many of the wrong sort of novel, and reading them indiscriminately. As for Emma Bovary—"Don't esk!" as Molly Goldberg used to say; Flaubert makes it plain that her ruination is owing in good part to too rich a diet of romantic fiction. Irving Kristol, who so far as I know has written no fiction, is reputed to have counseled young business students never to bring a novel to a job interview, lest they be taken as somehow distracted and dreamy. Sounds like good advice.

At the same time, some of the most interesting non-literary minds I know, and know about, are, and have been, passionate readers of novels. Justice Holmes read Conrad, Hardy, Henry James, and the other serious novelists of his day. (William James, Holmes's contemporary, had a hard go with the novels of his brother Henry.) Freud, who claimed to have acquired much of what he knew from "the poets"—by which he meant literary artists of all kinds—once wrote to Arthur Schnitzler, the Austrian novelist and playwright who had himself been trained as a physician: "The impression has been borne in on me that you know through intuition—really from a delicate self-observation—everything that I have discovered in other people by laborious work." John Maynard Keynes read novels. In our own day, Edward Shils has read a vast quantity of fiction, 19th-century, modern, and contemporary, and constantly rereads Balzac and Dickens, as one might think every good sociologist ought to do. The anthropologist Clifford Geertz makes it his business to keep up with contemporary fiction.

In the only case I know in any detail, my own, a heightened excitement accompanied the reading of novels from the very beginning. Not that I failed to get worked up by other books. My reading life began in earnest at the University of Chicago, where—in the most sensible of radical curricular reforms—no textbooks were used in the College and few books by living writers were taught, and so the intellectual diet was for the most part champagne and caviar. I can recall the deep pleasure of reading Herodotus, the intellectual provocation set in motion by Thucydides. Plato and Aristotle, both of whom were offered in plentiful supply, gave an unformed mind a good workout; and although I knew I had not the least chance of attaining anything like mastery here, I did come to adore Socrates, as Plato intended. I recall being devastated, at nineteen, by Freud's *Civilization and Its Discontents*, taking every dark word in that gloomy little tome to my youthful heart. I remember, too, the awe I felt upon first reading Max Weber's *The Protestant Ethic and the Spirit of Capitalism*—awe at the spectacle of a writer handling and shaping ideas and making intellectual connections with such easy virile brilliance.

But novels really set me aflame. "The main question as to a novel," wrote Sydney Smith, "is—did it amuse?" Although such novels as I had read as a child did amuse, else I would not have allowed then to detain me, even when quite young I sensed that something more than amusement was going on. In high school, I went through a brief jag of reading novels with slum settings; among their titles were *The Amboy Dukes, A Stone for Danny Fisher, The Hoods, Knock on Any Door.* These were all, I now realize, in the mode of a cut-rate naturalism whose chief message was that no one had much chance of rising above his environment. I lapped them up, not so much for the message (which I probably also swallowed) as for the details of slum and criminal life.

I remember finding these details not only exotic, as they would be to a boy born into the comforts of the middle class, but persuasive and, somehow, useful, though for what I could not with any exactitude say. Nevertheless, bits of these inferior works cling to my memory even today. ("The big boat pulled into the night, and Cockeyed Hymie thrilled to the sensation of the clutch.") If writers with names like Irving Shulman, Harold Robbins, Harry Grey, and Willard Motley could excite me like this at sixteen, imagine what lay in wait for me down the road at twenty from writers with names like Fielding, Stendhal, Dostoyevsky, Tolstoy, and Thomas Mann.

WHEN I FIRST ENCOUNTERED THE GREAT NOVELISTS, though I was far from being up to them, I nonetheless knew right off that what they wrote contained as high a truth quotient as I was likely to get from any other kind of writing. Philosophy, for which I had no natural bent, seemed to me to come at things at too high, too abstract, a level. Even so brilliant a writer as Plato struck me as ultimately playing a game—a complex and wondrous game, to be sure, played in splendid style, but in the end still a game. I had been born into a family where common sense was too greatly esteemed ever to take seriously any sort of schematic thinking. Thus the small portion of Marx offered at the University of Chicago was sufficient for me to understand only how other people could fall for it. Like many another student who read Freud too young, I was briefly taken with Freudian doctrine, until I tested it against my own sense of the world and my own sense of humor ("They were a tense and peculiar family, the Oedipuses, were they not?," Max Beerbohm once remarked) and found it wanting. I liked the exultation of poetry practiced on the highest plane, but I never for a minute felt I could live for long on that plane, where the air was so pure and thin. Perhaps I am speaking to no more than my temperamental and intellectual limitations, but the novel, I early felt, was the most fruitful form, literary or otherwise, going.

I read a great many novels at the University of Chicago, most on my own but some for the classroom, though I had no gifted teachers in this area. One, a nervous and highly irritable young assistant professor, had us read a survey of works from *The Princess of Cleves* to *Ulysses* and including novels by Dostoyevsky, Stendhal, Proust, and Thomas Mann. A more distinguished man, Morton Dauwen Zabel, who had been an editor of *Poetry* and was a friend of Edmund Wilson's, taught a course in the modern novel that introduced me to such writers as Ford Madox Ford, E. M. Forster, and Evelyn Waugh, but that otherwise, despite the impress left by Zabel as a cultivated man of letters, was not memorable.

I have since become a teacher myself, and one who frequently teaches courses built around novels, and I must say that I do not think of myself as doing much better than my own early teachers. I tend not to teach those abstruse or arcane books that permit a teacher to step proudly to the lectern and act as a guide to the perplexed. Instead I attempt to show how a given novel works, what moral issues and questions it raises, what is the particular quality of its artistry, and, finally, what its author thinks about the world. If one can do that much with clarity and force, I think one has done pretty well. Yet even when I have done this much, I always feel that I have left out a great deal that is important to the pleasure and point of the work. One can teach a poem so that every word, semicolon, and blank space is exhaustively accounted for, but, somehow, after having taught a novel one generally feels that many of the best parts have been left on the pedagogical equivalent of the cutting-room floor.

There are of course ideas embedded in novels and there are, as a subdivision of the form, those books called "novels of ideas." But when you have extracted or identified the ideas, I am not sure that you have a whole lot to show. If you determine that Proust in *Remembrance of Things Past* was operating with Bergsonian concepts of time, or that in *The Magic Mountain* Mann was able skillfully to represent the maelstrom of European political ideas of the day, what, really, have you determined? Perhaps that you would have done better to read Bergson directly, or that, having read Mann, you ought now to move on to a sound intellectual history of Europe between the wars. Which is a roundabout way of saying that, while novelists may have a plenitude of ideas, it is rarely their ideas that are the most interesting thing about them.

Or consider the case of Theodore Dreiser. Dreiser's ideas, at any rate those that ruled his life outside his novels, are generally appalling in their coarseness. A convert to Communism who found himself sympathetic to Hitler, he may have been the only man in America made happy by the Nazi-Soviet pact; he was an anti-Semite; he was a worshipper of power; he was a rather crude Social-Darwinist—ideationally, Dreiser was a mess. Yet within his novels, these and other ideas function, if at all, more on the level of notions, and they have little to do with Dreiser's very real power as a novelist. I am not altogether sure what does. On the occasions when I have taught a Dreiser novel to undergraduates, I have often wanted to begin by saying, "Look here, this guy Dreiser was homely and horny and born into a household where superstitious religion and shame ruled, all of which helped to render him into a writer who probably knew more about desire than any man who ever lived. So with that in mind, go home and reread this novel."

One day, in an essay by Desmond MacCarthy, I came across the following sentence: "It is the business of literature to turn facts into ideas." Exactly and just so, I thought, and handsomely formulated into the bargain. To turn the fact of Desmond MacCarthy's aphoristic sentence into an idea, he is saying that the method of literature, if method it has, is induction, reasoning that runs from the part to the whole, the particular to the general. Other branches of learning have claimed to operate inductively—science, social science—but there are grounds for thinking they do not, that in fact they are testing, hopefully, hunches. But novelists, unless they are corrupted by their own politics or pet views, are not out to prove anything. They tell their stories, and if they tell them truly and well, honestly and persuasively, somehow things will (as we used to say around the English Department) "resonate" into something more general and larger, and all those little frogs of fact that novelists concern themselves with will turn into princes of ideas—which, as MacCarthy says, is the business of literature.

WHY, IT MIGHT BE ASKED, does literature have to have a business at all? Is it not sufficient that it give pleasure, convey information, widen experience, provide flashes of insight? One reads the world's finest novels, plays, poems, and in time one becomes a more cultivated person, which means somehow more refined, subtler, deeper, possibly even—though this might be pushing it—better. You are what you read; and culture, like heredity and cheap paint, rubs off. I could go on with this catechism of once-hallowed assumptions, although at this point I feel the need to show slides or at least roll out a pumped-up quotation from Ralph Waldo Emerson. All these things may be true—with slight qualifications, I believe them—but they nowadays have an empty ring. As perhaps never before, the study of literature is being asked to justify itself, and thus far it has not done so very convincingly.

I know that I have felt the need for a justification of literary study, beyond the standard one of self-cultivation that is at the core of the liberal arts. As I stand there pointing out the intricacies of a novel by Joseph Conrad in a classroom that features a boy with a dangling earring and a girl in a spiky punk haircut, it occurs to me to ask what it is, exactly, that I am doing. Meanwhile, in a room down the hall, a colleague is giving a course in Third World writers much of which, I assume, is devoted to attacks on the West and especially the United States. Upstairs, other teachers are using literature to push their own particular lines: feminism, deconstruction, and the rest of it. Against the crude juggernaut of politicized teaching, which appears to have affected literature departments almost more than any others in the contemporary university, one wonders how effective traditional teaching, with its emphasis on the moral and aesthetic elements in literature, can continue to be.

The critic Robert Alter has, I suspect, felt doubts similar to my own, or so I judge by the appearance of his new book, *The Pleasures of Reading*, with its significant subtitle, "Thinking about Literature in an Ideological Age." Alter is now a senior professor at the University of California at Berkeley, where he teaches Hebrew and comparative literature. I mention especially the latter because, in today's university, departments of comparative literature, once the preserve of the multilingual and the erudite, have tended increasingly to become headquarters of academics priding themselves on what is now known as literary theory, or, as they call it in the trade, plain "theory." Theory in current literary studies usually means batting around the dependably less than lucid writings of Lacan and Derrida (*les frères Jacques*, as John Simon once called them), Michel Foucault and Roland Barthes, or some other Frenchman of the month. As for literary Marxists and feminists, they get on happily enough with the theorists, and together they form a jolly daisy chain of "isms." To all this, Robert Alter offers a happy exception.

Although "theory" has been in business for more than a decade now, modern literature theorists, so far as I know, have produced little in the way of brilliant books or essays. But then they tend to write exclusively for one another; and everything they turn out might as well be marked "to the trade only." As Alter notes in his introductory chapter, entitled "The Disappearance of Reading," the theory crowd does not much go in for reading actual literature; he states his suspicion that "many young people now earning undergraduate degrees in English or French at our most prestigious institutions have read two or three pages of Lacan, Derrida, Foucault, and Kristeva for every page of George Eliot or Stendhal."

Early in *The Pleasures of Reading*, Alter notes that, though his book is in part a response to the peculiarities of the new literary theory, "it is meant to be a good deal more than a polemic, for I am convinced that there are more interesting and more important things for a critic to do than merely expose fashionable absurdities." One understands Alter's unwillingness to stride into the Big Muddy of literary theory, though the element of his book that *is* polemical in intent does, it must be said, suffer as a result. But mainly what Alter chooses to do is to put on display the traditional modes of literary study, among them the investigations of character, style, allusion, structure, perspective, and interpretation. In so doing Alter still shows the enduring marks of having once been a student at Columbia (and subsequently at Harvard) at a time when Columbia was the gem of American English departments. Lionel Trilling, F. W. Dupee, Richard Chase, Andrew Chiappe, and others taught at Columbia then, and along with imparting a good grounding in literary study, they passed along a metropolitan spirit that for the vast most part seems absent from academic life today and especially from the crabbed style of contemporary literary academics.

Robert Alter has retained much of the Columbia spirit in the best sense. *The Pleasures of Reading* suffers more than seems to me absolutely necessary from a certain academic stuffiness or touches of classroom condescension. This does not detract from the fact that Alter's main points in *The Pleasures of Reading* are not academic but real ones. First among these is his insistence that "without some form of passionate engagement in literary reading, the whole enterprise of teaching and writing about literature becomes pointless"—and so, for that matter, does literature itself. Second is "that the language of literature is distinct from the use of language elsewhere in its resources and in its possibilities of expression," and that the investigation of how language is used in literature is not merely a game—however much it can be, as Alter says, "high fun"—but in various ways an aid to understanding the world.

These points may seem a bit obvious to anyone not in a university, but it needs to be reiterated that, within universities, ours is one of those times when, as Orwell once remarked, it is the duty of an intelligent man to repeat the obvious. For today the ascendant views in literary education hold that the language of literature is chiefly self-reflexive, that literature itself is either a game or a swindle, and that the best literary criticism is politics by other means, when it is not another technique for demonstrating that reality does not exist. By reiterating the older and greater truth about literature, and by demonstrating its enduring power through a series of highly intelligent readings of individual works, Alter's book is a reminder of why some of us were attracted to literary study in the first place.

WAYNE C. BOOTH, a professor of English at the University of Chicago, is not one of those professors out to prove that reality does not exist. In *The Company We Keep* he proposes, as his subtitle advertises, "An Ethics of Fiction," and he does so precisely in order to allow reality to obtrude on the reading and study of novels. Booth wishes to investigate the "ethical quality of the experience of narrative in itself," as well as the ethical consequences of various novels and the positions their authors take through the representations in their work. It is a large subject, and he has written a large book about it.

The Company We Keep, unfortunately, is also a vastly bloated book. Booth has the academic author's disease in extreme form. His idea of a chapter is to begin with five or six epigraphs, to include twenty or thirty discursive footnotes—he writes, incidentally, some of the best vanity notes in the business, directing us to other things he has written or is planning to write on connected subjects—and then to close with a bibliography often containing more than a hundred items. His is also one of those muddle-making books in which the author promises in Chapter 2 to discuss a related point in Chapter 11, while in Chapter 13 the reader is asked to recall a point raised some three hundred pages earlier in Chapter 3. Here, to give a small sample of the reigning tone, is a fairly typical footnote:

> 1. My article comparing the ethics of the "video" arts and the verbal arts (1982) has been read by some as a biased attack on "viewing" as opposed to "reading" and "listening." Not so. At one time I intended to include a revision as a chapter here, since obviously the different ethical effects of entire media are inherently a part of our subject. But on reflection, especially after W. J. T. Mitchell's *Iconology* (1986), I decided that the subject requires another book. Perhaps. Here I can simply assert that the experience of video *as now commercially determined* is in my view a cultural disaster.

To grasp the self-important and obvious spirit of *The Company We Keep* you have to imagine Dwight Macdonald without any of the wit.

In his attempt to delineate the complex ethical transaction between reader and novelist, Booth remarks that "the authors who become our lasting friends are those who offer to teach us, by the sheer activity of considering their gifts, a life larger than any specific doctrine we might accept or reject." This sounds sensible enough; yet in Booth's own practical criticism, it turns out, the "ethical" generally means only that a novel has to pass what is today considered OK liberal thinking in the academy, especially on such matters as gender and race. Thus Booth reports that his estimate of Ken Kesey's *One Flew Over the Cuckoo's Nest* "has diminished steadily on each new encounter, either with the text or in conversations about it, especially with female readers. . . ." The problem, he has come to realize, is with the character "Big Nurse," who, he now reports, "too crudely symbolizes not only 'female' domination of what 'should' be a man's world but also all civilized restraints."

My own guess is that Booth originally admired Kesey's far from first-class novel precisely for its general attack on society and on society's system of civilized restraints. He was, in my view, wrong about it then and he is wrong about it now—*One Flew Over the Cuckoo's Nest* has always chiefly been a book for a certain kind of teacher to put on his reading list to show students he is on their side. Nevertheless, Booth seems quite pleased with his own splendid flexibility, and adds: "Who can predict what a further reading, at age eighty, will yield?" In Booth's case, I believe *I* can predict what it will yield—namely, a rough congruence with whatever then passes for acceptable academic thinking. Still, the thought of Booth or anyone else reading a Ken Kesey novel at eighty does not go down easily, except perhaps as a peculiarly just punishment for a contemporary literary academic.

B︎UT THEN WAYNE C. BOOTH appears never to have read a book he did not like, or to have encountered a contemporary academic political or literary movement or idea he could not respect and learn from. He is, not to put too fine a point on it, a caring person, and the reason we know this is that he keeps telling us so. But he was not always thus, as he freely admits: as a young man, he recited what he now realizes were sexist passages from Rabelais "aloud to my young wife, as she did the ironing (!)," and he assigned Orwell's *1984* to his students in a spirit of self-congratulation at being "a passionate enemy of McCarthyism whose own life and opinions were in no need of change." Today, however, he is a more open fellow, confiding how he cried during the movie *The Color Purple*, or learned from Edward Said "to feel uneasy with the word [Oriental] even when it is enclosed in quotation marks." If he once excluded the novels of D. H. Lawrence from serious consideration, dismissing Lawrence as "a pretentious little preacher," now—thanks to his notion of thinking of writers as friends—"I even enjoyed talking with [Lawrence] about parenting."

To pause at this notion of authors as friends, is not the gong of self-congratulation struck rather too strongly in Booth's account of the transaction between great novelists and readers like himself?

> To dwell with you is to share the improvements you have managed to make in your "self" by perfecting your narrative world. You lead me to practice ways of living that are more profound, more sensitive, more intense, and in a curious way more fully generous than I am likely to meet anywhere else in the world. You correct my faults, rebuke my insensitivities. You mold me into patterns of longing and fulfillment that make my ordinary dreams seem petty and absurd. You finally show me what life can be, not just to a coterie, a saved and saving remnant looking down on the fools, slobs, and knaves, but to *anyone* who is willing to earn the title of equal and true friend.

This is all very prettily put, and it manages to suggest that Booth's reading of novels has made him a better man by far than Gunga Din. But I am reasonably sure that this is not, in fact, the case. No doubt he has read a great many novels, but I do not think doing so has necessarily turned him into a wise man, else how could he have written so vanity-ridden and swollen a book? I too have read a great many novels, but my guess is that Booth, for one, will not think they have made me wise, else how could I have written the last few paragraphs of this essay?

Booth appears to believe that in reading "ethically" we take the best each novelist has to offer, and that the sum of all this plays in our minds like some grand chorus, ultimately affecting our characters for the better. I prefer the more modest assessment set out by Robert Louis Stevenson in an essay entitled "Books Which Have Influenced Me":

The most influential books, and the truest in their influence, are works of fiction. They do not pin the reader to a dogma which he must afterward discover to be inexact; they do not teach him a lesson which he must afterward unlearn. They repeat, they rearrange, they clarify the lessons of life; they disengage us from ourselves, they constrain us to the acquaintance of others; and they show us the web of experience, not as we can see it for ourselves, but with a singular change—that monstrous, consuming ego of ours being, for the nonce, struck out.

This is far from the last word on the subject of what novels accomplish for those who read them regularly, but it is an excellent first word. Stevenson, who was a valued friend of Henry James, was, in James's view, one of the few practitioners of their shared craft who thought long and carefully about the assumptions behind the writing and the reading of fiction. Henry James was himself all but obsessed with such matters. For James, fiction was an authentic and, for him, the only real way of knowing. While he wrote yards and yards on the art of fiction—his own and that of his fellow novelists—no one ever formulated the essence of James's criticism and fiction better than T. S. Eliot, who, in a single jaunty sentence, wrote: "He had a mind so fine no idea could violate it." That splendid dictum would not have been misplaced on Henry James's tombstone.

Yet what does it mean? We can take it on faith that it does not mean that James could not comprehend ideas. Eliot refers to James's "mastery over, his baffling escape from, Ideas." I am not sure about the "baffling," but it is clear that to James, who could assuredly bounce the "isms" around with the best of them, the lifelong practice of writing novels had taught him that ideas were not where the important truths lay. There was a truth above ideas, an elusive, difficult to pin down, often inexpressible truth, but it was for James the only truth worth caring about—it was the truth of the novelist.

One does not begin reading novels with this kind of truth in view, any more than, when young, one marries a woman because she seems likely to make an excellent grandmother. When young, one reads novels in large part for information about the world. Much of what I know about the world of East European Jewry—of my own antecedents—I first learned from Sholem Aleichem, I. L. Peretz, Isaac Babel, the brothers Singer. Even not very good novels can supply useful information. I recently read Alison Lurie's *The Truth about Lorin Jones*, which I thought pretty thin stuff, but I did take away from it what seemed to me a persuasive portrait of feminism in present-day Manhattan, the kind of milieu in which one slips in and out of lesbianism as much through the force of the ideas in the atmosphere as through true feeling. The stories of Bobbie Ann Mason fill me in on a world from which I am far removed and which seems to me otherwise undescribed outside fiction: the world of the middle-Southern, unrooted, quasi-educated young who have grown up knowing chiefly the culture of the Pizza Hut, K-Mart, and community college, or what one thinks of as franchise culture. Except in squibs of journalism, generally journalism that prides itself on making use of fictional techniques, one cannot get this kind of news about contemporary American life anywhere outside fiction.

But news of this kind, very good to have for those of us who fancy ourselves students of our own and other societies, is only a charming if not necessarily valuable dividend that fiction pays out to its readers—and not, in my view, the principal reason for reading it. There are also the pleasures of plot, regrettably abandoned in much ostensibly serious fiction by writers more interested in working out their obsessions, intellectual conceptions, and relentless virtuosity, but pleasures that many serious readers return to 19th-century novels to recapture. Then, too, novels, along with history and biography, provide a fine laboratory in which to study character and thus attempt to make some small progress in that deepest of all deep subjects, human nature. H. L. Mencken once said that, when all the theorizing was done, it was chiefly a novelist's ability to create interesting characters that gave him any claim to our attention. Does the contemplation of character in fiction come under the rubric of pleasure or instruction? Or is such a bifurcation beside the point in great literature, where instruction is inseparable from pleasure and pleasure from instruction?

In his recent *Sketches from a Life*, a selection of entries from his diaries, George F. Kennan writes that many Americans "have engaged my admiration, along with a considerable number who have engaged the opposite."

Then, half-apologetically, he adds that "to depict them individually is the task of the novelist," whereas he himself has gone through life as a "traveler moving through regions where he has no personal acquaintances at all and where he sees, for the most part, only masses of anonymous figures with whom he has no possibility of interacting." Here we come, I believe, to the nub of the matter. The novelist deals in individual cases, and leaves the generalizations to the literary critics, sociologists, psychologists, journalists, and other fellows passing through town.

To CREATE A CONCEPT, said Ortega y Gasset, is to leave reality behind—not all of it, to be sure, but often the most interesting part. The world today is perhaps more concept-ridden than it has been at any other time, owing to the spread of rather mediocre higher education and the pervasiveness of the mass media. In contemporary politics, in social science, even in science, there appears to be no life beneath that of the theory, the concept. The study of literature was once an antidote to life lived at the level of theory and concept. Today, in universities, literary study is itself concept-plagued.

One of the usually unacknowledged but crucial tasks of the novelist, or so it has always seemed to me, is to demonstrate how reality almost always eludes too firmly drawn ideas. The novelist does this, when he is working well, by persuasively establishing that life is more surprising, bizarre, complex, and fascinating than any shibboleth, concept, or theory used to explain it. In that most famous of first sentences, Tolstoy began *Anna Karenina* by writing, "All happy families are alike, but every unhappy family is unhappy in its own way." Forgive my impertinence, but my own literary education leads me to believe that this splendid sentence is probably only half-true. I have learned from novels that every happy family, too, is happy in its own way.

To be educated by novels, then, is to be educated into a strong taste for the sheer variousness of life—Tolstoy himself said that the artist's purpose is "to compel us to love life in all its countless and inexhaustible manifestations"—and at the same time into a counterbalancing distaste for not only the easy but all generalization. To be educated by novels is to believe that human actions are best understood through individual cases, and to believe, further, that every individual case is itself immensely complex. "How astonishing reality was!" exclaims a character in Italo Svevo's novel *As a Man Grows Older*, and anyone educated by novels is likely to agree.

If the novel is finally obdurate before the best intellectual efforts to explain life—it is not for nothing that most novelists are anti-Freudians—it does, of course, yield lessons of its own, or at least the best novels do. These are neither explanations nor, really, revelations, but then, in the words of Borges, "this imminence of revelation which does not occur is, perhaps, the aesthetic phenomenon." Knowledge of the kind conveyed in novels may not, in any conventional sense, be useful. All that there is to recommend it is that it feels true, which, for someone educated by novels, is all the recommendation required.

Part Five

Education

A Case of Academic Freedom

(1986)

M
Y OFFICE IN THE ENGLISH DEPARTMENT at Northwestern University is in University Hall, an American gothic joke of a building whose architect might have been inspired by Charles Addams, if the building weren't much older than the cartoonist. Yet I have grown enamored of this absurd pile of limestone, where for the past twelve years I have had an office and done most of my teaching. Located on the second floor, my office overlooks what is known on campus as "the rock." The rock is a boulder, roughly seven feet high, perhaps six feet in diameter, and a marker and meeting place for undergraduates. Fraternity and sorority pledge classes regularly paint the rock, students set up tables near it to sell T-shirts or yearbooks or campus magazines or to collect for charities. From ten minutes before the hour until the hour is struck, there is fairly heavy traffic near the rock, with students passing on their way to classes or back to their apartments, dormitories, fraternities, and sororities.

Fancying myself old Mr. Chips(tein), sometimes I stand at the window of my office and gaze down upon the students as they congregate around the rock or on the steps of University Hall. I note especially students who have been in my classes, many of whose names, only a year or two later, I have quite forgotten or will soon forget. As I watch them pass, I wonder what plots life has in store for the two upper-middle-class girls from a suburb outside Minneapolis who are in Ralph Lauren duds, or for the punkily dressed theater major who was such an atrocious speller, or for the Chinese pre-med student who did so well in my course in advanced prose composition. I wonder, too, about the future of the students who are members of the campus political organization that is known as InCAR (standing for International Committee Against Racism), who frequent the purlieus of the rock perhaps more than anyone else and are always there on heavy political business: to collect funds for striking coal miners in the north of England, to aid the guerrillas in El Salvador, to crush the guerrillas in Nicaragua, to beseech the university to divest from South Africa, to halt a showing of the film *Birth of a Nation*, and more, always much more. Like the village idiot hired by the *shtetl* in which he lived to await by the village gates the coming of the messiah, the students of InCAR appear never to be out of work.

No one would ever accuse the InCAR kids of having flair. Say what you like against the sixties—and I would say a very great deal against them—the students who took part in the tumult of those years at least appeared hugely to enjoy the Dionysian fringe benefits that went along with their ostensibly Apollonian goals. The pleasure of the sixties, after all, was in doing exactly what one pleased while appearing at the same time to be doing good. This alluring combination has left many students of the current generation with what I think of as "60s envy," or regret at missing a whacking idealistic good time. But the students in InCAR in no way suggest those of the sixties. In their regression they jump all the way back to the 1930s, without the excuse of not knowing for certain what Stalin was doing in Russia during those years.

The students who belong to InCAR manage to achieve a grayness, a grimness, a joylessness that almost seems studied. There is a dimness about their dress, a bleakness about their response to the pleasant surroundings in which they live—Northwestern's is a lush campus set along the shore of Lake Michigan in Evanston, Illinois—that does not seem altogether natural. Whatever the season, winter seems to be in their faces as they stand near the rock, blaring the word through bullhorns or passing out leaflets for one or another of their causes—leaflets written in a tone and style that resemble not so much political argument as a ransom note. A local joke on campus asks, "How many members of InCAR does it take to change a light bulb?" "None," the answer is, "They don't change it—they smash it."

For the students who have joined it—and, undergraduate and graduate students together, they appear to number fewer than thirty—InCAR obviously gives something of the pleasure in collectivity that a fraternity or sorority provides, though much intensified. Among other pleasures, it gives that of being in total and permanent opposition on a campus whose student body is otherwise middle and upper-middle class in tone and feeling. Unlike a fraternity or sorority, InCAR gives its members a complete outlook on life: a way of understanding the world and a language to help explain it. There is also the sense of a "movement," for InCAR is not restricted to Northwestern University but claims an international membership in the thousands, ranging, or so it says, from coal miners in Kent in England to farm workers in the San Joaquin Valley in California. It is an offshoot—the impolite word is "front"—of the Communist Progressive Labor Party, which has been in existence for fifteen years.

But only in recent years has InCAR been a presence at Northwestern. A few of its members have wandered into my classes during this time. They tend to be very earnest, rather more passionate than the general run of Northwestern student, sometimes bright but never brilliant. The passion and the brightness, when they exist, come from the infusions of ideology that InCAR has given them. But what they gain on the straightaway they lose on the curve: that same ideology makes InCAR students leaden and mechanistic in their response to literature and ideas. They have minds so coarse no feelings can violate them. They have no notion that what seem to them hot new ideas are clichés pickled in the brine and blood of more than five decades. They write classroom papers with titles like "Sister Carrie as a Commodity" and "Joseph Conrad, Counter-Revolutionary." They will respond to a point made by a classmate by accusing him of being "imprisoned in bourgeois ideology," using the phrase as if it were quite as fresh and penetrating as an aphorism discovered in the middle of Proust.

THE RISE, if not to prominence then at least to high visibility, for InCAR came with the arrival at Northwestern of an assistant professor in the English Department named Barbara Foley. The daughter of a Columbia professor, raised in the affluent Riverdale section of New York, Barbara Foley had gone to Radcliffe and then for a PhD to the University of Chicago; she had taught previously at the University of Wisconsin; she is married and has two children. Somewhere along the line she was radicalized, and now, in her late thirties, she makes no bones about her politics: "Leninist" is for her an honorific term. Was it Barbara Foley that a student, in a course of mine on the sociology of literature, had in mind when, in a paper on the subject of the adversary culture, she wrote:

> As a writing major at NU, last year I took a course in American poetry which was taught by a certain Prof. X who claimed that Whitman was inherently racist and sexist in his naive representation of democracy, William Carlos Williams was racist in his depiction of individuals content within their socioeconomic positions, and that Dickinson, Frost, and other later New England writers were guilty of adhering to an ultimately "bourgeois" attitude of individualism combined with some sort of belief in religion, an after-life, and a sense of higher purpose: a belief which X considered "the opiate of the masses. . . ." X's message to aspiring writers was implicit; as writers, our goal should be to search out and criticize each and every fault in our culture. Any desire to affirm any aspect of that culture, we should stifle with our "critical intellects."

Although these views would seem to be congruent with Prof. Foley's, I cannot be certain that she is Prof. X, for there have been other professors in the English Department in which I teach who might also be pleased to claim the same views. I do not say that such views are dominant at Northwestern, or in the American university at large, but they do nowadays crop up with a fair frequency, and not in English departments alone. I recall three years ago taking two young men, graduating seniors who had been through two of my courses, to lunch, in the middle of which they unfurled a number of straightforwardly Marxist notions about American foreign policy. "Do you guys show slides with these clichés?" I inquired. I also asked where they had acquired such views. It turned out that they had just completed a course in American diplomatic history whose bottom, middle, top, and every other line was that all American foreign policy was a cover for the imperialist ventures of American business interests abroad. These were bright fellows, each of them with a fine sense of humor; one was headed for a career in journalism, the other for the foreign service; and I was disheartened to think that, as they were leaving my university, they were lugging such crude notions along with them.

A difference that never fails to astonish me between undergraduate education now and then—"then" being when I was an undergraduate at the University of Chicago—is that now university teachers who have strong political views feel no need to suppress them in the name of fairness or disinterestedness or a higher allegiance to the subject being taught. I may have been a political naïf when young, but thinking back upon my own undergraduate education I cannot recall the political opinions of any of my teachers. The reason I cannot, I suspect, is that they kept their politics to themselves. Their politics were nobody's business but their own, and, while they were in the classroom or lecture hall, not even their own.

Academic freedom, which earlier generations of professors had struggled to obtain, was about the right to hold any political views one wished *outside* the classroom. One of the most common meanings of academic freedom, in the words of Edward Shils, "refers to the freedom of university—and college—teachers to enjoy the freedom of speech and action that other citizens are constitutionally, legally, and conventionally empowered to exercise." But that meaning has in recent decades been extended to include the right to teach one's political views as part of the subject matter of one's courses. Not only is it considered a right, but, in many quarters it is thought a fine thing. University academic departments nowadays seek out feminists, Marxists, and others in whom the political impulse runs stronger than any other, to *teach their bias*—and to do so in the name of intellectual diversity. If a strong English-department chairman were today to learn about the teaching of Prof. X, quoted above, and tried to tell him or her to knock it off in the name of a higher seriousness, that chairman would no doubt be accused of interfering with Prof. X's academic freedom.

In the old days one can imagine a strong English-department chairman, in the approved English-professor manner, taking Prof. X aside to say, "Look here, X, do be a good fellow and forget that rot about the bourgeois attitudes of the New England writers I understand you are teaching. Publish it if you like—that is your business. But our business, as teachers, is sticking to the text." If Prof. X were tenured, the request would be a friendly one; if he were not yet tenured, the request would no doubt be more insistent. Today, however, our chairman would be accused, at a minimum, of McCarthyism, fascism, and troglodyticism. The American Association of University Professors might be called in. An article might appear in the *Chronicle of Higher Education*. Litigation might be set in motion. But, not to worry, no chairman is likely to suggest that Prof. X knock it off. It just isn't done.

It isn't done—not at least at large universities mindful of their prestige—because a college teacher's classroom has become his castle, and he is free to do there as he pleases. Colleagues do not make judgments about a fellow teacher's teaching. Instead, under the new dispensation, students do. Students always have done so, of course, but whereas earlier they did so informally, now, through something called evaluation forms, they do so formally. On the final days of a class, with perhaps ten or twenty minutes remaining, a professor passes out evaluation forms on which students remark on the strengths and deficiencies of his course. In cases where a professor is coming up for tenure, these evaluations are considered by his colleagues with some care. Tenured faculty, in these instances, do not directly judge the teacher; they judge the students' judgments, which is not quite the same thing.

NOT THAT JUDGING TEACHING IS EASY. As everyone who has been to college knows, a popular teacher can be inefficient and a dull teacher can sometimes leave a lasting impress. What seems exciting in one's youth, ten years later seems facile, if not silly. Teaching, especially teaching the large, so-called soft subjects in the humanities, where mastery of specific problems is not the chief business at hand, but asking the right questions is, is a subtle art. Student evaluations of one's own teaching do not help. These evaluations can capture real delinquency, citing a professor's many absences or his obvious unpreparedness. But beyond that, in the realm where useful distinctions might be made, they leave everything to be desired. Evaluations of my own teaching tend to be quite positive, and my teaching is almost always held to be—most ambiguous of words—"interesting." But how much gets through, how long it will remain, I haven't the least idea, and my guess is that neither does any other teacher. Undergraduate students can hardly be expected to be fit to judge this, and by and large they are not.

Barbara Foley, too, is thought to be an "interesting" teacher, some say an "exciting" teacher, some say the best teacher they have had at Northwestern. A small percentage of students—perhaps 10 percent—say that they are put off by what they term her "ideology." About this ideology she is apparently, as they say, "up front." She makes clear her political point of view and then teaches it. A bit of a Jenny One-Note, Prof. Foley teaches courses that feature the political; their titles have included "Race and Racial Attitudes in American Literature," "The Radical Tradition in American Literature," "Proletarian Writers of the 1930s," and "The American Dream: Myth or Reality?" (anyone out there who cares to bet that the dream is a reality, please get in touch with me immediately; there is some real estate in the Everglades I would like to show you). These courses, I have gathered from talking to students who have taken them and have since graduated, offer strong Marxistical readings of American books, with occasional eye-opening insights such as that, one of my former students recalls, Mark Twain was a "liberal racist." You don't have to believe Prof. Foley, you don't have to swallow her line to do well in her courses, but it is, evidently, no easy chore to buck her directly. Still, the vast majority of her students, according to student evaluations, walk away satisfied customers.

In the scuttlebutt way one picks up on these things, one hears occasional murmurs of reaction against the heavy dosage of politics in Prof. Foley's political teaching. A student who adored Emily Dickinson was greatly unsettled by Prof. Foley's announcement that Emily Dickinson had rendered herself permanently minor by ignoring the political subject in her work. In another case, a young black student, who had been in two of my courses, dropped in one morning to ask if I thought that he, an undergraduate, was intellectually prepared to take a graduate-level course taught by Barbara Foley. I replied that I thought if he took special pains he was indeed up to it. "There's only one thing I worry about, then," he said. When I asked what that was, he replied, "The word is out that Prof. Foley gives almost all black students A's. I really wouldn't want to get an A that way." Was this true? Was Barbara Foley practicing in her own classroom the redistributive justice she longed for in the world? Short of checking all her students' grades for the six years she has taught at Northwestern, there is no way of knowing. It is interesting, though, that this is the word among black students.

Something that no one in the English Department at Northwestern has had the ill manners to talk about is whether Prof. Foley uses her classroom to recruit members for InCAR. In a brief profile in the *Daily Northwestern* of an undergraduate InCAR member named Becki Huntman, the walls of whose rooms are festooned with pictures of Lenin, Stalin, Malcolm X, and Friedrich Engels, Miss Huntman is quoted as saying that she first learned of InCAR and Communist ideology during her sophomore year in a "Marxism in Literature" course taught by Prof. Foley. "It was the first class," Miss Huntman added, "where things made sense." I asked a former student of mine, who had taken one of Barbara Foley's courses, if the subject of InCAR ever came up in class. She replied that sometimes, toward the close of a class, Prof. Foley would pass out an announcement of an InCAR meeting, where, she would say, some of the things that had been discussed in class would be talked about in greater detail. Often, too, my former student said, InCAR members would be waiting at the beginning of a class outside the door with petitions to sign or leaflets to hand out. Once, when my former student called on Prof. Foley to discuss a forthcoming classroom paper, she found her extremely helpful, but on the way out Prof. Foley attempted to sell her the current issue of the Progressive Labor party newspaper. "Did you buy it?" I asked. "No," she said. "Was Prof. Foley angry that you didn't?" "Not at all," she said. "I guess she figured it was worth a try."

Something else that no one at Northwestern talks about is Barbara Foley's exact relationship with InCAR. The group is made up of students, but she is a professor. During the student tumult of the late sixties and early seventies there was many a professor who was in entire sympathy with groups such as Students for a Democratic Society, but were there any professors, above the level of graduate-student instructors, who were also members of student organizations? Such groups have generally had faculty advisers, but Prof. Foley's role in InCAR goes far beyond the advisory. If there is an InCAR picket, she is on the line; she puts in her time with the bullhorn; she works the rock. There is nothing of the standard dilettante, BMW-owning, Marxoid, let-the-kids-do-all-the-dirty-work contemporary radical university professor about Barbara Foley. The movement is neither an amusement nor an avocation for her. It is of her blood and bone; she is wedded to it; it is her life. Not many people at Northwestern seem to want to talk about this, either.

IN FACT, BARBARA FOLEY probably would never have been a subject of more than ordinary interest—her type, after all, is scarcely original—but for an incident that took place on the Northwestern campus on the evening of April 13, 1985, an incident that has come to be known locally as the Calero Event. On that night Adolfo Calero, then the commander-in-chief of the Nicaraguan Democratic Forces (FDN), the largest group of *contras*, as the guerrillas fighting against the Sandinista government in Nicaragua were known, was to speak at Northwestern under the auspices of two university organizations, the Conservative Council and the International Policy Forum. The Reagan administration's campaign to increase American support for the *contras* was already well under way, and one assumes that Adolfo Calero was to speak at Northwestern, as he would at other universities, to make the case for this policy.

One has to assume this, for in fact Calero never got to speak. His talk was scheduled for 7:00 PM and was open to the university community and to the public free of charge. Well before the talk, however, protesters from at least five different left-wing organizations—four from around the city of Chicago and InCAR from Northwestern—ranged themselves around Harris Hall, the place of the scheduled talk, some carrying pickets and shouting and chanting against Calero and the *contras*. In the room in Harris Hall in which the Calero talk was to be given—a room that accommodates roughly 300 people—some ten or fifteen minutes before Adolfo Calero was to appear, Barbara Foley walked up to the podium and began to speak. (The day before, she had discussed the forthcoming Calero talk in her English class and urged her students to attend.) She identified herself as a member of the International Committee Against Racism, and then announced, in the words of an ad-hoc panel document,* that "this was the first fascist rally on campus in some time, she suspected more were being planned and they should be stopped." She said that "Adolfo Calero was a monster who would be attempting to speak about freedom, democracy, and liberty. By that he meant the right to reappropriate his Nicaraguan business holdings"; that "Calero had the blood of thousands on his hands and no respect for the rights to life and free speech of the people he helped slaughter with the CIA's help"; that "He had no right to speak that night" and—the following are Prof. Foley's words—"We are not going to let him speak," and he "should feel lucky to get out of [Harris Hall] alive." She went on in this vein for two or three minutes. Other people followed her to the podium to offer their opinions.

When Adolfo Calero arrived there was a great deal of chanting and shouting in opposition to his presence. His talk was delayed some ten or fifteen minutes. Before he could begin someone—not Barbara Foley—rushed to the stage and threw a red liquid at him. This liquid had been variously described as paint and as animal blood. At this point, with a good deal of shouting in the hall, Adolfo Calero, his suit coat bespattered with the red liquid, was led from the hall by security men and did not speak that evening. Barbara Foley acknowledges joining in the chanting during the tumult. A witness claims that she also shouted that "the only way to get anything done would be to kill him [Calero]," though she and another witness, a graduate student who is also a member of InCAR, deny that she said this. In any case, what is apparently technically known as "a shout-down"—though the throwing of the red liquid went well beyond shouting—was successful. It was not a memorable night for "dialogue" at Northwestern University.

---

* I was not at Harris Hall on the night of April 13. My account of the events of that evening derives solely from a document entitled "Decision, Ad Hoc Panel of UFRPT-DAP, Northwestern University, In the Matter of Professor Barbara Foley." Both Prof. Foley's lawyer and the lawyer for the provost of Northwestern agreed to and signed a "Stipulation of Facts" about that evening. It is from the ad-hoc panel's presentation of those agreed-upon facts that I have drawn.

The Calero Event took place on a Saturday evening. The following Monday a photograph of the bespattered Adolfo Calero along with an account of the incidents surrounding the event appeared in the *Daily Northwestern*. The account quoted Barbara Foley as having said, "He has no right to speak here tonight and we are not going to let him. He should feel lucky to get out alive." (This quotation would come up again and again.) The account also mentioned that protesters later gathered outside the apartment at which Calero was staying, threatening violence, and had to be removed by police. Prof. Foley claimed that InCAR was not responsible for what had happened but that she did not regret that it happened. (She would never express regret, let alone offer apology, throughout the months that followed; nor has she done so since. But more about this presently.) She was also quoted as saying, "I think it's terrific that people saw the fascists."

Soon thereafter Arnold Weber, in his first year as president of Northwestern University, issued a strong but quite general statement about the impermissibility of any person or group invading the rights of students or faculty by disrupting regularly scheduled university events. Weber had previously been president of the University of Colorado and still earlier had worked for George Shultz at the Office of Management and Budget, but, apart from having a reputation as a strong and capable administrator, his general views or politics were not known. But a stronger and more specific statement came from the university provost, a man named Raymond W. Mack, a sociologist by training and, by all accounts, a liberal in politics. As a liberal should, Mack was said to be outraged by this violation of free speech and academic freedom, and, by way of a press release, he let it be known that he intended to propose that Barbara Foley be suspended for two academic quarters, and suspended without pay. Provost Mack also felt that the tenure procedure on Prof. Foley, which was to begin the following autumn, ought to be delayed for a full year.

Like Provost Mack, the majority of the faculty at Northwestern's College of Arts and Sciences are also generally liberal in their political views, with a sprinkling of Marxists and conservatives popping up here and there in various departments. But if most members of the faculty were outraged by the incidents connected with the Calero Event, they managed to keep it to themselves. When the autumn 1985 term began, such organizing efforts as were in evidence were on behalf of Barbara Foley. InCAR was firing up the Xerox machine with handouts headed "Foley Tenure Case Shows Need to Shed Liberal Illusions," pointing out that Northwestern University was clearly going the way of Nazi Germany. A group of faculty members in the English department wrote a lecture to Provost Mack on the subject of "due process" that ran as a full-page ad in the *Daily North-western*, signed by more than eighty members of the faculty. One would hear a good deal about "due process" in the days ahead. Except from the InCAR students, one would not hear much more about fascism and Nazi Germany. Liberals at a place like Northwestern are not so crude; they prefer instead to talk about "McCarthyism." One would also hear a great many sentences that began, "Of course I find Barbara Foley's views abhorrent, but. . . ." But, yet, still, and however. "The sin of nearly all left-wingers from 1933 onward," wrote George Orwell, "is that they have wanted to be anti-fascist without being anti-totalitarian."

THE FIRST REAL ACTION on what by now had come to be called "The Foley Case" took place on November 15 and 16, 1985, before the ad-hoc panel of a university body with the impossible acronym of UFRPT-DAP (standing for University Faculty Reappointment, Promotion, Tenure, and Dismissal Appeals Panel). The panel of five members—made up of two professors of medicine, one professor of material science and engineering, and a chairwoman and another professor from the School of Speech—met to hear eleven charges lodged against Barbara Foley for her conduct on the night of the Calero Event. At Prof. Foley's insistence, the panel met in open session, which (in my view) may have been a strategic mistake for Barbara Foley. The hearing was held on a dim Friday afternoon in an auditorium at the Kellogg School of Management called the Coon Forum. Modern in design, drab in appearance, the room ascends none too gently from its blackboard and podium and along its ascension double desks are arrayed behind which are swivel chairs. I have heard lectures in the Coon Forum, but I should say that it provides a better setting for, perhaps, a cockfight. The ad-hoc panel sat at the front, the bottom-most point of the room, with Prof. Foley and her lawyer to its right and

Provost Mack and his lawyer (both lawyers were women) and an associate provost to its left. Owing perhaps to its being a drizzly Friday afternoon, the crowd in attendance was sparse; perhaps we were sixty people in all—many fewer, in any case, than had come to hear or to shout down Adolfo Calero seven months earlier.

I found the ad-hoc panel impressive in its competence. As befits professors, its members had done their homework. Relevant documents had been exchanged between contending parties; the ground rules and procedures were clearly laid out. The chairwoman made plain that if there were any demonstrations or disruptions, she would clear the auditorium. The hearing was conducted with a certain gravity of spirit that was entirely appropriate to the business at hand. The business at hand was serious business—a young woman's career could ride on the outcome.

T HE HEARING PROPER began with Provost Mack reading his eleven charges against Prof. Foley. There is no need to list all eleven charges here. Suffice it to say that Barbara Foley was accused of disrupting a regularly scheduled university event by inciting the audience to a shout-down; that Prof. Foley did so willfully and premeditatedly, and thus contributed to an abridgment of freedom of speech and freedom of inquiry; that her behavior on that night constituted grave professional misconduct; and that this behavior violated principles of academic freedom and responsibility that are widely accepted and clearly expressed in statements issued by the American Association of University Professors (AAUP).

Before responding to the specific charges, Barbara Foley made a general opening statement. The political speech is a form with which she is at ease. To make a longish speech short, she said that subjecting her to these charges at all was farcical, and the charges showed that the administration at Northwestern University, in its accusations against her, was really aligned with the Reagan administration's policies in Central America. (I have to admit that this connection had not occurred to me.) After this statement, Barbara Foley's lawyer began calling witnesses. The first among them was a graduate student on whose dissertation committee Barbara Foley sat. A small and extremely tidy young woman, she shocked—at least she shocked me—with the quiet violence of her views. To her it was perfectly obvious that Adolfo Calero, being evil, had no right to speak, and she had no qualms either about the red liquid that was thrown at him. Others of Prof. Foley's students, graduate and undergraduate, agreed that Calero had been treated as he deserved and that shouting him down was a perfectly appropriate response to such a man. Allowing such witnesses to speak on Barbara Foley's behalf seemed to me a very foolish tack for her lawyer to take; the best defense can surely never be a bad offense.

As a university teacher, I am not sure I should wish to be judged by what my students thought they had learned from me. But in Barbara Foley's case, there was no question that her students had got it right; their views, at any rate, were perfectly congruent with her own on the subjects of freedom of speech, academic freedom, and political discussion: to those deemed enemies, none is permitted. While Prof. Foley was not being judged by the ad-hoc panel as a teacher, the sad show her students put on could not have helped her cause. The open hearing, too, made it impossible for Barbara Foley to express the least contrition for what she had done, assuming that she felt any or even wished to fake some. The best that could be got from her with her InCAR crowd in the audience was that—I am quoting again from the UFRPTDAP document cited earlier—"although she did not agree with a judgment that condemns her behavior, she would live within the limits prescribed and would not repeat the prescribed conduct. She acknowledged that were she to repeat it, she would do so knowingly and at full risk."

At the intermission of the first session of the ad-hoc panel hearing, I ran into a friend who is also a member of the English department at Northwestern. He looked very glum, not to say downright depressed. He told me that he was soon likely to lose the allegiance of some of his best graduate students, who were adamantly in Barbara Foley's camp. "After what I have just heard in that room," he said, referring to the ad-hoc panel proceedings, "there is no way I can ever hope to support Barbara." As things turned out, he, along with the majority of the faculty, would find a way.

It was not until January of 1986 that the UFRPTDAP ad-hoc panel delivered its report and recommendation on the Foley case. The report has a somewhat pompous tone, possibly owing to the panel members' repeated insistence on the scrupulosity of their procedures and bases for judgment. As for the judgment itself, it went crushingly against Barbara

Foley, sustaining eight of the administration's eleven charges against her. I quote from the summary of the panel's findings on the charges:

> The ad-hoc panel finds that Professor Foley's conduct on the evening of April 13, 1985, was violative of the speaker's rights to speak and be heard and of the audience's right to hear, and consequently constitutes "grave professional misconduct" as charged. We believe that the conduct was violative of academic freedom, a widely accepted principle essential to the central purpose of a university. We believe that the charges sustained describe conduct which is inimical to an atmosphere of open inquiry, antithetical to the principles of free speech, and unacceptable in a university community.

IF THE JUDGMENT AGAINST BARBARA FOLEY WAS SEVERE, the sanctions imposed upon her were not. "Despite the severity of Professor Foley's offense," the report ended, "we have weighed carefully possible sanctions short of two quarters of suspension without pay. The penalty we recommend is a formal letter of reprimand, accompanied by a warning that a repetition of the offense is actionable up to the point of dismissal, and placed in the permanent file of Professor Foley." Although she must secretly have been relieved at the lightness of these sanctions, Barbara Foley was quoted in the university newspaper as saying, "I was very disappointed by the stand taken by the panel, which failed to chastise the administration for its attempt to railroad me. In fact, the panel endorsed the essence of the administration's political position." The administration, in the person of Provost Mack, accepted the panel's recommendation, saying that its findings helped clarify university policy. Barbara Foley rejoined by saying that the administration had no choice but to accept the panel's recommendation, for "To react otherwise would've placed them in an antagonistic relationship with the rest of the faculty." She also said that she feared that faculty members reviewing her tenure case would be adversely influenced by the incident and would not concentrate on her academic performance.

That Barbara Foley was up for tenure the same year in which she was in effect tried for violations of academic freedom was a circumstance not without its ironies—for tenure, at its inception, was meant to protect the academic freedom of university teachers. Far from being the job-security arrangement it has since become, tenure began as a means of ensuring the rights of professors as citizens outside the university. Thus a university teacher might vote or speak or even organize on behalf of, say, labor unions and, with tenure, need not fear the retaliation of anti-labor men on his school's board of trustees. Academic freedom also ensured that a teacher would be able to pursue lines of scholarly or scientific inquiry that his colleagues or even the community might think odd or heretical. But academic freedom always carried certain responsibilities. Most obviously, it never included the freedom to abrogate someone else's freedom. It never included the freedom to turn the classroom into a political pulpit or guerrilla theater. It never included using the job of teacher to propagandize for political or religious conversions. The guardians of academic freedom were to be, precisely, its beneficiaries, the professors themselves, who might be expected to guard it jealously, at least if they knew what was good for their own interests.

Nowadays tenure is awarded, traditionally, after a young professor has been at an institution for two three-year terms, and on three bases: scholarship, teaching, and academic citizenship. The emphases laid on teaching and scholarship can differ from institution to institution. At some smaller colleges a teacher's publishing record may be of negligible import next to his performance in the classroom. At larger universities, especially those concerned about their prestige as research institutions, no publication, or insufficient publication, means no tenure. Although one hears the phrase less frequently now than formerly, "publish or perish" is still very much the rule at most larger universities.

The third basis for tenure, academic citizenship, is one that always has to be considered but is only in exceptional cases emphasized. It is a judgment, at least in part, of character; it is also a judgment about willingness to conform to the rules, explicit and implicit, that govern institutions of higher learning. If a young teacher shows himself irresponsible in his committee assignments, if he misses classes owing to drunkenness, if he seduces his young students, if he shows no regard for the fundamental beliefs of the institution, he could, theoretically, be faulted on academic citizenship and hence denied tenure. (With tenure, it occurs to me to add, the same teacher could now do any of the things mentioned in the previous sentence and probably keep his job.) Owing either to the widened tolerance for human misbehavior or to the lapse in standards of deportment on the part of professors, the category of academic citizenship is invoked in tenure decisions only in exceptional cases. Would Barbara Foley's be such a case?

Although I began teaching in the English department at Northwestern University in 1974, I continued to do so, largely by choice, without tenure. Since only members of the department who already have tenure are permitted to vote on tenure decisions, I did not attend the meeting at which the decision about Barbara Foley's tenure was made. On the other hand, had I been at that meeting, I should have been bound by confidentiality not to speak about it. What I know about this meeting, therefore, I know from things that have leaked out and from surmise. It quickly leaked out, for example, that the English department's vote was ten to five (with one member abstaining) in favor of recommending Prof. Foley for tenure. As such recommendations go, this was not a strong one; it is more usual for a candidate for tenure to get a unanimous recommendation, or one with only one or two votes of dissent.

It also transpired that, during the tenure vote, discussions of Prof. Foley's politics were ruled out of order. Whether she was pushing a clear and hard political line in her classes, whether it was appropriate for a member of the faculty to be a major figure in a radical student organization, whether the teaching of literature was a proper occasion for attacking what Prof. Foley deemed the rampant racism and brutalities of capitalism in American life—all this, apparently, was proscribed from discussion, lest politics be thought to determine a decision that ought to be made exclusively on grounds of scholarship and pedagogy. As for Prof. Foley's behavior during the Calero Event, this, too, was apparently ruled out of bounds for discussion.

I F ONE IS NOT PERMITTED to talk about the politics of so thoroughly political a woman as Barbara Foley, and forbidden to talk not only about her political views but (much more important) about her on-campus political activities, not much is left to talk about. There were the students' evaluations of her teaching, and these, as mentioned earlier, were vastly approving. There was her scholarship, as a teacher's publishing record is now conventionally called, and here she had clearly published in sufficient quantity to guard against her perishing: along with a fairly thick sheaf of reviews and articles in academic journals, she had a book on the documentary novel about to appear from Cornell University Press. Was Prof. Foley's academic citizenship discussed? I do not know, though afterward, in defense of the English department's decision, its chairman would say that he knew no better citizen of the English department than Barbara Foley. By this he meant that she was a willing and helpful member of department committees, attended meetings and other departmental events, was reliable in performing intramural house- and record-keeping functions. There is no reason to doubt his word on this, but his remains an astonishingly narrow view of academic citizenship. The vote, to repeat, was ten to five in favor of recommending tenure.

To plunge a bit further into the forest of surmise, what was in the minds of the ten faculty members who voted in favor of recommending Barbara Foley for tenure? None is a Marxist, though some have been known to mutter the cliché that "Marxism remains an indispensable tool of literary analysis." (Odd that the best literary critics have, without much difficulty, been able to dispense with it.) Some may have felt themselves crippled by the ground rules of the discussion. Almost all of them have said to me, singly, at one time or another, that "I find Barbara's views abhorrent, but . . . still . . . yet . . . however. . . ." *But* some find her abhorrent views useful for giving students a wide diversity of opinion. *Still*, some like her personally and say that in private she can be a charming woman. *Yet* some feel they have no right to claim that their own views are superior to the next person's, though I have never encountered anyone who finds his own views abhorrent. *However*, some feel that to censure even views and actions they find abhorrent is to be guilty of, yes, McCarthyism.

Of course, it is also possible that many members of the Northwestern English department were greatly impressed by Prof. Foley's scholarship, so greatly impressed that denying tenure to so considerable a scholar would have seemed grievously wrong (especially since there are now members of the English department who were given tenure before they even published a book). "Scholarship, scholarship, scholarship," said the chairman of the English department on another occasion in defending his department's decision on tenure, "that is what wins tenure at a place like Northwestern."

I fear that "scholarship" has in academic circles become one of those words that no longer means what it once did; "research" is another. Where scholarship once stood for the kind of work done by people like E. H. Gombrich, Arnaldo Momigliano, and Frances A. Yates, it now merely means published work. In this rather less impressive conception of scholarship, Prof. Foley had committed her share, and I decided to have a closer look at it (which, I believe, is called "research").

Reading Prof. Foley's book, *Telling the Truth: The Theory and Practice of Documentary Fiction*, I recalled that one of her graduate students, while defending her conduct during the Calero Event, remarked that she admired Prof. Foley's expertise in "social awareness literature" and added that Prof. Foley was at the forefront of "the theoretical debate that is shaping literature." There is something in what this graduate student said. In her book Prof. Foley sets out to demonstrate that she is very much *au courant* with the new literary theory but is not about to let it swamp the larger questions of social awareness that, when one gets right down to it, no one has posed with greater clarity, penetration, and wisdom than Karl Marx and Vladimir Ilyich Lenin.

Part of the difficulty with *Telling the Truth* is that one does not get right down to it very quickly. Its first 103 pages are given over to the new literary theory gradually becoming regnant in English graduate studies. Devotees of this theory will find many old friends cited in her pages: Foucault, Bakhtin, Derrida, Barthes, Lacan. The reliable Marxist gang is also there: Christopher Caudwell, Lucien Goldmann, Georg Lukács, and Louis Althusser. When either Marx or Lenin is quoted, he is given scriptural authority. The highest new jargonese is everywhere employed. The prose is consequently very dense. Few actual works of literature are cited in this first part of the book. Instead something called "the text" is continually mentioned; also such barbed-wire words as "intertextuality" and "extratextuality." Nonprofessionals will find it all very hard, almost impenetrable, going. Reading the first part of Prof. Foley's book I was reminded of Robert Frost's remark that writing free verse is like playing tennis with the net down; perhaps the best way to describe the new critical theory is to say that it is like playing ping-pong without the ball.

But the real purpose of the dense theoretical discussion of the first part of *Telling the Truth* is to make the point that the new literary theory cannot finally supplant that old indispensable tool of literary analysis, standard Marxism. In the second part of her book Prof. Foley puts the ball in play and discusses actual works in the genre she rather loosely defines as the documentary novel. "Contextualization," "hypostatization," "re-concretization of the referent," "fictionality"—the lyrics may be different but the melody is the traditional Marxist one. For, as long as we are telling the truth, the only documentary fiction Prof. Foley appears to approve is that which confronts the class struggle and the alienation she believes is the inevitable result of capitalism as part of an "oppositional program." Or, to put it in the not uncharacteristic prose style of *Telling the Truth*:

> Though some writers manage to make use of modernist de-familiarization as a powerful tool in the critique of reification, most accede to the thoroughgoing fetishization of social relations that characterizes what Lukács called the 'problem of commodities' in the early 20th century.

THAT, PATENTLY, IS NOT ENTERTAINMENT, but is it scholarship? Evidently, to judge by English-studies standards of the day, and by the subsequent career of Prof. Foley's tenure recommendation, it is indeed. Once such a recommendation leaves an academic department, its approval is far from certain. Not many years back the recommendation for tenure of an extremely popular teacher of philosophy was shot down at the level of the dean's office, presumably because the teacher's published work was felt by the dean not to have enough intellectual weight. But the recommendation for Prof. Foley sailed on through—from the university's ad-hoc tenure committee, thence to the College of Arts and Sciences Promotion and Tenure Committee, and thence to the dean of the College of Arts and Sciences—everywhere endorsed, and reputed to have been strongly endorsed. It was reported that where usually somewhere between eight and twelve outside readers are called in for judgment upon a tenure decision, in Prof.

Foley's instance there were between thirty-five and thirty-eight outside readers, and these endorsed her tenure overwhelmingly (a fact that by itself says a great deal about the fallen standards of English studies in recent years). Case, one would have thought, closed.

Not quite, as it turned out. On May 21, 1986, Barbara Foley received a letter from the dean of the College of Arts and Sciences whose first sentence read: "I must inform you that the Provost did not approve the recommendation to promote you to the rank of associate professor with tenure." The brief letter went on to say that she would be given a final year of employment as an assistant professor. Attached was a copy of Provost Raymond W. Mack's letter rejecting the appointment. In his letter the provost cited the fact that Prof. Foley "failed to receive a majority vote from her tenured colleagues in the department of English who had recommended her retention." (There are twenty-one members of the department with tenure, and five had missed the meeting.) But, obviously, a more significant item for the provost—and, clearly, for President Arnold Weber for whom he was also speaking—was Barbara Foley's behavior during the Calero Event:

> Professor Foley's record includes the fact that the administration of Northwestern University last year charged her with grave professional misconduct, in that she violated widely accepted principles of academic freedom and responsibility including those stated in the *Northwestern University Faculty Handbook* (p. 1). She asked for, and received, an open hearing on these charges before an ad-hoc panel of the elected faculty appeals committee.

The provost then quoted from the summary section of the ad-hoc panel's report, and ended by saying that he agreed with that summary. "I support the finding of the university faculty panel that her conduct is 'unacceptable in a university community.' I therefore have decided against offering her further appointment as a member of the Northwestern University faculty."

The faculty reaction to the administration's rejection of tenure for Barbara Foley was much stronger than its reaction to the Calero Event. The coolest reaction was perhaps Prof. Foley's own. Despite the cliché nature of her revolutionary rhetoric, she is no fool and far from being an unsavvy politician. She immediately sent around Xerox copies of the letter from the dean to her and the provost's letter to the dean, and she was quoted the following day in the university newspaper as saying that rejection of her tenure was "clearly a political attack that revealed nakedly the actual nature of power relations in the university," adding that the administration, not the faculty, is assuming control of "the academic business of the university."

Most professors at Northwestern tend to be essentially in business for themselves. They teach, they publish, they apply for grants, they go to their mailboxes ever hopeful that they will have a job offer from Stanford or Michigan, or—O my God, can it be?—Harvard, Yale, or Princeton. Not much in the life of the university community outside their own interests arouses them. But the Foley case did. Of course they almost all found her views "abhorrent," but still, yet, and however she was one of them, a professor, and the administration was still the administration, a historic enemy. A new issue, then, had arisen, and it went by the name of faculty governance. True, there was nothing illegal about the provost's action. The provost of the university is supposed to review all tenure decisions and under an active provost these reviews are never perfunctory. Still, in overruling the findings of the various faculty committees in the Foley case, wasn't the administration undercutting the faculty's own power? After putting the faculty through the entire rigmarole of tenure review for Barbara Foley, then rejecting its findings, wasn't the administration acting in bad faith?

Although it was near the end of term, with papers to grade and examinations to give, a flurry of meetings was called. A group of graduate students organized themselves into the Graduate Committee in Support of Barbara Foley. The graduate students and the faculty in the English department met to vote on a resolution first "demanding," then (in quieter language) "urging" the president of the university to reverse the provost's decision in the Foley case. Voted on solely by the English faculty in secret ballot, the resolution passed 17 to 2. (Whose was the other dissenting vote, I wondered.) Letters with lengthy lists of signatories explaining faculty governance were sent off to the metropolitan Chicago press in answer to editorials congratulating the administration for taking a strong stand on academic freedom in the Foley case. To add an Orwellian touch of doublethink, small posters began to appear on the walls of university buildings and in classrooms: "Support Diversity of Opinion, Back Foley!" and "Retain Civil Liberties, Keep Foley!"

Just before final-examination week, on May 28, a rally in support of Barbara Foley was held at what was described in a hand-out as the "Mandela/Crown Center." (The true name of the place is Rebecca Crown Center, the location of the university's administration offices, donated by the Henry Crown family.) It was, literally, a banner day. A podium was set up before a pink banner with black lettering carrying InCAR's initials. "Support Foley" banners were rife. A student carried a banner reading, "Fire Mack, Support Foley!" Four or five people came up to me with various petitions to sign. A faculty member wanted me to sign a petition urging the president to understand he was undermining faculty governance. She let me know—here was an original thought—that she found Barbara Foley's views abhorrent, but a larger issue was at stake. I told her that I didn't find Barbara Foley's views abhorrent, merely crude and preposterous; what I found abhorrent was what she had done and her refusal to offer anything approaching an apology for it.

S PEAKER AFTER SPEAKER came to the podium. Some were students, claiming that if the university did not retain Prof. Foley it would be shortchanging them on their education; some were from InCAR; some from anti-apartheid groups. A professor from the English department spoke about the importance of faculty governance and the sanctity of the procedure of tenure; a professor who is the representative on campus of the American Association of University Professors rose to say that the AAUP was likely to look askance at the administration's behavior in regard to the Foley case. A man with a ponytail hairdo arrived from the technology part of the campus to say that he had heard the College of Arts and Sciences was planning a "De-foleyation Program." A woman from the philosophy department explained at some length that she had been cheated in her own education by the depredations of the McCarthy years and she did not plan to let it happen again. I could not take my eyes off a very Germanic-looking character got up in a leather jacket, rimless spectacles, a short haircut and mustache, wearing a large gold medal around his neck. He was imitating someone, or something, but what? Of course, it was a Bertolt Brecht imitation; the getup was obviously meant to be a Berliner Ensemble ensemble. (The man turned out to be a local Marxist art historian, and the medal he wore was the medal that goes with his distinguished professorship.)

Meanwhile, everyone except those doing the talking was growing logy with boredom. Nearly two hours had passed. What we were all waiting for, of course, was for Barbara Foley to speak. At last she came to the microphone. There were perhaps a hundred and fifty people gathered. She was greeted by strong applause. For the most part, she spoke in pure clichés: about the administration's political motives in rejecting her for tenure, about its desecration of the principle of faculty governance, about the splendid work of InCAR around the country, about the evil of the *contras* whom she accused of torturing women and cutting off their breasts. Toward the close of her speech, she said, "When I got up on the stage in Harris 107, I had no idea all this would happen, but I have no regrets," and then she added, though I did not catch her exact words, that her only regret was that there hadn't been other faculty members with her on that night.

"You have to admit," Prof. Foley's friends say, "that Barbara has guts." I admit it. She also has a goofy kind of integrity. She calls herself a Marxist-Leninist, but the truth is that she is a poor Leninist indeed. A real Leninist would have apologized at some point—and I myself have little doubt that an apology would have made it very difficult for the provost to do what he did without seeming heartless—and then, in good Leninist fashion, would have gone on with whatever he thought would further the interests of the revolution. It may be that Barbara Foley cannot apologize even to the point of allowing that *perhaps* she went a bit far on the night of the Calero Event, lest she lose face among the students she has been revving up with her rhetoric over the past several years. My own suspicion is that she feels she has nothing for which to apologize. She is not in the least a phony. I think she is a real revolutionary, at least psychologically, and that, now headed toward forty years of age, she is probably in for the duration. As I walked away from the rally, I recalled that it was not her beloved Marx but Nietzsche who said that every idea has its autobiography, and I wondered what it was in Barbara Foley's own autobiography that had put the dark and fiery idea of revolution in her head, probably never to be dislodged within her lifetime.

There was to be one more meeting on the Foley case before, so to speak, school was out. With what I am quite certain was unconscious symbolism, the meeting of the College of Arts and Sciences faculty was held in Harris Hall in the same room where Adolfo Calero had been attacked and denied his right to speak. After the reading of various documents by the chairman of the Committee on Promotion and Tenure, the first speaker, a youngish man with a Russian accent, announced that Prof. Foley had outraged any serious conception anyone could possibly hold of the responsibilities of academic citizenship. His accent, which told that he had firsthand experience of totalitarianism and thus cherished freedom all the more, seemed to make little impression on his fellow teachers; another professor quickly rose to say that there was no way to gauge citizenship in a university. Another professor, a teacher of political science, spoke strongly against Prof. Foley's violation of free speech, and said that by this act she had disqualified herself as a member in good standing of the academic community. A few others rose to say that they did not have enough facts to make a careful judgment on the case.

But the reigning feeling in the room was overwhelmingly, if not pro-Foley, at least anti-administration. Much of the behavior I have come to think of as virtucratic was on display: people rising to speak chiefly to show that their hearts were in the right place. Not everyone apparently found Prof. Foley's views and actions abhorrent. A man in what I took to be a Swiss-German accent spoke against the *contras*, and ended by asserting that what Prof. Foley had done was courageous and correct. A left-wing sociologist chipped in with, "I'm sympathetic to speech acts against Mr. Calero." An economist who had served on the Council of Economic Advisers under Jimmy Carter allowed that he found Prof. Foley's views abhorrent, but felt she nevertheless deserved another chance; if she were to do something similar in the future, she should then be stripped of her tenure. A man in a page-boy hairdo and a mustache who looked like a minor character in Shakespeare ("poor Yorick," perhaps) reminded the meeting that Barbara Foley had not been found guilty of a shout-down but of "inciting to a shout-down," though the force of his distinction, of which he seemed rather proud, was lost on the audience. Another sociologist said that he wanted to hear nothing further about Prof. Foley's moral conduct, for surely everyone knew that "the morals of professors are lower than that of a snake." This remark was met with snickering laughter—a roomful of professors took it sitting down. Finally, a resolution was offered to the effect that the Promotion and Tenure Committee write a strong letter to the administration protesting its rejection of Barbara Foley's tenure as a violation of the principle of faculty governance. It passed by a vast majority.

WHERE WILL IT ALL END? Barbara Foley will be on campus all of next year, and no doubt petitions of varying degrees of stridency will be whirling around, the bullhorn will be blaring nearly full-time in front of the rock, acrimonious arguments will take place, old friendships will break up. Already the American Association of University Professors, which began its life as an organization to set standards of conduct for professors while protecting them against abuses, but has by now turned into a trade union of sorts for university teachers, has written a letter to President Weber calling on him to consider reversing the provost's decision to reject Prof. Foley's tenure. Further appeals may be made; perhaps there will be litigation, for which byzantine grounds will be discovered. Will the administration, the one body at Northwestern University to demonstrate a consistent concern for free speech and academic freedom, be able to maintain its position? With an imagination for disaster, I see myself opening the *Chronicle of Higher Education* in, say, 1991, there to read a three-inch story about one Prof. Barbara Foley being awarded $800,000 in damages and retroactive tenure at Northwestern. Then, again, perhaps the Foley case will slowly fade away, leaving in its wake a young professor who ruined her career because she followed the logic of her nihilistic politics, and leaving few of her colleagues any the wiser.

The Academic Zoo:
Theory—in Practice

(1991)

We have witnessed what amounts to a cultural revolution,
comparable to the one in China if not worse, and whereas the
Chinese have to some extent overcome their cultural revolution,
I see many signs that ours is getting worse all the time,
and no indication that it will be overcome
in the foreseeable future.

PAUL OSKAR KRISTELLER, "A Life of Learning"

66 **I**T'S NOT WHAT I HAD IN MIND," said my friend. He had just
returned from a Modern Language Association meeting in Houston, which he described in what for him was scarifying detail:
Marxists, professional lesbians, obscurantists were all over the joint—
they appeared not only to be in charge but to give the meeting, and hence
the occupation of teaching literature, its character. "It's not what I had in
mind," he repeated, wistfully, without irony or anger. He had studied at
Columbia toward the close of its glory days, under men of the intellectual quality and urbanity of Lionel Trilling and Jacques Barzun. Columbia, in the days of his graduate study there, retained an unmistakable and
immensely impressive metropolitan spirit, which years afterwards still
clung to my friend, who taught in a suit and wore a serious hat. But what
had once seemed the apogee of the "profession," as university teachers of
literature had come to refer to themselves in their collectivity, was now

clearly its anomaly. Then in his late thirties, my friend, with his metropolitan spirit and Arnoldian notions about literary culture, was a young fogey, already a dinosaur. Most distinctly, it was not what he had in mind.

What had I in mind when I began teaching in the English department at Northwestern University in 1974 at the age of thirty-seven? As someone who had never gone to graduate school, my expectations were much less precise than those of my friend. I had been a student of English myself as an undergraduate and the preponderance of contributors to the intellectual and literary magazines which had been so important a part of my education had themselves made their living teaching in English departments. I had been around enough not to expect Barzunian-Trillingesque suavity ("Ah, how did Wystan put it just the other evening . . . "), but I did expect adults for colleagues. It turned out to be not quite so. In 1974 the great period of student unrest (still one of my favorite euphemisms) may have been over in fact but it was far from dead in spirit. Youngish professors, which in academic life had come to mean anyone under sixty, now dressed and generally comported themselves like students. Beards and denim was the dress code for pedagogues, and fornication with one's undergraduate students was for many taken as a perquisite of the job (the pay, after all, wasn't that good). In the hall of the building in which I had my office, I would often hear a teacher address an undergraduate by his first name and then hear the student return the compliment. It all felt like Lord of the freakin' Flies.

But other things were cooking at the same time. One was a new tolerance for the absurd. For a while Northwestern had become the location of the summer School of Criticism and Theory, which at a vastly reduced intellectual level had become a replacement of sorts for the old Kenyon and then Indiana School of Letters. Such schools, institutes, centers (for things on the periphery) have never been my idea of a good time, and I generally steer clear of them. But I happened to see a notice that the Harvard philosopher Stanley Cavell was to give a lecture on the Howard Hawkes movie *His Girl Friday,* and, since I had been reading Professor Cavell for years, without either fun or intellectual profit, I thought I would drop around to see if he was any better in person. He wasn't, and in the flesh he was able to add pomposity to the oblique sententiousness I had already found so unprepossessing on the page. Yet I was astonished by the rapt reception his almost passionately boring, nearly frame-by-frame analysis of a delightfully lightweight little movie received on the part of graduate students and teachers in the standing-room-only audience. Professor Cavell ran past the normal lecturer's hour, which is probably longer than Ben Hecht and Charles Lederer spent on composing the screenplay for the movie but which to me felt longer than a bad fiscal quarter. I was the only one to leave the room at hour's end. The rest of the crowd remained, slack-jawed and agog, no doubt making innumerable intellectual discoveries that were clearly not available to me. This was the first but it would not be the last time that people putatively interested in the same things I was interested in would discover treasure where I found none buried.

Assembling these recollections, I recall, too, that I have been teaching just long enough to have been on the scene to witness a black woman denied tenure in an English department—my own at Northwestern. The scholarship of the woman in question was judged undistinguished, even drab, and her performance as a teacher wanting. The decision was not made without some nervousness—the fear of being accused of racism was already one of the leading social terrors of our time—but it was made. As an untenured member of the faculty, I was not in on the decision and so cannot say whether it was a just one. What I can say with some assurance, however, is that for a similar decision to be made today the woman would have had to set fire to at least a simple majority of all the university's trustees.

The hunt for minority group members—"minorities," they are rather barbarously called—to fill academic jobs has of course been on in earnest for some while now, owing not only to affirmative action laws but also, my guess is, to the desire on the part of most university teachers to do Spike Lee's "right thing." That the right thing isn't generally the correct thing from the standpoint of maintaining academic standards is not something that many academics who make these decisions wish to dwell upon. They say instead that minority students need "role models," that past injustices must be redressed, that different, even disparate views are much needed. As for the question of standards, well, they will tell you, if one is going to introduce standards into the discussion of who is fit to teach what, then the game really is up.

The notion that a multiplicity of points of view is a felicitous condition to which to aspire is one with a long and rather dreary history behind it. At least in part it stems from the bad academic historical conscience owing to the anti-Semitism of university English and philosophy departments that was regnant until well past World War II. When the generation of the sixties began to come into academic power the members of this generation not only wished to eliminate the old waspocracy, but tended to go about it in rather a crude way. I noted the crudity of it a number of years ago when I gave a lecture at Denison University, a school in the fastness of Ohio for the children of the upper-middle class who must have had rather lower-middle class SAT scores. At Denison I noted an altogether too tidy distribution of English department personnel: two blacks, one feminist, a homosexual, a Jew, and a bedraggled woman who was described to me as being "from the sixties," as if the decade were a country, like the Ukraine. When I returned from my visit to Denison I wrote to the chairman of the department, who was absent during my visit, asking why they weren't able to get a better Jew. Odd but he never answered.

The notion of a multiplicity of points of view was from the start more than a bit disingenuous. What was actually wanted all along was a multiplicity of left-wing points of view. It is only in the strange land of university humanities departments that Marxism—so heinous in dealing with people, so happy in dealing with texts—continues to find proponents. But then the university culture has never been known to let itself be put off or otherwise inconvenienced by reality. Nor put out by hypocrisy. To take a particular case, with all the great administrative passion to hire black professors, a man named Shelby Steele, a contributor to *Harper's*, the *New York Times Magazine, Commentary,* and the *American Scholar,* a university professor who is black and not afraid to examine the assumptions behind current black social psychology and political behavior, languished in the English department of San Jose State University until offered a job at the conservative Hoover Institution. Why wasn't this man working up the road at Berkeley, or across the country at Harvard, Yale, Princeton, or at Duke, Brown, or some other fashionable educational spas? *Engagé* and *enragé* is the way the better schools prefer their blacks and Professor Steele, poor chap, fails to qualify.

"All right, we are two nations," wrote John Dos Passos at the close of *USA,* by which he meant that he found the America of that day divided between rich and poor, executioners and victims, haves and have-nots. But when I think of his remark today I think, Yes, we are two nations: one made up of people who live within the university and the other made up of the rest of the country. Something very detached, remote, unreal there is about life in a contemporary university. More is entailed than the stale metaphor ivory tower can hope to convey. Standards of acceptable conduct, speech, humor, rationality are so different in the university than in the remainder of American life that, for one who travels back and forth between the two, as I do as a part-time university teacher, perspective at times becomes exceedingly difficult to maintain. Sometimes the university seems to me a comic zoo, filled with mildly deformed and largely disappointed bipeds; sometimes it seems a madhouse in which it is the staff (the faculty) and not the inmates (the students) which is insane; and sometimes it seems a strange collection of small businessmen, each trying to hammer out a living in a line of work where the rewards—of capital, of ego—are so skimpy that there is too little to go round, a condition that encourages very unpleasant behavior. Old-fashioned phrases to describe university faculties such as a "community of scholars" nowadays are not only drained of meaning but seem quite as oxymoronic as "a completely honest politician" or "a good kosher meal."

I don't mean to suggest that the fairly recent past was a prelapsarian period in which English departments were staffed exclusively by brilliant critics, profound scholars, serenely dedicated teachers. English departments have always been generously studded by snobs, fools, stuffed shirts, dreary one-ups-men, dipsomaniacs, and thumping deadly bores. Yet I doubt that the atmosphere around English departments was ever quite so snarly as it is today. People in them walk about in a state of high cussedness—ticked, as the kids say, to the max—ready at all times to be offended. Touchy, touchy, touchy. The least miscue and they book you for sexism, racism, homophobia, sexual harassment. Heaven forfend you should refer to a department *chairman* rather than to the neutral and sillily elliptical *chair,* or say "Negro" (instead of black or African-American or whatever is the OK nomenclature of the week), or enunciate an unacceptable political opinion—and you are done for, morally cashiered, banished forever from the land of the enlightened and virtuous.

All this might be entirely comical—it's still pretty damn ridiculous— if it didn't have real intellectual consequences. Life without a sense of humor, which is life as it tends to be lived in the contemporary university, is life without any sense of proportion or perspective. Where laughter has been abrogated, so has common sense, which is why much in current English department studies seems, not to put too fine a point on it, quite nuts. Thus I not long ago read a batch of student papers in which I learned that "English is a language of imposition for African-Americans, a language of slavery and domination"; that "Shakespeare and [Robert] Coover [what a jolly pairing!] are both products and propagators of a male-dominated capitalistic society and both use their mastery of rhetoric to reinforce the status quo"; and that Joseph Conrad, benighted fellow, shows "ethnocentric androgenism," which goes a long way toward explaining that Mr. Kurtz's problem, in *Heart of Darkness*, is apparently that he failed to acculturate sufficiently with the tribesmen he met up with in the Congo. "You don't like my brother," an old joke about cannibalism has it, "at least eat the noodles."

Given the atmosphere of endemic touchiness, it follows that every intellectual tendency in current academic life must be taken all the way out. In the contemporary university, there is every chance that the wildest possibility will eventually come about. Given time and the temerity of the goofy with tenure, the current interest in animal rights among certain academics figures one day to issue in a defense of bestiality, not to speak of many papers with titles like "Bambi Under Late Capitalism," and before long English departments will be running ads in *The Chronicle of Higher Education* (the *Pravda* of academic life), seeking a moose who can teach the Romantics ("We Are An Equal Species Employer"). I exaggerate, perhaps; but I wouldn't bet against the future existence of those papers on Bambi.

Although some of the zaniness I have been recounting has shown up in various forms throughout the humanities and in the softer social sciences, it has hit departments of English and Romance languages particularly hard. Why this should be so is a question calling for a complicated answer, or answers. My own would begin with the recognition that not so long ago English and comparative literature departments in America seemed to harbor some of the more interesting minds in universities. Erich Auerbach, R. P. Blackmur, Cleanth Brooks, Kenneth Burke, John Crowe Ransom, I. A. Richards, Allen Tate, Lionel Trilling, Robert Penn Warren, Rene Wellek, Yvor Winters, and a good many others found work in them. (F. R. Leavis and William Empson, in England, ought to be added to their number.) These were not original thinkers, or even (with the exception of Auerbach) great scholars, but they did have an indisputable seriousness about them that was impressive in their own day and seems no less so in ours. Cumulatively, they lent a dignity to the study of literature that guaranteed that considerations of literary matters would not fall below a certain level of seriousness.

This impressive academic cadre was never replaced. Or at any rate the great names in academic literary study that succeeded them were of a different sort. Geoffrey Hartman, Harold Bloom, George Steiner, Paul de Man, Fredric Jameson were more European-minded, ambitious on behalf of criticism, extravagant in their intellectual pretensions. They at once enlarged the scope of literary study and somehow at the same time managed to drain it of its gravity. Cumulatively, they stood for little. Each critic seemed to be pretty much in business for himself. A critic of their own generation wrote a book whose title might have stood in as the motto for them all: The Performing Self. They could be brilliant, they were often obscure, they were intellectually unattractive, they stood for nothing, with the exception of Fredric Jameson, who was a highly paid Marxist at tobacco-rich Duke University (talk about what Marx himself called "the objective contradictions of capitalism").

Yet the New Criticism of Brooks, Warren, & Co. gave way as easily as it did to this newer, flashier, partially imported (from France) criticism quite as much for industrial as for intellectual reasons. Careful, close readings of literary works, chiefly poems, which was the specialty of the New Criticism, would always be an integral part of literary training, though it soon became unfashionable to acknowledge this fact while the New Criticism was under attack. Perhaps the New Criticism could have been more historical or biographical than it generally was—though it was never quite so bereft of history or biography as its attackers claimed. Perhaps there was a conservative bias to the New Critical method of reading literature. But the real problem was not that the methods of the New Criticism were useless as that they seemed used up. The literary landscape had been picked clean by them. Could one really bear yet another close reading of yet another poem by John Donne or William Blake? Did the world truly need another explanation of any of Kafka's stories or novels? The people forced to write such stuff—for tenure, for promotion, for self-justification—must have been bored blue. Let us not speak of those asked to read the stuff.

And so the time had come, as they used to say on "The Monty Python Show," for something completely different. In a careful, rather arid, considerably tendentious study of the development of the teaching and study of literature in American universities, Gerald Graff has shown that there has been a series of intramural conflicts within English departments almost from the beginning. There had been the conflicts between the belle-lettrists and the philologists, between the philologists and the generalists, between the generalists and the literary historians, between the literary historians and the New Critics, between the New Critics and the cultural critics. Generally these conflicts ended in compromise arrangements whereby there occurred a shift in the alignment of power and popularity of one or another method of teaching and study within particular departments and within the so-called "field" at large. Somehow the conflicts were never quite allowed to come into the open, though power had nonetheless shifted and the newer method had gained ascendancy. Business, though changed a bit here and there, went on pretty much as usual.

But beginning in the 1970s a much more radical program emerged. It was more radical in two distinct senses: first, it tended to be much more openly political than other programmatic attempts to alter the teaching and professional study of literature; and, second, its methods were a direct challenge not alone to literary criticism but to literature itself. Whereas other, earlier disputes within literature departments were about methodologies, about how literature could most profitably be studied, what was now being proposed was the quite original notion that literature was itself inherently false, corrupt, in need of destruction. I say "destruction," but the official word was of course "deconstruction," which as Alvin Kernan, in *The Death of Literature*, noted has been "the covering term increasingly used for the broad range of literary criticism that discredited the old literature . . . and charged it with having been mystifying, illogical, and harmful rather than beneficial."

When it all began is a bit difficult to ascertain with precision. A large residue of resentment was left over from the revolution in the universities that never quite came off, and this resentment was reinforced by large reserves of contempt for life as lived outside the university (all those people who twice elected Ronald Reagan) and immediate sympathy for anyone who claimed victim status, both of which are among the chief legacies of the sixties. But perhaps the first significant bookish evidence of the new impulse to degrade literature came in 1970, with the publication of Kate Millett's *Sexual Politics,* which revealed that certain writers—Norman Mailer and Henry Miller prominent among them—did not treat women very kindly in their novels. What came to be known as "gender studies" were on their way, and would get goofier and goofier with the passage of time, though doubtless my view of the matter is, as the academic feminists would put it, "phallocentric." A new generation of Marxists began to work the class angle, fortified with large draughts of Foucault and other Frenchmen, and also pitched in on the unending project of discovering literature, and especially American literature, shot through with racism. Complaint had become the heavy motif of criticism. Everywhere one encountered papers, courses, conferences devoted to gender, class, and race. "Gender, class, and race," announced a wag (me, actually), "gender, class, and race, stop your blubbering and wash your face."

Much of this new higher thinking seemed to originate from Yale. At Yale there was, more than a changing of the guard, a blowing up of the castle. Brooks, Warren, Wimsatt, Wellek out; Bloom, de Man, Hartman, Miller (J. Hillis) in. Randall Jarrell had long before warned that "critics are now so much better armed than they used to be in the old days; they've got tanks and flame throwers now, and it's harder to see past them to the work of art. . . ." To hear some of the Yale critics talk—Geoffrey Hartman, in particular—the work of criticism had all but supplanted the work of art. How could they get away with such extravagant pretensions? Alvin Kernan is not far off the money when he answered this question by writing: "The sharp decline in the quality of novels, poems, and plays of recent years offered an opportunity for the critic to gain some ground on the author, and the 'adversary culture's' attempt to seize power in the 1960s offered the occasion." Some of the Yale critics would later disavow the kind of criticism they had helped to usher in. Harold Bloom has called the hodgepodge of critical schools that emerged in the 1980s "the school of resentment" and "Foucault with soda water" and "a rabblement of lemmings." That last, "a rabblement of lemmings," is very good, but it probably oughtn't to be forgotten that Professor Bloom helped show them the way to the cliff.

I do not know what sound lemmings make, but you could almost hear the gurgle of delight that this newer criticism—which now began to go under the generic name of "theory"—gave to refugee professors from the land of the sixties and to the younger professoriat and to many graduate students. Here was a form of criticism that gave everyone who went in for it plenty of fresh work, and lots of it; all readings of literary works, theory had established for its adherents, were misreadings, and so criticism became a game that anyone could play. The major impulse of theory was suspicion, for it was interested above all in what is covert and what is absent from literary works, and as such it was chiefly concerned with tearing down not only the assumptions of earlier criticism but works of literature that this earlier criticism had raised up. In this regard theory gave that portion of the professoriat who came through the sixties unfulfilled, and those younger professors who chose to squeeze all they could out of their self-created status of victimhood, a large and lovely outlet for their resentment. By attacking the works of the great writers, by arguing against the right of many of them to belong to the canon, they were able to attack the culture that had produced them, and to attack it at its roots. Under the regime of theory, the instability of language was often featured, and of course if one undermines the stability of language one is ultimately undermining meaning itself. Meaning, it had more than once been averred among the theory crowd, yes meaning, with its demands for order and its insistence on authority, was fascist.

I fear that I have made the adherents of "theory" seem more monolithic than perhaps they are. They in fact divide off into little groups, factions, schools, which go by the names of structuralists, speech-act theorists, reader-response critics, new historicists, and (most famously) deconstructionists; and to this partial roll call one can add feminists and multiculturalists. In *Professing Literature,* Gerald Graff writes: "Theory is what is generated when some aspect of literature, its nature, its history, its place in society, its conditions of production and reception, its meaning in general, or the meanings of particular works, ceases to be given and becomes a question to be argued in a generalized way." In this reading, criticism would be about the meaning of literature and theory about the meaning of meaning. Graff may be correct when he says that what theorists have in common is an interest in "an inquiry into assumptions, premises, and legitimating principles and concepts." But this is not how theory has tended to work in practice, where it is usually more aggressive than Graff's comments suggest. "The stakes are enormous," the now dead Paul de Man is supposed to have told J. Hillis Miller, one of the original Yale brotherhood who has not given up on deconstruction and has himself remarked that "the violence and irrationality of the attacks on theory" have "now taken the strange form of the almost universal triumph of theory."

Just how "violent" and "irrational" have been the attacks on theory? One might have thought that this new, presumably radical work would have divided the world of literary studies, both at the level of the Modern Language Association and at that of the academic department. But it is not my sense that it did. For the most part, theory rather quickly won the day. Not that it made so many converts, for, apart from graduate students— who, sensing it was the hot thing, leading to jobs, went in for it in a big way—I don't think that it did. What happened instead is that most people teaching in literature departments went along with it. Some thought it would soon pass, and while it was here what did it matter if it didn't interfere with their own work. When I tried to get some of the grander names in English studies to write about the advent of theory for the magazine I edited, I found that many of them felt it was likely to be a fashion without much staying power; and, besides, none had the appetite for reading the vast amount of hideous prose required to do the job. Others felt that not only was it not worth fighting theory but that it might be a bit unsafe to come out against it. The contemporary academic has a taste for the going thing that was whetted by theory. When my own English department made an attempt to hire Fredric Jameson, I remarked to a colleague that I thought he was quite unreadable. "Who reads him?" he replied. "The point is that he has the reputation of being the leading Marxist in literary theory just now." He went on to report that a friend remarked of Jameson's having written a well-known book titled *The Prison-House of Language* that he, Jameson, ought to know all about that, having long been an inmate of the place himself. None of which, you understand, would have caused this man to vote against the department's hiring Jameson if it could. *Au* bloody *contraire*.

Those who came out strongly against theory—and they were not many—were promptly put down. Walter Jackson Bate attacked theory and was declared a back number, a crank. Frederick Crews, who read a vast amount of wretched prose in order to launch detailed criticisms of the new theoreticism, was adjudged a fanatic. Peter Shaw's tough analysis of feminist criticism was easily dismissed on the grounds of its author being a neo-conservative. Others wrote against theory in various places and with various degrees of disbelief, petulance, and horror, but none of this was sufficiently sustained. Theory operated on the prestige of the avant-garde, the nouvelle vague, the cutting edge, and other (all) good things. To set oneself against it was to join the camp of blackest reaction, where dwelt the homophobes, misogynists, racist dogs, conservatives, and other bad persons.

However deep their doubts about the value of theory, not many teachers have been willing to risk being put in this camp of blackguards. The contemporary university is a place of deep conformity, despite its outward appearance of being an Elysian Field in which the spirit is allowed to roam freely, and one that has ways of punishing heterodoxy sharply and forthwith. Unlike the storied professor of yesteryear sinking gently into a fog of pedantic senility, the contemporary professor is terrified of nothing so much as seeming out of it. With-itry, bound up with whatever esteem he can muster for himself, is crucial to his academic existence. Theory has been very much with-it for some while, especially among graduate students, and the professor concerned about retaining his standing had best not forget it. Whereas professors once existed in a state of superiority to graduate students, it is now no longer quite clear that they still do so. God pity the poor professor about whom the word goes round among graduate students that he is insufficiently (shall we say) attuned to feminism or any of the other OK-isms. Out he goes to the academic equivalent of Coventry, Novosibirsk, Lapland. To be in good odor with graduate students by establishing one's bona fides as a theoretical allrightnik is one way of avoiding this sad condition of internal exile, even if one doesn't actually teach the stuff. In part, this is why not many senior professors have come out strongly against theory; in the souls of the cowardly there is, finally, no tenure.

For the most part, the teaching of theory, apart from feminism, seems to be done chiefly at the graduate level. Some of it seeps down to undergraduate courses, where notes about the new term's offerings are likely to include such enticing promises as that this course "will emphasize the frequency with which certain conflicts—involving power and justice, moral evil and social corruption, freedom and authority, gender and sexuality—recur in the plays," or that "close attention will be paid to representations of gender, class, and 'nature' in these novels." I have had a number of feminists show up in my own courses for undergraduates, but none has ever pushed the line with such insistence as to impede interesting classroom discussion. Once I had a most earnest engineering student, a Jewish lad from St. Louis with untameable hair, who had just returned from a year abroad at Sussex University, where he came under the influence of deconstructionists, ask if, for his class paper, he could be allowed to deconstruct George Orwell. After he was done, Orwell, I have to report, was still standing and the poor kid appeared to have become quite unhinged by his own self-imposed task.

If my experience is reliable, then, theory is largely a graduate school phenomenon, with only occasional incursions into the undergraduate curriculum (always excepting feminism, which is pandemic). Teachers freely politicize their subjects without any sense that doing so might be wrong or at least unfair, but this has been going on since the sixties, when the traditional conception of academic freedom was jettisoned. The deeper nihilism implicit (often explicit) in much theory—the destabilizing of language, the view of intellectual order as a form of oppression—is probably too complicated to teach to undergraduates. One cannot, after all, undermine a text without first knowing how to mine it; one cannot show what is absent without first showing what is there.

Theory has been slowed, too, by the fact that after all this while there are few essays or books written by its proponents that lucidly set out its methods and demonstrate its significance. Ask someone who has been swept away by theory, or even someone who has not but nonetheless claims to feel its cogency, what one ought to read to discover its attractions, and one is likely to be met with an embarrassing pause, or should one say an embarrassing paucity. "Parts of Derrida's *Grammatology* are awfully good," one will be told (which parts are never specified), or else one is sent to some tome that turns out to be filled with barbed-wire language about "foregrounding the metaphoricity" or the "vertiginous possibilities of referential aberration." Undergraduates need to consider less vertiginous possibilities, even the brightest among them, though this doesn't mean that many a newly minted assistant professor, still sailing along on a theoretical high, might not get in there and give it his best shot. Meanwhile, for those of us who are able to sight neither emperor nor new clothes, it is not pleasant to think that the preponderance of graduate students from the better—and even from the not so good—universities are being trained to study literature from the standpoint of what is false and rubbishy about it. And in departments where deconstruction and theory generally prevail, as Frederick Crews has written, "it will deprive a good number of students of the mental discipline that the older deconstructionists themselves received in an earlier phase of our profession. Weariness of rational standards in one generation becomes a pathetic ignorance of them in the next."

The academics who wish to change the canon and hence the curriculum, who have set out to shake confidence in language and hence in meaning, who insist on the indeterminacy of all literary interpretation, who tediously bang their kettles about patriarchy, Eurocentrism, late capitalism, elitism, and the rest have a political program, however inchoate it may be in the minds of some among them. It is an intellectual version of the Whole Earth Catalog—a pallid, boiled-down, warmed-over, unisexual, blandified Woodstockian vision of heaven on earth. Heaven for them, as I see it, hell for the rest of us.

My sense is that a reasonable quantity of traditional teaching continues to be done—old dogs, as some clever fellow once pointed out, aren't all that easily taught new tricks—at least to undergraduates. Some of this teaching is quite as dull and dreary as it ever was; some (always, inevitably, less) is genuinely impressive in its ability to inculcate habits of intellectual lucidity, critical thinking, and appreciation for both great works and the literary mode of thought. But it's the gaudy and the egregious that have been ringing the gong for some years now—that get the good jobs, the attention, the largest portions of the modicum of power available in academic life.

As for jobs, those who don't have an "ism" after their names need not apply. In the English department in which I teach a job candidate was recently proposed who was both a new historicist and a feminist, and in response to her candidacy it was pointed out that the department already has someone who combines these two "isms" and cannot "afford the luxury" of hiring someone with the same intellectual profile. Five or six years ago, I suggested to a professor influential in the department the name, of a highly intelligent man with a reputation as an excellent teacher as a possible candidate for a job in our department. "No hope," he said, without any irony that I could detect, "I'm afraid that X [the man in question] is merely serious."

X still couldn't get a job in our department—nor, my guess is, in any other English department that is still if not dominated then at least cowed by theory and the theorists. To this extent, the situation has not changed. "I find it hard to imagine," wrote Frederick Crews of deconstruction, "that such a fashion will last for long." Fashions do change in universities, bad ideas can be disqualified, but things take longer than they do elsewhere in the world. Universities are on slower timetables than other corporations and concerns. One learns one is fired from a university teaching job and so must find another job—within fifteen or so months. A teacher is given tenure and he hangs around the joint for life. Then there is the percolating effect: fashions percolate down and so endure even longer. At Knox College, in Galesburg, Illinois, they are just now writing books about Jacques Lacan, and at the University of Oklahoma, in Norman, they are writing blurbs for them. Here is a little lineup of subjects presented by graduate students in Comparative Literature and Theory, English and Foreign Language departments presented at Northwestern:

1. "Feminist Revisionist Mythmaking in Rosario Castellano's *Officio tinieblas*"

2. "Race and (De) Constructions of Female Sexuality in *Incidents in the Life of a Slave Girl*"

3. "Reading the Author Out of Text: Chapters 15 & 16 of Gibbon's *Decline and Fall*"

4. "Adorno's Paradox Reconsidered: The Name of Auschwitz in Tournier and Wolf"

5. "Rethinking Cultural Studies: Notes from a Seminar at the Center of Psychosocial Studies."

Read 'em, as the poker players say, and weep. Fashions change but people with a strong emotional investment in ideas of their youth often don't. The students who wrote those papers, it is discouraging to recall, figure still to be teaching forty years from now.

Yet there is some evidence that the ground is shifting, if slowly. Sound argument hasn't brought about the shift so much as have extraordinary events. And none has been more extraordinary than the revelations about the Yale literary critic and leading American-based guru of deconstruction, Paul de Man, having in his young manhood in Belgium written a vast amount of literary journalism for a pro-Nazi newspaper—and some of it, in the light of subsequent history, of a kind that ought to keep a man twisting in his sheets in deep shame every night for the remainder of his life. The Paul de Man scandal provided delicious hot copy: bigamy, a deserted family, deep deception, an entire secret life, all of which de Man took to his grave, no doubt thinking it would be buried there with him forever. In the department of statements people wished they never made, Professor Barbara Johnson, of Harvard, might like to enter the following, which she uttered at Paul de Man's memorial service: "In a profession full of fakeness, he was real."

Long after the Paul de Man revelations, two writers of considerable academic respectability, Helen Vendler, the literary critic at Harvard, and John Searle, the philosopher at Berkeley, weighed in with pieces that hum with the spirit of Enough Already! Helen Vendler, who is a past president of the Modern Language Association, wrote a quietly authoritative but finally quite scorching piece on the untenability—not to say unhinged quality— of contemporary feminist writing. John Searle's was a more general essay, which allowed a great deal that once would have been chalked up to conservative fantasies: first, that "literature [has] become the academic home of radical left-wing politics"; second, that the argument about the canon, which seems to agitate so many academics fired up by ethnic and genderesque passions, is largely bogus, since in Searle's "experience there never was a fixed 'canon,' [but] rather a certain set of tentative judgments about what had importance and quality"; and, third, that the academic critics who have worked so hard to show the indeterminacy of language, interpretation, and finally meaning itself have really called off the game, for "if you think there is no reality that words could possibly correspond to, then obviously it will be a waste of time to engage in an 'objective and disinterested search for truth,' because there is no such thing as truth." It is of no small interest that both Professor Vendler's and Searle's essays appeared in the *New York Review of Books,* a journal with certified left-wing credentials and perhaps the first bastion of contemporary academic snobbery. That hit 'em, in other words, where it ought to have hurt.

I say "ought to," but I am not sure that these impressively argued attacks, or any other for that matter, could dent the armor of people living in what are essentially intellectual bunkers. The various theorists continue to spin their webs, demystifying the reactionary delusions of the rest of us in what before the fall of socialism they liked to call "late capitalism," sharing among themselves their turgid little ironies. The feminists roll on, perpetually angry. Thus, attacking conservatives, Catharine R. Stimpson, who is dean of the graduate school at Rutgers, says that "under the guise of defending objectivity and intellectual rigor, which is a lot of mishmash, they are trying to preserve the cultural and political supremacy of white heterosexual males." This from the woman who is the outgoing president of the Modern Language Association. So many loony tunes, so few merry melodies.

In his history of the teaching of literature in the United States, Gerald Graff quotes a Germanist named Calvin Thomas who said that the literary generalists of the 1890s produced work that was apt to be "interesting but not true," while the philologists, who were their rivals produced work "which is apt to be true but not very interesting." The theorists of our day produce work in which one finds little that is either interesting or true; and no one, certainly, would argue that its charm is in its high readability or elegance. As for its content, the "open text" that many among them vaunt, with its endless indeterminate meanings, is finally rather like the "open marriage" of the early 1970s, providing as it does plenty of room for screwing around and with no ultimate responsibility.

The model for the contemporary literature department, I have come to believe, is the Russian Duma under the Kerensky government. By this I mean that, though liberals may be in the majority, Bolsheviks always win. They win because they are impelled by the spirit of cause that only true believers know; because they don't mind using rough tactics and dirty tricks to further that cause; and because, ultimately and crushingly, the Menshevik-liberals are terrified of being associated with anything that smacks of sympathy for any facet of the *ancien régime.* In many English departments—that of Duke University comes first to mind—the Bolsheviks have already taken over. Elsewhere they make it hot for liberals who would rather eat ground glass than not do what is construed to be the right thing.

Doubtless everyone associated with literary studies in the university will spend time struggling against the logical outrages of theory and its affiliated zaniness. Perhaps, in education, it was always and ever thus, periods of brief progress interrupted by dips or serious plunges into obscurantism and nuttiness, one step forward, two steps back.

Such is the goofiness of current academic life that restating the obvious—that most great literature is indeed separable from politics, that true culture is above gender, race, and class, that the point of view literature teaches is inherently anti-system, anti-theory, and skeptical of all ideas that do not grow out of particular cases also known as poems, stories, essays, and plays—restating all this has become nearly a full-time job and often a wearying one. Still, at moments of fatigue, when the absurdity outweighs the comedy, I find it comforting to recall an item from the notebooks of the biologist Jean Rostand. "*Les theories passent*," Rostand noted. "*La grenouille reste.*"

Long live that frog and literature with it.

Lower Education

(2011)

ORTHWESTERN UNIVERSITY, the school at which I taught for 30 years, has been visited by a delicious little scandal. A tenured professor, teaching a heavily attended undergraduate course on human sexuality, decided to bring in a woman, who, with the aid of what was euphemistically called "a sex toy" (uneuphemistically, it appears to have been an electric dildo), attempted to achieve a climax in the presence of the students. The professor alerted his students about this extraordinary show-and-tell session, and made clear that attendance was voluntary. The standard account has it that 120 or so of the 622 students enrolled in the course showed up. Questions about what they had witnessed, the professor punctiliously noted, would not be on the exam.

The professor, J. Michael Bailey, is a man with a reputation for specializing in the *outré*. (Northwestern ought perhaps to consider itself fortunate that he didn't teach a course in Aztec history, or he might have offered a demonstration of human sacrifice.) The word got out about the demonstration he had arranged, journalists quickly got on the case, and Northwestern found itself hugely embarrassed, its officials concerned lest parents think it was offering, at roughly $55,000 a year, the educational equivalent of a stag party.

The president of Northwestern, a man named Morton Schapiro, issued what might be termed Standard Response #763; every contemporary university president has a thousand or so of these equivocal responses in the kit that comes with the job. This one read:

> I have recently learned of the after-class activity associated with Prof. Michael Bailey's Human Sexuality class, and I am troubled and disappointed by what occurred.
>
> Although the incident took place in an after-class session that students were not required to attend and students were advised in advance, several times, of the explicit nature of the activity, I feel it represented extremely poor judgment on the part of our faculty member. I simply do not believe this was appropriate, necessary or in keeping with Northwestern University's academic mission.
>
> Northwestern faculty members engage in teaching and research on a wide variety of topics, some of them controversial. That is the nature of a university. However, in this instance, I have directed that we investigate fully the specifics of this incident, and also clarify what constitutes appropriate pedagogy, both in this instance and in the future.
>
> Many members of the Northwestern community are disturbed by what took place on our campus. So am I.

I have never met President Schapiro, but I have begun to establish a relationship with him. This relationship may be compared to that of a tsetse fly with a white settler in the Congo. As an emeritus faculty member, I have, in other words, decided, without waiting to be asked, to be a pest. When, for example, a month or so ago it was announced that Northwestern had selected Stephen Colbert for this year's commencement speaker, I sent President Schapiro the following email:

> I was a touch saddened, though not greatly surprised, to discover that you have chosen Stephen Colbert as this year's commencement speaker. In this you follow the low tradition of choosing commencement speakers from television journalism, show business, and the realm of minor celebrity. I know

> Mr. Colbert is a Northwestern graduate, and I am sure he
> will prove, in the cant phrase, a fun speaker. But the choice
> of Stephen Colbert is pure public relations, and not in any
> way an educational choice. I'm not sure you will grasp this,
> but I thought it worth mentioning.

President Schapiro wrote back to assure me that he had grasped my meaning and also to predict that the graduating students would arise from Mr. Colbert's talk "inspired." I replied, "I'm sure that Stephen Colbert will be every bit as inspiring as Julia Louis-Dreyfus was three or four years ago or as Diane Sawyer will be next year," and promised not to write to him soon again.

The current scandal over Professor Bailey's sex demonstration caused me to break my promise. Rosinante to the road again, I mounted my computer and tapped out the following: "I have just read your statement on what we may now term the Michael Bailey Dildo Scandal. I would have liked it a bit better if you'd added a final sentence, which read: 'And so I have decided to have Professor Bailey castrated, the schmuck deserves no less.' . . . Isn't the faculty lots of fun?" President Schapiro, who gets high marks for equanimity, wrote back: "Never a dull moment." And not many enlightening ones, either, I thought to answer but did not.

Professor J. Michael Bailey has a sex lab at the university, which turns out to be not at all like Masters and Johnson's lab, set up to do intricate physiological recording—"a blow-by-blow account of the clitoris in action," as one of their critics once described it—but a room with a few computers in it. A somewhat softish-looking man, balding, he was recently photographed in open-necked shirt and jeans (leisure cut, to be sure). But then perhaps a sexologist ought not to be too elegant, or even comely. Mrs. Johnson, of Masters and Johnson sexological fame, looked like nothing so much as a prison matron, and Dr. Masters resembled a little the evil Dr. Sivana in the old Captain Marvel comics. One of the founding fathers of sex studies, Alfred Kinsey, a serious masochist who in his spare time went in for self-circumcision, after a hard day at the office measuring the intensity of male orgasms, used regularly to be seen in Bloomington, Indiana, watering his lawn in a bikini. A strong tendency exists for sexologists to go native.

On his Northwestern home page, Professor Bailey provides a picture of himself in his high-school graduating class, when he wore his red hair shoulder-length. He lists his favorite albums—"I think you can tell a lot from someone by the kind of music they listen to," he writes—the symphonies of Shostakovich or the Beethoven late quartets not among them. Divorced and the father of a son and daughter, he also offers a picture of his former wife, whom he describes as "a generally cool woman" and Dave, her new husband or boyfriend, it isn't clear which, "who is equally cool." Thanks, professor, for sharing.

Professor Bailey wrote a book called *The Man Who Would Be Queen*, which apparently argues that homosexuality is innate, not the result of nurture, and which caused some controversy among politically minded homosexuals. The section of his book on transgendering especially inflamed transgendered readers, arguing as it did against the standard view that men who wish to cross genders are really the victims of a biological mistake; Bailey's view is that such men are instead motivated by erotic fantasies of themselves as females. The heat he took for this, mostly played out on the Internet, was hot and heavy.

The sex demonstration controversy is not the first to have visited Professor Bailey. Earlier a transgendered woman complained that she had had consensual sex with Bailey after discussions having to do with his research. Two transsexual professors on Northwestern's faculty filed a claim that he, who is not a registered psychologist—where, one wonders, does one go to register?—inappropriately wrote letters evaluating whether candidates were ready for sex-reassignment (happy phrase) surgery. In another instance four women claimed he failed to alert them that he was using discussions with them about their sexuality for a book. In each case, Northwestern concluded that Professor Bailey either was being harassed or was operating within scientific guidelines or else chose not to press the matter. A man with a penchant for smashing taboos, Professor Bailey enjoys pushing the envelope, but, like many another radical academic, prefers not to pay the postage.

As for the most recent controversy, Professor Bailey's first defense was to go on the offensive. "I think that these after-class events are quite valuable. Why? One reason is that I think it helps us understand sexual diversity." (Ah, diversity, the leading buzzword of the contemporary university.)

"Sticks and stones may break your bones," he said, "but watching naked people on stage doing pleasurable things will never hurt you."

"I regret upsetting so many people in this particular manner," he said. "I apologize. . . . In the 18 years I have taught the course, nothing like the demonstration at issue has occurred, and I will allow nothing like it to happen again," he said. Getting in a last shot, though, he added, "Thoughtful discussion of controversial topics is a cornerstone of learning." And for Fox News he noted, "Earlier that day in my lecture I had talked about the attempts to silence sex research, and how this largely reflected sex negativity. . . . I did not wish, and I do not wish, to surrender to sex negativity and fear."

"It's science, pal," Professor Bailey's defense in effect is, "and I am a courageous scientist, out there on the edge, so shut up and pass the K-Y, and grab a handful of Viagra pills on your way out." Bailey's remarks are the social-scientific equivalent of the old avant-garde blackmail. Bailey would have us know that he is doing edgy science; and the implicit blackmail here is that if we are not with him out there on the edge then we are intellectual philistines, no better than those people who, more than a century ago, attempted to scratch the paint off French Impressionist paintings. Disagree with Professor Bailey's views, in other words, and you are rearguard, a back number, one of those "fools in old style hats and coats, / Who half the time were soppy stern / And half at one another's throats."

What is of interest here is the professor's apparently genuine puzzlement that anything untoward was going on. Was there? Let us assume that human sexuality of the kind on display is a legitimate subject of social-scientific inquiry. The question is, why bring undergraduate students, who are neither scientists nor social scientists, in on the actual research itself? Might the justification be that watching an abnormal woman with the aid of an electrical device attempt orgasm before an audience of young strangers will make the students' own sex lives better? Or was Professor Bailey merely running a sideshow on the wackiness of human nature? Pretty flimsy, in either case.

One wonders if Professor Bailey isn't the heir all-too-apparent of decades of misunderstanding of the meaning of academic freedom. When did this understanding break down? The rough answer is: over many years, though it took its most drastic drop during the 1960s. Academic freedom is that unwritten body of assumptions and unspoken standard of ethics that has implicitly ruled university education from its earliest days. Without going into intricate detail on particulars, it is the freedom that scholars and scientists require if they are to pursue their studies and researches and their obligation to pass on their knowledge through teaching.

In earliest times, academic freedom's greatest opponent was religion, which in the nineteenth century felt its tenets being violated by biblical criticism and by the findings of geology. (Darwin, fortunately, was not attached to a university, nor was the great geologist Charles Lyell, so neither required academic freedom for his researches.) Earlier in the American twentieth century, academics were often under fire for their political opinions and causes they supported outside the classroom. Academic freedom would support a university teacher who thought himself a socialist or pro-union, or held nearly any other view, no matter how far out of the mainstream, so long as he did not argue for it or otherwise inflict his views on students in the classroom.

Northwestern has long boasted a stellar instance of the protection afforded by academic freedom by having on its engineering faculty a man named Arthur R. Butz, the author of *The Hoax of the Twentieth Century: The Case Against the Presumed Extermination of European Jewry*. Butz is an unembarrassed, in fact a rather aggressive, Holocaust denier, but because he doesn't express this view in the classroom, where, as a teacher of electrical engineering, he specializes in things called control system theory and digital signal processing, his job is safe. (In a world where side effects sometimes seem greater than central ones, Butz's position on the Northwestern faculty may even be said to have been good for the Jews. Partly owing to him, wealthy Jewish patrons have installed a Holocaust studies chair at Northwestern, and other Jewish alumni have set up Jewish centers of study at the school. One can almost hear them muttering, above the scratching of the pen upon their checks, "I'll show that S. O. B. Butz . . .") Meanwhile Butz, through the sufferance of academic freedom, keeps his job, and rightly so.

Academic freedom, though, works two ways. While it protects university teachers from outside forces that would inhibit them, it also sets a standard of conduct on what doesn't deserve to be protected by academic freedom. In "The Demand of the Academic Profession for Academic Freedom," Edward Shils wrote about this subject with great force and subtlety. Along with much else, Shils notes that academic freedom might be rightly abrogated "from a genuine conviction that [a scholar's or scientist's] research is unacceptable according to strictly intellectual standards," and that "academic freedom is primarily the freedom to do serious academic things without obstructions imposed with other intentions in mind." Academic freedom, as Shils also notes, is a specialized right that is "hedged about by obligations and conditions." Some of these have to do with academic behavior on the job, for not alone in dreams but in freedom begins responsibility.

When I began teaching at Northwestern in 1973, the smoke had not yet cleared from the student revolution. I recall at the time hearing gossip about a teacher who was sleeping with one of his students, and when I checked with a friend on the faculty, he confirmed that it was likely true. "Do many younger professors sleep with their undergraduate students?" I asked this same friend. "I don't know many who don't" was his rather casual reply.

Does sleeping with one's undergraduate students come under the shield of academic freedom, or was it instead an academic perk, or ought it, again, to be admonished, if not punished by dismissal? Although a youngish bachelor at the time, I eschewed the practice myself, chiefly because I thought sleeping with one's students was poor sportsmanship—fish in a barrel and all that—and my own taste happened to run to grown-up women; I also thought it was, not to put too fine or stuffy a point on it, flat-out wrong. I wondered, too, if in its taking unfair advantage—a teacher after all has the power of awarding grades to students—it wasn't an obvious violation of academic freedom, and not merely crummy.

Someone wishing to argue the other way might say that, by the end of the 1960s in America, there were not all that many college girls who could any longer be considered innocent. In these sexual transactions, they might go on to argue, it wasn't always clear who was seducing whom. That such an argument can be made shows how the culture impinges upon the university. In an earlier age, the university preferred to think itself as outside of, and if truth be told superior to, the general culture of the society in which it functioned.

For many people today, the more the culture impinges upon the university the better. From the 1960s and perhaps well before, they longed for the university to reflect the culture by being more open, democratic, multicultural, with-it, relevant. These people have seen their longings come to pass. Pursuing the old ideal of the university existing in splendid isolation, a place for the cultivation of the mind, where scholarship is garnered in tranquility and important scientific research done without the pressures of commerce or government—this ideal, the ideal of Cardinal Newman and Matthew Arnold, is no longer available. In the culture wars, the fall of the university was equivalent to the battle of Aegospotami in the Peloponnesian War: After it, Athens, and American culture, was never the same.

One of the most important things that departed from higher education with the old ideal of the university was intellectual authority. One of the first changes I noticed from my own undergraduate education when I began teaching at Northwestern—and this is certainly not true of Northwestern alone—was all the junky subject matter being taught. Courses in science fiction, in the movies, in contemporary or near contemporary writers already consigned to the third class, along with many courses that sounded more like magazine articles in quite boring magazines. At an earlier time, a powerful department chairman might have put the kibosh on the notion of courses on the Beat Generation or on secondary women writers or on soap opera as drama or on graphic novels or on videogames for the good reason that such things were insufficiently serious. Not anymore. No powerful department chairmen any longer existed—democratic departmental procedures had done them in—nor is there anything like a rough general consensus in the contemporary university about what is serious in the realm of culture and ideas. Who is to say that the films of Steven Spielberg are less important than the plays of Shakespeare, or for that matter that Shakespeare himself wasn't gay and a running dog of capitalism into the bargain?

Nor are there any figures higher up the academic ladder who can be counted upon to call a halt to the nonsense. No provost such as Jacques Barzun at Columbia, no university president such as Robert Hutchins at Chicago, now exists. If one is hard-pressed to name a single university president today, it is chiefly because none has much to do with actual education. The last major university president to concern himself with the educational content of his school—with appointments and with what was actually being taught—was John Silber of Boston University, and his efforts were far from appreciated by a large portion of his faculty. The contemporary university president's main tasks now, as everyone knows, are to siphon off money from the rich and put out little fires with wet public-relations blankets.

Higher education used to be an elite endeavor. The acquisition, in Matthew Arnold's formulation, of "the best which has been thought and said" was what it was supposed to be about. But one has to have the authority to know what really is best, and confidence in the belief that acquiring it is decisive. This, somehow, was lost. And once it was, great subjects in the university curriculum were increasingly replaced by hot ones; just as often, traditional subjects were corrupted by politics in ways that constituted a frontal assault on academic freedom, though not many people in the university seemed either to notice or much to mind.

There is always faculty ready to back up the most egregious behavior of colleagues. In the case of J. Michael Bailey, the *Chronicle of Higher Education* chimed in with an article by an assistant professor of sociology at Middlebury College named Laurie Essig, who finds the Northwestern sex scandal, as we now say, a great teachable moment. Professor Essig is of the view that shaking things up, attacking the status quo, is of the very essence of education, what the whole enterprise is really about.

"Clearly," Essig writes, "this 'live sex act' triggered a national conversation about what we can and cannot look at." She goes on to ask "what is it about the fact that there were people there on the stage that makes it different than a film with a sex scene or a book with a sex scene? . . . Why are we so damn uncomfortable with sex that is not mediated by film or text that ABC, CNN, and all the rest of the media outlets can't stop talking about it?" Essig even wonders if "the live sex act had occurred between a straight, vanilla, normatively gendered and married couple, would we have cared as much?" She concludes: "These all seem like important questions and questions that can be asked because a professor allowed something to happen in his classroom and triggered a national debate about the dangers of sex and education getting into bed together."

Professor Essig joins Professor Bailey as one of the university's shock troops. A student I talked with, who had earlier taken Bailey's human sexuality course and who did not otherwise speak harshly of him, noted that he seemed more than normally pleased to shock his audience of students. Does Professor Bailey, one has to wonder, thrill to his own acts of *épater les bourgeois*? Does he, so to say, get off in his combined role as Pied Piper, Krafft-Ebing, and the Diaghilev of the kinky?

Because of the great ruckus that his sex demonstration caused, Professor Bailey later allowed that, if he had to make the decision to stage the sex demonstration again, he probably wouldn't do it. But then he remarked: "Those who believe that there was, in fact, a serious problem have had considerable opportunity to explain why: in the numerous media stories on the controversy, or in their various correspondences with me. But they have failed to do so. Saying that the demonstration 'crossed the line,' 'went too far,' 'was inappropriate,' or 'was troubling' conveys disapproval but does not illuminate reasoning."

Allow here a small attempt at illumination. Because a subject exists in the world doesn't mean that universities have to take it up, no matter how edgy it may seem. Let books be written about it, let research be done upon it, if the money to support it can be found, but the nature and quality and even the sociology of sexual conduct—all material available elsewhere in more than plentitude for the truly interested—does not cry out for classroom study. Students don't need universities to learn about varying tastes in sex, or about the mechanics of human sexuality. They don't need it because, first, epistemologically, human sexuality isn't a body of knowledge upon which there is sufficient agreement to constitute reliable conclusions, for nearly everything on the subject is still in the flux of theorizing and speculation; and because, second, given the nature of the subject, it tends to be, as the Bailey case shows, exploitative, coarsening, demeaning, and squalid.

Difficult to understand how an expert in the field such as Professor Bailey missed the obvious analogy, but in the demonstration he arranged for his students the poor woman is little better than a prostitute, the students pathetic johns-voyeurs, and he himself, quite simply, the pimp. A curious role for a university teacher to play, but I guess it's a living.

English As It's Taught

(2011)

THE EDITORS OF *The Cambridge History of the American Novel* decided to consider their subject—as history is considered increasingly in universities these days—from the bottom up. In 71 chapters, the book's contributors consider the traditional novel in its many sub-forms, among them: science fiction, eco-fiction, crime and mystery novels, Jewish novels, Asian-American novels, African-American novels, war novels, postmodern novels, feminist novels, suburban novels, children's novels, non-fiction novels, graphic novels and novels of disability ("We cannot truly know a culture until we ask its disabled citizens to describe, analyze, and interpret it," write the authors of a chapter titled "Disability and the American Novel"). Other chapters are about subjects played out in novels—for instance, ethnic and immigrant themes—and still others about publishers, book clubs, discussion groups and a good deal else. "The Cambridge History of the Novel," in short, provides full-court-press coverage.

"In short," though, is perhaps the least apt phase for a tome that runs to 1,244 pages and requires a forklift to hoist onto one's lap. All that the book's editors left out is why it is important or even pleasurable to read novels and how it is that some novels turn out to be vastly better than others. But, then, this is a work of literary history, not of literary criticism. Randall Jarrell's working definition of the novel as "a prose narrative of some length that has something wrong with it" has, in this voluminous work, been ruled out of bounds.

Most readers are unlikely to have heard of the contributors to "The Cambridge History of the American Novel," the majority teachers in English departments in American universities. I myself, who taught in a such a department for three decades, recognized the names of only four among them. Only 40 or 50 years ago, English departments attracted men and women who wrote books of general intellectual interest and had names known outside the academy—Perry Miller, Aileen Ward, Walter Jackson Bate, Marjorie Hope Nicolson, Joseph Wood Krutch, Lionel Trilling, one could name a dozen or so others—but no longer. Literature, as taught in the current-day university, is strictly an intramural game.

This may come as news to the contributors to "The Cambridge History of the American Novel," who pride themselves on possessing much wider, much more relevant, interests and a deeper engagement with the world than their predecessors among literary academics. Biographical notes on contributors speak of their concern with "forms of moral personhood in the US novels," "the poetics of foreign policy," and "ecocriticism and theories of modernization, post-modernization, and globalization."

Yet, through the magic of dull and faulty prose, the contributors to "The Cambridge History of the American Novel" have been able to make these presumably worldly subjects seem parochial in the extreme—of concern only to one another, which is certainly one derogatory definition of the academic. These scholars may teach English, but they do not always write it, at least not quite. A novelist, we are told, "tasks himself" with this or that; things tend to get "problematized"; the adjectives "global" and "post"-this-or-that receive a good workout; "alterity" and "intertexuality" pop up their homely heads; the "poetics of ineffability" come into play; and "agency" is used in ways one hadn't hitherto noticed, so that "readers in groups demonstrate agency." About the term "non-heteronormativity" let us not speak.

These dopey words and others like them are inserted into stiffly mechanical sentences of dubious meaning. "Attention to the performativity of straight sex characterizes . . . *The Great Gatsby* (1925), where Nick Carraway's homoerotic obsession with the theatrical Gatsby offers a more authentic passion precisely through flamboyant display." Betcha didn't know that Nick Carraway was hot for Jay Gatsby? We sleep tonight; contemporary literary scholarship stands guard.

"The Cambridge History of the American Novel" is perhaps best read as a sign of what has happened to English studies in recent decades. Along with American Studies programs, which are often their subsidiaries, English departments have tended to become intellectual nursing homes where old ideas go to die. If one is still looking for that living relic, the fully subscribed Marxist, one is today less likely to find him in an Economics or History Department than in an English Department, where he will still be taken seriously. He finds a home there because English departments are less concerned with the consideration of literature per se than with what novels, poems, plays and essays—after being properly X-rayed, frisked, padded down, like so many suspicious-looking air travelers—might yield on the subjects of race, class and gender. "How would [this volume] be organized," one of its contributors asks, "if race, gender, disability, and sexuality were not available?"

In his introduction to "The Cambridge History of the American Novel," Leonard Cassuto, a professor of English at Fordham and most recently the author of "Hard-Boiled Sentimentality: The Secret History of American Crime Stories" (2009), writes that the present volume "synthesizes the divisions between the author-centered literary history of yesterday and the context-centered efforts of recent years." Yet context is where the emphasis preponderantly falls.

One of the better essays in the book, Tom Lutz's "Cather and the Regional Imagination," is only secondarily about Willa Cather. It is primarily about what constitutes the cosmopolitan ideal in fiction, which Miss Cather embodied and which turns out to be an imaginative mixture of wide culture and deep psychological penetration, lending a richness to any subject, no matter how ostensibly provincial. This is what lifts such novels of Cather's as *My Antonia* and *Death Comes for the Archbishop* above regional fiction and gives them their standing as world literature.

"The Cambridge History of the American Novel" could only have come into the world after the death of the once-crucial distinction between high and low culture, a distinction that, until 40 or so years ago, dominated the criticism of literature and all the other arts. Under the rule of this distinction, critics felt it their job to close the gates on inferior artistic products. The distinction started to break down once the works of contemporary authors began to be taught in universities.

The study of popular culture—courses in movies, science fiction, detective fiction, works at first thought less worthy of study in themselves than for what they said about the life of their times—made the next incursion into the exclusivity of high culture. Multiculturalism, which assigned an equivalence of value to the works of all cultures, irrespective of the quality of those works, finished off the distinction between high and low culture, a distinction whose linchpin was seriousness.

In today's university, no one is any longer in a position to say which books are or aren't fit to teach; no one any longer has the authority to decide what is the best in American writing. Too bad, for even now there is no consensus about who are the best American novelists of the past century. (My own candidates are Cather and Theodore Dreiser.) Nor will you read a word, in the pages of "The Cambridge History of the American Novel," about how short-lived are likely to be the sex-obsessed works of the much-vaunted novelists Norman Mailer, John Updike and Philip Roth or about the deleterious effect that creative-writing programs have had on the writing of fiction.

With the gates once carefully guarded by the centurions of high culture now flung open, the barbarians flooded in, and it is they who are running the joint today. The most lauded novelists in "The Cambridge History of the American Novel" tend to be those, in the words of another of its contributors, who are "staging a critique of 'America' and its imperial project." Thus such secondary writers as Allen Ginsberg, Kurt Vonnegut and E. L. Doctorow are in these pages vaunted well beyond their literary worth.

A stranger, freshly arrived from another planet, if offered as his introduction to the United States only this book, would come away with a picture of a country founded on violence and expropriation, stoked through its history by every kind of prejudice and class domination, and populated chiefly by one or another kind of victim, with time out only for the mental sloth and apathy brought on by life lived in the suburbs and the characterless glut of American late capitalism. The automatic leftism behind this picture is also part of the reigning ethos of the current-day English Department.

As a former English major, I cannot help wondering what it must be like to be taught by the vast majority of the people who have contributed to "The Cambridge History of the American Novel." Two or three times a week one would sit in a room and be told that nothing that one has read is as it appears but is instead informed by authors hiding their true motives even from themselves or, in the best "context-centered" manner, that the books under study are the product of a country built on fundamental dishonesty about the sacred subjects of race, gender and class.

Some indication of what it must be like is indicated by the steep decline of American undergraduates who choose to concentrate in English. English majors once comprised 7.6% of undergraduates, but today the number has been nearly halved, down to 3.9%. Part of this decline is doubtless owing to the worry inspired in the young by a fragile economy. (The greatest rise is in business and economics majors.) Yet that is far from the whole story. William Chace, a former professor of English who was subsequently president of Wesleyan University and then Emory University, in a 2009 article titled "The Decline of the English Department," wrote:

> What are the causes for this? There are several, but at the root is the failure of departments of English across the country to champion, with passion, the books they teach and to make a strong case to undergraduates that the knowledge of those books and the tradition in which they exist is a human good in and of itself. What departments have done instead is dismember the curriculum, drift away from the notion that historical chronology is important, and substitute for the books themselves a scattered array of secondary considerations (identity studies, abstruse theory, sexuality, film and popular culture). In so doing, they have distanced themselves from the young people interested in good books.

Undergraduates who decided to concentrate their education on literature were always a slightly odd, happily nonconformist group. No learning was less vocational; to announce a major in English was to proclaim that one wasn't being educated with the expectation of a financial payoff. One was an English major because one was intoxicated by literature—its beauty, its force, above all its high truth quotient.

In the final chapter of "The Cambridge History of the American Novel," titled "A History of the Future of Narrative," the novelist Robert Coover argues that, though the technologies of reading and writing may be changing and will continue to change, the love of stories—reading them and writing them—will always be with us. Let's hope he is right. Just don't expect that love to be encouraged and cultivated, at least in the near future, in American universities.

The Death of the Liberal Arts

(2012)

WHEN ASKED WHAT HE THOUGHT about the cultural wars, Irving Kristol is said to have replied, "They're over," adding, "We lost." If Kristol was correct, one of the decisive battles in that war may have been over the liberal arts in education, which we also lost.

In a loose definition, the "liberal arts" denote college study anchored in preponderantly Western literature, philosophy, and history, with science, mathematics, and foreign languages playing a substantial, though less central, role; in more recent times, the social science subjects—psychology, sociology, political science—have also sometimes been included. The liberal arts have always been distinguished from more specialized, usually vocational training. For the ancient Greeks, the liberal arts were the subjects thought necessary for a free man to study. If he is to remain free, in this view, he must acquire knowledge of the best thought of the past, which will cultivate in him the intellectual depth and critical spirit required to live in an informed and reasonable way in the present.

For many years, the liberal arts were my second religion. I worshipped their content, I believed in their significance, I fought for them against the philistines of our age as Samson fought against the Philistines of his—though in my case, I kept my hair and brought down no pillars. As currently practiced, however, it is becoming more and more difficult to defend the liberal arts. Their content has been drastically changed, their significance is in doubt, and defending them in the condition in which they linger on scarcely seems worth the struggle.

The loss of prestige of the liberal arts is part of the general crisis of higher education in the United States. The crisis begins in economics. Larger numbers of Americans start college, but roughly a third never finish—more women finish, interestingly, than do men. With the economic slump of recent years, benefactions to colleges are down, as are federal and state grants, thus forcing tuition costs up, in public as well as in private institutions. Inflation is greater in the realm of higher education than in any other public sphere. Complaints about the high cost of education at private colleges—fees of $50,000 and $60,000 a year are commonly mentioned—are heard everywhere. A great number of students leave college with enormous student-loan debt, which is higher than either national credit card or automobile credit debt. Because of the expense of traditional liberal arts colleges, greater numbers of the young go to one or another form of commuter college, usually for vocational training.

Although it is common knowledge that a person with a college degree will earn a great deal more than a person without one—roughly a million dollars more over a lifetime is the frequently cited figure—today, students with college degrees are finding it tough to get decent jobs. People are beginning to wonder if college, at its currently extravagant price, is worth it. Is higher education, like tech stocks and real estate, the next big bubble to burst?

A great deal of evidence for the crisis in American higher education is set out in *College: What It Was, Is, and Should Be*. Its author, Andrew Delbanco, a biographer of Herman Melville, is a staunch defender of liberal arts, as he himself studied them as an undergraduate at Harvard and as he teaches them currently at Columbia. The continuing diminution of the liberal arts worries him. Some 18 million people in the United States are now enrolled in one or another kind of undergraduate institution of higher learning—but fewer than 100,000 are enrolled in liberal arts colleges.

At the same time, for that small number of elite liberal arts colleges—Harvard, Yale, Princeton, Stanford, Duke, the University of Chicago, and a few others—applications continue to rise, despite higher and higher tuition fees. The ardor to get into these schools—for economic, social, and snobbish reasons—has brought about an examination culture, at least among the children of the well-to-do, who from preschool on are relentlessly trained to take the examinations that will get them into the better grade schools, high schools, colleges, and, finally, professional schools. Professor Delbanco is opposed to the economic unfairness behind these arrangements, believing, rightly, that as a result, "the obstacles [to getting into the elite colleges] that bright low-income students face today are more insidious than the frank exclusionary practices that once prevailed."

Whether students today, despite all their special tutoring and testing, are any better than those of earlier generations is far from clear. Trained almost from the cradle to smash the SATs and any other examination that stands in their way, the privileged among them may take examinations better, but it is doubtful if their learning and intellectual understanding are any greater. Usually propelled by the desires of their parents, they form a meritocracy that, in Delbanco's view, as in that of the English sociologist Michael Young whom he quotes, comprises a dystopia of sorts, peopled by young men and women driven by high, but empty, ambition. "Are these really the people we want running the world?" Delbanco asks. Unfortunately, they already are. I am not the only one, surely, to have noticed that some of the worst people in this country—names on request—are graduates of the Harvard and Yale law schools.

Attending one of a limited number of elite colleges continues to yield wide opportunities for graduates, but fewer and fewer people any longer believe that someone who has finished college is necessarily all that much smarter than someone who hasn't. With standards lowered, hours of study shortened, reports appearing about how many college graduates can no longer be depended upon to know how to write or to grasp rudimentary intellectual concepts, having gone to college seems to have less and less bearing on a person's intelligence.

Studies cited by Delbanco in his footnotes claim an increase among college students in cheating, drinking, and depression. In their book *Academically Adrift*, Richard Arum and Josipa Roska argue that the gain in critical thinking and complex reasoning among the majority of students during college years is very low, if not minimal. In an article in the *Chronicle of Higher Education* drawn from their book, Arum and Roska write:

> Parents—although somewhat disgruntled about increasing costs—want colleges to provide a safe environment where their children can mature, gain independence, and attain a credential that will help them be successful as adults. Students in general seek to enjoy the benefits of a full collegiate experience that is focused as much on social life as on academic pursuits, while earning high marks in their courses with relatively little investment of effort. Professors are eager to find time to concentrate on their scholarship and professional interests. Administrators have been asked to focus largely on external institutional rankings and the financial bottom line. Government funding agencies are primarily interested in the development of new scientific knowledge. . . . No actors in the system are primarily interested in undergraduates' academic growth, although many are interested in student retention and persistence.

What savvy employers are likely to conclude is that those who graduate from college are probably more conformist, and therefore likely to be more dependable, than those who do not. Paul Goodman, one of the now-forgotten gurus of the 1960s, used to argue that what finishing college really meant is that one was willing to do anything to succeed in a capitalist society. In getting a college degree, Goodman held, one was in effect saying, I want in on the game, deal me a hand, I want desperately to play. Education, meanwhile, didn't have a lot to do with it.

Not everywhere in higher education have standards slipped. One assumes that in engineering and within the sciences they have been maintained, and in some ways, owing to computer technology, perhaps improved. Relatively new fields of learning, computer science chief among them, have not been around long enough to have lost their way. Medical and legal education are probably not greatly different than they have traditionally been. Chiefly in the liberal arts subjects do standards seem most radically to have dropped.

Apart from eliminating corporal punishment and widening the educational franchise, we can't be sure if, over the centuries, we have made much progress in education. At the moment there is great enthusiasm about "advances" in education owing to the Internet. Two teachers at Stanford, for example, put their course on Artificial Intelligence online and drew an audience of 160,000 students from all around the world. But science, which deals in one right answer, is more easily taught without a physical presence in the room, and probably works better online than humanities courses, whose questions usually have many answers, few of them permanently right. The *Washington Monthly*, in its May-June issue, has a special section called "The Next Wave of School Reform," a wave that, in the words of the editor, aims to "improve students' ability to think critically and independently, solve complex problems, apply knowledge to novel situations, work in teams and communicate effectively." The problem with these waves of school reform, of course, is that a new one is always needed because the last one turns out to have tossed up more detritus on the shore than was expected.

The fact is that we still don't know how to assess teaching—trial by student test scores, except in rudimentary subjects, isn't very helpful—and we remain ignorant about the true nature of the transaction between teacher and student that goes by the name of learning. In undergraduate education, we may even have retreated a step or two through the phenomenon known as grade inflation and through the politicization of curricula.

The division between vocational and liberal arts education, which began during the 19th century with the advent of the land-grant state universities in the United States, is today tilting further and further in favor of the vocational. Even within the liberal arts, more and more students are, in Delbanco's words, "fleeing from 'useless' subjects to 'marketable' subjects such as economics," in the hope that this will lend them the practical credentials and cachets that might impress prospective employers.

Delbanco reminds us of Max Weber's distinction between "soul-saving" and "skill-acquiring" education. The liberal arts, in their task to develop a certain roundedness in those who study them and their function, in Delbanco's phrase, "as a hedge against utilitarian values," are (or at least were meant to be) soul-saving. Whether, in the majority of students who undertook to study the liberal arts, they truly were or not may be open to question, but what isn't open to question is that today, the liberal arts have lost interest in their primary mission. That mission, as Delbanco has it, is that of "attaining and sustaining curiosity and humility," while "engaging in some serious self-examination." A liberal education, as he notes, quoting John Henry Cardinal Newman, "implies an action upon our mental nature, and the formation of our character." Delbanco warns that it won't do to posit some prelapsarian golden age when higher education approached perfection. Surely he is correct. A good deal of the old liberal arts education was dreary. The profession of teaching, like that of clergyman and psychiatrist, calls for a higher sense of vocation and talent than poor humanity often seems capable of attaining. Yet there was a time when a liberal arts education held a much higher position in the world's regard than it does today. One of the chief reasons for its slippage, which Delbanco fails directly to confront, is that so many of its teachers themselves no longer believe in it —about which more presently.

I MENTIONED EARLIER that the liberal arts were for a good while my second religion. Here let me add that I had never heard of them until my own undergraduate education had begun.

When I was about to graduate from high school as an amiable screw-off, ranked barely above the lower quarter of my class, my father, who had not gone to college, told me that if I wished to go he would pay my way, but he encouraged me to consider whether my going wouldn't be a waste of time. He personally thought I might make a hell of a good salesman, which was a compliment, for he was himself a hell of a good salesman, and a successful one. I eschewed his advice, not because it wasn't sound, but chiefly because I felt that, at 18, I wasn't ready to go out in the world to work.

In those days, the University of Illinois was, at least for residents of the state, an open-enrollment school. If you lived in Illinois, the school had to take you, no matter how low in your high school class you graduated. Lots of kids flunked out, and my own greatest fear on the train headed from Chicago down to Champaign-Urbana, in white bucks and reading *The Catcher in the Rye*, was that I would be among them.

Most of my friends, Jewish boys from the rising lower-middle class, went to the University of Illinois to major in business. "Business major" nicely rang the earnestness gong. Yet the courses required of a business major struck me as heart-stoppingly boring: accounting, economics, marketing, advertising, corporation finance, also known as "corp fin," which sounded to me like nothing so much as a chancy seafood dish. I was especially nervous about accounting, for I had wretched hand-writing and a disorderly mind, which I viewed as two strikes against me straightaway. Wasn't there something else I might study instead of business? A fellow in the fraternity that was rushing me suggested liberal arts. This was the first time I had heard the phrase "liberal arts." What it initially stood for, in my mind, was no accounting.

In my first year at the University of Illinois, I had slightly above a B average. I attained this through sheer memorization: of biological phyla, of French irregular verbs and vocabulary, of 17th-century poems. I also discovered, in a course called Rhetoric 101, that I had a minor skill at prose composition, a skill all the more remarkable for my excluding all use of any punctuation trickier than commas or periods.

After this modest success, I decided that I was ready for a more exotic institution, the University of Chicago, to which I applied during my second semester at Illinois. What I didn't know then, but have since discovered, was that my demographic cohort, those people born toward the middle and end of the Depression, were lucky when it came to college admission, for our small numbers made colleges want us quite as much as we wanted them. In short, I was accepted at the University of Chicago, though I would never have been accepted there today, and that is where I spent the next, and final, three years of my formal education.

The University of Chicago had a reputation for great teachers, but I managed, somehow, to avoid them. I never sat in a class conducted by Leo Strauss, Joseph Schwab, Norman Maclean, David Greene, or Edward Shils. (Of course, great teachers, like great lovers, can sometimes be overrated. Later in life, I met a few men and women reputed to be great teachers and found them pompous and doltish, their minds spoiled by talking too long to children.) I attended a lecture by David Reisman, who was then *Time* magazine-cover famous, and was impressed by what then seemed to me his intellectual suavity. I sat in on a couple of classes taught by Richard Weaver, the author of *Ideas Have Consequences*, but left uninspired. I was most impressed by teachers from Mittel-Europa, Hitler's gift to America, whose culture seemed thicker than that of the native-born teachers I encountered, and could not yet perceive the commonplace mind that sometimes lurked behind an English accent.

I took a course from Morton Dauwen Zabel, who was the friend of Harriet Monroe, Marianne Moore, and Edmund Wilson. Although not a great teacher, Zabel was an impressive presence who gave off whiffs of what the literary life in the great world was like. I took a summer course from the poet and critic Elder Olson, who kept what seemed a full-time precariously long ash on the end of his cigarette, and who, after reading from "The Waste Land," ended by saying, "How beautiful this is. Too bad I can't believe a word of it."

The students at the University of Chicago were something else. In his book, Delbanco, defending the small classroom, refers to something he calls "lateral learning," which refers to what a college student learns in class from his fellow students. He cites Cardinal Newman and John Dewey on this point, and quotes Nathaniel Hawthorne:

> It contributes greatly to a man's moral and intellectual health, to be brought into habits of companionship with individu- als unlike himself, who care little for his pursuits, and whose sphere and abilities he must go out of himself to appreciate.

A great many of my fellow students in the College at the University of Chicago seemed to come from New York City, several others from aca- demic families. They appeared to have been reading the *Nation* and the *New Republic* from the age of 11. Their families argued about Trotsky at the dinner table. A few among them had the uncalled-for candor of psy- choanalysands. I recall a girl sitting next to me at a roundtable in Swift Hall volunteering her own menstrual experiences in connection with a discussion of those of the Trobriand Islanders.

Some among these University of Chicago students had an impressive acquaintance with books. One morning in Elder Olson's class in modern poetry, Olson began quoting Baudelaire (*mon semblable—mon frère!*)

and a student next to me, named Martha Silverman, joined him, in French, and together, in unison, the two of them chanted the poem to its conclusion. This was one of those moments when I thought it perhaps a good time to look into career opportunities at Jiffy Lube.

"I invariably took the first rank in all discussions and exercises, whether public or private, as not only my teachers testified, but also the printed congratulations and carmina of my classmates." So wrote Leibniz about his own classroom performance. Reverse everything Leibniz wrote and you have a fairly accurate picture of my classroom performance at the University of Chicago. None among my teachers there ever suggested that I had intellectual promise. Nor should they have done, for I didn't show any, not even to myself. I made no A's. I wrote no brilliant papers. I didn't do especially well on exams. I was not quick in response in the classroom.

Only years later did I realize that quickness of response—on which 95 percent of education is based—is beside the point, and is required only of politicians, emergency-room physicians, lawyers in courtrooms, and salesmen. Serious intellectual effort requires slow, usually painstaking thought, often with wrong roads taken along the way to the right destination, if one is lucky enough to arrive there. One of the hallmarks of the modern educational system, which is essentially an examination system, is that so much of it is based on quick response solely. Give 6 reasons for the decline of Athens, 8 for the emergence of the Renaissance, 12 for the importance of the French Revolution. You have 20 minutes in which to do so. Begin now.

At the University of Chicago I read many books, none of them trivial, for the school in those years did not allow the work of second- or third-rate writers into its curriculum. Kurt Vonnegut, Toni Morrison, Jack Kerouac, Adrienne Rich, or their equivalents of that day, did not come close to making the cut. No textbooks were used. You didn't read "Karl Marx postulated . . ."; you read Karl-bloody-Marx. The working assumption was that one's time in college is limited, and mustn't be spent on anything other than the first-rate, or on learning acquired (as with textbooks) at a second remove.

Nor did Chicago offer any "soft" majors or "lite" courses. I remember, in my final year, looking for such a course to fill out a crowded schedule, and choosing one called History of Greek Philosophy. How difficult, I thought, could this be? Learn a few concepts of the pre-Socratics (Thales believed this, Heraclitus that), acquire a few dates, and that would be that. On the first day of class, the teacher, a trim little man named Warner Arms Wick, announced that there was no substantial history of Greek philosophy, so we shall instead be spending the quarter reading Aristotle and Plato exclusively.

How much of my reading did I retain? How much does any 19- or 20-year-old boy, whose hormones have set him a very different agenda, retain of serious intellectual matter? How much more is less than fully available to him owing to simple want of experience? What I do remember is the feeling of intellectual excitement while reading Plato and Thucydides and an almost palpable physical pleasure turning the pages of Max Weber's *The Protestant Ethic and the Spirit of Capitalism* as he made one dazzling intellectual connection after another.

The idea behind the curriculum at the College of the University of Chicago was the Arnoldian one, abbreviated to undergraduate years, of introducing students to the best that was thought and said in the Western world. Mastery wasn't in the picture. At least, I never felt that I had mastered any subject, or even book, in any of my courses there. What the school did give me was the confidence that I could read serious books, and with it the assurance that I needed to return to them, in some cases over and over, to claim anything like a genuine understanding of them.

I was never more than a peripheral character, rather more like a tourist than a student, at the University of Chicago. Yet when I left the school in 1959, I was a strikingly different person than the one who entered in 1956. What had happened? My years there allowed me to consider other possibilities than the one destiny would appear to have set in grooves for me. I felt less locked into the social categories—Jewish, middle-class, Midwestern—in which I had grown up, and yet, more appreciative of their significance in my own development. I had had a glimpse—if not much more—of the higher things, and longed for a more concentrated look.

Had I not gone to the University of Chicago, I have often wondered, what might my life be like? I suspect I would be wealthier. But reading the books I did, and have continued to read throughout my life, has made it all but impossible to concentrate on moneymaking in the way that is required to acquire significant wealth. Without the experience of the University of Chicago, perhaps I would have been less critical of the world's institutions and the people who run them; I might even have been among those who do run them. I might, who knows, have been happier, if only because less introspective—nobody said the examined life is a lot of laughs—without the changes wrought in me by my years at the University of Chicago. Yet I would not trade in those three strange years for anything.

I turned out to be a better teacher than student. In fact I took to saying, toward the close of my 30-year stint in the English department at Northwestern University, that teaching provides a better education than does being a student. If he wishes to elude boredom among his students and embarrassment for himself, a teacher will do all he can to cultivate the art of lucid and interesting presentation and the habits of thoroughness. Thereby, with a bit of luck, education may begin to kick in.

Yet even after completing three decades of teaching, I am less than sure that what I did in the classroom was effective or, when it might have been effective, why. Of the thousands of inane student evaluations I received—"This guy knows his stuff" . . . "Nice bowties" . . . "Great jokes"—the only one that stays in my mind read: "I did well in this course; I would have been ashamed not to have done." How I wish I knew what it was that I did to induce this useful shame in that student, so that I might have done it again and again!

Student evaluations, set in place to give the impression to students that they have an important say in their own education, are one of the useless intrusions into university teaching by the political tumult of the 1960s. Teaching remains a mysterious, magical art. Anyone who claims he knows how it works is a liar. No one tells you how to do it. You walk into a classroom and try to remember what worked for the teachers who impressed you, or, later in the game, what seemed to work best for you in the past. Otherwise, it is pure improv, no matter how extensive one's notes.

As a testimony to the difficulty of evaluating the quality of teaching, Professor Delbanco includes a devastating footnote about student evaluations. One study found that students tend to give good evaluations "to instructors who are easy graders or who are good looking," and to be hardest on women and foreign teachers; another, made at Ohio State University, found "no correlation between professor evaluations and the learning that is actually taking place." As Delbanco notes, the main result of student evaluations is to make it easier for students to avoid tough teachers or, through harsh reviews, punish these teachers for holding to a high standard.

I was not myself regarded as a tough teacher, but I prefer to think that I never fell below the line of the serious in what I taught or in what I asked of my students. What I tried to convey about the writers on whom I gave courses was, alongside the aesthetic pleasures they provided, their use as guides, however incomplete, to understanding life. Reading Joseph Conrad, Henry James, Leo Tolstoy, Fyodor Dostoyevsky, Willa Cather, and other writers I taught was important business—possibly, in the end, though I never said it straight out, more important than getting into Harvard Law School or Stanford Business School. When I taught courses on prose style, I stressed that correctness has its own elegance, and that, in the use of language, unlike in horseshoes, close isn't good enough; precision was the minimal requirement, and it was everything.

How many students found helpful what I was trying to convey I haven't the least notion. If anything I said during the many hours we were together mattered to them, I cannot know. Not a scholar myself, I never tried to make scholars of my students. A small number of them went on to do intellectual work, to become editors, critics, poets, novelists; a few became college teachers. Did my example help push them in their decision not to go for the money? Some of the brightest among them did go for the money, and have lived honorable lives in pursuit of it, and that's fine, too. A world filled with people like me would be intolerable.

When I taught, I was always conscious of what I thought of as the guy in the next room: my fellow teachers. During my teaching days (1973-2003), I could be fairly certain that the guy in the next room was teaching something distinctly, even starkly, different from what I was teaching. This was the age of deconstruction, academic feminism, historicism, Marxism, early queer theory, and other, in Wallace Stevens's phrase, one-idea lunacies. A bright young female graduate student one day came to ask me if I thought David Copperfield a sexual criminal. "Why would I think that?" I asked. "Professor X thinks it," she said. "He claims that because of the death in childbirth of David Copperfield's wife, he, Copperfield, through making her pregnant, committed a crime." All I could think to reply was, "I guess criticism never sleeps."

While not wishing to join the dirge-like chorus of those who write about the fate of higher education in our day, Andrew Delbanco does not shy from setting out much that has gone wrong with it. He highlights the importance everywhere accorded to research over teaching among faculty. He notes the preeminence of science over the humanities, due to the fact that science deals with the provable and can also lead to technological advancement, and hence pays off. (He mentions the sadly mistaken slavishness of the humanities in attempting to imitate science, and cites the advent of something called the "literature lab" as an example.) He brings up the corruption implicit in university presidents sitting on corporate boards, the fraudulence of big-time college athletics, some of whose football and basketball coaches earn more than entire academic departments, and much more.

Delbanco, a secular Jew and a man of the Vietnam generation, is nonetheless ready to allow the pertinence of the earlier Protestant view of higher education in the liberal arts:

> The era of spiritual authority belonging to college [when it was under religious auspices] is long gone. And yet I have never encountered a better formulation—"show me how to think and how to choose"—of what a college should strive to be: an aid to reflection, a place and process whereby young people take stock of their talents and passions and begin to sort out their lives in a way that is true to themselves and responsible to others.

College: What It Was, Is, and Should Be gives a clear picture of all the forces, both within and outside the university, working against the liberal arts. Yet Delbanco lets off the hook the people who were in the best position to have helped save them—the teachers, those "guys in the next room." Much could be said about teaching the liberal arts before the Vietnam generation came to prominence (which is to say, tenure) in the colleges: that it could be arid, dull, pedantic, astonishingly out of it. But it never quite achieved the tendentious clownishness that went into effect when "the guys in the next room" took over.

Not that the ground hadn't been nicely prepared for them. Universities had long before opened themselves up to teaching books and entire subjects that had no real place in higher education. Take journalism schools. Everyone who has ever worked on a newspaper knows that what one learns in four years in journalism school can be acquired in less than two months working on a newspaper. But as journalism schools spread, it slowly became necessary to go through one in order to get a job on a large metropolitan daily. Going to "journ" school became a form of pledging the fraternity. Everyone else in the business had pledged; who are you, pal, to think you can get in without also pledging? And so journalism schools became mainstays of many universities.

Then there is the business school, especially in its MBA version. Business schools are not about education at all, but about so-called networking and establishing, for future employers, a credential demonstrating that one will do anything to work for them—even give up two years of income and pay high tuition fees for an MBA to do so. As with an American Express card, so with an MBA, one daren't leave home without one, at least if one is applying for work at certain corporations. Some among these corporations, when it comes to recruiting for jobs, only interview MBAs, and many restrict their candidate pools to MBAs from only four or five select business schools. Pledging the fraternity again.

Soon, the guys in the next room, in their hunger for relevance and their penchant for self-indulgence, began teaching books for reasons external to their intrinsic beauty or importance, and attempted to explain history before discovering what actually happened. They politicized psychology and sociology, and allowed African-American studies an even higher standing than Greek and Roman classics. They decided that the multicultural was of greater import than Western culture. They put popular culture on the same intellectual footing as high culture (Conrad or graphic novels, three hours credit either way). And, finally, they determined that race, gender, and social class were at the heart of all humanities and most social science subjects. With that finishing touch, the game was up for the liberal arts.

The contention in favor of a liberal arts education was that contemplation of great books and grand subjects would take students out of their parochial backgrounds and elevate them into the realm of higher seriousness. Disputes might arise from professor to professor, or from school to school, about what constituted the best that was thought and said— more Hobbes than Locke, more Yeats than Frost—but a general consensus existed about what qualified to be taught to the young in the brief span of their education. That consensus has split apart, and what gets taught today is more and more that which interests professors.

Columbia still provides two years of traditional liberal arts for its undergraduates. The University of Chicago continues to struggle over assembling a core curriculum based on the old Robert Hutchins College plan. St. John's College, both in Annapolis and in Santa Fe, has, from its founding, been devoted to the cult of the liberal arts, even to the point of having its students study medieval science. The hunger among students for the intellectual satisfaction that a liberal arts education provides is not entirely dead. (At Northwestern, a course in Russian novels taught by Gary Saul Morson attracts 600 students, second only to the recently canceled notorious course in sex education offered by the school.) But the remaining liberal arts programs begin to have the distinct feel of rearguard actions.

The death of liberal arts education would constitute a serious subtraction. Without it, we shall no longer have a segment of the population that has a proper standard with which to judge true intellectual achievement. Without it, no one can have a genuine notion of what constitutes an educated man or woman, or why one work of art is superior to another, or what in life is serious and what is trivial. The loss of liberal arts education can only result in replacing authoritative judgment with rivaling expert opinions, the vaunting of the second- and third-rate in politics and art, the supremacy of the faddish and the fashionable in all of life. Without that glimpse of the best that liberal arts education conveys, a nation might wake up living in the worst, and never notice.

Part Six

Language

My Fair Language

(2012)

THE LANGUAGE WARS date from the beginning of language—the beginning, one suspects, of every language. A language is invented, new words added, a grammar devised, an approved syntax established, and in one of countless possible ways it proves inadequate, opponents gather, snipers fire verbal shots, polemical grenades are flung, canons lined up, and war is underway. The reigning rule of language is change, endless bloody change; it was forever thus, and always will be. Case—far from closed—permanently open.

In his richly informative book Henry Hitchings chronicles the language wars of English, its continuous skirmishes, its controversies, its often rancorous disputes. *The Language Wars* is impressively comprehensive, its author immensely knowledgeable. He takes up the subjects of spelling, grammar, punctuation, pronunciation, metaphor, regional speech, jargon, the influence on language of the internet, and profanity, both lyrical and gross. One cannot but admire his learning and high spirits as he makes his way through material that in a less deft hand would have drooped into pedantry or become inflamed with bad temper.

In writing about language one must prove that one can oneself manipulate language. Hitchings passes this test. His prose is lucid, nicely dappled with irony, and if not elegant then attractively virile. The only complaint I have against his prose style is that he tends to overuse the word "intriguing," and uses it to mean interesting, sometimes fascinating, thereby ignoring what for me is the word's root sense of making secret plans to do something illicit or harmful to someone. Spies have traditionally been thought to be intriguing, not authors of books on grammar and spelling. Many contemporary dictionaries approve Hitchings's use of the word, often these days according it primary position in their numerical list of definitions. But dictionaries, as we know, are cowardly institutions, which tend to go along with the changed meaning of words, and hence are not to be trusted.

My argument against Hitchings's use of *intriguing* is on two grounds: First, it is an act of verbicide, for if more and more people use the word as he does, its older, more specific meaning will soon pass out of existence, which would be both a loss and a pity. After all, there is no other word for the older meaning of *intriguing*, whereas interesting or fascinating will always cover the case in the sense that Mr. Hitchings and so many others now use the word. Second, people who use the word *intriguing* wish to be taken as not merely interested or fascinated by phenomena but—you should pardon the expression—*intrigued* by them; they tend through its use to suggest that they are themselves interesting or fascinating, *intriguing*, if you will, though I won't.

I have deliberately incited this small skirmish to convey that people are nutty about language, and to establish that I am, proudly, among those who are. We take pride in our own use of words, and judge others by theirs, sometimes admiringly, more often to their detriment. I once heard a woman disqualify another, or so she thought, by remarking that she was one of those people who habitually misuse "hopefully." I have myself in recent years grown tired of hearing people describe life, their job, their marriage, even cancer as "a journey." If it is, how come so few first-class tickets are dispensed? "As soon as one begins to analyze the idea of what is correct and what incorrect [in language]," Hitchings writes, "one sees how entangled it is with notions of what's appropriate, felicitous, effective, useful and socially acceptable."

*T*HE *LANGUAGE WARS* does not take up the question of *intriguing*, though it does take up *hopefully, expert, benchmark, whatever*, and many other words about which people contend. Hitchings himself, alas, uses *input, feedback, process, proactive, supportive*, and *seminal*. I find that *seminal*, a word used chiefly by academics to overpraise one another, tends vastly to underrate the power of semen. I'm fairly certain, not at all by the way, that Hitchings would not approve my *alas*.

The parade of warriors in the English language wars all make an appearance in Hitchings's book. Among them have been Ben Jonson, Daniel Defoe, John Dryden, Jonathan Swift, Thomas Hobbes, Joseph Priestley, John Locke, Samuel Johnson, Richard Steele, Joseph Addison, Noah Webster, William Cobbett, William Hazlitt, George Bernard Shaw, H. G. Wells, H. W. Fowler, H. L. Mencken, Kingsley Amis, and Ferdinand de Saussure. Some of these figures line up in the prescriptivist (or tradition-minded) and others in the descriptivist (or change-accepting) trenches. I use the metaphor trenches because the language wars resemble nothing so much as World War I in having lots of charges back and forth but no clear victor.

Eighteenth-century England, Hitchings maintains, was the first time that a noticeable slippage in the use of English was felt among the educated classes. At this time the battle between the prescriptivists and descriptivists was joined. Hitchings neatly formulates the essential difference between the two sides. The prescriptivists "believed that language could be remodeled, or at least regularized; they claimed that reason and logic would enable them to achieve this." The descriptivists, on the other hand, "saw language as a complicated jungle of habits that it would be impossible to trim into shape," and thus was perhaps best left to grow slightly wild, rather like an English garden.

YOU CANNOT ALWAYS TELL THE PLAYERS without a scorecard. Most people would assume that Samuel Johnson, given his famous peremptoriness, would be a prescriptivist. According to Hitchings, who wrote *Defining the World* (2005), an excellent book on the making of Johnson's *Dictionary*, he wasn't—at least not straight out. Johnson began as a prescriptivist, or perhaps more of a proscriptivist, citing many words as "low" or "cant" or "barbarous." His original plan was to be a lawgiver: to "embalm the language," as Hitchings writes, "yet by the time he completed it [the *Dictionary*] he was conscious of the necessary mutability of English; he had also come to recognize the need for lexicography to say how things are rather than to specify how they ought to be."

Two key names likely to be unknown to amateurs in this landmine-strewn field—they were hitherto unknown to me—are Robert Lowth (1710–1787) and Lindley Murray (1745–1826). A bishop, a Professor of Poetry at Oxford, a Fellow of the Royal Society, Lowth published a *Short Introduction to English Grammar* (1762) based roughly on Latin rules. Lowth's book, Hitchings reports, was in use in Anglophone classrooms as recently as 100 years ago. In it Lowth adjudicated upon the use of *shall* and *will*, *would* and *should*, the crime of ending sentences with prepositions, the duration implied by marks of punctuation, and other such matters that since their invention have driven schoolchildren comatose with boredom. Lowth enjoyed finding errors, grammatical and semantical, in famous authors, Shakespeare notably among them.

"The *Short Introduction*," Hitchings notes, "represents the general condition of English grammars up until the twentieth century: there is a reluctance to wrestle with difficult questions, an emphasis on using literature to illustrate aspects of language, an affection for example and learnable points rather than larger rational procedures, an inherited set of labels that are variably used, and a rarely explored awareness that there is something wrong with all of this." Hitchings will from time to time toss up a curveball sentence, whose surprising final clauses get one's attention as it pops resounding into the catcher's mitt.

Unlike Robert Lowth, who had a nice sense of humor, Lindley Murray brought the point-of-view of the moralist into the language wars. An American who took up residence in England, he was the author of the *English Grammar* (1795), which represents the *ne plus ultra* of conservatism in this realm. Everything for Murray needed to be buttoned up, locked down, iron certain. His "doctrine," writes Hitchings, "was that the rules of usage should not allow choice." He did not think that children deserved the relative pronoun *who*, not yet being fully sentient beings. He could write: "Sentences, in general, should neither be very long, nor very short," which leaves one to wonder if they should not also be very medium. He felt a strong link, as Hitchings writes, "between sound grammar and virtue, and . . . between mistakes and vice," and even imagined "a connection between proper syntax and moral rectitude."

ALONG WITH PHYSICAL APPEARANCE, language is one of the primary ways we have of taking one another's measure, and as such measures go it is not entirely an inferior one. A person's speech is often a strong clue to his region and his social class, his choice of vocabulary to his education and point of view. My not having written that last sentence "A person's speech is often a strong clue to his or her social class, his or her vocabulary to his or her education or point of view" offers clues to my own disposition, even my politics, in preferring a smoothly rhythmical sentence over a politically correct one.

As an argument for why language not only changes but needs to change, Hitchings offers the example of the word *everyone*, a word that takes a singular pronoun, as in "Everyone is certain that he is correct." The rise of female sensitivities in these matters has now forced one to write "Everyone is certain that he or she is correct," or to alternate between "he" and "she" in the sentences that follow, or to lapse into the odious s/he. Why not, then, drop the rule, and where everyone is used revert to the plural pronouns *they, them, their*? The precedent for doing so is found in the works of great writers; Shakespeare, Fielding, Swift, Johnson, Byron, Ruskin, George Eliot, and Lewis Carroll, as Hitchings points out, availed themselves of plural pronouns in this connection. "Some usages," he writes, "regarded as illiterate are really acts of discretion," and this strikes me as one of them.

Usually it is the prescriptivists who grow moralistic about language, but Henry Hitchings frequently takes out his own moral trumpet in *The Language Wars* in the hope of blowing away the strict prescriptions he contemns. He is not above imputing the motive behind prescriptivist thought to fear, finding "a sense of life's encroaching chaos and myriad uncertainties" expressed in their outrage at the changes that language naturally undergoes. He can also shift into high dudgeon, as when he accuses prescriptivists, this time under the name of "purists," of attempting "to repel lexical invasions," adding that "it's a repression of life itself. For now, as for all the recorded past, languages are able to cross-pollinate, and as they do so the achievements, visions, philosophies and memories of different cultures interfuse, enriching our expressive resources and making our experience more intricate." Might Hitchings be a multiculturalist in descriptivist's clothing? Or does one position lead naturally, even inexorably, into the other?

That language has political content is a point Hitchings makes repeatedly. Orwell made the same point earlier and more forcibly in his famous essay "Politics and the English Language." (You might want to check the difference between forcibly and forcefully; you will find, I believe, that my using the former suggests I am—within elegant limits, you understand—a prescriptivist in reasonable man's clothing.) Hitchings cites those who are strict in their insistence on the enforcement of grammatical rules, for example, as liking "*the idea* of grammar because they see in its structures a model of how they would like society to be—organized and orderly, governed by rules and a strict hierarchy."

A less complimentary picture of a descriptivist is that of a man who comes in with his hands up. Claiming to grasp that the essential point about language is that it changes, relentlessly, he thinks it a waste of time to fight change. He is not alarmed when old meanings or usages or rules are jettisoned. (Hitchings, for example, believes that, given the quick communication required by texting and internet writing the days of the apostrophe and the semi-colon may be numbered; one might throw in the hyphen along with them. Farewell, old pals.) The descriptivist goes with the flow, thinks of language as existing in an ecosystem. The descriptivist view is the linguistic equivalent of the free marketeer; as the invisible hand of the market will in the end cause all things to work out for the best for the free marketeer, so the invisible lexicographer will turn the same trick for language for the descriptivist.

A descriptivist Henry Hitchings indubitably is, but he is not an uncritical one. He views political correctness, for example, as an attempt to legislate language usage—in most contemporary universities it is now all but the law—and feels that its use has no more point than "allow[ing] us to applaud our own sensitivity while evading the redress of real evils."

IS THERE AN HONORABLE POSITION between that of the prescriptivists and the descriptivists? There is, and you will be shocked to learn that that position is my own. The position entails the tacit agreement that language is mutable, but reserves the right to loathe certain changes, however widely accepted they may be.

In his *Studies in Words*, C. S. Lewis remarks on our "responsibility to the language," and adds that "it is unnecessary defeatism to believe that we can do nothing" about language change. Lewis affirms that "language which can with the greatest ease make the finest and most numerous distinctions of meaning is the best." The question for Lewis is always does a new word add to the richness of the language or does it diminish it. He also cautions his readers to be on the *qui vive* for words that suggest "a promise to pay which is never going to be kept," which applies to three-quarters of the language of psychology and fully half that of contemporary social science.

Inspired by Lewis, I am for putting a 20-year moratorium on the use of the inflationary word *icon* to describe anything other than a small religious painting. Nothing to be done about it, I realize, but it is worth noting that the perhaps perfunctory phrase "You are welcome" has now been replaced with "No problem," which does not seem a notable advance in elegance or manners. I'm for banishing the word *workshop*—which is also available as a verb—to describe what is little more than a classroom discussion of undergraduate poems or stories; "workshop" used in this sense, Kingsley Amis once remarked, implies all that has gone wrong with the world since World War II. Allowing the word *issue* to stand in for *problem*—"I have issues with that"—is as pure a case of verbicide as I know: a useful word, *issue*, distinctly different in meaning from *problem*, describing a matter still in the flux of controversy in a way that no other word does. *Impact* and *focus* deserve a long rest from overuse, and *process* is surely one of those words that never keeps its promise. Perhaps, too, the time has come to call a halt to people describing people as "highly literate," given that literate means no more than that one can read and write; what they really mean, presumably, when they say literate is "literary" or possibly "cultivated," which is not at all near the same thing.

Or consider the word *disinterested*, with its core meaning of impartiality or above personal interest, which has now all but melted into the condition of a pathetic synonym for *uninterested*. If we lose *disinterested* do we not also lose the grand ideal that it represents? I fear we may already have done so, at least insofar as I find it impossible at present to name a single disinterested figure on the stage of world politics. *Ideas Have Consequences* is the title of a once famous book, but words, being the substance out of which ideas are composed, turn out to have even greater consequences.

Heavy Sentences

(2011)

FTER THIRTY YEARS OF TEACHING a university course in something called advanced prose style, my accumulated wisdom on the subject, inspissated into a single thought, is that writing cannot be taught, though it can be learned—and that, friends, is the sound of one hand clapping. A. J. Liebling offers a complementary view, more concise and stripped of paradox, which runs: "The only way to write is well, and how you do it is your own damn business."

Learning to write sound, interesting, sometimes elegant prose is the work of a lifetime. The only way I know to do it is to read a vast deal of the best writing available, prose and poetry, with keen attention, and find a way to make use of this reading in one's own writing. The first step is to become a slow reader. No good writer is a fast reader, at least not of work with the standing of literature. Writers perforce read differently from everyone else. Most people ask three questions of what they read: (1) What is being said? (2) Does it interest me? (3) Is it well constructed? Writers also ask these questions, but two others along with them: (4) How did the author achieve the effects he has? And (5) What can I steal, properly camouflaged of course, from the best of what I am reading for my own writing? This can slow things down a good bit.

All sorts of people write books that promise shortcuts to writing well, most not particularly helpful, if only because shortcuts are not finally available. Over the years, I have consulted many of these books, on rare occasions taking away a helpful hint or two, but not much more. The most famous is Strunk and White's *Elements of Style*, which is devoted to teaching the composition of prose clear, crisp, and clean of excess verbiage or tricky syntax, served up in what is called the active voice. Nothing wrong with clear, crisp, and clean prose, or with the active voice, but *The Elements of Style* is limited in its usefulness, if only because there are more ways of writing well than the ideal advocated by its authors. On the Strunk and White standard, for example, I suspect my opening sentence would have to be heavily edited, if not deleted.

The best book on the art of writing that I know is F. L. Lucas's *Style* (1955). Lucas was a Cambridge don, a Greek scholar, and an excellent literary essayist, especially good on eighteenth-century writers, who wrote a once-famous book called *The Decline and Fall of the Romantic Ideal*. *Style* is filled with fine things, but the most useful to me in my own writing has been Lucas's assertion that one does best always to attempt to use strong words to begin and end sentences. Straightaway this means eliminating the words "It" and "There" to begin sentences and dropping also the pompous "Indeed." This advice also reinstates and gives new life to the old schoolmarmish rule about not ending a sentence with a preposition, for a prepositon is almost never a strong word.

F. L. Lucas wrote the best book on prose composition for the not-so-simple reason that, in the modern era, he was the smartest, most cultivated man to turn his energies to the task. He understood the element of magic entailed in great writing—and understood, too, that "faulty greatness in a writer stands above narrower perfections." He also knew that in literature style can be a great preservative, and "how amazing it remains that . . . perfection of style can still do much to immortalize writers of the second magnitude like Horace and Virgil, Pope and Racine, and Flaubert himself." Pause a moment to consider the wide reading required to have written that last sentence.

Style, according to F. L. Lucas, "is simply the effective use of language, especially in prose, whether to make statements or rouse emotions." That it is, but it is also of course much more. Even though there have been national (English, French, German) and historical (baroque, rococo, plain) styles, style itself is not finally about ornamentation or its absence. In its subtlest sense style is a way of looking at the world, and an unusual or sophisticated way of doing so is not generally acquired early in life. This why good writers rarely arrive with the precocity of visual artists or musical composers or performers. Time is required to attain a point of view of sufficient depth to result in true style.

In a chapter boldly titled "The Foundation of Style—Character," Lucas writes that "the beginning of style is character." I write "boldly," for what, one might at first think, has character to do with composition. "The fundamental thing," Lucas explains, "is *not* technique, useful though that may be; if a writer's personality repels, it will not avail to eschew split infinitives, to master the difference between 'that' and 'which,' to have Fowler's *Modern English Usage* by heart. Soul is more than syntax."

Lucas didn't hold that good character will make an ungifted person write better, rather that without good character superior writing is impossible. And, in fact, most of the best prose writers in English have been men and women of exceedingly good character: Samuel Johnson, Edward Gibbon, Jane Austen, William Hazlitt, Charles Lamb, George Eliot, Matthew Arnold, Anthony Trollope, Henry James, Max Beerbohm, George Orwell, T. S. Eliot, Willa Cather. Even those excellent writers with less than good character—compose your own list here—seem to have been able to have faked good character, at least while at their desks.

F. L. Lucas fought and was wounded in World War I, opposed the British policy of appeasement, was properly skeptical of the Soviet Union, and, along with H. W. Fowler, had acquired the most interesting point of view of those who have attempted books on the art of writing well. A paragraph from Lucas' first chapter, "The Value of Style," will suffice to render his point of view, with its fine sense of perspective and proportion, plain:

> It is unlikely that many of us will be famous, or even remembered. But not less important than the brilliant few that lead a nation or a literature to fresh achievements, are the unknown

many whose patient efforts keep the world from running backward; who guard and maintain the ancient values, even if they do not conquer new; whose inconspicuous triumph it is to pass on what they inherited from their fathers, unimpaired and undiminished, to their sons. Enough, for almost all of us, if we can hand on the torch, and not let it down; content to win the affection, if it may be, of a few who know us and to be forgotten when they in their turn have vanished. The destiny of mankind is not governed wholly by its "stars."

First day of class I used to tell students that I could not teach them to be observant, to love language, to acquire a sense of drama, to be critical of their own work, or almost anything else of significance that comprises the dear little demanding art of putting proper words in their proper places. I didn't bring it up, lest I discourage them completely, but I certainly could not help them to gain either character or an interesting point of view. All I could do, really, was point out their mistakes, and, as someone who had read much more than they, show them several possibilities about deploying words into sentences, and sentences into paragraphs, of which they might have been not have been aware. Hence the Zenish koan with which I began: writing cannot be taught, but it can be learned.

In *How to Write a Sentence and How to Read One*, Stanley Fish, in his jauntily confident manner, promises much more. Fish's central key to good writing, his Open Sesame, is to master forms of sentences, which can be imitated and later used with one's own content when one comes to write one's own compositions. Form, form, form, he implores, it is everything. "*You shall tie yourself to forms,*" he writes, "*and forms will set you free.*"

By forms Stanley Fish means the syntactical models found in the sentences of good writers, or sometimes even in grabber lines from movies, or even interviews with movie stars: "If you want to see the girl next door," he recounts Joan Crawford saying, "go next door." He serves up John Updike's sentence about Ted Williams's last home run in Fenway Park—"It was in the books while it was still in the sky"—as a form that can be made use of in one's own writing by wringing changes on the original. "It was in my stomach while it was still on the shelf" is Fish's example of such a change.

Fish's first bit of instruction is that one practice wringing changes on these forms, over and over again, as a beginning music student might practice scales. "It may sound paradoxical," he writes, "but verbal fluency is the product of hours spent writing about nothing, just as musical fluency is the product of hours spent repeating scales." He adds: "For the purposes of becoming a facile (in the positive sense) writer of sentences, the sentences you practice with should have as little meaning as possible." Is this true? Taking the Updike sentence for my model, allow me to kitchen-test the method: "My *toches* was still in Chicago while my mind was in Biarritz"; "My mind was still in Vegas while my *toches* was in the Bodleian." I fear it doesn't do much for me, but perhaps I am too far gone for such warming-up exercises.

The larger point for Fish is that one learns to write

> not by learning the rules [of grammar, syntax, and the rest], but by learning the limited number of relationships your words, phrases, and clauses can enter into, and becoming alert to those times when the relationships are not established or are unclear: when a phrase just dangles in space, when a connective has nothing to connect to, when a prepositional phrase is in search of a verb to complement, when a pronoun cannot be paired with a noun.

That ungainly Fishian sentence is of course itself built on reciting a few rules, but let that pass. The first thing that one might argue with in Stanley Fish's method is that the number of relationships that words, phrases, and clauses can enter into is not limited, but nearly inexhaustible. In art, anyone writing a book on how to write ought to remember there are no rules except the rule that there are no rules. One does come upon a sentence with a fresh form from time to time, and makes a note to abscond with it, but learning the forms of sentences alone will not take one very far. The argument of *How to Write a Sentence* is that it will take you all the way: "Hence the formula [of this book]: sentence craft equals sentence comprehension equals sentence appreciation."

Some well-established sentence forms are, in fact, better neglected. Those sentences that begin with the word "Although," or those sentences requiring a "however" somewhere in their middle, are almost always dead on arrival. If a form is imitable, it is probably stale, and hence best avoided. Superior writers do not seek out old forms. They create forms of their own devising.

Fish's notion that "without form, content cannot emerge" is not very helpful either, and, except in the most blatant way, untrue. Content obviously needs to be given form, but in my experience it dictates form rather more than the other way round. Form too well fixed, in fact, is ripe for comic response. "The world is everything that is the case," wrote Wittgenstein, "So stop your blubbering and wash your face," added, several years later, the poet Donald Hall.

If one is to write a solid book on how to write, one ought on every page to demonstrate one's own mastery of the skill. H. W. Fowler, the author of *Modern English Usage*, a writer with great powers of formulation, dressed out in witty peremptoriness, was easily able to do so. Here he is on the delicate matter of the split infinitive: "The English-speaking world is divided into (1) those who neither know nor care what a split infinitive is; (2) those who do not know, but care very much; (3) those who know and condemn; (4) those who know and approve; and (5) those who know and distinguish."

Ernest Gowers, who revised *Modern English Usage* and wrote an excellent book called *Plain Words* intended to eliminate the pompo-verbosity of bureaucrats, commanded a fine common-sense style suitable to his message. Writing early in the history of the feminist incursions on language: Gowers noted: "*chairperson* and other new words ending in *person* have yet to win general approval. Meanwhile, it is safer for official writers to be cautiously conservative, and to take evasive action where possible."

Stanley Fish is not a writer of this caliber. He is a fluent, sometimes a lively (for an academic), but finally an undistinguished writer. A self-advertised sophist, he is most at home in polemic. Sentence by sentence, this would-be connoisseur of sentences is insufficiently scrupulous. He often roams deep into cliché country. "You can talk the talk," he writes, "but you can't walk the walk." Earlier he writes that "the very thought of putting pen to paper, an anachronism I find hard to let go of, is enough to bring on an anxiety attack." An anachronism isn't the same as a cliché, and pen to paper, as clichés go, is blue ribbon, and let go of it, gladly, Fish should have done. His diction, or word choice, is commonplace: those worn-out vogue words "focus," "meaningful," and "bottom line," come to him all too readily. "But, far from being transparent and incisive," he writes, "these declarations come wrapped in a fog; they seem to skate on their own surface and simply don't go deep enough." Take three metaphors, mix gently, sprinkle lightly with abstraction, and serve awkwardly. These infelicities are from Fish's first twenty pages. Many more, to stay with my salad metaphor, are peppered throughout the book.

U NLESS ONE IS CONSIDERING aphorisms or maxims, the study of the sentence, by itself, has its severe limits. After one has charted simple, complex, and compound sentences, mentioned sentences dominated by subordinate clauses and sentences that are additive, or add one clause after another on their tail end, there isn't all that much useful to say, except that one sentence is ill- and another well-made, one tone deaf and another sonorous.

Fish ignores the crucial fact that sentences owe their form and their language to their place in that larger entity, the paragraph. One cannot know the form one sentence is to take until having taken into cognizance the sentence, or sentences, that precede it. As the principle of poetry is— or once was—uniformity of meter, so the reigning principle of prose is variety, which means avoiding uniformity of syntax, rhythm, repetition of words, sameness of syntax. A sentence, every sentence, is a tile in a briefer or lengthier mosaic known as a paragraph. No sentence, like no man, as the poet said, is an island.

Here is a paragraph from that brilliant prose mosaicist Evelyn Waugh from his biography *Ronald Knox*, in which I can descry seven artless— which is to say perfectly artistic—sentences and no clear forms whatsoever:

> Ronald had no desire to grow up. Adolescence, for him, was not a process of liberation or of adventure. Manhood threatened him with tedious duties and grave decisions.

His mind had flourished and matured while his heart was still a child's. He grew up slowly. Each stage of his growth imposed a burden; each enlargement of spirit, the loss of something fond. Perhaps some instinctive foreboding of the heaviness of the coming years years tinctured his love of Eton and sharpened his longing to delay.

The only sentences that stand alone—that is, that are not utterly dependent on what has come before them—are the first and, to a lesser extent, the last sentences in a composition. Fish defines the missions of first and last sentences thus: "First sentences . . . are promissory notes," prefiguring what is to follow. Last sentences "can sum up, refuse to sum up, change the subject, leave you satisfied, leave you wanting more, put everything into perspective, or explode perspectives." I should put it differently. Excellent first sentences are about seduction, seducing the reader, at a minimum, to read the second sentence. Fish chose to ignore the best first sentence in literature, which is Tolstoy's in *Anna Karenina*: "Happy families are all alike; every unhappy family is unhappy in its own way." Often first sentences aren't composed as first sentences at all, and rare, I should say, is the writer who has never had the experience of discovering that his initial first sentence was a misfit and that his composition starts better by opening with the sentence beginning his second or third or fourth paragraph.

As for last sentences, along with that of *A Tale of Two Cities* ("It is a far, far better thing that I do than I have ever done before; it is a far, far better rest that I go to, than I have ever known") of which Stanley Fish doesn't approve, the best in my opinion is that which ends on *Madame Bovary*: "Monsieur Homais received the legion of honor," which signals a victory for all that its author wants his readers to despise. The task of a fine last sentence is to set the plane down safely, without any bumps, and the satisfying sense of a trip completed.

Stanley Fish refers to himself as a "sentence nut" and at one point refers to "the wonderful world of sentences," reminding me of nothing so much as of the Erpi Classroom Films of my boyhood, which contained lines like "Wonderful world of fungus," with the public-school camera generally grinding to a slow breakdown on the word fungus. In his chapter "What

Is A Good Sentence?" he neglects to tell us what, precisely, it is, perhaps because there is no convincing solitary answer. He teaches, as the old proverb has it, by example—the example of a few score sentences scattered through his book.

WHAT THESE OSTENSIBLY EXEMPLARY SENTENCES prove is that, in the realm of sentences, tastes differ. Fish exults over sentences by Leonard Michaels, D. H. Lawrence, Virgina Woolf, and Ralph Waldo Emerson that I find without power or charm. He cites an abstruse sentence from Joseph Conrad's *The Nigger of the "Narcissus"* on the composition of sentences when much better, and more efficient, sentences were available to him in the preface to that same story: "My task which I am trying to achieve is, by the power of the written word, to make you hear, to make you feel—it is, before all, to make you see," followed by the clincher close, "That—and no more, and it is everything."

Fish quotes a few sentences by Gertrude Stein—he ends his book on her writing about the seduction of diagramming sentences—and is under the impression that she was a great writer. (He also quotes from that most useless, for the real writer, of essays, Edgar Allan Poe's "The Philosophy of Composition.") What Gertrude Stein attempted was to make prose do what the great avant-garde art of her day—that of painting—did, by writing in the continuous present and using boring repetitions as if filling in a canvas. She failed in her attempt, and a good thing, too, for English prose.

Perhaps the reason for the rather poor choices of so many of Fish's sentences is that they allow him, in obeisance to his subtitle, which promises how also to read a sentence, to do rather elaborate riffs—*explications du texte*, in the old New Criticism phrase—on these sentences. While many of these heavy-breathing exercises allow Professor Fish to work himself up into a fine pedagogical lather, their chief effect on this reader is to remind him that it is good no longer to be a student.

I seem to have written more than three thousand words without a single kind one for *How to Write a Sentence and How to Read One*. To remedy this, at least partially, let it be noted that, at 165 pages, index and acknowledgments and biographical note on the author included, it is a short book.

The Personal Essay: A Form of Discovery

(1997)

THE PERSONAL ESSAY is a happy accident of literature. I call it an accident because it seems to have come into the world without anything like a clear line of descent. Michel de Montaigne (1530–1590) was its first great practitioner, the first man to make plain that he did not intend to be either exhaustive or definitive in his writing and to use the first-person singular in a fairly regular way. Montaigne once referred to himself, in fact, as "an accidental philosopher."

Writing that comes very close to the personal essay appears in the letters of the Roman philosopher Seneca; and of course the first person was used in great autobiographies such as Saint Augustine's. But neither Seneca's letters nor Augustine's autobiography is quite the same as the personal essay. Both were written under the constraints of very different forms. I have called the personal essay "a happy accident," and invoked the word happy because it is free, the freest form in all of literature. A form that is itself intrinsically formless, the personal essay is able to take off on any tack it wishes, building its own structure as it moves along, rebuilding and remaking itself—and its author—each time out.

Adding to its accidental quality, no one, I think, sets out in life to become an essayist. One might, at an early age, wish to be a poet or a dramatist or a novelist, or even possibly a critic. One somehow wanders or stumbles into becoming an essayist. But, given the modest reputation of the essay and the way it has tended to be taught in schools, it is quite amazing that anyone should ever again wish to read essays let alone write them. My own introduction to the personal, essay—one, I suspect, shared by many in my generation—was by way of the bloated, vatic, never less than pompous Ralph Waldo Emerson and the sometimes rather precious Charles Lamb. Few things are more efficient at killing the taste for a certain kind of literature than being force-fed it in school at an early age. Although I have come to have a higher opinion of Lamb and an even lower one of Emerson, having to read them at an early age all but effectively killed the essay for me.

WHEN I THINK ABOUT my own reintroduction to the personal essay, it is connected with my having begun to read, in my junior year at the University of Chicago, the so-called little magazines. This was in the late 1950s, when these magazines—among them *Partisan Review, Kenyon Review, Encounter* (in England), and *Commentary*—were going through a rich period. These magazines contributed more to my education than anything that went on in the classroom, and classrooms at the University of Chicago weren't all that bad. (Like Mark Twain, I was one of those students who tried never to allow school to get in the way of his education and generally seemed to find more interesting things to read outside the classroom than those offered within it.) The little magazines ran political articles, short stories, much literary criticism, but also occasional memoirs and personal essays. The last, with their strong personal note, especially excited me.

I came too late to read George Orwell when he was still alive and regularly wrote a personal essay of a sort under the rubric of "London Letter" for *Partisan Review.* But through that magazine's pages I learned about Orwell the essayist, who was much greater, if less famous, as a writer of essays than as a novelist or, more precisely, as the political novelist who wrote *Animal Farm* and *1984.* But even as a critic, Orwell invariably struck the personal note: every word he wrote outside his fiction bore his beliefs, his point of view, his strong personal trademark.

Orwell is not alone in being a writer who—though famous for work in other forms—was really at his best as an essayist. With the single, towering exception of *The Adventures of Huckleberry Finn,* a strong case can be made for Mark Twain's having been a greater essayist than novelist. About Edmund Wilson, who also wrote fiction, no such argument need even be made. James Baldwin was stronger in the essay than as either a novelist or a playwright.

I'm not at all sure how any of these writers would take the judgment that they are better essayists than novelists. Literary forms, like stocks, rise and fall, not in value of course but in prestige. Until very recently, the prestige of the essay was much lower than that of the novel. The novel was the art of the imagination; it was, in the loaded term taken up by university writing programs, "creative" writing. The essay, in contradistinction, was thought mundane, earthbound, pedestrian—cut it any way you like, nowhere near so elevated. This, one begins to sense, is changing.

Of course, poetry once held first place in the form, or genre, sweepstakes, rivaled only by drama. The prestige of any single kind of writing is in good part dependent upon who its practitioners are at any given moment in history. The appearance of another Shakespeare would doubtless catapult drama back to the top position it held in Elizabethan England. Yet a Shakespeare of our day might not choose to write drama at all. He might just possibly discover a new form not yet known but perfectly suited to our times. Why certain forms rise and fall as they do is itself a question of immense complication.

V. S. NAIPAUL HAS SAID that lucky is the writer who has found his or her true form. What makes this remark especially interesting is that V. S. Naipaul, who in such books as *A House for Mr. Biswas* and *A Bend in the River* has written some of the best novels of the last half of the twentieth century, has recently announced that he no longer considers the novel a useful form for conveying the complex truths of our day. I myself tend to doubt that this is so. What I think may be the case is that people do not seem to have the patience for so lengthy a form as the novel, which is a shame. Naipaul, meanwhile, has said that he plans to write no more fiction.

Near the beginning of the twentieth century, Georg Lukács, the Hungarian critic, prophesied that the essay was likely to be the reigning form of the modern age. He had in mind less the personal than the cultural-philosophical essay, but behind his prophecy was the notion that the essay, with its tentativeness and its skeptical spirit, was really the ideal form for those times when people were less certain about matters that were once thought fundamental and fixed: family, love, religion, loyalty, happiness among them. Theodor Adorno felt that the essay was well suited to the modern spirit because it shied away from what he called "the violence of dogma." The essay, in short, was—and perhaps remains—the ideal form for ages of transition and uncertain values. Such an age, for better and for worse, is the one in which we now live.

The personal essay has this single quality of difference from fiction: it is bounded—some might say grounded—by reality. There are no unreliable narrators in personal essays; in a personal essay an unreliable narrator is just another name for a bad writer. We believe—we have to believe—what the writer tells us, though we are of course at liberty not to be persuaded by the way he tells it. We believe, too, in the facts in his essay as facts that have an existence in reality, unlike the "details" ("caress the details" Vladimir Nabokov instructs all writers of fiction) in stories and novels, whose ultimate existence resides in their authors' minds, whatever their origin in reality. The subject matter of the personal essay, then, is actual, palpable, real, and this, from a reader's standpoint, can be an immense advantage.

The first personal essay I ever wrote was written when I was thirty-one and was, in fact, closer to a memoir than to a personal essay. But I found myself greatly elated in writing about that sweetest of subjects—my own experience. Thirty-one, it occurs to me now, may be young to write personal essays. The personal essay is perhaps intrinsically a middle-aged or older writer's form in that it calls for a certain experience of life and the disposition to reflect upon that experience. Since that time, I have written perhaps two hundred personal essays, and I wonder if I mightn't convey something of what, from the writer's point of view, has gone into the making of these essays.

I agree with Phyllis Rose who, writing about Montaigne, called him "the father of jazz." By this she meant that he was "the inventor of the verbal riff, the man who elevated organic form over inherited structures and first made art by letting one thing lead to another." That is, in my own experience, precisely how writing the personal essay works. I sometimes make notes recalling anecdotes, facts, oddities of one kind or another that I wish to include in an essay, but where precisely in the essay they will be used I cannot say in advance. As for a previous design or ultimate goal for my essays, before I write them I have neither. I would no more use an outline in writing a personal essay than I would take a thesaurus to a pro-basketball game.

THE PERSONAL ESSAY IS, in my experience, a form of discovery. What one discovers in writing such essays is where one stands on complex issues, problems, questions, subjects. In writing the essay, one tests one's feelings, instincts, and thoughts in the crucible of composition.

I plan to write an essay on the subject of talent. Just now I know very little about the subject apart from the fact that it fascinates me. "We need a word between talent and genius," Valery once said. He may well be correct, but I am myself not even clear on the precise definition of the word "talent." I know only that talent tends to be something magical, or at least confers magic on its possessors, no matter in what realm: art, athletics, crime. In this essay, I intend to speak of my own admiration for the talented, question the extent to which I may myself have any spark of talent, try to figure out the meaning of talent in the larger scheme of existence. Through this essay I hope to learn what I really think about this complex subject and, while doing so, to learn perhaps something new about myself and the world. Talent, in any case, seems to me a fine subject for a personal essay—a fine subject, that is to say, for personal exploration.

I also write short stories, which has caused me to wonder why certain kinds of material seem better suited to essays than to stories. As with my writing of essays, when I begin a story I generally do not have anything like a clear notion of its direction. I suspect the same may be true of poetry. I have always been impressed by a remark of Robert Frost's to the effect that whenever he knew the ending of a poem in advance of writing it, the poem turned out to be a damn poor one.

When I set out to write a story, I am usually motivated by a strong yet somewhat vague curiosity; often behind this curiosity lies complex emotion of a kind that I have felt but not yet sorted out, at least not in any way I find satisfactory. Sometimes in a story a character will be at the center of my attention, sometimes a question still in the flux of controversy.

Consider a live and rivening issue of our day—that of abortion. It is not a subject upon which I brood, and my "political" position on it, if I were pressed to give it, is that I am "pro-choice"; I believe a woman ought to be allowed to decide if she wishes to go through with a pregnancy; I also believe that there are too many instances in which to deny the possibility of abortion is to bring about unhappiness of a kind that is avoidable—unhappiness for the unborn child as well as for its parents. I do not believe that the decision to have an abortion ought to be entered into frivolously, though I rather doubt that many women who choose to have abortions do so without giving it serious thought. I guess my true position on abortion is that I am not against it, yet I also think it a private matter that people do well to keep to themselves.

Having said this, I have to go on to say that, if I had a young daughter, I would hate to learn that she had had an abortion. It would more than bother me; it would tear me up. Why? I have no religious objections to abortion. I do not believe that an early fetus is quite truly human. I do not even believe that all people must accept the responsibility for their actions, especially when this acceptance entails possible hardship for an entirely innocent third party, the poor child. Medically meticulous abortion, thoughtfully entered into, therefore seems to be intelligent, sensible, even enlightened. All very well, except, as I say, I would be torn apart if I learned a still young daughter of mine had put herself through an abortion.

I suppose I could write an essay—even a personal essay about abortion, but I am certain it would be a flop. My opinions and point of view on the subject are not all that interesting; my personal experience of the subject is nil. Still, how to resolve my inchoate feelings on the subject? The way I chose to do it was through a short story. What I did was draw a character, a serious businessman, to whom I gave a daughter whom he much loved and also supplied him with my own general views on abortion and sat back and watched how he would react when he learned that his nineteen-year-old child, so dear to him, had had an abortion. Whether I succeeded in this story is not for me to say, but I do think I was correct in deciding that this was material appropriate for fiction.

On the other hand, when my mother died, it did not for an instant occur to me to put her into a short story. Instead I wrote an essay about the remarkable woman who was my mother. Nothing would be gained—a good deal might have been lost had I chosen to disguise my mother through the transformative powers of fiction. Behind my decision was my belief that writing about my mother, about whom I felt uncomplicated love, was best done directly—that is, in the form of the personal essay; while writing about things about which I had somewhat confused, unresolved, less than fully formed thoughts was best done indirectly—that is, in the form of fiction. All this may be a roundabout way of saying that stories are about what happens to characters, while essays are about what happens to one character: the essayist him- or herself.

None of this is meant to circumscribe the territory of the personal essay. "My idea of a writer," Susan Sontag has written, is "someone who is interested in everything," and it is true that the field of subjects available to the essayist is as wide as life itself.

Whatever the ostensible subject of a personal essay, at bottom the true subject is the author of the essay. In all serious writing, no matter how strenuous the attempt to attain objectivity, the author leaves his or her fingerprints. But in the personal essay, all claims to objectivity are dropped at the outset, all masks removed, and the essayist proceeds with shameless subjectivity. This direct presentation of the self, when it comes off, gives the personal essay both its charm and its intimacy.

Perhaps it is this intimacy that makes the personal essay an almost irresistible form. The novelist Rosellen Brown, who edited a collection of personal essays for the magazine *Ploughshares,* makes this same point when, in the preface to the issue of the magazine, she wrote: "Mediocre essays, I can swear after months of reading, are never as boring as mediocre fiction because, even in the hands of the inept, the lives we actually live or witness are more interesting than the ones most of us can (or dare to) invent from scratch." Brown adds that "essays can be badly written and banal, too, but (to mix metaphors wantonly) the wildly unpredictable movements of real event and outcome tend to poke through and make a lively choreography."

Which brings us to the matter of how a personal essay ought to be written. The obvious answer, to mimic those old jokes about how do you feed a seven hundred-pound gorilla, is as carefully and as well as possible. But to take things a step further, there is a general style for personal essays, and it is that which William Hazlitt, one of the great practitioners of the personal essay, termed, nearly two centuries ago, "familiar style." In his essay "On Familiar Style," Hazlitt notes that, to write in a truly familiar style "is to write as anyone would speak in common conversation, who had a thorough command and choice of words, or who could discourse with ease, force, and perspicuity, setting aside all pedantic and oratorical flourishes." A familiar style, in other words, is a natural style natural to conversation, very superior conversation to be sure, and without artifice, pomposity, any bull whatsoever. To be natural in prose, it turns out, much practice is required. The first thing one must learn—and here the exercise of the personal essay is a help—before one can be oneself is who oneself really is.

Not, let me hasten to add, that there is only one familiar style. The styles employed by essayists range widely, from the plain to the ornate, to the sensitive, to the anti-nonsensical, to the aggressive, to the penetrating, to the bemused. There are as many styles as there are different temperaments. What unites all the styles of the best personal essayists, though, is that they have found the best way, for them, to recount their experience with the greatest honesty.

What the personal essayist must do straightaway is establish his honesty. Honesty for a writer is rather different from honesty for others. Honesty, outside literature, means not lying, establishing trust through honorable conduct, absolute reliability in personal and professional dealings. In writing, honesty implies something rather different: it implies the accurate, altogether truthful, reporting of feelings, for in literature only the truth is finally persuasive and persuasiveness is at the same time the measure of truth. One might think this would be easy enough to do, but it isn't, especially when one is under the added pressure of making both the feelings and the reporting of them keenly interesting.

Two of the chief ways an essayist can prove interesting are, first, by telling readers things they already know in their hearts but have never been able to formulate for themselves; and, second, by telling them things they do not know and perhaps have never even imagined. Sometimes the personal essayist is, in effect, announcing: "Please to notice that I am not so different from you in my feelings toward my father [music, food, sleep, aging, etc.]." When this happens, an amiable community is built up between essayist and audience. Sometimes the personal essayist is announcing, also in effect: "Something truly extraordinary has happened to me that I think you will find no less extraordinary than did I." When this happens, the reader, through the mediation of the essayist, finds his or her own experience enlarged. Sometimes, too, the essayist will admit to ignorance, which is a way of asserting sincerity, and this also makes for an atmosphere of congeniality between essayist and reader. On the matter of a writer's audience, Gertrude Stein once said that she wrote for herself and strangers. The personal essayist writes, I think, for himself and people—even though he has never met them—he assumes are potentially his friends.

Often the personal essayist will begin with a small subject, which grows into something much larger. A perfect example of this phenomenon is Max Beerbohm's essay "Something Indefeasible," which begins with the essayist observing a child building castles in the sand and leads gently but firmly into a profound observation about the need for destruction in human nature. This magical trick of the personal essay of turning the small into the large has been well described by the essayist Philip Lopate in a nice reversal of an old metaphor: "The personal essay is the reverse of that set of Chinese boxes that you keep opening, only to find a smaller one within. Here you start with the small . . . and suddenly find a slightly larger container, insinuated by the essay's successful articulation and the writer's self-knowledge." Yet from where, the question is, does this self-knowledge derive?

Many years ago I read, in a biography of the philosopher Hannah Arendt, that every afternoon, in her apartment in Manhattan, Arendt would lie down on a couch for an hour and do nothing but think. What a sensible arrangement this seemed! I thought to test it myself but when I set myself down on my own couch, I discovered that I could come nowhere near an hour's concentrated thought on a specific subject. Five or six minutes seemed my outer limit. Soon my mind would drift off to stray subjects, irrelevant preoccupations, food, fantasies, sheer dreaminess. I suspect that I am not entirely alone in this deficiency.

I HAVE OFTEN FELT, in fact, that the only coherent, consecutive thought I am capable of comes about through my own writing and through reading other writers. Here I return to my earlier point about the personal essay as a mode or method of discovery—of discovering such truth as is available to the essayist and to his readers. Some writers do not begin a composition—be it a magazine article or a full-blown book—until all the fact-finding that goes by the pretentious name of research is completed. The personal essayist—if my own experience is in any way exemplary—stumbles into facts as he goes along. He writes out of his experience, seen through the lens of his character, projected onto the page through the filter of his style. Experience, character, style—these things, if the personal essayist is lucky, will come together to supply a point of view.

A point of view, very different from a collection of opinions, is a distinct way of viewing the world. It is the *sine qua non* of the personal essayist. It can be the making or the breaking of him. All the strong personal essayists—from Montaigne through Hazlitt through Beerbohm through George Orwell have had a clear and strong and often subtle point of view.

If one has a defect in one's personality, the personal essay is likely to show it up. (Self-congratulation, or the imputation of virtue to oneself, is one of the great traps of the personal essay.) Just possibly all personal essayists suffer from the defect of wishing to talk—or what is much the same thing, write—about themselves. Apart from those whose egotism is entirely out of control, every personal essayist has had to have thought about this. "I think some people find the essay the last resort of the egoist," wrote E. B. White, "a much too self-conscious and self-serving form for their taste; they feel that it is presumptuous of a writer to assume that his little excursions or his small observations will interest the reader. There is some justice in their complaint."

When the complaint is most just, of course, is when the experience described by the personal essayist has no generalizing quality. By this

I mean when the essay isn't really about anything more than the essayist's experience, merely, solely, wholly, and only. The trick of the personal essay—I call it a trick, but I really think true magic is entailed—is to make the particular experience of the essayist part of universal experience. The subject of the personal essay—one's self—may be one in which the personal essayist is the world's leading expert, but if that is his only subject of expertise, the essayist won't remain in business long.

For more than twenty years, I wrote a personal essay every three months for the *American Scholar* magazine. Each time I did so I wondered if the readers of the magazine didn't pick it up and, with a half-exasperated sign, mutter to themselves, "Him again" to be followed, if they decide to read the essay anyway, by such unhappy (for me) exclamations as "Give him the hook!" "Enough already!" and (most terrifying of all) "Who cares!" Where, the question is, does the personal essayist acquire the effrontery to believe—and, more astonishing still, to act on the belief—that his or her interests, concerns, quirks, passions matter to anyone else in the world? If you happen to write personal essays, it's rather an embarrassing question. The answer, at least for me, comes in part out of two utterly contradictory beliefs. The first is my complete confidence that I am, in the larger scheme of things, an altogether insignificant and fairly ordinary being; the second is my belief that, even in my insignificance and ordinariness—possibly even because of it—what I think is worthy of interest. Another contradiction: I am a man committed to understanding the world and how it operates, all the while knowing that I haven't much chance in succeeding in this endeavor. What I do know is that the world is too rich, too various, too multifaceted and many-layered for a fellow incapable of an hour's sustained thought to hope to comprehend it. Still, through the personal essay, I can take up one or another of its oddities, unresolved questions, or occasional larger subjects, hoping against hope to chip away at true knowledge by obtaining some modicum of self-knowledge.

"The world exists," said Mallarmé, "in order to become a book." For the personal essayist, the first use for experience is for it to be translated into essays. In struggling to make sense of personal experience, the essayist must also fight off adopting the notion of being in any way a star, at center stage. By its very nature, the essay is modest in its assaults upon the world. It is modest, to begin with, in being an attempt (*essayer*, in French, of course, means just that: to attempt) and, to end with, in being content not to answer anywhere near all the questions the essayist's own work, let alone the world, raises. Like the painter Vermeer, the personal essayist is most profound, at least for me, when his intentions are most modest.

An element of confession resides in the personal essay, but, in my view, it ought not to dominate. Confession leads to excessive self-dramatization, and behind most literary work in which self-dramatization plays a key role is the plea, not always entirely out in the open but always hovering in the background, for the sensitivity, soulfulness, and sweet virtue of the essayist. The etiquette for confession in the essay, again in my view, ought to be the same as that for confession in religion: be brief, be blunt, be gone.

What the essayist confronting a subject usually has to confess is that he or she is not quite like other men or women—but then, it turns out, neither are most men and women like other men and women. That seems to me perhaps the chief value of the personal essayist: by displaying his individuality, he reminds readers of their own individuality. If he succeeds at his task, he also reminds them that their own lives exist in a world never dreamed of by social science, journalism, or any sort of academic thought.

Part Seven

Magazines

New Leader Days:
Can You Have a Political
Magazine without Politics?

(2006)

S OMETIME EARLIER THIS YEAR the *New Leader* magazine, after
82 years in business, ceased publication. Not all that many people
could have known of the magazine during its existence. The tag
line in a full-page ad that it once ran in the *New York Times Book Review*
seeking new subscribers, as I remember it, was "Habitual coupon clip-
pers please don't clip this one." The ad went on to say that not everyone
read the magazine and cited a statistically infinitesimal number of people
who did—only the intellectually best people, to be sure. John F. Kennedy
read it, Hubert Humphrey read it, T. S. Eliot read it, and I forget the
other rather rarefied names who did. In its house ads, the magazine used
to carry a blurb from Eliot that went (again, I'm quoting from memory):
"Of all the journals that cross my desk, the one I should most sorely miss
is the *New Leader*."

I worked as a sub-editor for the *New Leader* for nearly two years, 1962–
1963. If that ad were to have been re-run later, it could not have said that
Joseph Epstein reads it, because for more than 40 years I scarcely glimpsed
it. Now that the magazine is gone, I suppose the best I can say is that I shall

miss not missing it. But my brief adventures there, I have always known, were of considerable significance, to me if not at all to the rest of the world.

The first article I published was in the *New Leader*. The year was 1959, I was in the Army, an enlisted man typing up physicals in a recruiting station in Little Rock, Arkansas. Two years before, Little Rock had been at the center of the world's attention, when President Eisenhower sent in federal troops to insure the safety of the black children who, by court order, integrated Little Rock's Central High School. I wrote a piece on race relations in the city two years later from the standpoint of an outsider. I have just reread it, and it strikes me as in the category I think of as sensitive-pretentious, and rather cheaply moralistic, with ornate vocabulary thrown in at no extra charge: "Gallimaufry," "blague," and "panjandrum" were among the words I used.

I had learned of the *New Leader* only a few months before I sent off my article. I discovered it in a tobacco store on Main Street in Little Rock that sold out-of-town newspapers and foreign magazines, including the London *Spectator*. I had discovered the little magazines and intellectual journals a few years before, while a student at the University of Chicago. *Encounter*, *Commentary*, *Partisan Review*, *Sewanee Review*, *Kenyon Review*, these magazines opened up a new world to me, and an entirely new cast of writers—among them Dwight Macdonald, Sidney Hook, Irving Kristol, Robert Warshow, Midge Decter, Isaiah Berlin, Leslie Fiedler, Irving Howe, and a great many others. I must have been the only soldier who went off on bivouac with copies of *Partisan Review* and *Dissent* in his backpack in the icy November of 1958 at Fort Leonard Wood, Missouri.

The *New Leader* of those days, even though published on slick paper, was a weekly and impressively drab. The logo—small n, capital L—was in white surrounded by a black box. A news photograph usually appeared on its cover; there was nothing seductive about its typeface or layout. (The general appearance of the magazine was revamped in 1961 by a gifted designer named Herb Lubalin, who changed its typeface to Times Roman, pitched out dreary photographs in favor of line drawings, and added lots of elegant—if slightly funereal—thick black lines above the titles of articles and reviews. With a bit of sprucing up here and there, it retained this look till its dying day.) I was beguiled by the grandeur of some of the names I discovered in its pages. An early issue I read carried a debate between Bertrand Russell and Sidney Hook over whether, with the possibility of an atomic war hovering over the world, it was better to be Red than Dead. Hook argued that life without freedom such as was offered by communism wasn't worth living; without freedom, he declared, better dead than red—better to be a dead lion than a live jackal. He easily defeated Russell. British Labour MPs wrote articles for the magazine; so did a number of writers whose names I knew from other intellectual magazines.

I was 22 years old and thrilled to have my article published in a New York magazine, even if no one I knew read or had ever heard of the *New Leader*. In identifying the magazine, I could always say that Bertrand Russell wrote for it. After the pleasure of first publication began to wear off, I wondered about what I would be paid for the article. Surely it couldn't be less than $100—and then I began to imagine it as much more, up around $500, maybe an even thousand.

After three or four weeks, a few contributor's copies arrived, but no check. So I wrote to the editor, a man named S. M. Levitas, telling him (a lie, of course) that the mailboxes in the building I was living in had been broken into, and I wondered if perhaps his check for my article "A Stillness at Little Rock" had been stolen. Less than a week later, Mr. Levitas wrote back to inform me that I was a young man and thus, as I recall his phrasing, "unaware that the truth has no price tag. The *New Leader* does not pay its contributors." He ended by saying that he encouraged me "to do more writing."

Funny, I seem never to have realized the obvious point that "the truth has no price tag." But what I did realize from this letter was that Levitas, a former Menshevik who had briefly been vice mayor of Vladivostok, was a man with a fine touch. He was in fact a *schnorrer* extraordinaire, which would have to be part of the job description of anyone running a small intellectual magazine without a generous angel behind it. I subsequently learned that Levitas smoked two packs of cigarettes a day and rarely bought any. Editors were said to enter his office demanding a raise, and depart with no raise but a review copy of an unreadable novel.

One quiet day in the office, after I had come to work for the *New Leader*, I discovered in the files a folder marked T. S. Eliot. As I remember it, the correspondence between the famous poet and the Menshevik editor began with a letter from Levitas inviting Eliot to review some entirely inappropriate book. Levitas must have known that Eliot's was a powerhouse name without knowing much more about him. Not Eliot but his secretary wrote back on exquisite light blue stationery, saying that Mr. Eliot was on holiday just now and thus wouldn't be able to accept Mr. Levitas's kind invitation. Levitas replied straightaway by telling Eliot how he envied him his ability to get away, and that he was only the other day saying to Mrs. Levitas that they, too, must find time for a vacation. He may or may not have suggested another inappropriate book for review. Eliot's secretary replied by saying that Mr. Eliot was still on holiday and would perhaps answer this letter upon his return. To which Levitas, now presuming on an old acquaintanceship, wrote to say that there was nothing finer than a lengthy holiday. . . . Finally, there is a letter from Levitas to Eliot in which he announces that he and Mrs. Levitas will soon be in London and he wonders if Eliot and Mrs. Eliot could "break bread" (quotation marks around the cliché supplied by Levitas) with him and his wife. T. S. Eliot may have officially been an anti-Semite, but he was, from all reports, a kind man, and he and Levitas must indeed have broken bread. The result was no T. S. Eliot reviews or essays but that blurb: "Of all the journals that cross my desk the one I should most sorely miss is the *New Leader*." He'd perhaps miss it, I used to think, even if he ever actually read it, which was difficult to imagine.

I never met S. M. Levitas, who died before I arrived at the *New Leader*, and I'm here making him out a clownish figure. He must of course have been much more than that. He was able to garner, after all, the support of such men as Sidney Hook and Reinhold Niebuhr, Hugh Gaitskell and Walter Reuther, all of whom wrote for him. He ran a magazine that for many years was the most persistently courageous voice of the anti-Stalinist left in America and maybe in the non-Communist world—and he did it with little in the way of financial backing. He attracted an impressive run of European writers, many of them, like himself, Russian émigrés. Most of the great names on the anti-Stalinist left at one time or another wrote for him. When the rest of the world didn't want to hear about it, he and the contributors to the *New Leader* kept reminding that portion of the world prepared to listen that the Soviet Union was one large prison; and the magazine kept the pressure on in separate pamphlet studies of the Soviet doctors' plot, show trials, Khrushchev's "secret speech," and a great deal more.

Not long after I first became aware of the magazine, I acquired, from the Little Rock library, a copy of one of its special issues, "Jews in the Soviet Union." I found myself immensely impressed by the seriousness and usefulness of it. (Not long before, I had read a collection of Sidney Hook's essays, *Political Power and Personal Freedom*, which turned me away from ever thinking that communism was anything but a menace to those upon whom it was visited.) Reading this "Report by the Editors," I recall thinking how pleased I was to be, in my small way as a onetime contributor, connected with the *New Leader*.

After my discharge from the Army, I returned to Chicago. I wanted to be a writer, but realized that I had all the equipment for the job except for subjects to write about, and so searched out editing jobs. The best I could find in Chicago at the time was an assistant editorship on the *Kiwanis Magazine*, which I, already an inveterate highbrow, condescended to take. In fact, a very decent man named Richard Gosswiller patiently taught me how to put together and put out a magazine. I had stayed in touch with Myron Kolatch, the man I had dealt with at the *New Leader* on my Little Rock article, who had himself, after S. M. Levitas's death, risen to be the magazine's executive editor. When a vacancy occurred on the editorial staff, I wrote to ask if I might be a candidate for the job. I learned that the job, if I wanted it, was mine.

I was then 24, married, and had a child; my wife was pregnant with our second child. The pay was low, even for those days—$6,000 a year— but the benefits nonexistent. (I was even dismayed to learn that, should the need arise, I could not collect unemployment, for the *New Leader* did not pay the employer's share; only on a socialist magazine was this possible. But the magazine arranged another $1,000 a year for me as copy editor for *Labor History*, an academic journal published by the Tamiment Institute.) I felt I couldn't let the opportunity pass. In those years, if one had intellectual or artistic ambitions, Manhattan was thought the only true testing ground for them. New York, New York, if you could make it there, etc., etc.

I wasn't sure what to expect when I arrived at the *New Leader*'s office at 7 East 15th Street, between Fifth Avenue and Union Square. On one of its floors the building housed the old Rand School library, filled with books about socialism and the various strains of American radicalism, including the Eugene V. Debs papers. The offices of labor union agents were on another floor. The magazine, if I remember correctly, was on the third floor. On the ground floor was the Tamiment Institute, a foundation brought into being (I believe) by the ILGW and other clothing workers' unions. Tamiment ran a summer camp in the Poconos and was also one of the *New Leader*'s chief financial backers; when the camp was sold, much of the money derived from the sale was used to keep the magazine afloat.

Adult clothes were still the order of the day, and I came to work that first day in a blue suit, white button-down collar shirt, rep (as they used to be called) tie. Noel Coward, arriving at a party in a lounge suit when everyone else was in white tie and tails, is supposed to have said, "Please, I don't want anyone to apologize for overdressing." But I hadn't overdressed. My two fellow editors, Mike Kolatch and Joel Blocker, were also besuited. Kolatch was a smallish man, with a serious mustache, a pipe-smoker, tidy of mien and mind, who in those days jokingly called people, in his New York accent, "Doc-tah." He gave off the aura of being unsurprisable.

Joel Blocker, a fellow University of Chicago graduate, was darkly good looking, a Brooklynite, a man passionate about culture. I once heard him say that anyone who didn't love Bernard Malamud's novel *A New Life* could not possibly be his friend—a remark emblematic of how much culture and ideas seemed to matter to intellectuals in those days. The translator of an about-to-be-published book of Israeli stories, Joel knew Isaac Bashevis Singer, just then ascending to his fame, and it was at his apartment that I first met Singer. I liked Joel, though sensed he was touchy, under pressure of some (to me) mysterious sort. He came in latish every morning, because he was in psychoanalysis.

In those days in New York it seemed as if everyone was in psychoanalysis. Not to be was, somehow, to seem a touch callow, as if fearful about exploring one's inner yearnings, terrors, repressions. Albert Goldman, the magazine's music critic, based his jumpy, hipster personal and literary style on a combination of jazz and psychoanalytic banter. He talked openly about his various therapies, including his group sessions. He once told of a woman who confessed that she slept with every man she ever went out with and then felt degraded afterwards. "How did you react to that?" I asked. "Oh," he said, "I introduced her to Phil, a horny friend of mine."

Al taught at the School of General Studies at Columbia, which he called "working the lounge at Columbia." I edited a book he wrote on Thomas De Quincey that demonstrated De Quincey's having plagiarized from Germans. Al hungered for more than academic success, and went on to write biographies of Lenny Bruce, Elvis Presley, and John Lennon (in response to the last, Elton John called him "human vermin," a fine blurb, I've always thought). He died in his middle sixties. Had he lived longer, he would doubtless have had to add to this triptych of popular culture figures by producing as a fourth panel a book on Michael Jackson. He could be hard on women, and yet he had an odd sort of refinement, wore expensive clothes, had some of the mustache-and-small-spectacles elegance of S. J. Perelman, and required lots of attention at any table or in any room he occupied.

Not long after I arrived at the *New Leader*, John Simon signed on as the movie critic. A PhD in comparative literature at Harvard, the student of Harry Levin, John had a heavy armor of learning. He once reviewed a film with segments by six directors from different countries, each segment in a different language, and remarked on the quality of the subtitles of all but the one in Japanese, a language he allowed— owing to a busy schedule, one gathers—he had never learned. Tall, speaking careful English with a slight Mittel-Europeanish accent, John had determined to earn his living writing criticism. Not an easy thing to do at any time; his being able to do so has perhaps been all the more remarkable in that he curried no favor from anyone, anywhere. Instead he often curried rage with the harshness of his own unmediated opinions. As I recall, John concluded his first movie review for the magazine, on David and Lisa, which was about two emotionally disturbed adolescents, by suggesting that perhaps the Lacedaemonians (not your mere Spartans) were probably correct in their practice of burying the deformed soon after birth.

John invited me out for a few evenings of what I took to be, for him, normal critical jousting. I remember his telling me that he had run into Pauline Kael one evening, who told him that she disagreed strongly with his review about some movie or other but she much admired the style in which it was written. "Oh, my dear," he told me he replied, "I had no idea that you were in the least interested in style." Distinctly not, this, my idea of a swell time, but nonetheless amusing to hear about in John's recountings.

The *New Leader*'s art critic was Hilton Kramer, whose name I first encountered in *Commentary*, where he wrote a no-hostages-taken review-essay of James Thurber's *The Years with Ross*. After Joel Blocker left the magazine for a job at *Newsweek*, Mike Kolatch asked Hilton if he knew of anyone who might be interested in a job as an editor at the *New Leader*. "Actually I do," Hilton said. "Me." After editing his own magazine, *Arts*, Hilton had been freelancing, writing reviews for the *Nation* and the *Progressive*, and other places where the checks for contributors were written in longhand and tended to be in the low or middle two figures.

Hilton in those days looked rather like the best of the modernism he has long admired: He was well-turned out, sleek in an understated way, a touch severe (owing to large round spectacles), and wildly witty. Kolatch once asked him if every piece of art criticism had to contain the word *oeuvre*. Hilton answered he wasn't sure, but could promise that every one of his would. He had a New England accent, and a comic vision of the world. "Scandalous!" was a word he used a great deal; and "shameless," always accompanied by a sly smile, he used even more. Detached amusement was his general tone. He knew all the strange crew of odd scribblers who attempted to eke out a living writing for the *New Leader* and other of the intellectual magazines of those days: Edouard Roditi, George Woodcock, Keith Botsford, Edward Seidensticker, and other intellectuals now entirely forgotten. He once told me about Roditi, a homosexual who was under pressure to leave France during the Algerian war because he was living with an Algerian boy, that his cancer was the only subject upon which Roditi was less than fully candid with him. Hilton had a laugh that I loved to be able to evoke. Knowing he would be sitting at the desk across the room from me made me look forward to coming to work. He left the *New Leader* after I did, to become the primary art critic of the *New York Times.*

Stanley Edgar Hyman, who was at the top of the second echelon of critics during what has been called the Age of Criticism, wrote the lead book review in each issue. His reviews were the most read item in the magazine. Stanley wrote brief book notes for the New Yorker and taught at Bennington. He was married to Shirley Jackson, famous in those days for her macabre story "The Lottery," about a village stoning. Stanley's specialty was literary theory *avant la lettre,* which he used chiefly to show how other critics became ensnared in the presuppositions of their own methods. As a reviewer, he availed himself of all the critical methods: anthropological, mythological, New Critical, Freudian, and the rest. Every two weeks he sent in a piece that required no editing, fit space requirements perfectly, and was rarely dull—an impressive performance that he kept up for many years.

Bearded, overweight, a man of great bonhomie, Stanley came into the office only a few times during my days on the magazine. When he did, we all went to lunch with him, and listened to his stories about the legendary figures around the *New Yorker.* He wore three-piece brown suits and used a gold cigar cutter. Between his *New Yorker* and *New Leader* jobs, he was said to read a book a day and drink a bottle of booze a night. Stanley died at 51, his wife at 49.

A young woman who came in part time, chiefly to proofread and do odd editorial jobs, was Diane Ravitch. Diane in those days was, through marriage to the scion of an enormously successful construction company, a poor little rich girl, but a highly intelligent version of the species. She was one of eight children of the family of a Houston liquor-store owner. Good at school, she went off to Wellesley, where she complicated her life by becoming interested in intellectual things. She now had two sons of her own. I adored joking with her. I used to imitate various movie stars reading the staid titles on *New Leader* articles; Lauren Bacall, for example, saying "Agonizing Opportunity in Southeast Asia." One of our specialties was coming up with absurd titles of our own, a contest Diane won going away one morning by giving the title "Days of Whine and Neuroses" to a review of a complaining memoir about growing up in India. The title was turned down as insufficiently serious.

Diane had a strong streak of common sense, and, what usually goes along with it, an equally strong distaste for nonsense. In those days, hers was a good mind that had not yet discovered the right subject to which to apply itself. Toward the end of her *New Leader* days, she found it, through the encouragement of Lawrence Cremin at Columbia Teacher's College, in education, its history and contemporary practice, upon which she has since written with great energy and distinction.

My own role on the *New Leader* was distinctly minor. While working there, I was never asked to write for the magazine; nor did I step forward to request to do so. I brought in a few new writers, though none whose presence greatly altered the tone or general direction of the magazine. Mostly, I worked on manuscripts, trying to edit them into readability. Many of the magazine's contributors in those days were European émigrés who had not yet mastered English. Walter Lacqueur, who has long since become an elegantly efficient writer on contemporary history, in 1962 was not yet confident in his English composition. Boris Nicolaevsky, the Sovietologist, wrote, as I recall, rather Pninesque English, which needed to be put on a gurney and sent into the operating room. Writers on such abstract subjects as arms control, Sovietology, and foreign policy were not much interested in lilting prose style. Some of the magazine's English contributors—a then young Labour MP named David Marquand comes to mind—would send in pieces written in longhand on yellow foolscap that didn't need a word or comma changed.

A man then in his middle eighties named William Bohn, who had served as nominal editor during S. M. Levitas's time, had a column that required heavy reworking, sometimes near total rewriting. His column presented what I thought of as "a typewriter job," in which one put a fresh sheet of paper in the typewriter and rewrote from scratch. Bohn never complained; maybe he never read himself, at least in my version. Dwight Macdonald, a writer I then much admired, wrote a letter to the editor calling one of William Bohn's columns—a column I completely rewrote—a small classic. This was my biggest thrill in copyediting.

I frequently edited Reinhold Niebuhr, the Protestant theologian whose name still had intellectual cachet and who continued writing for the *New Leader* probably long after he had much to say. He had had a stroke, and one of its effects was to cause him much of the time to forget that a typewriter has a space bar. Many of his sentences read as if they were multiple-choice propositions, permitting an editor to go any one of three different ways with it or eliminate it entirely (none of the above). The novelty singer Chubby Checker was then in his brief heyday, and, Niebuhr's raw copy on my desk, I would sometime rise, and, going into a brief dance, sing a few lines of "Come on Reinie, let's do the twist."

I owe to the *New Leader* two things: first, a small skill for working with other people's writing, which, perhaps, helped me in shaping my own prose style; and, second, certain knowledge that I had no deep interest in the intricacies of foreign policy. Although I edited articles about polycentrism in the Communist world, one-party rule in Africa, the activities of Falangists in Spain, revolutionary parties in Peru, debates about the Common Market, and economic trends in the Benelux countries (are there still Benelux countries?), once the articles left my desk they also left my mind. The rhythms of the news were not my rhythms.

My own politics in those days were what I would now call a lazy leftism. I thought of myself as vaguely socialist, if still anti-Communist, a man interested in social justice without any particular plan on how to acquire it, an automatic (if not very happy) Democratic voter. Voting for a Republican, for anything, was more than I, otherwise not an unimaginative person, could conceive. Not many politicians or policies could pass my lofty lefty standard; in this I resembled the man who complains about every synagogue he's ever been in, and when asked his own affiliation, replies, "Unobserving Orthodox."

John F. Kennedy was president of the United States when I was at the *New Leader*, and my own view of him was that he was a business-as-usual politician, perhaps a bit better tailored and more carefully managed than most others, but not much more: weak on doing anything about civil rights in the South and not notably courageous in taking unpopular positions generally. (I still believe this, and continue to find the relentless apotheosis of this politician whose father's money bought him the presidency hard to fathom.) On the Friday afternoon that word came into the *New Leader* office that he had been shot in Dallas, my first thought was, "Hell, we'll have to remake the whole damn magazine." That, I have long since confirmed, is not a bad example of how journalists really think.

I'm not sure exactly how long I remained at the *New Leader*, but I was mentally no longer fully there when, sometime after the conclusion of my first year, the editor called me in to say that he appreciated all my efforts, adding that without my help he couldn't have brought the magazine out. Joel Blocker, he told me, was obviously looking for another job, and he realized that he couldn't any longer rely on him, and so many of Joel's tasks fell to me. He was grateful to me, and he was giving me an $800 raise, and only wished it could have been more. (When I recently told this story to someone, she asked, "You mean $800 a year?" Yep, a year.)

A week or two later, over drinks after work, Blocker told me that he was indeed looking for another job, and had been for some time. There was no place to go at the *New Leader*, and he didn't think the magazine was likely to go anyplace either. "Besides," he said, "Kolatch gave me a lousy thousand-dollar raise, which is pretty damn pathetic." That last sentence put *fini* to my own days at the *New Leader*; emotionally at any rate, I was out of there. I myself began to think about looking for a new job.

I began shopping myself around as an editor at other magazines, with a textbook publisher in Chicago, at NBC television news. (Roughly a year later, owing to domestic complications, I returned to Little Rock, where I worked in an urban renewal agency and then as the director of the Pulaski County anti-Poverty program.) A magazine editor noted for the directness of his views, after gazing down at my résumé during a job interview, looked up and said, "I consider anything good in the *New Leader* is there by accident." I did not, I regret to say, have a triumphant comeback. The magazine, true enough, apart from occasionally interesting criticism in its back pages, was pretty dull.

The obvious reason was that not many of its articles were sought by the editors; most things came in over the transom, with others commissioned for altogether too obvious reasons: the dull piece on midterm elections from the dullish man who was then CBS's White House correspondent, the bundle of articles reporting on youth around the world by an Indian

who wrote for the *Christian Science Monitor* and other regular contributors, the usual Sovietological extrapolations caused by the absence of
some Politburo member from the photograph taken at the most recent
Communist party congress (interesting that no Sovietologist came close
to predicting the demise of the Soviet Union). The phrase "he could have
mailed it in," in its current meaning of half-hearted effort, applied to lots
that appeared in the magazine during the time that I worked there.

The one exciting piece I recall from my days there was initiated by
Mike Kolatch. After reading an essay of Irving Howe's about how Ralph
Ellison and other black (then Negro) writers ought to be more out in the
open with their protests about racial injustice in America, Kolatch got
in touch with Ellison to invite him to respond in the pages of the *New
Leader*. Ellison's response was a whiplash blast at Howe for his effrontery
in telling another man what opinions he ought to have and how he should
express them and, ultimately, what kind of writer he needs to be. Howe
replied, wanly, and Ellison, replying to the reply, body-slammed Howe
onto the mat once again. It made for superior intellectual journalism.

In defense of the *New Leader*'s dullness, it had almost no money to pay
its contributors—some professional journalists received $25 or $50 for
their contributions—and so it had to print what it was offered or could
scare up, after an editorial rinsing, of course. When there was a contribution from a well-known writer, there was a slight odor of the bottom of
the desk drawer about it. I once wrote to Dwight Macdonald, praising
him and suggesting he write something—I don't remember what—for
the magazine, apologizing for the smallness of the fee we could offer. He
thanked me for the praise and suggested that, to arrive at his customary
fee, I attempt fund-raising.

Then, too, the magazine's reason for being, anti-communism, or the
defense of freedom vis-à-vis communism, was losing its old motive force
as the magazine's central interest: Stalin was dead, the Soviets had been
backed down in the Cuban missile crisis, Khrushchev and the shabby
characters who followed him in leading the Soviet Union seemed a good
deal less menacing than their precursors.

But the true reason for the dullness of the *New Leader* I think was
revealed in an interview that Mike Kolatch gave to Charles McGrath

of the *New York Times* at the announcement of the magazine's ending publication. "I'm essentially an apolitical person," Kolatch said in that interview. "I can't stand ideologies." Everyone of course hates ideologies, and an ideologue is usually what you call the person who, in a political argument, doesn't agree with you. But for a man who has edited a political magazine for more than 40 years to say that he is "essentially apolitical" seems striking.

Let me quickly say that I believe Mike Kolatch. He had no line, and, apart from a steadfast anti-communism, took few strong positions. Still, his saying that he "is essentially apolitical" is rather like the editor of *Poetry* saying, "Poems—I can take 'em or leave 'em"; or the editor of *Field & Stream* saying that he doesn't get out-of-doors all that much.

Mike Kolatch's idea, then, was to run a magazine that was liberal (in the older, civilized meaning of the term), centrist, and educational in the sense of setting out the great political questions and issues of the day without a strong political *parti pris*. "I guess I had this naive notion that we had a very intelligent audience that didn't need to be told how to think, how to vote, what to do," Kolatch told the *Times*.

Within the *New Leader*'s serious limitations—of money, brilliant contributors, a large readership—the magazine may, for all I know, have accomplished what it set out to do. I say "for all I know" because on those occasions when I saw a copy, scanning its contents and contributors' names, I found myself easily able to resist buying it. The question that the recent history of the *New Leader* poses is, Can you run a political magazine without having firm political beliefs, demonstrating political passion, and taking clear positions? The *New Leader* shows it can indeed be done, so long as you don't expect many people to read it.

Commentary

(2010)

M UCH OF MY EDUCATION, such as it is, is owing to intellectual journalism. I first discovered the intellectual journals—*Partisan Review, Kenyon Review, Sewanee Review, Dissent, Encounter*, and others—in my wanderings in the periodical room of William Rainey Harper Library in my junior year at the University of Chicago. These magazines functioned for me as a continuation of the Great Books education served up, with vastly uneven allure, in the school's dour classrooms.

They also allowed me to link the past with the contemporary. Among their contributors were Dwight Macdonald who in his comic devastations of middlebrow culture—he wrote strong takedowns of the *Great Books of the Western World*, the *New English Bible*, and *Webster's Third New International Dictionary*—seemed a successor to H. L. Mencken; Edmund Wilson who in his biographical and encyclopedic interest in literature seemed a successor to Sainte-Beuve; and Sidney Hook who in his logic and rationality, a successor to the thinkers of the Enlightenment. ("Voltaire with a mustache," is what my friend Edward Shils once called Sidney.) Reading these and other contributors to the intellectual journals provided its own little lesson in how intellectual influence and tradition work.

As it happened, I came upon the intellectual magazines in 1957, one of the high points in their history. Among their contributors, along with those I've already mentioned, were Lionel Trilling, Allen Tate, Clement Greenberg, John Crowe Ransom, Saul Bellow, Hannah Arendt, Randall Jarrell, Leslie Fiedler, Ralph Ellison, Mary McCarthy, Delmore Schwartz, James Baldwin, Robert Lowell, Alfred Kazin, and Irving Howe; contributors from abroad included André Gide, Jean-Paul Sartre, Ignazio Silone, Bertrand Russell, George Lichtheim, Nicola Chiaromonte, Arthur Koestler, Raymond Aron, F. R. Leavis, and Gershom Scholem. The outlook of the intellectual journals of that time was international, the reigning feeling fraternal: The contributors were a fraternity, if a highly disputatious one, of intellectuals.

None of these magazines had a large circulation. Fees paid to contributors were almost derisory, sometimes not reaching the high two figures, often sent out in handwritten checks. All the editors could promise contributors was a serious audience and the opportunity to have their work appear in excellent company. Good writers did not have all that many other places to go, at least if they were serious intellectuals not willing to lower their sights. By this time the war of the brows was underway in earnest, with the intellectual journals being strictly highbrow, or high culture, and the notion of "selling out" was very much in play. Selling out, among the intellectuals who wrote for these magazines, included appearing in the *New Yorker*, about which Robert Warshow, an editor at *Commentary*, wrote a devastating piece whose main point was that the *New Yorker* wasn't about understanding the subjects it took up but about inculcating the proper attitude to take on those subjects.

Of all the intellectual magazines, *Commentary* was the one of most importance to me. Discovering it was a great intellectual event in my life. Alongside publishing many of the leading intellectual figures of the day, *Commentary* offered a serious and critical perspective on Judaism and Jewish life in America unavailable anywhere else. The magazine ran contributions from such Jewish theologians as Martin Buber, Abraham Joshua Heschel, and Emil Fackenheim and historians such as Salo Baron and Lucy Dawidowicz. Bernard Malamud, Saul Bellow, and Philip Roth—the Hart Schaffner & Marx of American literature, as Bellow bitterly jibed—

published some of their early stories in its pages; so, too, did such old world Jewish writers as Isaac Bashevis Singer and Chaim Grade.

One of the magazine's regular features was called "From the American Scene," which included accounts of American Jewish institutions, stories of the assimilation of immigrants, and odd and interesting aspects of the lives of Jews throughout the country. One such piece I recall, written by a woman named Grace Goldin, was about her father, an immigrant and a grocer in Tulsa who loaned money to an oil wildcatter. When the latter's well came in, the grocer, whose loan made him part-owner of the well, found himself a wealthy man. With his newfound fortune, he built a house, one wing of which he used as a private synagogue behind which he planted a large rose garden, because on Saturdays, the Jewish Sabbath, he wished, he said, "to see nothing but Jews and roses."

I have been reading *Commentary* since 1957, and writing for it, as Benjamin Balint, in *Running Commentary* (Public Affairs, 304 pp., $26.95), a critical history of the magazine, informs me, since 1964. I was also interviewed by Balint, and my name is mentioned in his book several times. Balint himself was a sub-editor at *Commentary* between 2001 and 2004. *Running Commentary*, though, is far from an in-house history where life has been, as Grace Goldin's father wished it, all Jews and roses.

Balint has gone through *Commentary*'s archives with great care, and I shouldn't be surprised to learn that he has read his way through the entire 65-year run of the magazine. His book contains a vast amount of useful information, some of the best of it about the magazine's founding and its early days. But it suffers from the want of a clear point of view. In the end, one is not altogether sure where Benjamin Balint stands in regard to *Commentary*, itself one of the most continuously contentious magazines ever produced in America.

Running Commentary begins with the career of the magazine's first editor, Elliot Cohen, who set the parameters and tone of the magazine. The editorial masthead of the early *Commentary*, which was founded in 1945, just after the war, included, along with Robert Warshow, a brilliant writer on popular culture, the writer Irving Kristol, the sociologist Nathan Glazer, and the art critic Clement Greenberg. A smart and witty woman named Sherry Abel was the managing editor, and a 23-year-old woman named

Midge Decter worked as Elliot Cohen's secretary. I should like to add that the janitor was Alexis de Tocqueville, but fear no one would believe me.

Elliot Cohen had been born in Mobile, Alabama, in 1899, and graduated, precociously, from Yale in 1917. He soon was hired as managing editor of a magazine called the *Menorah Journal*, to whose pages he brought luminaries of the day from the world of Jewish thought and belles-lettres. One of his contributors, whom he subsequently hired as an assistant editor, was Lionel Trilling. Six years younger than Cohen, Trilling would later say that Elliot Cohen, who he claimed was "the only great teacher I have ever had," was "a man of genius."

Cohen left the *Menorah Journal* in 1931 because he thought it insufficiently critical in spirit, especially about the complex situation of Jews in America. *Commentary*, his new magazine, was published under the auspices of the American Jewish Committee, which picked up the bill for its perennial losses. The AJC is an organization that was formed at the turn of the 20th century by a small group of wealthy American Jews of German descent to protect the rights of Jews round the world. In Elliot Cohen they found the right man, but also someone who, with his insistence on complete editorial freedom, would sometimes give the organization conniption fits.

One of the chief differences between *Commentary* and *Partisan Review*, though they shared many of the same contributors, is that the former had a direct stake in Jewish issues, questions, problems. "*Commentary* would be," as Balint correctly puts it, "less avant-garde than *Partisan Review*: less enamored of Ezra Pound, T. S. Eliot, James Joyce, and Gertrude Stein; less European in orientation." Yet the preponderance of contributors to both magazines were Jewish intellectuals born and living in New York, causing Edmund Wilson to call *Partisan Review* the *Partisansky Review*.

In his new magazine, Cohen published some of the sharpest things written about the then-recent near genocide of the Jews in Europe. This was at a time when people didn't want to believe in the scale, which is to say the true horror, of the Holocaust. Balint notes that two excerpts from the diary of Anne Frank were published in *Commentary*, acquired from Doubleday for the piddling sum of $250 because, at the time, not all that many people were interested in it. One of the first copies of *Commentary*

I happened to pick up had a gripping portion of *The Notes of Emanuel Ringelblum* about the last days of the Warsaw Ghetto.

As with so many intellectuals in New York in the thirties, Cohen was a leftist; for a period, according to Balint, he was a fellow-traveler. But by the time he founded *Commentary*, at age 46, he was strongly anti-Communist and a liberal. Elliot Cohen's anti-communism was of the take-no-prisoners kind. In the pages of *Commentary*, the execution of the Rosenbergs for treason was unequivocally approved. Balint reports that Cohen turned down a brilliant piece by Robert Warshow on Charlie Chaplin because he didn't want any fellow-travelers praised in his magazine.

Cyril Connolly—himself editor of *Horizon*, a splendid English intellectual journal that ran from 1939 to 1949—distinguished between dynamic and didactic magazines. Dynamic magazines published the best material they could find with no further motive than providing superior literary entertainment; didactic magazines published with a larger program or plan in mind. They had, as we should say today, "a line," which didn't of course preclude providing superior intellectual entertainment, without which the program or plan would of course never have had a chance to succeed. Connolly's *Horizon* was dynamic, and Cohen's *Commentary*, as would be true of the magazine under his successors, was didactic.

Elliot Cohen was very much what we should today call a "hands-on" editor. He instructed his contributors about what their articles should contain and how they should be organized and with what emphasis— and then, when the articles arrived, often rewrote them. The tradition of heavy editing continued well after Cohen's editorship. The advantage of heavy editing carefully done is that no *Commentary* articles fell below a certain standard; the disadvantage was that much of the magazine read as if written by one person.

Balint, who admires Elliot Cohen's achievement, characterizes the articles and reviews in *Commentary* "under Cohen's steady hand" in the following admirable formulation:

> *Commentary* treated politics with a literary sensibility. It balanced treatments of Jewish and general subjects, journalistic topicality with large-bore analysis. Neither pretentious nor patronizing, it joined the rigorous with the personal, passion

with intelligence, brainy heft with fluency. It clamored to go
beyond the immediate subject to larger questions of culture.
It brought religious intensity to secular expression. It was writing *con brio*.

In 1959, at the age of 60, Elliot Cohen, who was a manic-depressive,
took his life by tying a plastic dry-cleaning bag around his head. The
American Jewish Committee briefly considered Alfred Kazin, Daniel
Bell, and Leslie Fiedler for the editorship of *Commentary*, then offered it
to Irving Kristol, who turned it down. The job was then offered to Norman Podhoretz, who, disregarding his friend Kristol's advice also to turn
it down, accepted the job. The precocious Podhoretz, who was 29 at the
time, had been a contributor to the magazine under Elliot Cohen, and
worked there as an assistant editor under difficult conditions during the
interregnum between Cohen's illness and death and his own appointment. No one expected him to be a dull editor; but then, no one could
have predicted, either, on what a wild ride he would take the magazine.

Anyone interested in intellectual life in America over the past half-
century cannot be neutral about Norman Podhoretz. I am certainly not
myself; I admire him greatly, for his intellectual courage, his logic and
clarity, and—a quality less known to his readers than to his friends—his
kindness and generosity, of which I have had ample evidence in my dealings with him as both editor and friend. Yet most of Norman Podhoretz's
life has been spent in intellectual combat. He is the last man to run away
from a fight, which has earned him many enemies.

When younger, Podhoretz was a magnet attracting envy. When I lived
in New York in the early 1960s, the contemporaries of Norman Podhoretz
whom I knew were all envious of him. Not only had he made that longest
of trips, as he once described it, from Brooklyn to Manhattan, traveling
from the working class (his father was a milkman) to the educated—let us
make that the *bien pensant*—class; but he seemed, at least from the middle distance, to have done it so easily. As an undergraduate at Columbia
he became known as Lionel Trilling's favorite student. Off to Cambridge
on a Kellett Fellowship he studied under F. R. Leavis and published at any
early age in Leavis's magazine *Scrutiny*. After he returned to the United

States, his literary criticism appeared in *Partisan Review* and in all the other okay places. He was a younger member, but one in good standing, of the group of New York intellectuals he himself has called "the Family," a term suggesting the coziness yet argumentativeness of an actual family, and the potential for internecine viciousness of a Mafia family.

Once he had attained the editorship of *Commentary*, Podhoretz gave it a violent lurch, ending the magazine's celebration of America under Elliot Cohen and steering it, as Balint puts it, "sharply leftward into a decade of anti-establishment iconoclasm." He began by publishing three lengthy excerpts from *Growing Up Absurd*, a book by Paul Goodman arguing, essentially, that America was not a country worthy of young men to grow up in. Staughton Lynd, a kind of domestic Noam Chomsky, found welcome in the new *Commentary*; and so did H. Stuart Hughes, a Harvard historian who argued for America's taking up a position of unilateral disarmament. Norman Mailer, then a close friend of Podhoretz's, wrote, quite incomprehensibly as I recall, on Buber's *Tales of the Hasidim* as if he were a secular version of a Hasidic rebbe, which he clearly was not.

These leftist years at *Commentary*, from 1960 through roughly 1968, may have been the only phase in the career of Norman Podhoretz, who has been a lifelong nonconformist, when he traveled with the horde, or herd, of independent minds. Leftism was at that time nothing if not fashionable, and the only question among intellectuals on the left was how to out-radical one's fellow intellectuals. A proof of the fashionableness of leftism is that at no time was *Commentary*'s circulation higher (rising to 62,000, according to Balint) than during its most leftist period.

While still in his leftwing mode, Norman Podhoretz published his memoir, *Making It* (1967). The book argued the case for ambition, for exposing "the dirty little secret" that having power, money, and fame was much to be preferred over not having them. These are things that, however obvious, are not supposed to be averred publicly, especially by liberal-left intellectuals. Nor was Podhoretz permitted to get away with averring them. I don't recall a book having been so thoroughly lambasted by reviewers in my day as was *Making It*. The subtitle for an attack on the book in *Esquire* read, as I recall: "Norman Podhoretz's dirty little secret may not be all that dirty but it sure is little."

Some people have suggested that the crushing reviews *Making It* received helped push Podhoretz politically rightward. Perhaps. But the more decisive element in turning Norman Podhoretz were the events of the late 1960s and early seventies. Even in his leftist days, Podhoretz found the writers of the so-called Beat Movement—Allen Ginsberg, Jack Kerouac, William Burroughs, et al.—third rate and, in their dedication to immaturity, not finally to be taken seriously. The drugging and political wildness represented by the coalition of students, old lefties, and liberal hangers-on that went by the name of the Movement he found even less congenial. Some of the menacing utterances about Israel on the part of the Black Panthers must have reminded him that the one thing the extreme left and the extreme right can always agree upon is hatred of the Jews.

Benjamin Balint has a Norman Podhoretz problem. He appears not to have been able to decide if Podhoretz is a good or bad hombre. The only clearly unequivocal thing he says about him is that he has "a marvelous baritone voice," which in fact he doesn't: He has the raspy voice of the ex-smoker, Camels, unfiltered, four packs a day. Balint's portrait of Podhoretz is of a figure of aggression: He uses words such as "hard-charging," "brusque," "pugnacious" to describe him. What Balint cannot quite make up his mind about is whether Norman Podhoretz is a main-chancer looking to promote himself through his magazine or, instead, a man of high principle devoted to his country, to fellow Jews round the world, and to staving off barbarians who, often during the years of his editorship of *Commentary* between 1960 and 1995, seemed not at but well inside the gates.

Podhoretz never disguised his ambition; *Making It* is proof of that. The question—a question Balint never gets around to answering satisfactorily—is what has been behind that ambition? I believe the right things have been behind Norman Podhoretz's ambition. Time after time, as editor of *Commentary*, he has taken up strong positions that went against the grain not of mainstream America but of mainstream American intellectual life. In "My Negro Problem—and Ours," an essay of 1963, Podhoretz pushed against black psychological bullying, which was to grow much more rampant and intense in the years ahead, and claimed that the most likely solution to the country's race problem was miscegenation. (Lo, today we have not a black but a biracial president; and indeed biracialism—not only of the black-and-white but of the Asian-Caucasian varieties—looks to be the order of the future.) He took on Hannah Arendt and her heartless book about Jews in the Holocaust, when sentiment among the *New York Review of Books* crowd went strongly the other way—and again he has been proven correct. He held *Commentary* to a strong anti-Communist line so long as communism—a truly evil empire, in case anyone failed to notice—continued to exist, even though so many among the old liberal anti-Communists gave way to the plague-on-both-your-houses politics of anti-anti-communism. He was early to label the current Western conflict with Islamic fundamentalism as World War IV (World War III was the Cold War), and in this, as we are learning, he was not wrong, either.

One of the striking changes in *Commentary* under Norman Podhoretz was that the magazine became more political and less cultural in its interests. This is all the more noteworthy since Podhoretz began his career as a literary critic. Irving Kristol, in his warning not to take up the editorship, told him that if he continued writing literary criticism, "you'll end up replacing Edmund Wilson in our pantheon." (Others warned that he would be the next Clifton Fadiman.) But of course, not even Edmund Wilson could have replaced Edmund Wilson, for literary culture has been slowly dying—choked off by academic idiocy, by politics, and by the blurring of high culture generally. Podhoretz's ambition required the larger arena of politics in which to exercise itself.

Not that *Commentary* was devoid of cultural interest. Robert Alter published serious literary criticism in the magazine; so did Ted Solotaroff and Cynthia Ozick (whose general importance to the magazine Balint overrates). For a brief while, a dazzling writer named Alfred Chester wrote memorable attacks on J. D. Salinger and John Updike and other pieces. Sam Lipman wrote brilliant music criticism for the magazine, Richard Grenier wrote in an insiderish way about the movies. Hilton Kramer wrote less regularly for the magazine but always powerfully about the visual arts.

Yet at a party at the Rainbow Room at Rockefeller Center, marking Norman Podhoretz's 25th anniversary as editor of *Commentary*, those who spoke about the significance of the magazine included George

Shultz, Daniel Patrick Moynihan, Jeane Kirkpatrick, Ed Koch, and Henry Kissinger. At this party I found myself at a table with Hilton Kramer, John Gross (editor of the *Times Literary Supplement*), Cynthia Ozick, Gerard Schwarz (conductor of the Seattle Symphony), and Sam Lipman. Midway through the dinner, with several Secret Service and other security men leaning against the walls and near the entrances, Sam Lipman leaned over to me and said, "I see we are seated at the children's table." By which witty remark he meant, among other things, that culture was no longer central to the magazine.

Commentary remained very much a Jewish magazine. Of course, the plight of the Jews in America had changed radically from Elliot Cohen's editorship to Norman Podhoretz's—from the days of concern about anti-Semitism and assimilation in America to those of worry about too great assimilation ending in loss of Jewish identity through intermarriage. Elliot Cohen and many of the intellectuals who wrote for his magazine in its earliest days were not in favor of a Jewish state, Balint reports, though once Israel became a *fait accompli* they rallied to its defense. Under Norman Podhoretz's editorship, and later Neal Kozodoy's, the defense of Israel became a major priority.

I write "under Norman Podhoretz's editorship, and later Neal Kozodoy's"—but in fact the two were nearly coterminous. In 1966, at the age of 24, Kozodoy, who had been a graduate student at Columbia, had been hired as a sub-editor at *Commentary*. He soon developed a nearly perfect rapport with Norman Podhoretz such that, during all my years as a *Commentary* contributor, who dealt chiefly with Neal Kozodoy, I thought of the two men as co-editors. Kozodoy had the authority to make assignments and decisions on manuscripts as if he were himself the principal editor. If one disagreed with him, one never thought to take the matter to a higher authority because it didn't feel as if there were any higher authority. True, because he wrote more—Neal Kozodoy published little—and his name appeared atop the masthead, Norman Podhoretz received most of the glory the magazine attracted, and also most of the not inconsiderable contumely that came its way. In the late 1960s, I can recall more than one person asking me why I wrote for *Commentary*, "that vulgar magazine." "Vulgar" is the word intellectuals use when they really mean "vile," by which they actually mean in disagreement with their own views.

Neal Kozodoy was the principal editor of *Commentary* for 13 years. During that time, the magazine's line did not much change: Defense of Israel from its enemies (not all of whom bore Arab names), criticism of anti-Americanism and anti-Americans, attacks on thin culture passing itself off as serious, remained the order of the day. Plenty of room remained in the magazine for the nonpolitical: I was myself permitted to write in its pages during Kozodoy's editorship about Montaigne, John R. Tunis, life at the National Endowment for the Arts, and other not centrally political subjects. Kozodoy brought on board new contributors—David Gelernter, David Berlinski, Arthur Herman, Michael J. Lewis notable among them—and used some contributors (Terry Teachout, Hillel Halkin, Joshua Muravchik) more than Podhoretz did.

During Kozodoy's editorship, *Commentary* joined corporate independence to editorial independence by breaking away from the American Jewish Committee, and this imposed an additional fundraising burden that Kozodoy worked at sedulously and successfully. The chief difference between the Podhoretz and the Kozodoy editorships—under the latter the former continued to be a featured contributor—is that Neal Kozodoy retained his amazing, I would say heroic, self-effacement. He kept the magazine to the highest standard of seriousness and literary scrupulosity, and required no public recognition for his achievement.

In *Running Commentary*, Balint notes that I have published one hundred and thirty essays, stories, and reviews in *Commentary*. I would add that I never sent one of them off to the magazine without worrying about its acceptance, for under the editorships of Neal Kozodoy and Norman Podhoretz having been a frequent contributor or sharing their politics, or having a famous name, was never sufficient to guarantee publication in *Commentary*. The quality of what one wrote was always the chief element.

As the fourth editor of *Commentary* in its 65-year history, John Podhoretz, the son of Norman, is under the curse of what a friend of mine called the Brooks Robinson Factor. Robinson was the greatest fielding third baseman in the history of baseball, and his successor at third base for the Baltimore Orioles was an excellent ballplayer named Doug

DeCinces. DeCinces might dive into the dugout in a superhuman effort to catch a foul ball; but if he missed, one Orioles fan was sure to turn to another and mutter, "Brooks would've had it." Whenever John Podhoretz attempts something new or different in *Commentary* many of the magazine's old-line readers are likely to mutter, "Neal [or Norman or even Elliot] would never have permitted it."

My sense is that John Podhoretz, the only editor of *Commentary* who comes to the job after working as a professional journalist, intends the tricky balancing act of making the magazine livelier without draining it of its seriousness. The magazine, let it be said, could become dour under its earlier editors—we have, after all, lived through some dark times—and the injection of a brighter note, if its current editor can bring it off without diluting the content and high editorial quality of the magazine, has to be viewed as welcome.

The times make magazines more than magazines make the times. John Podhoretz takes up his editorship at a period when many of the old working assumptions of intellectual magazines no longer hold. One of the important tasks of the old intellectual journalism was, through its criticism of the arts, to serve as a stern gatekeeper, keeping out all that was shoddy, thin, ersatz. In 1958 Dwight Macdonald wrote an essay in *Commentary* called "By Cozzens Possessed" that put a dent in the literary reputation of James Gould Cozzens from which it has yet to recover. I remember being with Saul Bellow and Harold Rosenberg as they agreed that Philip Roth's *Portnoy's Complaint* was passable as blue stand-up comedy, but had no real standing as literature. How useful it would be today to have critics who might let it be known that what passes for great writing, serious art, beautiful music, shouldn't be allowed to pass at all. Without strong intellectual journalism, the culture is all the more likely to lapse—actually, it long ago lapsed—into what Santayana called "a second-class standard of firstness."

As the bar for High Culture has been taken down, so has the old intellectual journalistic approach to politics changed. When he began his intellectual journal the *Criterion*, T. S. Eliot said that it was committed to a conservative program but would be hostage to no party. Many years later Dwight Macdonald, in describing the two major American parties, called them Tweedledumb and Tweedledumber. American politics seemed too trivial for the capacious minds of the intellectuals of Macdonald's generation; American politicians were mainly crooks and clowns—case closed. The intellectuals of that day dreamt of socialism and dabbled in revolution. Of course, it came to nothing more than dreaming and dabbling, but it lent to their lives a feeling of grandeur.

"In general," Balint writes, "an imaginative impoverishment seem to set in [at *Commentary*] as Podhoretz led the magazine deeper into neoconservative sensibility." Norman Podhoretz and Neal Kozodoy probably had less choice than they might have realized in taking *Commentary* further out into the heavy political waters that led the magazine to become one of the spearheads of neoconservatism. With America under intellectual attack at home, Israel under military threat abroad, anti-Semitism on the rise in Europe, educational and intellectual and artistic standards slipping everywhere, where else could the magazine honorably have gone but into the defending or conserving mode that has been at the heart of neoconservatism.

The chief problem facing John Podhoretz in his editorship of the current-day *Commentary*, I would say, is not the distraction of the Internet or the isolation of neoconservatism, but how to run an intellectual magazine without genuine intellectuals. For it is far from clear that we even have intellectuals any longer—at least not in the old sense of men and women living on and for ideas, imbued with high culture, willing to sacrifice financially to live the undeterred life of the mind. Intellectuals of the kind that T. S. Eliot sought as contributors to the *Criterion*—Ortega y Gasset, Paul Valéry, E. R. Curtius, Arthur Eddington—no longer exist. Nor do the intellectuals, of lesser fame and distinction, who helped fill Elliot Cohen's pages.

Instead, we have so-called *public* intellectuals, a very different, much less impressive, type, whom I have always thought should be called Publicity Intellectuals. Public intellectual is another term for talking head—men and women who have newspaper columns or blogs or appear regularly on television and radio talk shows and comment chiefly on politicians and political programs; they tend to be articulate without any sign of being cultured, already lined and locked up politically, and devoted to many things, but the disinterested pursuit of the truth not among them. Frank

Rich is a public intellectual, so too are Andrew Sullivan and Christopher Hitchens and Dinesh D'Souza.

At the end of his book, Balint describes the neoconservatives "gathered around *Commentary* [as] both chosen and reviled, both vanguard and anomaly. For all their prominence, they found themselves isolated, a minority of a minority." I should put it rather differently. The neoconservatives gathered around *Commentary* are a minority among the majority of standard Jewish liberals, they are reviled by leftist *bien pensants*, and they are an anomaly in not caring about being in intellectual or political fashion. Not the least dishonor that I can detect attaches to any of these conditions.

The *New York Review of Books*

(1993)

I AM A THIRTY-YEAR, GREATLY DISSATISFIED SUBSCRIBER to the *New York Review of Books*. From the beginning, despite the savings a multiple-year subscription could bring, I have renewed one year at a time—partly because, in the event of my death, I do not wish to complicate my estate, let alone have the thing coming into the house after I am gone; and partly because I do not want the journal to have the advantage of the minuscule additional interest my long-term subscription would earn. Fair to say that I do not wish the *New York Review (NYR)* well, even though I expect to continue reading it for the foreseeable future—during which indefinite period of time, I have no doubt I shall continue to be dissatisfied.

I am also the author of a single piece in the *New York Review*, which appeared as far back as 1970, and I have had one book of mine reviewed (harshly) in its pages. That was, I believe, in 1974. Because I have published nine more books since then, none of them reviewed in the journal, I suspect I may be under a boycott. But I am not complaining, and I do not in the least mind things remaining this way, for I know it would be difficult for my books to be treated fairly in *NYR*, I am, after all, the fellow who said, in print, sometime in the 1970s, that the contributors to *NYR*, were made up of mad dogs and Englishmen. I would emend that today to read chiefly sly dogs and Englishmen, but I doubt the emendation would help matters.

In expressing dissatisfaction with a journal to which I have subscribed for so long, I feel rather like the man who complains to the restaurant owner that everything about the meal he has just eaten was too cold or too hot, too sour or too sweet, too over- or too underdone—and besides, the portions were awfully small. It would be ungracious not to admit that I have had some memorable intellectual meals in the pages of *NYR*: Joseph Brodsky on Odessa; V. S. Naipaul on Argentina; Edmund Wilson and Vladimir Nabokov putting the finishing touches to their friendship in arguing over the quality of Nabokov's translation of *Eugene Onegin*; John Searle on the breakdown in higher education; Malcolm Muggeridge on the hagiography of John F. Kennedy and on pornography.

But the same establishment has over the years turned out some powerful ptomaine as well: a then-young journalist named Andrew Kopkind condescending to instruct Martin Luther King, Jr., in paraphrase of Mao Zedong, that "morality, like politics, starts at the barrel of a gun"; Tom Hayden approving the 1967 race riots in Newark, New Jersey, on essentially Leninist principles ("the worse the better") and because they helped create the "conscious guerrilla" who, "if necessary, can successfully shoot to kill"; Mary McCarthy, in her reporting from Vietnam, making the Ho Chi Minh Trail seem like the Yellow Brick Road; the famous instructional drawing of how to make a Molotov cocktail that appeared on the journal's cover for its issue of August 24, 1967, a piece of radical porn that no one ever fails to mention.

To retain the restaurant metaphor a moment longer, *NYR*, is a place where one clearly does best to order *à la carte*. And so, for many years now, I have done: reading the pieces on literature, music, art, and science, and devoting less and less attention to the political side of the menu. Yet, I would guess, it is the *table d'hôte*, sloshed together and served up in a gumbo, that attracts most of the journal's readers. Many of these people have treated it, from its very beginnings, as an all-you-can-eat joint, and they cannot seem to get enough.

I RECALL THOSE BEGINNINGS WELL. A brainchild of the Random House editor Jason Epstein, *NYR* came into being during the New York newspaper strike of 1963. The timing was more perfect than even the journal's founder and principal editors could have known. Anyone with any intellectual interests had long ago given up on the *New York Times Book Review* as a serious forum for the discussion of books. (It was edited in those days by a man who used to refer to reviews as either "up" or "down" and who much preferred the former, as did the publishers he saw himself as servicing.) But other vacuums, which not only nature but journalism abhors, were also beginning to open.

Partisan Review, the great intellectual journal of the 1940s and '50s, was coming unstrung; its chief editors, William Phillips and Philip Rahv, would soon split up, the latter to form a short-lived magazine called *Modern Occasions*. *Encounter*, the young but already splendid magazine published in London, would presently lose many of its most distinguished contributors with the revelation that some of its funds were derived from the American Central Intelligence Agency. Around this time, it is true, the *New Yorker* and *Esquire* were opening their pages to Dwight Macdonald and Harold Rosenberg, who previously had written exclusively for such intellectual magazines as *Partisan Review*, *Encounter*, and *Commentary*. But here, suddenly, was a new biweekly American journal, the *New York Review of Books*, playing the intellectual equivalent of catcher in the rye, gathering in all these people with a taste and talent for highbrow journalism and few places to exercise it.

At its upper reaches, the masthead of *NYR* has not changed since its inception. Its two principal editors have been notable in not allowing themselves, at least in a public way, to be very notable. Of the two, Barbara Epstein, previously an editor in book publishing, was the wife of Jason Epstein when the journal was founded; and Robert B. Silvers had worked as an editor at *Harper's* and before that at *Paris Review*. Neither Mrs. Epstein nor Mr. Silvers writes; neither signs proclamations, provides book-promotion blurbs, or announces political positions (not that they need to). So much an anonymous *éminence grise* has Silvers been that Edmund Wilson, a long-time and much-honored contributor to *NYR*, could recount, in his journal (*The Sixties*), spending an evening at a dinner party in the company of the publisher Robert Giroux and mistaking him all the while for Silvers.

Whether Silvers or Mrs. Epstein has been the greater force in the shaping of *NYR* is not a subject one hears much about. Scuttlebutt has it that

Silvers is more passionately interested in the political side, Mrs. Epstein in the cultural. Silvers would also appear to be the more actively engaged in the day-to-day running of the journal. Probably only a bachelor, monomaniacal and with limited outside ambitions, could have brought out such a journal over so long a stretch of time with a limited staff and—until recently, when it was bought by a millionaire Southerner from a newspaper-publishing family named Rea Hederman—fairly moderate financial resources. Silvers, too, appears to be the journal's main man in London, where the *New York Review* has become so fashionable that an Englishman of my acquaintance describes Silvers's visits as having something of the aura of the Viceroy of India home on furlough.

ALTHOUGH THE MEASURE OF *NYR* is best taken through its political and cultural positions, both discrete and cumulative, it is not by these alone that one is likely to understand its remarkable success. The journal has a large social component. Take, for example, its first major contributors. These prominently included Igor Stravinsky, W. H. Auden, Edmund Wilson, Robert Lowell, and Isaiah Berlin. All were bona-fide figures from the world of art and intellect, but they also represented culture with cachet—the cachet in this instance being international, cosmopolitan, in good part English. If culture can be said to have a class hierarchy, *NYR* was clearly upper-class in its intellectual pretensions, a place where Bunny (Wilson) spoke only to Isaiah, Igor spoke only to Wystan (Auden), and Cal, a Lowell after all, only to God.

These contributors served as a powerful magnet to draw in others. Writers are great snobs—perhaps the greatest of snobs. If there is guilt by association, why not glory by association? To have one's prose appear in *NYR* between a Stravinsky interview and an essay by Edmund Wilson was enough to cause a writer to quiver and swoon, overcome with the belief that he had arrived. Many writers indeed have appeared in *NYR* who dissent more or less strenuously from its politics yet have not been able to resist the temptation, as if the journal were a party which, even though one dislikes much of the company, one nevertheless cannot afford to miss.

But the larger point is that *NYR* began life as the journal of a special kind of American establishment. This establishment was neither economic nor political but cultural and social. Here the English connections helped. Although England today may be enfeebled in many ways, Anglophiliac snobbery still rings the gong here in the colonies. At American universities, a sound estimate is, a good English accent can still bring its bearer anywhere from $10,000 to $20,000 more in professorial salary than he would get without it. And *NYR*, at least as these things run, had some fairly tony Englishmen among its contributors, including various lords— Dacre (also known as H. R. Trevor-Roper), (Noel) Annan, (Solly) Zuckerman—as well as classicists, art historians, medievalists, and scientists who added to the journal's social as well as its intellectual luster.

In the early days, the cultural pieces contributed by these figures seemed very close to a cover for the review's politics. A very good cover they made, too. E. H. Gombrich and Isaiah Berlin rattling on about Renaissance pictorial values and the history of ideas gave legitimacy to defenses of the Black Panthers and Vietnam war protesters. Of course, the division between culture and politics within the same journal is hardly a new story. In the old British *New Statesman* under Kingsley Martin, the front of the book, with its defenses of Stalinism in Russia and arguments for Fabian socialism at home, and the back of the book, with its high literary sensibility and defenses of traditional culture, seemed almost at war with each other—and the wonder always was why this division was allowed to persist. Something similar existed in America at the *Nation* in the 1940s.

No such division, however, seemed to obtain at *NYR*. The artistry in the editing lay in making the cultural component seem to be not separate from but in easy harness with the politics; the combination seemed to suggest that culture of this splendid and elevated kind issued naturally out of, and also led back into, the Left politics that gave the journal its true bite and was, many felt, its true reason for being.

ONE DOES NOT GET A VERY GOOD SENSE OF THIS from *The First Anthology*, a collection of pieces from *NYR*'s first 30 years. As an anthology the book is rather disappointing, both in itself and especially as an accurate reflection of the journal's history. Although many of *NYR*'s most valued contributors do appear—Isaiah Berlin, Elizabeth Hardwick, W. H. Auden, Hannah Arendt, Gore Vidal, V. S. Pritchett,

Susan Sontag—reading the anthology in isolation from the magazine conveys the quite false notion that *NYR* has been chiefly a publication devoted to intellectual and cultural life.

True, politics is more ephemeral than culture, and hence less the stuff of which lasting anthologies are made. True, too, even in these carefully culled pieces there are interesting little lapses into political snobbery or politically-correct hyperbole. Susan Sontag leads the way here in her essay, "On Photography," in which she writes that "taking pictures is a soft murder, appropriate to a sad, frightened time," and calls the Korean War "an ecocide and genocide in some respects even more thorough than the ones inflicted on Vietnam a decade later." But such lapses aside, *The First Anthology* reads like conversation at high table in an Oxford college. This may be one characteristic note of *NYR*, but it is far from the full scale.

Every magazine or journal, I sometimes think, should also publish an anthology of the pieces it has run in the past of which its editors are, or ought to be, thoroughly ashamed. *NYR* could, on this basis, put together an impressive volume. The entries would come almost exclusively from the political realm, and would demonstrate the journal's support of student uprisings and race riots; its ingrained distrust of Israel; its defense of human rights without feeling the need (until fairly late in the game) to take the offensive against Communism, the greatest abuser of human rights in our era; its persistently negative attitude toward the policies of its own country no matter who the foe or what the objective ("My country, wrong or wrong," might have been *NYR*'s motto); and its great care in walking any number of lines, fearful of stepping on mines that might lose it one or another of its prized constituencies. Such an anthology would not make delightful but it would make more interesting reading than the one the editors have, with diplomatic delicacy, put together.

The great days of *NYR*—which were far from being the great days of the country—were those of the Vietnam war, the assassinations of public leaders, and the race riots in American cities. These were the days when the featured pieces were by Noam Chomsky, Paul Goodman, Barrington Moore, Jr., I. F. Stone, Richard Barnet, and other intellectuals of the radical Left. A great rush was on, too, to reform primary education, getting it off the track of warmongering capitalist values, and so the journal was full of the words of John Holt, Edgar Z. Friedenberg, Ivan Illich, and Herbert Kohl. The old society was caving in, the new waiting to be built. Bliss was it in that dawn to be alive,/ And if you could not write for *NYR*,/ At least you could subscribe.

As one runs through back issues of *NYR* one is reminded how relentlessly and consistently it played at the game of revolution. Its steady line was that America was one just about unrelieved hell. Here were Gar Alperovitz assigning much of the blame for the cold war to the United States; Stokely Carmichael (right on the heels of Sir Stuart Hampshire writing about Virginia Woolf) informing his readers that black neighborhoods in American cities were essentially colonies; Berkeley sociologists arguing that the contemporary university, as currently constituted, did not deserve to survive; Andrew Kopkind laying the troubles of the world on the CIA; the Berrigan Brothers recounting their travails as Vietnam-war protesters; Paul Goodman ending his throat-catching account of the "We Won't Go" anti-draft movement by saying that among these young men "I did not hear a sentence that was not intelligent, nor a tone that was not beautiful"; Noam Chomsky referring to the Pentagon as "the most hideous institution on earth"; Robert Heilbroner waiting for the death of capitalism as if for a bus into utopia; Philip Rahv trying on the role of an American Plekhanov, advising that, during a time of revolutionary ferment, constructive ideas may only get in the way; Murray Kempton idealizing the Black Panthers; F. W. Dupee exulting in the student uprising at Columbia; Christopher Lasch calling for a third American political party "based squarely on radical principles"; Mary McCarthy finding George Orwell's political virtue wanting, because less impressive than her own; James Baldwin, with his talent for apocalyptic phrase-making, dubbing the United States "this most sinister and preposterous of Edens"; regular and extended coverage of political trials; and the caricaturist David Levine, who somehow did not quite turn out to be our Daumier, drawing Lyndon Johnson and Dean Rusk as Bonnie and Clyde, the late Mayor Richard J. Daley of Chicago as a pig, and Richard Nixon as a rabid dog.

A good time, it seems, was had by all.

THAT *NYR* WAS, IN RETROSPECT, WRONG about almost all these matters is perhaps less interesting than why its wrongness attracted so many readers. A piece by Ronald Steel on a Black Panther conference in Oakland (September 11, 1969) provides part of the answer. Steel writes that "the Panthers' Marxist-Leninist language combined with their Fanonist theories of psychological alienation and third-world solidarity [makes] them particularly appealing to middle-class white militants, who share their ideology but lack their discipline."

But "discipline" is not really the correct word here; what Steel means is that the Panthers really did seem to be putting their lives on the line for their beliefs. My guess is that while this is something neither the writers nor the readers of *NYR* ever, for a moment, considered doing, through its pages they could imagine themselves capable of doing it; they could even imagine they *were* doing it.

Such politics must have been all the more attractive for not costing anything. Thinking Left and living Right is an old story—at least as old as Henry James's *The Princess Casamassima*. But never has the story played so successfully in a magazine as in *NYR*, which at its inception even had, in a man named Michael Field, a superior writer on the subject of food. When Stokely Carmichael declared in the journal's pages that America was a racist nation, "top to bottom," he did not, it was clearly to be understood, intend quite to include the readers of *NYR* in his sweeping condemnation; and besides, that was a lovely new poem by Auden in the same issue, was it not?, and V. S. Pritchett was awfully good, was he not?, on the new Malamud novel.

For a single-paragraph encapsulation of *NYR*'s politics, one might look at the ending of Ronald Steel's piece on the Black Panthers:

> America is not now a "fascist" country, nor is it likely soon to become one, although this is not impossible. Probably it will continue to be an advanced capitalist society in which cruel inequalities and repression, unlivable cities, and inhuman conditions of work continue to exist along with considerable liberty to take political action, while our rulers control an empire of poor nations abroad. It is the duty of the Left to find ways to change this system: to educate people rather than simply

abuse them; to use the universities as places where the complex problems of replacing repressive capitalism and imperialism with a better system can be studied seriously; to stop playing Minutemen and begin acting like radicals. If there is ever going to be a revolution in this country, it will have to happen first in people's heads. What takes place in the streets of a society like this one has another name. It is called repression.

That was written during the Vietnam war, but I should not be surprised to learn that, minus the invocation to activism, many of *NYR*'s most devoted readers still believe it to be a substantially accurate depiction of the United States. Although the journal has greatly toned down the radical note in its latter years, as recently as its issue of November 4, 1993, one finds Gore Vidal reviewing the final volume of Edmund Wilson's journal and writing, apropos of Wilson's earlier book, *The Cold War and the Income Tax*:

> The American people were kept frightened and obedient by a fear of the Soviet Union, which their government told them was on the march everywhere, as well as by the punitive income tax, which was needed in order to pay for a military machine that alone stood between the cowed people and slavery. It was better, we were warned, to be dead than red—as opposed to in the red.

S O MUCH FOR POLITICS in the pages of the *New York Review*. As for culture, that too has been of a very particular kind. What is once again noteworthy in this connection is how thoroughly of the elite have been—and remain—the contributors to *NYR*, for all its radically egalitarian passion. Its English writers have been preponderantly Oxbridge, its American academics chiefly from Ivy League schools. In these institutions, too, the journal has found its most satisfied readership. As others have remarked, *NYR* has never been a place where new talent is discovered; on the contrary, appearing in its pages has been a sign that a contributor—Bruce Chatwin, Julian Barnes, Robert Stone, *et al.*—has now arrived.

But if, in politics, the elitism of *NYR* has gone hand in hand with radical revolutionism, in culture the same elitism has taken a different form altogether. The journal has been careful never to risk straining its muscles by jumping on every passing cultural bandwagon. In literary criticism, it has steered clear of post-structuralism, deconstruction, and other zany English-department dalliances. (In part, this may be owing to the fact that writing of this kind is fundamentally unreadable, and *NYR* can at least claim a continuous tradition of clarity.) Nor has it gone gaga over Derrida, Foucault, and the rest of the French gang. While feminist in its general stance, it has also shied away from the madder kinds of academic feminism that see a phallo under every centrism. *NYR* has treated the issue of the normalization of homosexuality the way one treats a thousand-pound gorilla—very gingerly. It is for tolerance, which is easy; but while it has not aligned itself with the stridency of the gay/lesbian-liberation movement, neither has it uttered a word of criticism against it. The editors will print Gore Vidal engaging in homosexual gossip but not in explicit homosexual polemic.

In culture generally, then, *NYR* has kept its skirts clean. During the wildest of its political flights in the 1960s, it never mistook rock and roll for art, nor proclaimed the music of the Beatles to be the cultural equivalent of T. S. Eliot's *Four Quartets*. It has lost its head neither over movie directors nor over contemporary visual artists. The detritus of publicity culture has not attracted it. Quite properly, *NYR* prizes all those dear dead white males whose works comprise the chief treasures of Western civilization. Far from being trendy, in its approach to culture the journal has if anything tended to be conservative, even a little staid.

That may be part of the reason why the feeling among most intellectuals and academics these days is that *NYR* was at its best when it was at its worst—that is, when it was playing at revolution and cheering on the North Vietnamese, the Black Panthers, and the draft-card burners from its bunker in the Russian Tea Room. The journal has long since pulled back from those horrendous days. Middle-aged now (its editors are in their mid-sixties), *NYR* retains its taste for rather selectively raking muck, for jabbing at people in economic or political power from the standpoint of people who cannot really envision themselves out of intellectual or social power. *NYR* seems decidedly less than eager to take another shot at revolution and perfectly content to let Theodore Draper and others with a taste for such sport shoot off eyeball-glazing articles that seem only a bit shorter than the Thirty Years' War, with footnotes intended to take little nicks out of the reputations of larger men.

WHEN ITS EDITORS RETIRE, the *New York Review* figures to slide from prominence. By their own lights, though, they had a terrific run. They have made a great and lengthy stir. Prose from some of the best minds of our time has appeared in their pages: scholars, artists, perhaps the last generation of free-ranging belletristic intellectuals. The result has been a journal that even people who have detested its politics felt they had to read; I can produce 30 canceled checks in evidence.

The *New York Review* holds a place in the history of modern journalism, constituting as it does one of the four genuine innovations in periodical publishing in this century. First, there were Henry Luce and Briton Hadden, who at *Time* invented the newsmagazine, packaging accounts of current events in peppy and concise form for impatient readers. Second, there was Hugh Hefner, who, at *Playboy*, brought the Bible into the whorehouse by publishing ostensibly serious material— interviews with Bertrand Russell, stories by Graham Greene—alongside what we should today call soft porn. Third, there was Clay Felker, who, at *New York*, invented the magazine dominated by the consumer spirit, with its unrelieved interest in status, money, and scandal, and not really much else.

Finally, there is *NYR*, which has been able to make an unrealistic and damaging politics not only more than palatable but, in many quarters, immensely appealing by interweaving it with, by causing it to seem indistinguishable from, high culture. Thanks to this extraordinary innovation, *NYR*, now thirty years old, has become the representative intellectual journal of our age, with the important qualification that it has not been a great age and the *New York Review of Books* has done more than its share to diminish it.

Postscript

THE *NEW YORK REVIEW OF BOOKS* recently celebrated its fiftieth anniversary, and I wasn't invited. Might it have been because I've written critically about it, or was it because last year, after forty-nine years, I cancelled my subscription. I canceled my subscription, not in high dudgeon, the way outraged subscribers tend to do, but because the *NYR* had been boring me a fine Matisse blue for at least a decade and maybe longer.

I felt no need to read any of its political articles, which came to constitute more and more of the journal, and whose conclusions held no surprises. I found myself reading in each issue at most two or three of its 14 or 15 articles, and these only on nonpolitical subjects, and even here usually without much pleasure or any advance in insight. The *NYR* had become dishwater dull, without so much as a hint of its old glorious, once infuriating self.

At the outset, and for many years thereafter, all the established names in Anglophone culture were pleased to write for it—and impressive names they were. Among the stellar contributors to the *NYR* in its early days were W. H. Auden, Edmund Wilson, Igor Stravinsky, Isaiah Berlin, Mary McCarthy, Robert Lowell, E. H. Gombrich, Malcolm Muggeridge, V. S. Pritchett, Virgil Thomson, H. R. Trevor-Roper, Vladimir Nabokov, Hannah Arendt, Arnaldo Momigliano, and others. Literary culture was only half the story at the *NYR*. As the bus of the 1960s advanced into the chaos of the student revolt and the anti-Vietnam movements, and as the civil-rights movement turned into the black-power movement, the *NYR* jollily jumped aboard. On the political side of its ledger—the mad dogs admixed with its Englishmen—were Paul Goodman, Noam Chomsky, I. F. Stone, Tom Hayden, and such now deservedly forgotten names as Barrington Moore, Jr., Richard Barnet, Edgar Z. Friedenberg, Gar Alperovitz, Stokely Carmichael, and two anti-war priests who went under the corporate name of the Berrigan Brothers.

In the pages of the *NYR*, the great cultural figures in effect lent their imprimatur to the political radicalism. The journal was what Wolcott Gibbs long ago called "salvationist": It was out to save America's political soul. The combination—high culture admixed with radical politics—made a fine blend upon which the *bien pensants* in the media and academic life happily puffed. When I taught at Northwestern University, every two weeks the professorial mailboxes filled with fresh copies of the *NYR*.

In its heyday, the *NYR* was a radical chic publication. Its collapse came quite as much because of the fall of high culture as it did owing to the distaste for extreme radical politics after the terrorism of 9/11. Muslim terrorism has taken some, though not all, of the bloom off old-fashioned anti-Americanism. More important, the great figures of high culture are no longer there to write for the *NYR*, to lend the drearily predictable articles against Republicans and in favor of Barack Obama the cultural support they obviously require.

In the advertisement for the 50th anniversary celebration in New York, the writers promised to be in attendance were Joan Didion, Michael Chabon, Mary Beard, Daryl Pinckney and Daniel Mendelsohn. How the mighty have not so much fallen as disappeared! If I may be allowed a touch of snobbery, this group wouldn't even constitute a mildly interesting dinner party. The *New York Review of Books* may have a lingeringly radical politics, but there is no longer anything the least chic about it.

The *TLS*

(2001)

I AM, I BELIEVE, THE IDEAL READER for the London *Times Literary Supplement* (*TLS*), which I have been reading for roughly forty years. What makes me ideal is my high standing as a serious dilettante: that is, someone who feels he needs to know nearly everything, but not all that much of any one thing in particular and certainly nothing in the kind of depth that will weigh him down.

I, for example, do not need but am nevertheless pleased to know about the reception of Nietzsche's work in France, Lord Esher's plan to save the artists before the Second World War, and the history of cricket in Jamaica, all items I could only have acquired a smattering of information about in the *TLS*. I find I can read endlessly about Socrates, Montaigne, Gibbon, Tolstoy, Proust, Henry James, and Wittgenstein, and the *TLS* has over the years supplied me with a rich abundance of items on these figures, though perhaps rather more than I require on James Joyce, D. H. Lawrence, and the Sisters Stephen and those of their friends who gathered at 29 Fitzroy Square.

I am a pushover for eccentricity, comical snobbery and slashing polemic, all of which have always found a place in the *TLS*. I turn first to the correspondence columns, sniffing for rage and hoping to find libel, or the possibility of an invitation to a duel. As Prufrock measured out his life in coffee spoons, so I measure mine, or at least the orderliness of mine, by how many issues of the *TLS* I am behind at the moment. Just now I am two-and-a-half issues behind, which isn't all that bad; at various times, it has been as many as eleven.

Now the *TLS* is almost 100 years old, and to celebrate it and its centenary Derwent May has written *Critical Times: The History of the Times Literary Supplement*, an excellent and honorable book, alert alike to the *TLS*'s weaknesses and strengths and filled with information both significant and charming about the inner workings of the paper. May has read through millions of words in order to set out, in a way that somehow eludes tedium, nearly a century of *TLS* opinion on literature, politics and other subjects, and has done so in an even-handed manner, accompanied by a sly but never obtrusive wit.

Along with being an important history of a central periodical, *Critical Times* casts a cool light on the history of literary reputation and the ephemerality of ideas. Look on this work, ye intellectuals and artists, and despair. *Critical Times* is organized around the terms in residence of the *TLS*'s eight principal editors: Bruce Richmond (1903–1937), D. L. Murray (1937–1945), Stanley Morison (1945–1947), Alan Pryce-Jones (1948–1958), Arthur Crook (1959–1973), John Gross (1974–1982), Jeremy Treglown (1982–1990), and Ferdinand Mount (1990–).

During this same period its parent publication, the *Times*, has had six owners: Arthur Walter, Lord Northcliffe, John Jacob and later David Astor, Lord Thomson, and Rupert Murdoch. Apart from Northcliffe, who was blustery and profit-minded and would have lowered the paper's standards but for fear of being identified as the philistine he indubitably was, the *TLS*'s various proprietors pretty much left it alone, and Murdoch, in his coup at Wapping, did it the great service of getting the then restrictive printers' union off its back.

This is all the more remarkable when one considers that the *TLS* never had a circulation of more than about 49,000 readers (a high-water mark hit in 1950)—half of these overseas readers, two-thirds of those being Americans—and that it never made anything like large profits for its owners, and in some years lost money. A literary man who himself worked for the *TLS* in the 1960s under the editorship of Arthur Crook, Derwent May is knowledgeable, un-stuffy, and for the most part admirably self-effacing. Only occasionally in chronicling the treatment of a particular writer or episode in the pages of the *TLS* does he intervene with a bracing flick of ironic comment. After recording the review of John Rewald's *The History of Impressionism*, a review written by Anthony Blunt, later revealed as the fifth man in the Burgess-Philby spy ring, for example, he writes: "The impressionists were not for him—though he did not give any hint that the Social Realists were."

Strong politics on the part of the author could have killed this book, but May doesn't allow his own politics—whatever they may be—to obtrude. The *TLS*'s own political record over the past century has been no worse (and perhaps even a little better) than other publications: getting many things wrong and many important ones right. Of course, its opinions on the major issues were rendered for the most part at one remove through its reviewing of political books. *Critical Times* demonstrates that the *TLS* rarely had a clear political or literary line. A grave flaw, this, in other magazines, but not here, because the *TLS* has always had the standing of a national publication—in some genuine sense, even an international one, as headquarters of the Anglophone Republic of Letters.

To have closed its pages to all but what its editors deemed good sense— the prerogative and delight of most other editors—would have been intolerable. Good sense must be preponderant, and over its lifetime, it could be argued that in the TLS it generally has been. But in such a publication even nonsense, where taken seriously elsewhere, must be given a hearing. "Eclectic hospitality," in the phrase of the paper's current editor, must be shown to all sides in a debate, and this the paper has generally provided.

"All the Reviews in the world begin with the intention of being virtuous," Flaubert wrote to Louise Colet in 1853, "none have been." The *TLS*, to be sure, has had its lapses. As May shows, its early reviewers could be prudish, or tended to disqualify poetry and fiction that did not strike the upbeat note. It missed the boat on early James Joyce, but, from the start, got Proust right. Between the 1930s and 1950s E. H. Carr reviewed many of the books on the Soviet Union. With his historiographical notion that history is the record of the winners, this put him squarely—and as time showed incorrectly—in the camp of the Soviet Union, which Carr (certain that Collective Man was next in line in political evolution) egregiously thought to be the winner hands down. I have heard it said that the megalomaniacal collector and connoisseur Douglas Cooper was, similarly, permitted too much influence in the realm of reviewing books on the visual arts, one of the few items that isn't touched on in May's history.

But for the most part, the *TLS* has also been magisterial in the best sense: calm, elevated, disinterested. During the First World War, the paper ran a regular series of articles reminding its readership not to give way to coarse anti-German feeling, and invoked a moratorium on self-righteous chauvinism.

If *Critical Times* can be said to have a hero, it is Bruce Richmond, its first Editor, who is rightly revered by May for setting the *TLS* on a high level, and keeping it there for more than thirty years. Richmond had the good fortune to be at the helm when a rich array of excellent writers were at work. But his eye for spotting talent was impressive. He brought the very young Virginia Woolf on board, encouraging her in every way, even, after a while, setting up a special higher fee for her work. He cultivated the youthful T. S. Eliot, who wrote to his mother in St. Louis that being invited to write for the paper was "the highest honor possible in the critical world of literature." Richmond was also able to solicit work from nearly every great writer of the day. Henry James, agreeing to write about Emile Faguet's biography of Balzac, noted: "I rather think that I shall like your maximum amount of space." When Richmond found it necessary to cut the review, James grudgingly consented, but was unable to resist remarking that the review "thereby bleeds. But it's a bloody trade."

Despite rare attempts to raise circulation by popularizing the contents, the paper has never really fallen off the pedestal on which Richmond placed it. "I have made the *Supplement* hard to read again," announced Stanley Morison, with exultation, though he had earlier set out to make it easier. T. S. Eliot, in a tribute on Richmond's ninetieth birthday, wrote: "Bruce Richmond was a great editor: fortunate those critics who wrote for him."

The editors who followed widened the range of the *TLS*. An editor has no control over the issues with which his time confronts him, though he must determine what those issues truly are. Over the past century, the *TLS* has dealt, often amusingly, sometimes exhaustingly with various literary controversies: from those about Shakespeare to Booker Prizes, from censorship to the Two Cultures debate and the place of literary theory in university teaching.

Intramurally, the paper's greatest single issue—that of whether or not to continue the policy of reviewing anonymously—was presented to John Gross. Against real pressure to retain anonymity, Gross abandoned it. Eliot, among others, was an advocate of anonymity, thinking it good discipline for a writer to "subdue himself to his editor"; he also thought that anonymity brought its own natural restraints, causing him personally as a young writer "to moderate my dislikes and crotchets, to write in a temperate and impartial way." Anonymity also allowed the editor to enlist the expertise of people working in government and other sensitive jobs who were not in a position to sign their work. No doubt it tended to give an authoritativeness to reviews that a signed piece often does not carry.

"Anonymous statements," E. M. Forster wrote in an essay titled "Anonymity"—which, by the way, he signed—"have . . . a universal air about them." During the reign of anonymity, more knowing readers of the *TLS* used to play the game of guessing the authorship of reviews. This implies contributors with a strong, idiosyncratic style and probably inflexible opinions. On the other side, anonymity had its own corrupting influence. How many reviewers unfairly attacked rivals or enemies while hiding behind the cloak of anonymity? (Derwent May mentions a few glittering instances.) In anonymous reviewing, the first persons, both singular and plural, were entirely off limits. John Gross finally decided the issue—rightly, I would say—on the matter of accountability: a reader, he felt, was "entitled to ask on what authority a judgment or opinion is being advanced." So, beginning with the *TLS* of January 7, 1975, every review in the paper was signed.

The ideal is to create a magazine or paper whose format will allow its editor to accommodate almost all that is interesting in the world, and dropping anonymity was of immense help here. But each of the paper's editors, in his own way, helped shape and give it its character. Alan Pryce-Jones and John Gross, especially, widened the scope of the paper's interests—Gross brought in many more American contributors—and each had a nice taste for the purely pleasurable and the eccentric. Jeremy Treglown was more hospitable (some felt, too hospitable) than previous editors to academics. Ferdinand

Mount has attempted to broaden the coverage of the paper and engage it more in the political issues confronting an England whose power has been greatly diminished. Under Mount, the *TLS* circulation gained 10,000 readers, after a slump in the 1980s, to its current level of roughly 35,000.

The readership of the *TLS* has been eaten into by competition from, first, the *New York Review of Books* and then the *London Review of Books,* though both are vastly different in nature: more directly (left-wing) political, much less wide-ranging. But no paper over the past century has done more than the *TLS*, in Bruce Richmond's phrase, to "irradiate the humanities." It has been unrelenting in its insistence on a high standard of scholarship and on the primacy and autonomy of culture. As Alan Pryce-Jones once put it, in another connection, the *TLS* is for those who "find themselves looking at pictures, hearing music, reading in other languages, travelling, correlating as far as possible the whole plan of civilization in which the English faculty at a university occupies only one corner."

The perfect paper, in other words, for the serious dilettante, of which, one would like to think, there must be at least three or four hundred thousand in the world. Let them delay no longer and write their subscription checks now.

There at the *New Yorker*

(2011)

T HE *NEW YORKER*, like New York itself, is always better in the past. In the present, it seems always to be slipping, never quite as good as it once was. Did the magazine, founded in 1925, have a true heyday? People differ about when this might be. The *New Yorker*'s heyday, it frequently turns out, was often their own.

I began reading the magazine in 1955, at the age of 18—not my heyday, which, near as I can tell, has yet to arrive—drawn to it originally because someone told me that the then-current issue had a story by J. D. Salinger. Harold Ross, the magazine's founder and tutelary spirit, had died four years earlier. William Shawn was on the first stretch of his 35-year tour (1952–1987) as editor in chief. The writers Harold Ross had hired remained in place—the big four among them were James Thurber and E. B. White, Joseph Mitchell and A. J. Liebling—and the ethos of the magazine was still that which Ross had imprinted.

Ethos is a word that Harold Ross, even if he knew it, probably wouldn't have permitted in the pages of his magazine. Urban sophistication, emphasizing life's eccentricities (and often featuring its eccentrics), with an amused view of human ambition, was the spirit with which Ross imbued the *New Yorker*. The magazine was apolitical, serious without being heavy-handedly so. During World War II its war reporting was first-class, and it gave over an entire issue, in 1946, to John Hersey's account of the devastation caused by the atomic bombing of Hiroshima. Yet when I came to the magazine there were still columns devoted to horse-racing, Ivy League football, jazz, and night-club entertainment. The general tone of the proceedings was casual, playful, and yet, somehow, withal adult.

An impressive roster of contributors, who in those days had their names printed not under the titles of their articles and stories but at the conclusion, popped in and out of the *New Yorker*'s pages each week. S. J. Perelman, Mary McCarthy, Janet Flanner, Edmund Wilson, Dorothy Parker, Robert Benchley were part of the magazine's literary vaudeville. Many *New Yorker* writers began their professional lives as newspapermen, lending them an anchor in reality, if not cynicism, before turning to the unpretentious belles lettristic journalism practiced at the magazine.

If in those years there were a representative *New Yorker* writer, his name was Wolcott Gibbs. Gibbs, too, began writing for newspapers. A man of all work, he contributed Talk of the Town pieces, Notes & Comments, profiles, light verse, short stories, drama and movie and book criticism, and delicious parodies. (The most famous of his parodies—a parody-profile, actually—was *Backward Ran Sentences*, which was about the rise of Time, Inc., written in *Time* magazine style.) In the foreword to a collection of his pieces called *More in Sorrow*, Gibbs claimed to have contributed more words to the magazine over its first 30 years than any other writer. In *Here at the New Yorker*, Brendan Gill notes that Gibbs was also the magazine's best editor of other people's copy. As an editor, deletion was his specialty; he was a cut man in the corner of less elegant writers.

Wolcott Gibbs is not a name any kid taking next year's SATs need be concerned about. He wrote a play that had a modestly respectable run on Broadway, and three collections of his various writings appeared in book form (*Season in the Sun and Other Pleasures*, *More in Sorrow*, and *Bed of Neuroses*). Today he seems a man of another era, unlikely to arouse interest in a world clamorous with so many other demands on its attention.

Gibbs might have slid into oblivion but for the fact that an editor and journalist named Thomas Vinciguerra, much taken with Gibbs's writing, has gone to the work of assembling an impressive, and substantial, collection of his prose, the preponderance of it from the *New Yorker*. Reading through Vinciguerra's book sets off many observations, notions, insights into the world of smart journalism, criticism, and the writing life, both now and then at the *New Yorker*.

As we Americans reckon such matters, Wolcott Gibbs was well-born. One of his paternal forebears, Vinciguerra informs us, signed the Declaration of Independence; another was secretary of the Treasury under John Adams; both were governors of Connecticut. On his mother's side he was descended from Martin Van Buren. Yet the family was tapped out financially before Gibbs was born, in 1902, owing to bad investments, among them a bungled land purchase in New Jersey.

Sent to the Hill School, in Pennsylvania, where Edmund Wilson also went to prep school, Gibbs took a pass on college, as did many of the good writers of his and the preceding generation. Brendan Gill remarks that Gibbs suffered feelings of inferiority for not having gone to university, though this seems unlikely. H. L. Mencken, who similarly didn't bother with college, claimed that between listening to boring German professors and working as a journalist covering fires, executions, and bordello raids, there really wasn't any choice. Vinciguerra reprints a mock commencement address to non-college-graduates Gibbs wrote that establishes his awareness of the inanity of much college education.

Wolcott Gibbs died at 56, in 1958, in bed, cigarette in hand, a batch of galley proofs of a collection of his writings on his lap. In his introduction, Vinciguerra leaves open the question of whether he was a suicide, which was what Gibbs's third wife suspected. He was a dedicated drinking man, a serious boozer, as were many of the staff assembled by Harold Ross. The *New Yorker* of those days was a place where, in the mornings, it wouldn't at all do to tell people to have a great day.

While he could cause laughter in others, Wolcott Gibbs was not himself a notably cheerful man. ("I suppose he was the unhappiest man I have ever known," wrote his friend the playwright S. N. Behrman.) When a newly arrived writer at the *New Yorker* asked him if he had had a pleasant New Year's, Gibbs instructed him to practice an anatomically impossible act on himself. This same want of conviviality found its way into his drama criticism, but with winning effect. He came across as the very opposite of the enthusiast—as a man much put upon, giving the clear impression that he wished he could have departed most plays after the first act; or better still, never left his apartment and gone to the theater in the first place.

All this might result in mere glumness if Gibbs didn't write so well. Of the great and gaudy snob Lucius Beebe's early days in journalism—Beebe later made his mark as the chronicler of café society—Gibbs wrote: "He had an apathy about facts which verged closely on actual dislike, and the tangled wildwood of his prose was poorly adapted to describing small fires and negligible thefts." Gibbs described the mustache of Thomas E. Dewey as "bushy, dramatic, an italicized swearword in a dull sentence." He referred to posterity as "the silly bitch," to Eugene O'Neill's "involved and cosmic posturings," to the liberal newspaper *PM* as "a journal of salvation," to the "genial condescension of an Irish cop to a Fifth Avenue doorman."

Gibbs claimed to be "comparatively accomplished only in the construction of English sentences," but he also had a nicely angled point of view and the courage of his opinions. Intellectually, he was hostage to no one, not even Shakespeare. He thought *Romeo and Juliet* an ill-made play: "There are too many innocent misunderstandings and staggering coincidences, too many potions and poisons; in the end, far too many bodies cluttering up the Capulets' not so very quiet tomb." Sacred cows, he felt, made good hamburger. Paul Robeson, he wrote, overacted in the part of Othello.

To the gods of modernism, he brought no sacrifices but, instead, a heavy dose of useful philistinism. Of *Waiting for Godot*, he wrote: "All I can say in a critical sense is that I have seldom seen such meager moonshine stated with such inordinate fuss." Jean-Paul Sartre's *No Exit* he called "little more than a one-act drama of unusual monotony and often quite remarkable foolishness."

On lighter matters, writing about Maurice Chevalier's stagey pursuit of women, he compared French seduction to women's basketball: "There is a lot of squealing and jumping up and down, but certainly not much in the scoring department." In explaining the breakup of the old Algonquin Round Table group, he wrote:

Those who didn't move away [to Hollywood, to Connecticut or Bucks County] were by now temperamentally unfit for the old close association, since there is nothing more enervating to the artist than the daily society of a lot of people who are just as famous as he is.

One of Gibbs's few idols was Max Beerbohm, also a literary man of all work, with great skill as a caricaturist added. Gibbs and Beerbohm shared the quality of sublime detachment. No man of his day was less *parti pris* than Wolcott Gibbs. After reading the more than 600 pages of his writing in *Backward Ran Sentences*, I cannot characterize his politics. A. J. Liebling, his colleague on the *New Yorker*, claimed that his own politics were "let Paris be gay," which turned out not to be true in the case of Liebling (who was a fairly standard liberal) but was, I believe, true of Gibbs, although gaiety, clearly, was scarcely his specialty.

In a fine formulation, Vinciguerra writes that Gibbs "embodied [the *New Yorker*'s] archetypal combination of blunt honesty, sly wit, exacting standards, and elegant condescension." The *New Yorker* of those days seemed mildly aristocratic, making everything seem easily within the grasp of its writers and, perhaps as important, of its readers. Hilton Kramer, in an essay-review of James Thurber's *The Years with Ross*, recounts that a *New Yorker* fact-checker called him countless times to get straight the positions of various French art critics for a piece the magazine's own art critic, Robert Coates, was writing about the European art scene. When the piece appeared, Kramer was struck "at the absurdity of the feigned ease" with which it was presented in Coates's published copy: "I marveled at the discrepancy between the pains taken to get the facts of the matter as accurate as possible, and the quite different effort that had gone into making the subject seem easy and almost inconsequential to the reader." What was going on? "For myself," Kramer wrote,

> I don't see how we can avoid concluding that the principal reason for the *New Yorker*'s method is ignorance: the ignorance of writers first of all, and ultimately the ignorance of readers. In a society which could assume a certain level of education and sophistication in its writers and journalists—which could

make the assumption because it shared in that education and sophistication—there would be more of a public faith that writers knew more or less what they are talking about.

But, then, the magazine has never been without its critics. Robert Warshow, in 1947, wrote: "The *New Yorker* has always dealt with experience not by trying to understand it but by prescribing the attitude to be adopted toward it. This makes it possible to feel intelligent without thinking, and it is a way of making everything tolerable, for the assumption of a suitable attitude toward experience can give one the illusion of having dealt with it adequately." The charge here on the part of Kramer and Warshow, of course, is middlebrowism—the pretense of culture when the efforts behind attaining true culture have been efficiently eliminated for the reader.

The charge of middlebrowism became more difficult to prove as the *New Yorker* began, under William Shawn, to load up on certified intellectual contributors. Edmund Wilson was the first of these, writing regularly for the magazine's book section. Dwight Macdonald soon joined Wilson, and his assignment was, precisely, to attack such middlebrow cultural artifacts as Mortimer Adler and Robert Hutchins's *Great Books of the Western World*, the *New Revised Standard Version of the Bible*, and *Webster's Third International Dictionary*. Harold Rosenberg signed on as the magazine's regular art critic; Susan Sontag wrote for the magazine. Vladimir Nabokov, Isaac Bashevis Singer, Saul Bellow, and other highbrow novelists regularly published stories in the *New Yorker*. Two of the great controversial intellectual publishing events—Hannah Arendt's *Eichmann in Jerusalem* and James Baldwin's essay "The Fire Next Time"—first appeared in the magazine's pages.

The reason so many intellectuals, in effect, went over to the *New Yorker* is no more complicated than that they were asked. The money the magazine paid was much greater than that paid by any other even semi-serious magazine. Quite as important, the *New Yorker* had the best of all American audiences. Anything published in its pages was certain to be read by everyone a writer cared about. Even people who didn't much like the magazine felt obliged at least to glimpse it. Writing for the magazine, one discovered an America one could not be sure existed until one heard from its readers: the cardiologist from Tacoma, Washington, who kept up his ancient Greek, the lady from Tyler, Texas, who read Proust in French and with intellectual penetration, and many more.

William Shawn's regular contributors not merely appreciated but adulated him, a writer's editor. Two of my friends who were staff writers under his reign never referred to him as other than Mr. Shawn. Editorially, Shawn was immensely tolerant, allowing writers to take years to complete assignments (he could also hold back pieces for decades and not run them at all). He permitted his writers to run on at great, sometimes stupefying, length: Long John McPhee pieces on geology or E. J. Kahn pieces on corn were notable winners in the eye-glazing boredom category. A man who does not press a writer about deadlines, never suggests that length might be a problem, and pays him handsomely—that, from a writer's point of view, is an immortal editor.

William Shawn was the editor responsible for changing the *New Yorker*, taking it from the realm of smart into that of intellectual journalism. Was it a happy change? Under it, Wolcott Gibbs was replaced as drama critic after his death by Kenneth Tynan, a man much more attuned—some would say too well attuned—to the avant-garde. Arlene Croce, along with Edwin Denby the best dance critic America has known, covered ballet. Movies, which had hitherto been treated as, at best, trivial entertainment became, under Pauline Kael, quite literally the talk of the town, with Miss Kael's opinion on the latest movie weighing more heavily among the so-called educated classes than the opinions of the chairman of the Federal Reserve.

The magazine also became more political. Earlier, E. B. White would occasionally write Notes & Comments editorials urging the need for world government, an idea always up there among the Top Ten dopiest political ideas of all time. Under Shawn, political ideas became more specific. He ran Rachel Carson on pollution, Lewis Mumford on city planning, and several pieces highly critical of American involvement in Vietnam. The magazine's politics were liberal but—an important qualification—liberal without being hostage to any political party, professing to speak on behalf of the greater good of the nation.

During his long editorship, Shawn held to an unvarying policy of no profane words or descriptions of sex in the *New Yorker*. (Whenever one saw a John Cheever or John Updike story in *Harper's* or *Esquire*, one could be fairly certain that it contained bits of fancy fornication.) Harold Ross's advice upon hiring editors for the magazine was "Don't f— the contributors," which Wolcott Gibbs claimed was the closest Ross came to enunciating an editorial policy. This was a policy violated by, of all people, Shawn himself; after his death it was revealed by Lillian Ross, one of the magazine's longtime reporters, that she and the married Shawn had had a love affair of many years' standing.

Much to the consternation of the *New Yorker*'s staff, in 1987 William Shawn's retirement was forced, at the age of 79, by S. I. Newhouse, who had bought the magazine for his Condé Nast publishing empire. Robert Gottlieb, a successful publisher's editor, replaced Shawn. His major contribution to the magazine was to allow profane language and sexy stories in its pages. He departed five years later, to be replaced by Tina Brown, who set out to make the magazine genuinely with-it. She had a taste for épatering the genteel with gaudy covers and photographs, and also made it seem, through her selection of articles, as if the most important things in the world were Hollywood, designer culture, and royalty.

After Tina Brown left in 1998 to begin a short-lived magazine called *Talk*, the magazine was taken over by David Remnick, an earnest journalist who had written well on the Soviet Union and other matters. *New Yorker* staff members, seeing this as a return to seriousness, were pleased. Remnick's ascension also meant a turn toward a more specific politics. The politics were liberalism now distinctly aligned with the Democratic party. A large number of its general articles made American foreign policy seem what the left calls "the imperialist project," and its "Comment" editorials, written most weeks by Hendrik Hertzberg, read with all the complexity of old western movies: Good guys wear Democratic hats, villains wear Republican ones, and that isn't the Lone Ranger but Barack Obama riding to the rescue.

Relevance has its costs. In its covers, its coverage of events, its need to seem *au courant*, and its insistent politics, the *New Yorker* has begun to seem more and more like a weekly news or opinion journal ("of salvation") than the magazine once adored by earlier generations of readers. The *New Yorker* Wolcott Gibbs wrote for—elegant, literary, ironic, laced with a bracing skepticism—was the spiritual house organ for people looking for relief from the clang of rivaling opinions, the barkering of each Next New Thing, the knowingness of haughty punditry, the maelstrom of the world's unrelenting noise. The *New Yorker* of the current day flourishes financially, its circulation said to be in the ascendant. The *New Yorker* of Wolcott Gibbs's time, published in the world we now live in, would probably not last out the year.

Part Eight

Intellectuals

Leo Lerman

(2007)

THERE IS AN OLD JOKe about a man named Sam, who knew everyone and was known by everyone, so that, Easter morning, on St. Peter's Square, when Sam appears on the balcony of the Vatican, a number of people in the crowd are heard to murmur, "Who's the guy in the white yarmulke with Sam?"

For nearly 50 years a writer and editor for various Condé Nast and other slick magazines, Leo Lerman was a lot like Sam. Born in 1914, Lerman was a New Yorker by spirit, temperament, and outlook. He was also unabashedly Jewish, gay, and very smart. Such was his glittering web of acquaintance that one could almost say that, if you lived in Manhattan between 1940 and 1994, and Leo Lerman didn't know you, you have to consider the possibility that you were not worth knowing.

The great frustration of Leo Lerman's life was a long-planned but never executed great book, a Proustian chronicle of his life and times. Lerman was a devoted admirer of Proust, and thought himself well positioned to be the American Marcel Proust. Off on one journalistic project or another—he was, briefly, the second editor-in-chief of the revived *Vanity Fair*, between the original editor, a man named Richard Locke, and Tina Brown—and with endless social engagements intervening, Lerman really hadn't the *sitzfleish*, or bottom patience, to sit down to the composition of this book, which was at first to be a novel, then an extensive memoir, then an autobiography, and ended being nowhere near a reality.

Lerman did make a number of abortive runs at writing his phantom book. He was also the keeper of a journal, in the form of many notebooks filled with gossip and introspection, found after his death. In these notebooks he chronicled the lives of the talented, with a special eye toward their character, not excluding their foibles. Now, through the good and patient work of Stephen Pascal, for many years Lerman's assistant at Condé Nast, the bits of Lerman's uncompleted memoir, many items from his journal, and parts of his correspondence, the book Leo Lerman longed to write has come into the world in a form its author would never have imagined. The title *The Grand Surprise* is taken from the second name of the Camberwell Beauty, a rare and exotic butterfly, lepidoptery being a boyhood love of Lerman's. The title is a good one, its point being that Leo Lerman's days were given over to the endless pursuit of another grand surprise, this one in the form of the perfect social life.

"Among New York's movers and markers of art," Stephen Pascal writes in his Introduction, "Leo Lerman grew legendary as a man who knew everyone and had seen everything. For fifty years, it seemed he attended every debut, opening, and *vernissage* in the city and had the crowd at his place to celebrate afterward."

Many of the usual suspects were among his guests: Truman Capote, Paul and Jane Bowles, Carson McCullers, Virgil Thomson, Anaïs Nin, Katherine Anne Porter, the Trillings, Diana and Lionel, the Bernsteins, Leonard and Felicia, and several others. His circle of friends and acquaintances was also highly Europeanized, and included Marlene Dietrich, George Balanchine, Maria Callas, Noel Coward, Margot Fonteyn, and Gertrude Lawrence.

Bald early, heavyset (weight was always a problem), wearing a beard because of a serious car accident that scarred the bottom part his face and left him with serious health problems as he grew older, Lerman in midlife resembled the Henry James whom others have described as looking like a sea captain. Perfectly at ease with his homosexuality, his Jewishness, his autodidactical education (he went to Feagin School of Dramatic Art in New York, where he trained to become a stage-manager, though he always read widely and with taste and penetration), he seemed altogether at ease in the world of high fashion, performing arts, visual art, and smart journalism.

Lerman lived with two men during his adult life, both painters, the second, a man named Gray Foy, who is alive today. His partners tended to do the heavy lifting of organizing his domestic life, while he paid the brunt of the expenses and brought in the great names for his famous parties. Those portions of his book that take up the emotional complications of his relationships with these two men are the dullest parts of *The Grand Surprise*. What is of much greater interest is, in Stephen Pascal's words, Lerman's continuous pursuit of "powerful beauty, performance, and character through a long life." Lerman died at 80.

The Grand Surprise is a very homosexual book. At its center are portraits of powerful women—*monstres sacrés*—whom he cultivated and who were attracted to Lerman in great part because of his kindness and charm, in lesser but not insignificant part, one supposes, because he posed no sexual threat to them. The first of the powerhouse women in Lerman's life were Betsy Blackwell, Carmel Snow, Diana Vreeland, the editors of *Mademoiselle*, *Vogue*, *Harper's Bazaar*, and other women's magazines. But Lerman was also a close friend and confidant of Eleonora von Mendelssohn (herself the lover of Walter Rathenau, Max Reinhardt, and Arturo Toscanini), Marlene Dietrich, Maria Callas, Diana Trilling, and Mina Curtiss (sister of Lincoln Kirstein). To take up with such women, divas of the spirit, is to put oneself in a permanently secondary, largely subservient position—subservient, that is, to their own tireless self-absorption. This Lerman was willing to do, which didn't preclude his taking the measure of their gloriousness and wretchedness both. "Adoration nourished her," he writes of Marlene Dietrich, "the way health food sustains others."

THE GOSSIP QUOTIENT in *The Grand Surprise* is marvelously high. Lerman cites Capote for genius in this line, remarking that "Truman told so many dreadful things about everybody. It's wonderful how Truman acquires bits of information and then passes them off as his own." Whether Lerman confined his own best gossip to his notebooks or passed it out along with the canapés at his parties, is difficult to know.

Some of the gossip is purely amusing, such as Lerman's reporting that Frieda Lawrence, widow of the novelist, mistook Lionel Trilling for Diana's son. He lunches with Dame Rebecca West, claiming it was if he had dined "with the most brilliant gossip columnist in the world." He reports that, in conversation, Cary Grant went in heavily for four-letter words. Here, from a letter to his brother, is a perfect three-cushioned name-drop: "I had a lovely, lively encounter with Princess Margaret last week at Cecil Beaton's party for Audrey Hepburn. . . ." The index to *The Grand Surprise* reads like the Yellow Pages of intellectual and artistic society between 1940 and 1990.

A lot of the gossip is about people's sex lives. Nice to know, for example, that while Leonard Bernstein chased boys, his wife Felicia had an affair with Goddard Lieberson, president of Columbia Records. Yul Brynner, we learn, was bisexual, as was Vladimir Horowitz. If Truman Capote is to be believed—a case of gossip at the second remove, of which *The Grand Surprise* contains a fair amount—so was Steve McQueen; another piece of second-remove gossip features Claudette Colbert as a lesbian. Maria Callas tells Lerman that Aristotle Onassis slept with Lee Radziwill before Jacqueline Kennedy nabbed him (and his money) off for herself.

"I adore gossip of all kinds," Lerman writes in 1970, but then adds that "I gossip less and less, save to myself. Of course these notebooks are extreme narcissism. This is a search to find myself and my times in my own looking glass, and in looking glasses held up by others." If Leo Lerman were a retailer (and re-teller) of gossip merely, or a Vogue magazine scribbler only, he would not be of much interest. But he was more than that—he was a serious person, caught between his ambitions and his fantasies. His fantasy was to live among the famous and talented; his ambition to prove himself as a member among them in good standing by giving evidence of his own talent. His was a rare case of a man able to realize his fantasy but never—unless now, posthumously—achieve his ambition.

"I am a born voyeur," Lerman wrote in his journal, "which in the most positive sense means: I love life." His curiosity was wide and so was his appreciation. "I admire industry in people and courage and quiet and devotion and humor and a sense of irony and laughter and a loving heart and optimism and genuine *douleur* and style and panache," he wrote. "I detest negativism and destructiveness and niggardly-stingy ways. Energy exults me."

Enamored of the high life though Lerman was, he was also skillful at seeing beneath its sheen. In Mary McCarthy he recognized "a self-afflicted scourge," ungenerous, heartless, chiding. He views Alvin Ailey's famous work *Revelations* as entertainment passing itself off as art, an interesting distinction. Ballet, which he loved, he perceives as "dedicated people, ultimately as ill-fated as butterflies, the living symbols of transience." He spots the avariciousness of Stravinsky: "Always the eater, not the eaten." Gore Vidal he finds "complacent, pompous, assured that his every platitude is an apothegm, a witty wisdom."

Self-doubt plays through these pages. Lerman regularly blames himself for the self-indulgence of his life. "I have wasted my life," he wrote, when still in his thirties. "A sloppy, sloppy life—mostly notions and remarks and little achievement." The "dressy life I now experience," he realizes, keeps him from doing the serious work he ought to be doing. What good, after all, would Proust be without the justifying achievement of *Remembrance of Things Past*?

He realizes that one of the major aspects of his life has been building up other people, "trying to make everything and everyone glamorous, a star" through the efforts of his journalism in *Vogue* and elsewhere. He fears he may be no more than a *naches-schlepper*, a Yiddish phrase meaning a hanger-on, someone who trails after the gifted and fortunate. The pursuit of artificial glamour at times gets to him. "Suddenly," he writes, "I am bone-tired—from coping with neurotics."

Commenting on the sale of Proust manuscripts to the University of Texas, he notes how fantastic is the very notion of Proust in Texas: "I see how possible it is to live in a fantasy world and become stranger and stranger. See! I've lived that way all of my life." Leo Lerman had a seat in the dress circle of the fashionable life of his time, though he knew that he paid a high price for it.

And yet there is something redeeming in Lerman's kindness ("tactlessness," he writes, "is always cruel") his ardor for life (his constant curiosity, he felt, made suicide an impossibility for him), his preference always for the personal and the palpable. ("It is depersonalization I hate, and this is why

I am against so much of 'modern' art and psychoanalysis.") His relentless sociability reveals not a social climber but a truly gregarious soul.

That a social life of the kind Leo Lerman lived is no longer possible is more than a touch sad. Politics today are too divisive to make such a life any longer likely among artists and intellectuals; and then there are the further divisions, even in the hollow world of celebrity, into youth culture, black culture, academic culture, and more, all working against the formation of a coherent world of the smart and talented such as Lerman enjoyed.

Leo Lerman discovered the Grand Surprise. And he was smart enough to recognize that behind the Grand Surprise was, as he put it in his notebook one night, the home truth of "how gay and sad life is simultaneously." His rich book provides charming and irrefutable testimony that this is so.

Walter Cronkite

(2012)

But, gee, to depend on somebody to tell you the absolute truth
every night and give you The Word every night, that's a bad thing,
a serious problem in a democracy.

WALTER CRONKITE

H ERE'S A LITTLE SECRET: Walter Cronkite, during his life
billed as the most trusted man in the nation, the conscience
of his country, the sagacious old uncle to us all, wasn't very
smart, and not especially wise either. He was instead a man making a living out of television journalism—a very good one—by pretending to be
serious and objective, when it is far from clear that he was either.

I had my first clue of this when, in 1971, I attended a talk Cronkite
gave at the University of Chicago under the auspices of an institution
there known as the Urban Journalism Center. Such panjandrums from
journalism and academic life as Chicago was able to turn out were there
to hear him. He proceeded to speak about the importance of professors
imbuing their students with the spirit of dissent. With an air of perfect
confidence, without a hem or haw, the slightest sputter or stutter, he
emitted an assemblage of platitudes, utterly unaware that this same spirit
of dissent he was urging had in recent years just about ended in setting
fire to universities, as he might have said, "across this great land of ours."
A professor at my table looked at me, his eyebrows just about transcend-
ing his forehead, and asked: "Where has this guy been?"

My second clue came when I read a preface Cronkite wrote to a paper-back edition of George Orwell's *1984*, and discovered he thought that the target of the novel was not the brutal devastation of life, private and public, under totalitarianism, but chiefly the danger posed by the technology of modernity. "*1984* is an anguished lament and a warning that vibrates powerfully when we may not be strong enough nor wise enough nor moral enough to cope with the kind of power we have learned to amass," Cronkite wrote. Throughout this preface, the Soviet Union and China, whose governments treated their respective populations as conquered nations, go unmentioned. The preface was written in 1983, and by then Cronkite had entered that phase of liberalism that finds no country more dangerous than one's own.

I never met Walter Cronkite, but one day in 2003, I was sitting in the dining room of the Hotel Sacher in Vienna when he sauntered in. He was in Vienna to introduce the program of warhorses played by the Vienna Philharmonic for its annual New Year's concert, a telecast of which ran on PBS. It was a regular gig for him, who, so far as one could determine, knew nothing about serious music. The flutter in the room as people recognized his presence was that accorded a movie star. Cronkite was indeed a star, not of the stage or screen but of that more pervasive medium of television. In his day he was the most powerful and famous figure in mass media.

Now that there are scores of cable channels, and that the Internet has become the major news source for younger generations, such power and fame as Cronkite enjoyed in his lifetime are no longer possible. The three major networks still offer their versions of the evening news, but as one can conclude from their sponsors—Viagra, Cialis, Nexium, Boniva, and the rest—their audience is an older one, aging fast. With the advent and success of Fox News and MSNBC, which play directly to their audiences' already formed politics, the older news offerings seem even less in demand.

If one wants a perfectly ideal picture of how the world—that great ninny, as Henry James called it—took Walter Cronkite, one cannot do better than this note he received from Lady Bird Johnson not long after his retirement:

We love you so much. A stalwart with whom we've shared moments that touched depths of despair and the farthest reaches of space. We've mourned with you some of America's saddest days and soared as we celebrated some of mankind's highest aspirations and achievements. You've been an advocate for what is best in the United States, and we are better for it.

Douglas Brinkley, a historian and Walter Cronkite's new biographer, claims that Cronkite's role was that "of a steadying presence in frightening times. He was a national leader of a new sort: the healer in chief." What was more, according to Brinkley, "even when he was announcing tragic news, he was himself a reminder that America would persevere."

When Cronkite retired as anchorman of the *CBS Evening News* in 1981, the novelist Kurt Vonnegut, in an article in the *Nation* called "A Reluctant Big Shot," worried that democracy was henceforth at risk. "So now a kindly teacher has left our village," Vonnegut wrote. "I'm not a religious man," Jack Paar noted. "But I do believe in Walter Cronkite."

How did it happen that this hardworking, highly competitive, but otherwise far from brilliant or even especially thoughtful man attained such prominence and fame? This question will be uppermost in the mind of anyone who plunges into the more than 800 pages (text and scholarly apparatus included) of Brinkley's *Cronkite*. There he will find several answers, none of them satisfactory.

An infelicitous writer, Brinkley has produced a cliché-laden work: oil in his pages is "black gold," museums are "world class," memories are like "steel traps," rivalrous journalists come "loaded for bear," and "push," surprising to report, generally "comes to shove." Imprecise and awkward phrases stud his pages, where people are never given jobs but are "tasked with" them and "enormity" and "masterful" and "fulsome" along with other words are blithely misused. Brinkley seems to think that Billy Wilder and not Alfred Hitchcock directed the movie *Foreign Correspondent*, that Virgil Thomson is "America's premier composer," that Melville's "Bartleby the Scrivener" is a story about endurance on the job. At one point he remarks that *The Lucy Show*, *Perry Mason*, and *See It Now* "were genuine highpoints to applaud for the ages," which suggests both the range of his mind and the fundamental unsoundness of his judgment. Matters are not much helped by Professor Brinkley's comfortable assumption that political liberalism and moral goodness are one and the same.

Brinkley finds Cronkite guilty of various character flaws: cheapness, excessive competitiveness, an unforgiving nature (he resented Edward R. Murrow, Barbara Walters, and Dan Rather all his days). He accepted free travel junkets, served up softball questions as an interviewer of presidents and others, and often played it safe in corporate wars, protecting his own job and status before all else. But through the length of *Cronkite*, which reprises assassinations, space launchings, presidential conventions and elections, intramural power struggles at CBS, and which provides biographical bits about nearly everyone who has ever done or been associated with national television news, Brinkley never attempts to take the measure of Walter Cronkite's mind.

Cronkite's occupation was that of anchorman. The very word came into being when, in the first telecast of a national political convention, in 1952, it was assigned to him upon becoming CBS's central figure, reported to by television newsmen bringing in tidbits of news from the convention floor. So exclusively was the term *anchorman* associated with his name that for a time in Sweden, he tells us in *A Reporter's Life* (1996), his autobiography, anchormen were called "cronkiters."

An anchorman is a man who reads news that other men and women have probably written for him. In France the anchorman is known by the more accurate name of *speakerine*, suggesting an instrument through which others speak. The chief requirements for the job seem to be two: a good voice and a good hairdo. Once, when Cronkite appeared on *The Mary Tyler Moore Show*, Ted Baxter, that sitcom's wonderful send-up of inept anchormen, said to him: "Let's talk shop. What words do you have trouble pronouncing?"

Cronkite did the *CBS Evening News* for 19 years, from 1962 to early 1981, along with doing various television news specials and being the main voice for CBS's coverage of anything of national newsworthy significance. Along with anchorman at *CBS Evening News*, he had the title of managing editor, which meant that, with his various executive producers, he decided which news stories were to run each evening and in what order of priority.

Cronkite's skill as an anchorman was his ability to ad-lib at great length on camera without a script (something Edward R. Murrow wasn't able to do) and to boil complex questions, issues, and problems into capsule summary in a way that the average person could understand (something Murrow had no wish to do). He also brought a sense of gravity to the proceedings; he himself took the news very seriously, and he would later mock the advent of Barbara Walters and others who tended to meld news and entertainment into a stew he called "infotainment" that brought high ratings.

And then there was his face: Framed by his parted and combed-back graying hair, he had earnest blue eyes under bushy eyebrows that late in life required waxing and a carefully groomed military mustache that diminished a rather large and fleshy nose, all of which made him look like Walt Disney, but for adults. His wife claimed that people liked him because he looked like their dentist, but who likes their dentist? His 40th high school class reunion came closer when it voted him the man from whom you were most likely to buy a used car (the very antithesis of Richard Nixon). Cronkite's was a face best seen on glass, through a screen; it was a face only a nation could love, and in his case did, emphatically. Between 1967 and his retirement in 1981, with him as its anchor, *CBS Evening News* easily led the other two major networks in the ratings.

Cronkite's presentation of the news, and of news events, was not to everyone's taste. I, for one, preferred the team of Chet Huntley and David Brinkley, whom he displaced as number one in viewer ratings. Cronkite took the news too straight; he admired American politicians too much, whereas Huntley and Brinkley, and Brinkley especially, tended to view them and politics generally in a more Menckenesque light—that is, as carnival, a carnival in good part to be sure of bunkum, which seemed not only more charming but more realistic. Cronkite, solid and humorless, never made that mistake.

66 IT ALL STARTED in a little 500-watt radio station in Fresno, California," Ted Baxter of *The Mary Tyler Moore Show* was fond of saying. Cronkite's beginning was in St. Joseph, Missouri, where he was born in 1916, the son of a dentist, whose alcoholism caused his divorce from his wife when Cronkite was 16. By that point, the Cronkites (the name is

Dutch) had moved, first to Kansas City and thence to Houston. Walter, a perfectly ordinary kid, worked on the school paper. He became greatly enamored of newspaper work owing to a teacher who inculcated the principles, such as they are, of journalism in all his students: a respect for facts, a need to check sources, the importance of making oneself understood through plain style.

The young Cronkite got a job on the *Houston Post*. His would be the purely spectatorial life, not making news but reporting it, though some would say that, once he attained his great eminence, he made a certain amount of news on his own by pushing events in a way he wanted them to go. "I used to think that life wouldn't be worth living if I wasn't in on the action," he remarked late in life, though, as we shall see, he never really stopped thinking it.

Cronkite lasted two years as a student at the University of Texas, for he hadn't much interest in bookish things. While there he wrote freelance articles about the university, which he placed in the *Houston Post* and elsewhere, and got a job on an Austin radio station. He cultivated his radio voice: sonorous yet unpretentious, dramatic yet familiar, portentous when need be. After giving him a tryout for a job on a radio station in Kansas City, the man who hired him took him into the station manager's office to announce, "Here is a man with the best radio voice I've heard in my years in radio." That voice was rich beyond its years, without accent, and a perfect vessel for conveying seriousness.

At 26 Cronkite married a woman who also worked on newspapers in Kansas City and then for Hallmark Cards. Brinkley remarks that Cronkite's wife was a better writer than he. No surprise here, for Cronkite was a pure journalist, and journalists for the most part aren't truly writers but instead collectors of information. The essayist Midge Decter, when working at *Harper's* magazine with David Halberstam, Larry King, and others who had acquired their training on newspapers, once explained the difference to me. "When you and I decide to write about a subject, we read what has already been written about it, we read things connected with it, we think about it, we brood over it, and only then do we begin to write about it," she said. "When a journalist gets an assignment, he does none of these things; instead he picks up the phone." The problems only begin when journalists start thinking, and in recent decades, alas, they have been thinking more and more.

Cronkite's big break as a journalist came in 1935, when he got a job at the Kansas City bureau of United Press, one of the leading wire-news services of the day. UP had a tradition of tough journalism, done on a shoestring, with high standards and a relentless focus on scoops. The company used Cronkite at its different bureaus, and eventually he went off to cover World War II for it. He had, as they say, a good war. He became known as "the Dean of Air-War Writers," having gone along on a few bombing missions over Germany. (He was himself rejected for military service owing to color-blindness.) He would later be the UP's man at the Nuremberg Trials and its chief Moscow correspondent. The United Press may be said to have put the blacking on Cronkite's journalistic training; CBS would apply the polish.

At one point during the war, Murrow attempted to lure Cronkite away from the UP to join him and his circle of reporters known as Murrow's Boys (a circle that included Robert Trout, Eric Sevareid, Howard K. Smith, Charles Collingwood, and Richard C. Hottelet) working at CBS radio. Murrow was every journalist's ideal of the great foreign correspondent. Cronkite was among Murrow's early admirers, and he was tempted, but a large raise from UP caused him to refuse Murrow's offer. Murrow and Cronkite would always remain wary of the other, each jealous of his own prerogatives.

Murrow had flash and flair, Cronkite stability and steadiness. If Murrow was television news broadcasting's Babe Ruth, Cronkite was its Lou Gehrig. Gehrig was known in his day as Iron Horse for his durability in never missing a game; among his colleagues, Cronkite was called Iron Pants for his ability to work a microphone for hours on end, as he did during the aftermath of the John F. Kennedy assassination and funeral and during the sometimes extensive delays before space launchings.

People remember Cronkite taking off his thick-frame black glasses, fighting back tears, before announcing, definitively, that John F. Kennedy was dead in Dallas. They remember his crying out "Go, Baby, Go!" when spaceships made successful launches from Cape Canaveral. They remember his declaring, after a two-week visit to Vietnam during the

Tet Offensive, that our war there was a "stalemate," and thus unwinnable, to which many attributed great significance. They remember his role in bringing together Anwar Sadat and Menachem Begin for a combined television interview.

But no one, I think, will recall a memorable, or penetrating, or original statement made by Walter Cronkite during his 50-odd years on television, and this is because he never made one. Nor was he any better in prose. His memoir *A Reporter's Life*, though a bestseller in its day, is a dullish, matter-of-fact book. One of Walter Cronkite's real advantages was that he had the common touch; and the most certain way of acquiring that touch is to have a commonplace mind.

Cronkite began his career as a man without strong politics. During World War II he had no qualms about supporting American troops. He thought the NASA space program one of the great American endeavors and hero-worshipped the early generation of astronauts, and through his career was even thought a shill for NASA. He much admired Dwight David Eisenhower, so much so that many Democrats, John F. Kennedy among them, thought him a Republican. Unlike Murrow, or Howard K. Smith, or Eric Sevareid (also known as Eric the Red and Eric Clarified), early in his career he showed no taste for editorializing, for inserting his own opinions into stories, and he preferred to think himself purely a purveyor of the news.

This began to change, as did so many things, with the 1960s. Cronkite first faced criticism of the media from the contingent that backed Barry Goldwater at the 1964 Republican convention at San Francisco. Even former President Eisenhower, in a speech to the convention, inserted a paragraph about the press's antipathy to the Republican Party. Cronkite himself was wary of Goldwater, and CBS, as even Douglas Brinkley allows, treated the Goldwater campaign unfairly, making out its candidate to be "a kind of neo-Nazi" and "the horn-rimmed face of the John Birch Society, a sagebrush reactionary even more unfit for White House command than Joe McCarthy."

The 1968 Democratic convention, at which the Chicago police and the hippie protesters confronted each other directly, drove Cronkite further to the left. At one point during the proceedings, he called Mayor

Richard J. Daley's security men, who had manhandled an aggressive Dan Rather on the floor of the convention, "thugs." Later he would, as his colleagues felt, give the mayor a pass in a too-gentle interview. "We used to call Walter 'Mr. Softball,'" the CBS correspondent Robert Pierpoint said. "If you were a president or a general, Walter turned submissive."

Vietnam, however, was the great turning point in Cronkite's career. At first he was hawkish on the question of that war, feeling it was necessary and certainly winnable. A trip to the country during the 1968 Tet Offensive staged by the North Vietnamese caused him to believe it was neither. CBS organized a special on the subject, "Report from Vietnam," whose conclusion, read though not written by Cronkite, ran:

> To say that we are mired in stalemate seems the only realistic, yet unsatisfactory conclusion. On the off chance that military and political analysts are right, in the next few months, we must test the enemy's intentions, in case this is indeed his last big gasp before negotiations. But it is increasingly clear to this reporter that the only rational way out then will be to negotiate, not as victors, but as an honorable people who lived up to their pledge to defend Democracy and did the best they could.

The reverberations from this have been disputed. Some claim that President Lyndon Johnson said, in slightly different variations, "If I've lost Cronkite, I've lost the country"; and that Cronkite coming out against the war was the determining factor in Johnson's not running for reelection in 1968. In his book *The Powers That Be*, David Halberstam wrote that "it was the first time in history that a war had been declared over by a commentator."

Cronkite's view was largely formed by R. W. Apple, David Halberstam, and other *New York Times* journalists. His conclusion about the viability of the war in Vietnam after Tet wasn't exactly a minority position in 1968. Little if any courage had been required in the rendering of his verdict. If anything, it brought him enormous personal dividends. "He entered the main-game annals of American history," to quote Brinkley's bloated language. "With white streaks in his closely cropped hair and mustache, Cronkite had come to epitomize old-fashioned values in an era of rote lies. America asked for the truth about Vietnam, and Cronkite dutifully delivered." What Cronkite dutifully delivered was the standard media line of the moment.

CBS Evening News didn't do much in the way of original reporting with the Watergate scandal. But it did regularly recapitulate the findings of Woodward and Bernstein at the *Washington Post*, and this was enough. Doing so lent imprimatur, or as Brinkley says, "high-octane credence," to the newspaper's efforts. Ben Bradlee, the *Post*'s editor, told Brinkley, "When Cronkite aired the Watergate bits, the sun came out for me. It was just like being blessed; if Cronkite was taking the Watergate story seriously, *everyone* in journalism would."

After his enshrinement as a hero in history, helping end the Vietnam War and helping bring down Richard Nixon, Cronkite increasingly became a pontificator. He spoke out about the shortcomings of television news, which he considered, rightly, little more than the announcement of headlines. He began lecturing on the subject of that old Jeffersonian saw of a well-functioning democracy requiring a well-informed electorate. (A true enough statement, but it is far from clear if the United States, or any other country, has ever had such an electorate.)

After his Vietnam stalemate declaration and his aid in bringing down Nixon, the honors and awards flooded in: Emmys, Peabodys, honorary degrees—Cronkite, Arthur Schlesinger Jr., and John Kenneth Galbraith used to joke about who had more of the latter—and a Medal of Freedom bestowed by Jimmy Carter. New York City made him one of its "living legends." A journalism school at Arizona State University was named after him. When Cronkite sold his four-story townhouse at 519 East 84th Street, his wife said that her main regret was losing the backyard, "for I had a plot of land where I could bury all of Walter's plaques."

Why? Why was Walter Cronkite somehow selected as the great man of the media? It wasn't his intelligence, it wasn't his learning, it wasn't his charm or wit, it wasn't his penetration or high style or courage, for over a long career he demonstrated, insofar as one can make out, none of these things. When Cronkite retired from *CBS Evening News* in March 1981, an article in the *New Republic* cited him for being "heroically honest," the nation's "one incorruptible guardian, who has won the kind of trusted admiration our leaders ought to have deserved," but obviously didn't. For years, the article went on, he "managed to keep alien realities at a safe distance, putting the world in order every weeknight. In short, his charisma partly results from a long record of apparent objectivity." Not a word of this tribute is backed up, of course, and what is that word apparent doing in its final sentence?

Others claimed that it was Cronkite's rootedness in America that gave him his magical attractiveness. He was Midwestern, small-town, never forgot his Kansas City origins. People responded to that, or so the claim goes. Brinkley writes: "This was a key to all the great TV newsmen's success: Never forget your hometown folks. Cronkite's hometown just happened to be the whole damn United States." Yet as early as the middle 1950s, Walter Cronkite had elided from working journalist to major celebrity. He would soon become a naturalized New Yorker, where people stopped him on the street for autographs. On Martha's Vineyard, at Edgartown, he kept a large house and private harbor for his yacht, and his social circle there included Jacqueline Onassis, John Lehman, William F. Buckley Jr., and Joseph Heller, not exactly your local Rotary Club.

In an interview with a boating magazine given in 1976—sailing was his passion—Cronkite averred:

> I don't understand my appeal. It gets down to an unknown
> quality, maybe communication of integrity. I have a sense of
> mission. That sounds pompous, but I like the news. Facts are
> sacred. I feel people should know about the world, should
> know the truth as much as possible. I care about the world,
> about people, about the future. Maybe that comes across.

Whether it did or not is difficult to say, but one thing that isn't is that any person who vaunts his own integrity probably doesn't have much, nor is anyone who publicly claims to care about people really likely to care much at all. No, the reason for Cronkite's appeal needs to be found elsewhere.

When Walter Cronkite retired, at the age of 64, from the *CBS Evening News*, he continued on as an employee at the network at a handsome salary. The vague plan was that he was to do documentaries on serious subjects, he would be on hand for continuing crises, he would be an ever-burbling fount of experience and wisdom. Along with unleashing him from the daily grind of a news show, it would also free him from his centrist pose with its need to hold back his true opinions. He would no longer be, as he told the *New York Times*, "an ideological eunuch."

What Cronkite turned out to be was a very standard left-winger, *Nation* magazine division. The older he got (he died at 92), the more liberal-left he became. At 88, he began a King Features newspaper column that was syndicated in 153 papers, which he used to berate anyone to the right of him. His judgments were less than solid. He claimed that in retrospect the Soviet threat was overrated. Of Jimmy Carter, he told an interviewer in *Rolling Stone*, "I think he's got one of the best brains of anyone I've known." He said that Bill Clinton has "Carter's intelligence, Johnson's experience, and Kennedy's gonads," a mixed compliment if ever there was one. He became a world-government man, deciding that "unlimited national sovereignty" could only end in "international anarchy," a sentiment that won him the Norman Cousins Global Governance Award. He was of course a great George W. Bush hater, suggesting at one point that Bush ought to be impeached for incompetence. His last great cause was the decriminalization of marijuana. "Nobody," as Brinkley writes, "held his overt liberalism against him." But in a media and intellectual culture dominated by liberalism, who might imagine anyone would?

What if, after his retirement from *CBS Evening News*, Cronkite, free from ideological constraints, had turned out to be a rock-ribbed Republican, a free-marketer, anti-big-government, anti-abortion, strongly pro-Israel? The honorary degrees would have had to be rescinded, the Freedom Medal returned, the journalism school in Arizona renamed The Brokaw School, all the encomia choked back. Katie Couric would have missed out on that "cathartic" feeling just knowing Walter Cronkite was around, but then George Clooney would not have to "hate the world" without him, as he said at Cronkite's death in 2009. The man who Douglas Brinkley claims "walked the plank for our nation," he who "in the last analysis became the TV conscience of Cold War America and beyond," would have been quickly and quietly swept into the dustbin of history. Nor would we ever have had Professor's Brinkley's otiose biography. And, as Walter Cronkite himself might have said, that's the way it is.

Paul Goodman in Retrospect

(1978)

6 6 **A** **VOICE A GOOD DEAL UNDERVALUED** is that of Paul Goodman," wrote a reviewer in *Book Week,* in 1968—or precisely
at the time when, far from being undervalued, Paul Goodman's
career was very much in the ascendant. In 1968 Goodman was easily this
country's best-known radical thinker, a spokesman for all who wanted
change in the United States, a prolific writer and lecturer, a man more
than any other admired by the young. "Goodman is, quite simply, inde-
fatigable," our reviewer in *Book Week* continued. "How characterize him?
The Pied Piper of the American Welfare State? Our St. Paul of the Inspiring Radicalism? The Intellectuals' Martin Luther King, Jr.? In some loose
sense Paul Goodman is all these things and more. He is an extraordinary man—decent, patient, incredibly learned—who has some extraordinary things to say about the way we in America live." Was our bubbling
reviewer perhaps being ironical, or was he altogether sincere in his enthusiasm? He was quite sincere, allow me to assure you, for I am in a privileged position to know, since I wrote the review.

I was about to complete that last sentence by writing, "since, to my
chagrin, I wrote the review." But I am less chagrined than amazed at what
time will do to a body of writing such as Paul Goodman's and to one's
own opinion of it. That review, of a book entitled *Like A Conquered*

Province: The Moral Ambiguity of America, about which I can remember almost nothing, ends by announcing that Goodman is "a man whose life restores honor to the word 'citizen.'" I believe that the book's paperback edition carries that line as a blurb, along with blurbs from a few other enthusiasts. If truth-in-advertising laws were enforced in the publishing business, I should be, if not in jail, then under heavy fine, for the fact is I no longer believe anything of the kind about Paul Goodman.

How, then, account for all that gushing enthusiasm? I suppose there would be no public need to account for it at all, but that the possibility of a resurgence of interest in the work of Paul Goodman, who died in 1972, may be under way. Three collections of his essays and occasional writings—*Drawing the Line, Nature Heals,* and *Creator Spirit, Come!*— have recently been published, edited by Professor Taylor Stoehr, who is also at work on a biography of Goodman. Yet a second Goodman biography is said to be in the works, this one by Raymond Rosenthal, the critic and translator from the Italian. Is it possible, then, that Paul Goodman's career might be gaining not its second but indeed its third wind?

One speaks of Goodman's career gaining not its second but indeed its third wind because the period of his greatest prominence, the 1960s, marked something of a comeback for Paul Goodman. After what looked to be a promising beginning as a literary man (critic and novelist, poet and playwright) and social theorist (psychologist and city planner, philosopher and anarchist), Goodman's career suffered its first serious reversal when, during World War II, the principal editors of *Partisan Review,* to which Goodman had contributed frequently, could not accommodate his conscientious objection—indeed active opposition—to the war. According to Professor Stoehr, Goodman "regarded the loss of *Partisan's* backing as fatal to his literary career," and came to believe that the magazine's editors, Philip Rahv and William Phillips, froze him out of other places of literary prestige and power.

If Paul Goodman's politics were troublesome, his sexual activities were scarcely less so. Technically, Goodman was a bisexual—he was married and the father of two children—but as with most men who call themselves bisexual, much of his energy seemed to be engaged in the pursuit of younger male lovers. Such at all events was the aggressiveness of Goodman's homosexuality that it caused him to be fired from jobs even at such morally flexible institutions as the University of Chicago during the early years of Robert Hutchins; the Manumitt School, an offshoot of A. J. Muste's Brookwood Labor College; and Black Mountain College. When Goodman was a strong Reichian, which in some respects he always remained, Wilhelm Reich himself claimed that Goodman was giving "Orgonomy" a bad name. Reading about Goodman's homosexual escapades, or hearing anecdotes from people who knew him, one is reminded of no one quite so much as the minor character in Clancy Sigal's last novel who was "expelled from Summerhill for behavior offensive to A. S. Neill."

Politically difficult, sexually impossible, Paul Goodman nevertheless plowed on. He collaborated with Fritz Perls on the book *Gestalt Therapy*, saw patients as a lay analyst, wrote his ambitious if not very readable novel, *The Empire City*. But generally, as he recorded in *Five Years*, the journal he kept from 1955 through 1960, Goodman felt frustrated, purposeless, out-of-it. *Five Years* carries the subtitle, "Thoughts During a Useless Time." In one of his journal entries, remarking that he did not leave *Partisan Review* but that it left him, Goodman notes: "I have never left *anybody* who has access to a printing press!" He had in the meantime written a book, purportedly about juvenile delinquency, entitled *Growing Up Absurd*, for a publisher who rejected the completed manuscript. The story has it that the book went the rounds of sixteen different publishers till it was picked up by Norman Podhoretz, the then newly appointed editor of *Commentary*, who ran large segments of it in the magazine while also persuading Jason Epstein of Random House to bring it out in hard covers. Published in 1960, *Growing Up Absurd* was to prove a book of considerable importance for the decade ahead; it was also to provide the ass upon which Paul Goodman would ride into the Jerusalem of a popularity greater than any he had hitherto known, or even possibly dreamed of.

R ETURNING TO OUR ENTHUSIASTIC REVIEWER, I had read Paul Goodman in *Dissent* and other magazines, but it was in the pages of *Commentary* that I first came upon *Growing Up Absurd*. The year was 1960, I was a year away from having taken a BA at the University of Chicago, and was an enlisted man in the US Army stationed in Arkansas. Even now I can recall reading those *Commentary* pages in a sweat of approbation: yes; yes; yes; exactly; yes; yes; yes; perfect! Most of us take from books and articles that which we need, or want, leaving the rest, often including the author's intentions, behind. While *Growing Up Absurd* was chiefly about the young Spanish and black kids of New York slums and the Beat generation of San Francisco, and how social arrangements worked to exacerbate rather than alleviate their conditions, I read into the book the message that there was no honorable work for the young in America. This was one of the book's principal points. But I, who wanted no part of graduate or professional school, and who had been trained into a rather easy contempt for business, took it for the book's reigning point, and applied it to myself. I wished to earn my living writing, but had serious doubts about being able to bring it off. If I were to fail, as I had every reason to believe I would, I could then contend, as I no doubt would have done, that there was no honorable work in America.

Surely not everyone put this rather special construction upon the pages of *Growing Up Absurd*. A less personal reading of the book was certainly possible, one linking it to its time, of which it was very much a part. Consider that time: the late 1950s, toward the end of the second Eisenhower administration. The great sociological tracts of the day were *The Organization Man*, which attacked the corporations and the suburbs; *The Lonely Crowd*, which pointed up the deadly new conformity among the young; *The Affluent Society*, which scolded a rich country for its misarranged priorities. In intellectual circles, most political argument was then about foreign policy, and chiefly about whether anti-Communism had run its course. Domestically, nearly everyone claimed to be Left, at least after a fashion, though what being Left meant, apart from being for civil liberties and civil rights and a more planned economy, was less than clear. Along came Paul Goodman, whose indictment of American life, radical though without the taint of Marxism to it, was pretty near complete yet had nothing vindictive about it. Holding out the possibility of alternative social arrangements, he seemed to rouse the discussion about domestic policy again after long intellectual slumber. He wanted a more humane, a less repressive society—one, as he kept repeating, less wasteful of human resources, built more to human scale. That there was some truly hideous writing in *Growing Up Absurd*, or that there was what seemed perhaps an undue emphasis on sex, could be let pass. This man cared about the young, about America, about mankind. Or so it then clearly seemed.

How seems it now? Not quite the same, it turns out. Fish and visitors, said Franklin, begin to stink after three days; radical writing dependably rots after a decade. Right off there is, as one rereads it today, an odor of datedness about *Growing Up Absurd*: "... the problems I want to discuss in this book," Goodman writes in his opening chapter, "belong primarily, in our society, to the boys: how to be useful and make something of oneself. A girl does not *have* to, she is not expected to, 'make something' of herself." Perhaps one cannot blame Goodman for not including the women's movement in his vaticinations. One can blame him, though, for the tremendous jumble of his book. So many statements in it are made *ex cathedra*. (Of modern marriages, for example: "We are all in the toils of jealousy of our own Oedipus complexes, and few of us can tolerate loneliness and the feeling of being abandoned.") Frequently Goodman will clinch an argument with a quotation from the earlier work by that noted authority—Paul Goodman. Arguments often lead nowhere; subjects founder in obscurity, as when, talking about the community culture of the Beats, Goodman writes that they would do well to ponder, as a model, "the Balinese dances." As befits its anarchist author, *Growing Up Absurd* may be one of the few books organized along anarchist lines; that is to say, without any organization at all.

The language of *Growing Up Absurd* was a compound—compost?—of the purest psychobabble overlaid by sociological barbarisms. No one who so regularly cited himself as an artist ever wrote so poorly. "Depersonalized" was a big item in his vocabulary, as was "structure." He could refer to one's "own meant world"; "needs" were inevitably "felt"; and it nearly goes without saying that he was for "growth," "dialogue," and "feelingful sex." True, such phrases were not then the clichés they have since become, but they served the same purposes, then as now, of evasion, obfuscation, and self-deception. But Goodman's book contains clichés of thought as well as of language. "Community" was one he regularly fell back upon, as in this dubious statement in *Growing Up Absurd*: "children of all classes are equally deprived of the human community." ("With us," he notes in his journal, "the Absurd has become so huge that I feel justified in the Arbitrary.") He availed himself of the even more commonplace clichés of social criticism, complaining of freeways, suburbs, supermarkets; and at a higher level of generality, though certainly no deeper a level of penetration, of Wall Street and Madison Avenue and Hollywood.

Paul Goodman was famously eclectic, which seemed to give him the authority to speak out in several different voices. At one point, he spoke as a psychologist; at one point, as a literary critic; at one point, as a city planner (co-author, with Percival Goodman, of *Communitas*); and always as an artist ("Consider the case of the artist," he writes, "my own."). While the variety of Paul Goodman's accomplishments seemed to make him more appealing in his role as a social critic, the harsh fact is that he was not a very incisive psychologist, an original city planner, an interesting literary critic, or a good novelist, poet, or playwright. That he did all these things is impressive, but as Samuel Johnson once said, "A horse that can count up to ten is a remarkable horse, not a remarkable mathematician."

Although many of the notions in *Growing Up Absurd* anticipated those of the New Left later in the 1960s, as Goodman's vaporous language anticipated the therapeutic view of life still much in the air today, there remains a sense in which Paul Goodman was not himself conventionally doctrinaire. "I have felt the power of my disinterestedness," he wrote, "since indeed I have no ax to grind and don't want anybody's money." To come on as he did well above the ruck, all disinterest and deep feeling, was surely a great part of the appeal of Paul Goodman. After talking with a group of young men outside Hamilton, Ontario, for whom the future, because bereft of useful work, seems hopeless, Goodman, in *Growing Up Absurd*, writes: "I turned away from the conversation abruptly because of the uncontrollable burning tears in my eyes and constriction in my chest." He was very good, in the same vein, at conveying the sense of squandered energies and their cost. Goodman had his voice, his characteristic tone, and when served up in an unadorned syntax, shorn of clotted language, it could be very winning. At the close of a *New Republic* piece on television, for example, after delivering the standard jeremiad against television, Goodman plaintively wrote: "This is too beautiful a medium to be thrown away like this."

Allied to Goodman's sadness at the prospect of waste was the Rousseauism that was one of the major motifs in everything he wrote. Almost everywhere in Paul Goodman's work not men but institutions are at fault. In literary matters, to cite an almost comical example, Goodman felt that the problem with our novelists is not that they are inferior in understanding society but that society is not good enough for them: "The burden of proof is not on the artist but on society." Who is to blame is always left rather vague in Goodman. "Writing *Growing Up* [*Absurd*]," he notes in his journal, "I rapidly sketched out an enemy, the Organization." Sometimes he called this enemy the System, or the Organized System; sometimes the Establishment. "Of course," he wrote, "I sometimes generalize outrageously for rhetorical effect; I assume the reader is not a moron and does not think that I am."

PROFESSOR STOEHR, in his introduction to *Creator Spirit, Come!*, Goodman's literary essays, remarks that "it would not be far afield to read through his entire work of the 1960s as a kind of literary criticism applied to social problems." Such a case can perhaps be made, but it leaves out a decisive aspect of Paul Goodman's work—his hope, through that work, to dismantle, as Professor Stoehr puts it, "a hardened status quo." Goodman's method was to criticize existing arrangements, always making sure to suggest alternatives: decentralize here, organize from the bottom up rather than the top down there, change an existing law elsewhere. Some of his alternatives were interesting, some superficial, some silly. But were these alternatives made in the name of a large vision? Socialism, strictly speaking, was not the name of Paul Goodman's desire. What, then, was?

In his brief foreword to *Five Years*, Goodman writes: "When I speak of 'psychology' I am speaking about 'society.'" The two, for him, were interchangeable. When Goodman spoke of "repression," he did not mean the word metaphorically, a borrowing from psychological discourse to be put to political or social uses. He thought that people were quite literally repressed, their natures twisted and thwarted by life in modern society. The roots of this repression were psychological, even if its consequences were political. D. H. Lawrence and Wilhelm Reich were his intellectual mentors. "Consult Your Deepest Impulse" was his working principle for his own behavior. Goodman's own Deepest Impulse impelled him to extol freedom and despise constraint. He once told Professor Stoehr that, so hot did its ideas make him, he used to masturbate with Freud's *The Interpretation of Dreams* open in front of him. Evidently no one ever suggested he take *Civilization and Its Discontents* with him into a cold shower.

The sexual element in Paul Goodman's work was more than merely pronounced. He never hid it. His admirers—myself of a decade ago among them—simply never wished to recognize it. The fact that Paul Goodman was a roughhouse homosexual—"trade's trade," as he once described himself—was not in any case considered a fit topic for polite intellectual talk. Professor Stoehr claims that "More than any other single person, he [Goodman] helped make present-day honesty and the gay liberation movement possible." Yet Goodman's homosexuality was of a very different order from what one thinks of as characteristic of the gay liberation movement today. His was not homosexuality as a matter (as they say nowadays) of "lifestyle," but rather as a pressing need. As Goodman himself envisioned it, there was something "manly," or at least "comradely," about his homosexuality. It was connected, if vaguely, with work, and with athletics. In his journals, he recorded his debt to homosexuality in relieving him of the burden of snobbery: "I think my homosexual needs, involving rough company, catch-as-catch-can chances, and dirty practices, got me out of a lot of snobbery, though homosexuality does not seem to have this effect on the tribe of uptown queens whose reaction against their drives makes them more squeamish and snobbish still."

When, in 1966, *Five Years* was published, its pages rife with Goodman's cruisings, his bathhouse and lavatory adventures—"my abject sexuality, quite beyond humiliation"—Goodman was praised for his candor. But he had always been candid in this regard. It was his readers who hid in the closet. *Growing Up Absurd* is filled with sexual references: "The fellows are interrupted in growing up as men; their homosexuality threatens them as immaturity. They are afraid of going backward to boyhood status, admiring the model penises and powers of their seniors and adults." And so on. But somehow such stuff retreated to the background, lost in the attacks on President Eisenhower or the dreariness of life in corporations.

Goodman felt that his homosexuality gave him a certain edge as a writer. "As one grows older," he wrote in an essay entitled "The Politics of Being Queer," "homosexual wishes keep one alert to adolescents and young people more than heterosexual wishes do. . . ." He was also, to put it gently, sexually highly charged: "There have been few days back to my 11th year when I have not had an orgasm one way or another." Among his admirers, there was a tendency to treat Paul Goodman's homosexuality as peripheral, perhaps as imbuing him with a greater hunger for social justice, but otherwise not really central to his chief concerns. He was, in this view, a cogent critic of modern American life who *happened* to be homosexual.

"DO NOT PRACTICE WHAT YOU PREACH," Paul Goodman wrote, "preach what you practice." Goodman practiced homosexuality, and as intensely as any man. "I have cruised rich, poor, middle class, and petit bourgeois; black, white, yellow, and brown; scholars, jocks, Gentlemanly C's, and dropouts; farmers, seamen, railroad men, heavy industry, light manufacturing, communications, business, and finance; civilians, soldiers and sailors, and once or twice cops. (But probably for Oedipal reasons, I tend to be sexually anti-Semitic, which is a drag.)" Having practiced homosexuality, did Goodman preach it? Not explicitly, though he was an ambassador for sexuality generally. "Needless to say," he wrote, "if we had better community, we'd have better sexuality too." What is not needless to say, and what is implied in so much of Goodman's writing, is that if we had better sexuality, we would have better community. Thus his young men in *Growing Up Absurd* are often violent as a result of repressed homosexuality. Everywhere the enemy is repressed sexuality. "Most sexual behavior would give more satisfaction and do lasting good, and would certainly result in far less damage, if any, if it were completely ignored by the police and not subject to any social disapproval *qua* sexual." Again, on the subject of education, Goodman believed that what he termed "a functional sexuality" is probably incompatible with our mass school systems, and concluded: "This is one among many reasons why they should be dismantled." For Goodman, the "coercive society" was one that not alone repressed sexuality but also failed to encourage it. The good society, for Goodman, started at the groin.

Many of the things Paul Goodman asked for in his essays and books of the 1960s have now come about, and with rather pitiful consequences; and this as much as anything, when one rereads him today, diminishes his stature. In *Growing Up Absurd,* he complained, for example, that "the powerful interests have the big presses." He should be alive today to read the New York *Times* and the *Washington Post.* In "Pornography, Art, and Censorship," an essay first published in *Commentary* in 1961, he complained about "the forbidden topic, the mockery of sacred public figures." He should be alive today to read the novels of E. L. Doctorow and Robert Coover, the journalism of Garry Wills and Gore Vidal. He believed that if the legal restrictions were lifted from pornography, it would "ennoble all our art," "humanize sexuality," have "beautiful cultural advantages." He should be alive today to walk the 42nd Street of every large American city. He believed in decentralizing everywhere, getting back to the land and artisanship. He should be alive today to see the squalor of youthful communalism, the triviality of boutique culture. One could go on. Many of the things Paul Goodman asked for have come about—and with the result that he now seems a voice a good deal overvalued in his own lifetime.

Saul Steinberg

(2013)

A T A CELEBRATION AT UCLA of the career of Eugen Weber, the Romanian-born historian of France, I made the mistake of describing Eugen as an exile. In his response to the tributes paid him, Eugen corrected me, remarking that he had never considered himself an exile. "From the moment I attained consciousness," he said, "I wanted to leave Romania. The place is a dump."

Tristan Tzara (né Samuel Rosenstock), one of the founders of Dada, was a Romanian. Eugenè Ionesco, perhaps the most famous Romanian artist of the last half of the 20th century, was a surrealist playwright prominently associated with the Theater of the Absurd. E. M. Cioran, the Romanian aphorist, wrote: "An acute sense of absurdity makes the merest action unlikely, indeed impossible. Lucky those who lack such a thing! Providence has indeed looked out for them." Dada, surrealism, absurdity—Romania seems to have encouraged such responses on the part of its writers and artists.

Another Romanian, Saul Steinberg (1914–1999), the cartoonist, illustrator, and artist, called the country of his birth "a sewer." Feeling stymied by Romanian anti-Semitism, well on the increase in the late 1920s with the advent of the fascist Iron Guard (for whom the Nazis were moving all too slowly), in his adolescence Steinberg escaped, going off to Milan to study architecture. (A fine education, he averred, for everything but the practice of architecture.) He did not escape Cioran's curse of an acute sense of absurdity. If there are mixed blessings, so, too, may curses be mixed. Absurdity was Steinberg's stock in trade, his manner of looking at the world. Without it, he was out of business; with it, however, happiness was always out of his reach.

Outwardly, Saul Steinberg's was an immensely successful life. And this success did not come only after great travail. He drew, and the world was eager to have him continue to do so. On the artistic front, warm welcome met him all of his days. Money, fame, honors fell into his lap. "After nearly forty years of looking at his work," said William Shawn, then editor of the *New Yorker*, "I am still dazzled and astounded by it. His playfulness and elegance are of a sublime order."

While a student in Milan, Steinberg published cartoons in Italian satirical journals. When Mussolini began rounding up Jews, he was briefly interned in an Italian concentration camp, which, by his own account, was more a disorganized detention depot. With the help of relatives and friends, he won his freedom and made his way to Portugal. Because American immigration quotas for Romanians were filled, he was turned away at Ellis Island and had to spend a year awaiting a visa in the Dominican Republic. While there, he published drawings in the *New Yorker*, which was to prove a lifelong and lucrative connection. Over the years he provided the magazine with nearly 90 covers and hundreds of drawings.

Soon after his arrival in New York in 1941, Steinberg went to work for the graphics division of the Office of War Information. Once naturalized as an American citizen, he was drafted into the Navy, where he was made an ensign. He served in China, North Africa, India, and Rome, illustrating instructional manuals and turning out drawings used as propaganda dropped behind enemy lines. During this period, he continued to contribute to the *New Yorker*, where he had a "first-look" contract giving the magazine initial refusal rights on all his drawings.

In his early days in New York, Steinberg met Hedda Sterne, a Romanian émigré, an abstract painter, and a woman of intelligence, beauty, and sympathetic understanding. She invited him to lunch, and, in her words, "he stayed six weeks." They married, though Steinberg persistently betrayed her through adultery, and they eventually separated. But they never divorced. She remained someone he called on in times of confusion, anxiety, and depression, and these times were neither few nor far between.

A Jew in Romania, then a Romanian in America, Saul Steinberg was an outsider by fate but also by choice, forced to think in a language to which he was not born. He saw the world in the coolly detached way of an artist. This allowed him to capture it in his drawings in its illogicality, its unconscious comedy, its silly pretensions. In Steinberg's drawings the figure 5 makes love to a question mark, a Don Quixote-like figure attacks a pineapple, the earth is seen in parochial diminishment when viewed from Ninth Avenue in Manhattan.

"I don't quite belong in the art, cartoon, or magazine world," Steinberg claimed, "so the art world doesn't quite know where to place me." Was he major or minor, a high- or middlebrow figure, a mere cartoonist and illustrator or a major artist? Even now, fourteen years after his death, this question has yet to be resolved.

Deirdre Bair's well-researched biography of Saul Steinberg is less a work of interpretation than of reporting. Bair chronicles the year-by-year facts of her subject's quotidian life. Her book records an odyssey of success played in counterpoint to an iliad of woe. As she builds up her details, in pointillist fashion, patterns emerge. Hedda Sterne claimed that "the mystery over his [Steinberg's] work was always 'where did it come from?'" Deirdre Bair's biography does not finally solve the mystery but, in helpful ways, greatly lessens it.

As for Steinberg's success, along with artistic honors and critical approval, he made a vast amount of money. This came not through sales to magazines, where his drawings were much in demand, but from Hallmark, Ford Motors, Neiman Marcus, Noilly Prat vermouth, and other companies for which he made drawings to accompany their ads; he also designed wallpaper and fabrics, and created dust jackets for books and murals for restaurants. The demand for Steinberg's work was always greater than the supply—though the supply itself never ran out, for his facility as a draftsman was unremitting and his production prodigious.

Yet artistic and commercial success could not stay Steinberg's depression. He blamed much of his gloomy outlook on Romania and his family.

His mother, the implacable Rosa, was one of those women for whom no act of generosity, no accomplishment on her son's part, was ever satisfactory. She drove her husband, Moritz, into psychological retreat and her son to early desertion, though a highly qualified desertion it was. Little as he could bear to be in his mother's presence, listening to her cacophony of nagging and complaint, witnessing its shriveling effect on his father, Steinberg nonetheless supported his parents and his sister Lica and her family until their deaths. He also sent money to relatives who had emigrated from Romania to Israel, and who always had a fresh list of requests for him to fulfill. He kept his first lover, a married Italian woman, on his payroll for much of her life long after he left her.

If Steinberg's generosity seemed more dutiful than heartfelt, it was because expansive emotions were not in his psychic portfolio. He tended to be in business for himself, emotionally as well as artistically. In conversation, he was a monologist, offended if not given the floor at dinner parties. "I am not a listener," he acknowledged. "I am a talker." In relationships, things had to be weighted in his favor. "We are the two people in the world who love you most," Hedda Sterne told him, and, in their almost daily phone conversations after their separation, she claimed that "we talked only about him."

Steinberg was a relentless woman chaser. A small man, bald, with thick glasses and a chosen nose, he must have made up for what he lacked in animal magnetism through the aphrodisiac of his artistic fame. As he grew older, he chased younger and younger women. Friends could not leave him alone with their attractive adolescent daughters. At one point, he seduced the babysitter of painter Ad Reinhardt's children. While still living with his wife, he began a love affair with the wife of a couple with whom he and Hedda Sterne were friendly and whose child he liked, and so he proposed, in all seriousness, a *ménage a cinq*.

"In a way," Hedda Sterne said, "sex was [Steinberg's] life. He deprived himself of a true union because he was not ever in love." His friend the art critic Dore Ashton seconded the motion, telling him, "Saul, you do not love women. What you love is *your* reaction to them. . . . I well know that deep sentiment is alien to you, that somewhere you are lamed, and that secretly you are afraid of and despise love." Had there been an attractive woman in the room when Ashton said this, Steinberg wouldn't have heard a word of it.

The saddest of Steinberg's love affairs, recounted in detail by Deirdre Bair, was the longest lasting. This was with a German émigré named Sigrid Spaeth, which began in 1960, when he was 46 and she 24. At first besotted by her, he shaved off his mustache at her request—for a vain man, the ultimate sacrifice. As Bair puts it, "The thirty-five years war began." Sigrid, who called herself Gigi, was psychologically fragile, given to deep depression. He moved her in and out of his apartment in Greenwich Village and house in East Hampton. He took her to Europe and paid for her many trips to Africa. He gave her an allowance, paid her tuition for courses at Columbia, and provided her with everything except what she really wanted: marriage and children. He made plain that he was up for neither—and added that, in any case, he wasn't in love with her. A bit of a hippie, with lots of love affairs of her own, and a druggie, she eventually killed herself, at the age of 60, by jumping off the roof of the Riverside Drive building in which Steinberg had bought her an apartment.

In her bill of complaint against Steinberg, Sigrid Spaeth claimed that he often shut her out, and that he didn't include her in his social life. She embarrassed him, he countered, by not being sufficiently sophisticated, socially or intellectually. Steinberg was often invited to the dinners and parties of those rich given to dabbling in art. As an intellectual who read in a serious way, he also had entrée to the *Partisan Review* crowd. Two figures in that circle, Mary McCarthy and Dwight Macdonald, pushed him politically further to the left than he might otherwise have gone. A closer friend was Harold Rosenberg, a high-powered schmoozer who wrote art criticism for the *New Yorker* and who championed Steinberg's work.

On his frequent trips to Europe, Steinberg met with Alberto Giacometti, Vladimir Nabokov, Henri Cartier-Bresson, Nicola Chiaramonte, Carlo Levi, Janet Flanner, Igor Stravinsky, and Pablo Picasso. He bought Stravinsky's Cadillac, and described Picasso as resembling "an old Jewish man in the Florida sun—all torso and shorts. The voice of a cigar smoker . . . the falsetto of a cello."

Steinberg thought of his own art as in the tradition of James Joyce and Nabokov. If so, it would have been the Joyce of *Finnegans Wake* and the Nabokov of *Pale Fire*, farcical works built on the mockery of the vagaries of language. Nabokov, Bair reports, reciprocated Steinberg's admiration, and said of him that, in his drawings, he "could raise unexpected questions about the consequences of a style or even a single line, or he could open up a metaphysical riddle with as much wit as Escher or Magritte and with far more economy." Steinberg also admired Picasso, and thought he and Picasso were the two most important visual artists of the 20th century—an assertion that, at best, may be half true.

Resisting all attempts to get him to explain his art, Steinberg said: "The sort of people who need an explanation deserve a mystery." He claimed to be "a writer who draws," by which he must have meant that he was a visual artist of ideas. Anton van Dalen, his studio assistant, maintained that Steinberg "was all about ideas." Steinberg's notion of his own art was that it was "only an indispensable way of showing a poetic invention. Notice the drawing."

The first things worth noticing about his drawings are their immediate fascination and infinite charm. "Don't underestimate your God-given ability to enchant and delight," Hedda Sterne told him during one of his many glum periods. And so his endlessly inventive talent does. Steinberg held that one of the aims of the artist should be to keep alive the childlike ability to see things innocently and afresh. He was aided in this attempt by being an outsider in every culture into which fate had tossed him—Romanian, Italian, American—which gave him his peculiar off-center slant on things.

What to American eyes might be ordinary was to Steinberg's often astounding. He could be amusing in his representations of American ambitions and vanities, and took particular note of the contradictions that ran up the center of American culture. In a famous *New Yorker* cover showing an American monument, the figure of Prosperity sits atop the highest pedestal, flanked by statues of Freud and Santa Claus, while at the bottom Uncle Sam shakes hands with Uncle Tom; in the middle, under a banner reading "The Pursuit of Happiness," a snake and a crocodile are biting off each other's tails.

Death was always much on Steinberg's mind. He has drawings in which he sets out life as a series of ascending steps from childhood to a paunchy retirement in Florida, which he called a "concentration camp for old people." In one drawing, a man appears enclosed on the right side of a parenthesis, a bird about to place a wreath over his head, with the date 1905 followed by a dash occupying the left side of the parenthesis. In another drawing, a Quixotesque figure on horseback, lance at the ready, chases a crocodile down an incline, unaware that a large boulder (death itself) is in pursuit of, and certain to kill, him and the crocodile both.

The autobiographical element in many of Steinberg's drawings is not difficult to grasp. A drawing of a man earnestly dancing with a girl crudely limned in crayon recalls a photograph, reproduced in this book, of Steinberg dancing with Sigrid Spaeth. The subject of many of his drawings is drawing itself, and the comedy of artistic creation generally. In several of these, styles from different art-historical periods—from cubism to childish scrawlings—appear in the same drawing, just one of the many instances (as he put it) in which he combined "ideas in unpredictable ways."

A splendid calligrapher, Steinberg was able to bring letters of the alphabet, as well as numbers, to life. In one drawing, the letter "H" from the word "Who" pushes over the word "Did," which crushes the letter "I" in the word "It" in the phrase "Who Did It"—with the question mark off to the side presumably asking the question. In another, a man sits before a desk while the authoritative man behind the desk fills the large balloonish letters "N" and "O" with much indecipherable writing, all of which of course adds up to "NO." Owing to their construction, he thought the numbers 5 and 2 erotic, and 1, 4, and 7 quite without sex appeal, though he felt the number 4 might be of interest to cats.

Cats with human countenances—many of them resembling that of Franz Kafka—in Steinberg drawings slyly observe people solemnly pursuing their ridiculous ambitions. He drew false documents in which he substituted fingerprints for faces. In other drawings, human beings are lost in mazes and labyrinths; military men are given severely geometrical faces; women are all legs in whorish high heels or else menacingly birdlike; rococo architecture looms in the background (he drew the Chrysler Building over and over); a vinyl record, on the Sphinx label, shows the head and bosom of a woman attached to a cat's body, with the song on the record called "Kumming Tango."

In an *oeuvre* so large as Steinberg's, not everything succeeds. Late in life he began producing the tops of desks and their contents, and these, apart from being tidy compositions, seem of slight interest. His postcards, often of landscapes with rubber stamps on them, fail to engage the imagination. In the 1960s, his view of America darkened, and so did his drawings. They began to be filled with menacing Mickey Mouse-like figures toting guns, hookerish women, fierce dogs, rats, bums, menacingly bearded Black Panther types. Of all his drawings, these seem most like the doodlings of a frightened neurotic, and hence are of the least interest.

Steinberg was best as a humorist, though one who went in less for jokes than for puzzles, paradoxes, and visual parodies. "I try to make [people who view my drawings] jittery by giving them situations that are out of context and contain several [possible] interpretations," he said. He even claimed that he published a few drawings in the *New Yorker* "that I myself didn't quite understand." He rendered the watercolor painting of a palette of watercolors; a man under the hood of an old-fashioned camera photographing a woman in a burka; men and women carrying portraits, statues, busts, and pennants of themselves; a parade of avant-garde painters like so many soldiers in Red Square, marching in lockstep past a building marked the "National Academy of the Avant-Garde."

As "a writer who draws," Saul Steinberg also claimed that "drawing is a way of reasoning on paper." Had he been born "in a place with a good language, a good vocabulary," he told a *New York Times* reporter,

> I would have stayed there, I would probably have become a writer. This was my inclination. But being deprived of this thing, and having what I considered a modest talent, gave me from the beginning a *métier*. I transformed this *métier* into something much more complex and much more to my own needs.

That "something" was illustration at the service of ironic observation.

Steinberg's uniqueness resides in the fact that we do not enjoy his work in the way we do most art—considering its elements, examining the feeling it evokes, gauging its power—but instead tend to read it for meaning. He himself sometimes referred to his audience as "readers." These drawings force us to ask, *What's going on here? What is the true subject? Why is it amusing?* And, finally, *What makes it all so Steinbergian?*

Like "Orwellian" or "Kafkaesque," "Steinbergian" is a personal adjective of a kind assigned to only a few exceptional modern artists. The Steinbergian figure is a man who, like E. M. Forster's description of the poet Cavafy, stands "at a slight angle to the universe." In Steinberg's various drawings, he is a male figure with a rabbit inside his head, or a man able to detach his nose from his face, or a man photographed holding the hand of a life-size photograph of his 8-year-old self. Fairly certain that life is a joke, Steinbergian Man anxiously awaits its punchline.

Because he published his drawings chiefly in the *New Yorker*, Steinberg probably had the largest audience for his art of any visual artist in the 20th century. Print was his preferred medium, and magazines the preferred venue for his work. Of that work, Harold Rosenberg, in an essay accompanying the collection of drawings that appeared at a Steinberg retrospective at the Whitney Museum in 1975, wrote: "Steinberg is the only major artist in the United States who is not associated with any art movement or style, past or present."

Because of this, Steinberg's art is not easily categorized. I think of him as belonging to that small but lustrous school of artists—Alexander Pope, Honoré Daumier, Maurice Ravel, Max Beerbohm are of this same school—who do not overpower, but instead charm through the mastery of their craft and the unalloyed pleasure they provide.

Saul Steinberg's considerable success—financial, critical, social—wasn't sufficient to offset the depression that scorched his last years. As a hypochondriac who was more than a bit paranoid, a heavy drinker, and a man more than normally terrified by death, Steinberg found life drearier and darker as he reached his seventies. As his friends died off, Steinberg's depression deepened. So strong was its hold on him that, in the hope of shaking its grip, he submitted to electroconvulsive therapy. Being diagnosed with slow-growing lymphoma didn't lift his spirits. Pancreatic cancer took him in his 85th year.

Saul Steinberg was not the first, and doubtless will not be the last, of those artists who gave the world much more pleasure than he was able to derive from it.

Hilton Kramer

(2012)

I READ HILTON KRAMER before I met him. When I was in the Army, in response to an essay he published in 1959 in *Commentary* on the subject of James Thurber's book on Harold Ross and the *New Yorker*, I wrote a letter-to-the-editor arguing against his attack on the magazine and its founding editor. Fortunately, Hilton did not respond to my letter, else I should have required a scalp transplant and might today be wearing a hairpiece, for he was, among his other talents, a powerful polemicist, one of the best in the business.

A few years later, working now at the *New Leader* magazine in New York, I edited Hilton, who worked briefly as that magazine's art critic. I write that "I edited" him, but in truth there wasn't much to edit, for his copy, as we call it in the trade, was lucid and free of errors. Although Kramer was often a Jewish name, the name Hilton was not. His first name and the formality of his prose left no ethnic or other clues. Hilton was indeed Jewish, and I later learned that he was given his name in honor of a Miss Hilton, a Gloucester, Massachusetts, grade-school teacher who brought homework every night for one of his two older brothers who had rheumatic fever, a service that prevented the boy from having to repeat the grade.

One day Hilton appeared to drop off his copy in person in the shabby *New Leader* offices on Fifteenth Street, just east of Fifth Avenue, in the old Rand School building. The building also housed union agents, a labor-union-financed organization called the Tamiment Institute, the local headquarters of the International Association of Machinists Union (the site of much boozy partying), and the Rand School Library. An associate editor of the magazine had just given notice, and the principal editor, a man named Myron Kolatch, asked Hilton if he knew anyone who was looking for a job as an editor. "Actually, I do," said Hilton. "Me."

The following week Hilton came to work at the *New Leader*. Suddenly my drab job, one chiefly entailing rewriting Sovietologists whose first language distinctly wasn't English, became filled with laughter and high spirits. I liked Hilton straightaway, and at lunch together on his first day of work I filled him in on the oddities of life in the *New Leader* office. I found myself looking forward to returning to work each morning, reluctant to leave in the evening.

We worked in the same room, our desks perhaps twelve feet apart. Hilton was then thirty-four, I twenty-five. He was of medium height, tending toward the stocky, a build not at all athletic yet suggesting strength nonetheless. He wore Brooks Brothers suits and interesting neckties; he had large-framed round glasses, black hair slicked back. His New England accent was distinctive, and could hit high C when he said, as he not infrequently did, the words "Shameless!" and "Scandalous!"

Before taking this job, Hilton had been the chief editor of *Arts*, formerly *Arts Digest*, a magazine devoted to criticism of the visual arts. He knew a great many artists, and knew even more about the corruption of the art world, which he tended to view with a detached amusement. He was also on the periphery of the group now known as the New York Intellectuals, having published in *Partisan Review*, *Commentary*, and other of their magazines, though he was younger than most of them.

After *Arts*, Hilton had tried to live the free-lance life, not easy to do when a review in the *Nation* might pay $25, one in *Commonweal* or the *Progressive* even less. The checks from these magazines were usually handwritten, which somehow made their derisory sums even more dispiriting. Still, it was a time in which one could live in decent poverty. Hilton had a place for a while at the Chelsea Hotel, where Virgil Thomson and other musicians, artists, writers, and members of the higher bohemia lived. It was at the Chelsea that Delmore Schwartz, under the paranoid illusion that Hilton was sleeping with his wife—Schwartz also thought Nelson Rockefeller was sleeping with her—banged on Hilton's door with a pistol, demanding to be let in. When I met him, Hilton lived in Hoboken, in an inexpensive apartment large enough to house his already ample collection of books.

AMONG HILTON'S CIRCLE OF FRIENDS in those days were enough odd types to fill three more volumes of Anthony Powell's *A Dance to the Music of Time*. There was Vernon Young, an English highbrow film reviewer, who wore Bertrand Russell-like high-collared shirts and lived off the hospitality of women, in on whom he regularly moved. He once asked Hilton, with great *hauteur*, what he thought Americans meant when they said, upon parting, "Have fun." There was Edouard Roditi, a homosexual Sephardi Jew who wrote poetry, a book on Oscar Wilde, and translations from the Turkish, German, and French. Roditi once published a quite hopeless piece in the *New Leader* about some controversy within the Olympic Committee over volleyball. Hilton and I laughed at the spectacle of this international aesthete, hounded at the time by the French government for consorting with Algerian boys, trying to wangle a $25 check from the magazine for a piece on a subject on which he could scarcely have cared less. There was Sydney Freedberg, who wrote for Hilton at *Arts* and went on to a professorship in art history at Harvard. Hilton once told me of being at Harvard with Sydney, who, though born in America, adopted an English accent ("sheer pretension" was the reason he gave Hilton when queried about its provenance). They were there for the dedication of a new sculpture garden and, as it turned out, a heavily platitude-laden speech by Derek Bok, the university's president. "President of Harvard," Sydney Freedberg whispered in his English accent to Hilton midway through the speech. "Bet you didn't think he could be so fucking stupid."

Hilton had innumerable stories, most having to do with outrageous behavior ("Scandalous!") and ill-hidden ambitions ("Shameless!"). When I once mentioned a rather gaudy woman I had met at a party, he replied, "Next to Jack Kroll's prose [Kroll was then a very with-it writer on culture for *Newsweek*], she's the vulgarest thing in New York." He was absolutely

Jamesian at spying out people's motives, and therefore not a man whom one did well to attempt to con.

If Hilton had a cultural hero, a figure on whom he may be said loosely to have modeled himself, it was Henry James. He knew and loved James's fiction, but he also had great regard for James as a critic of art and literature. He admired his cosmopolitanism, his Olympian detachment, and he never lost sight of what many people forget—that Henry James could be an immensely funny writer. In its obliquity, some of Hilton's own wit was distinctly in the Jamesian mode.

Hilton seemed to me smart not only about art but about the world. He was as far as possible from being a Freudian, but I recall him telling me never to underestimate the power of sexual attraction among human motivations, especially among those who fancy themselves high-minded. Once, talking about the novels of Theodore Dreiser, he told me that all writers could be divided between those who relied on irony and those who didn't—and those who didn't were better.

During those *New Leader* days, we mostly laughed at that capacious book known as the human comedy, specifically at its intellectual chapters. I had assigned a few book reviews to Richard Howard, the translator and poet, and a man so stuffed with literary knowledge that his own prose was clotted and mottled with endless allusions. I recall the laugh I got out of Hilton when I told him that Richard Howard is the only man I knew who might choose to begin a piece with a parenthesis. He filled me in on stories about Mary McCarthy, Philip Rahv, and the *Partisan Review* gang. When Mary McCarthy left Rahv, with whom she was living, to marry Edmund Wilson, Hilton said that it was perfectly understandable; after all Wilson was the better and more powerful critic. The calculating cold-bloodedness of Miss McCarthy was of course the point of the story.

I was once invited to dinner at the loft apartment (before lofts were fashionable) in Hoboken of Hilton's friend—and later wife —Esta Leslie. Esta was a serious cook, who would drive twenty miles for better tomatoes or delay dinner for two hours while a pepper properly marinated. (The food, let me add, was always worth the wait.) I remember the meal, leg of lamb nicely underdone, beautiful vegetables perfectly cooked, good wine, all accompanied by a fine flow of talk. The only distraction was a life-size nude painting of Esta on a bed, placed on a wall directly in my line of vision, done by her first husband, the Abstract Expressionist Alfred Leslie, who had not long before entered his figurative painting phase.

F OR REASONS TOO ELABORATE AND BORING to go into here, I left the *New Leader* roughly a year after Hilton arrived there. By then our friendship was solidified, and continued by letter and by his occasional postcards written in a minuscule but always legible hand. I cannot vouch for my letters to him, but his to me were informative, penetrating, amusing, always with a nice touch of indiscretion, which T. S. Eliot claimed that every good letter should contain. I don't have the letter before me, but in a characteristic touch I recall Hilton writing: "Saw Ted Solotaroff [an editor at *Commentary*, later the founder of the *New American Review*] yesterday; he seemed mildly depressed. Things must be looking up for him."

In 1965 Hilton took a job at the *New York Times*, where he soon replaced John Canaday as the paper's first critic of the visual arts. In an attempt to go upmarket intellectually, the paper hired Hilton to write about art and Stanley Kauffmann to write about theater. Hilton was interviewed for the job by Clifton Daniel, Harry Truman's son-in-law and then the editor of the paper. In describing his interview with Daniel, Hilton mentioned that he had brought along a number of his essays, but Daniel wasn't much interested in talking about them. "He opened a copy of *Partisan Review* to a piece of mine, and his pencil landed on an idea," Hilton said, "which he apparently was not up to discussing."

While Hilton was at the *New York Times* it was like having a friend at the Kremlin. He had rollicking stories about various *Times* characters: Sydney Gruson, a former bellboy who kept race horses when he was the paper's Mexico City correspondent and was the first man to wear colored shirts with white colors and cuffs; Arthur Gelb, who served as the editor Abe Rosenthal's hatchet man, keeping reporters and editors in line with bullying; Charlotte Curtis, the paper's society editor whose own social-climbing antics were always worth recounting; Howard Taubman, once the paper's drama critic, now left to sit in expensive suits writing paragraph-long squibs on old movies; the great publisher himself, Arthur

Ochs Sulzberger, whom Hilton never referred to in conversation with me as other than "Punchy."

Hilton's friends on the paper tended to be the other arts writers. He had genuine respect for the architectural criticism of Ada Louise Huxtable. He brought the critic John Russell in from London to work on the paper, and he did a nice imitation of Russell's appallation when being told that the *New York Times* was planning a special weekly section called "Home." His best friend on the *Times*, though, was Grace Glueck, a woman of acuity and a sense of humor to match Hilton's own. I once met Grace for a delightful breakfast in Evanston, and as we were parting, she asked me how to get to Oak Park, where she had an appointment. I started to draw a map for her. "No, no," she said. "Just point the way. I'm always forty-five minutes late wherever I go. It doesn't matter."

The reason it didn't matter, of course, was that she worked for the *New York Times*. The power of the *Times* in those days was unsurpassed. I recall that the Art Institute in Chicago mounted a major show a day early for Hilton because its originally scheduled opening conflicted with his schedule. My wife and I once traveled to New Orleans to meet Esta and Hilton in New Orleans, where Hilton was giving a talk and covering a show. When we arrived, we discovered that a wealthy arts patron in town had been assigned to the Kramers, and took them, and us with them, to Antoine's, Brennan's, and other of the more famous restaurants where she had her own personal waiters—such was the power of the *New York Times* and of *Times* men.

At the *Times* Hilton wrote lengthy, strong pieces on the fraudulent piety surrounding the blacklisted Hollywood writers, on the Hiss-Chambers case, on the pressures put upon Russian artists in the Soviet Union, on the heroism of Matisse, and on many other subjects. Such was the reputation for integrity Hilton acquired while at the *New York Times* that Aleksandr Solzhenitsyn, then living in Vermont after having been sent into exile by the leaders of the Soviet Union, agreed to be interviewed by only one man on the paper—Hilton Kramer. The respect of Solzhenitsyn, I have always thought, was one of the greatest of all tributes to Hilton.

This tribute was much greater, surely, than the Pulitzer Prize in arts criticism, which Hilton never won but should have, since no one, apart perhaps from Virgil Thomson in his days writing on music for the *New York Herald-Tribune*, wrote arts criticism so well as he. In a less politicized world, Hilton would have been elected a member of the American Academy and Institute of Arts and Letters, though I don't know whom among the stiffs who are members he would have found to talk to there.

N OT, SO FAR AS I KNOW, that Hilton yearned for such recognition from so thin an establishment. His intellectual independence set him apart. This same independence caused him to leave the *New York Times* in 1982 to found, with his friend the music critic Sam Lipman, the *New Criterion*. I have heard people say that his doing so was a mistake, for at the *Times* he had a forum like no other in the country, perhaps in the world. Yet it is doubtful that Hilton's strong views, his utter unwillingness to go along with the show, could have survived the regimes at the paper under the editorships of Howell Raines and Bill Keller.

Impossible to imagine Hilton trimming his sails by altering his positions, or modifying his views, to accommodate a changing management, or even a changing zeitgeist. Hilton said what he thought, even if it worked against him. He hated a lie, despised fraudulence, always shot from the hip. He never looked over his shoulder to discover who did or did not approve. He knew what he knew, and said what he felt needed saying.

Once, at Northwestern, I was in the audience when he was on a panel with the critic Erich Heller, the biographer Richard Ellmann, and an academic-painter named George Cohen discussing some lofty topic; it might have been "Technology and Modernism." Hilton was the last to speak. "As I look about me," he began, "I note that I am the only non-academic on this panel, for I am a mere journalist, a sojourner in the epiphenomena of the everyday . . ." (Did he lift that, I wondered, from Henry James?) And then he proceeded intellectually to dismantle and blow up the presentations of the other three men on the panel.

Later that same evening Hilton was assigned a sorority house on campus, where he was to answer questions about the night's proceedings. I went along, and marveled at how gentle and instructive he was in answering what seemed to me the vague and uninteresting questions posed to him by undergraduates. When I told him so, he replied that it wasn't made any easier by the prospect before him of a young man in the hallway kissing his date goodnight with his hand down her blouse.

On another occasion, Hilton and I were on a panel at a conference of small-circulation magazine editors in Los Angeles sponsored by the *Nation*. At one point, a woman in the audience rose to ask Hilton a question. He replied by saying that, though she may not have realized it, every assumption behind her question was false; and he then went on, point by point, to demonstrate how this was so. After this, a man in the audience got up to say that Hilton treated her so severely only because she was a woman. In a calm voice, Hilton, who rarely used profanity, announced: "You, sir, are full of shit. I treat everyone alike. If the woman whose question I answered would prefer that I treat her differently because she is a woman, let her stand up now and say so."

For the most part, the obituaries greeting Hilton's death were generous and gracious. The one in the *New York Times* written by William Grimes was especially so, since Hilton was an unrelenting critic of the *Times* in what he considered its fall into the slough of liberal despond. But a few spoke of him as a "pugnacious writer on the arts" or "a polarizing critic," and one ignorant blogger even took out after him for being against "the civil rights movement" and homosexuals. The fact was, as Hilton said that day in Los Angeles, he treated everyone alike. He was very much for the civil rights movement, and only opposed to such charlatans as Jesse Jackson, Al Sharpton, and Cornel West who tried to ride their blackness into profitable careers. As a man entirely comfortable in the art world, Hilton had innumerable gay and lesbian friends, some among them dear friends: James Mellow, with whom he had grown up in Gloucester, the biographer of Gertrude Stein and Nathaniel Hawthorne, was a lifelong friend, and so was Josephine Herbst, whose literary executor he was. But he didn't see this as any reason to give a pass to the poisonous views of Gore Vidal or pretend that the secondary poetry of Adrienne Rich was first-class. He loathed the crude intrusions of racial and sexual politics in art, and had no hesitation in explaining why in public and in a forthright way. Vaunting the shoddy in literature and visual art he considered no mere venial sin. He paid culture the respect of taking it with the utmost seriousness. Witty, wise, intellectually courageous, a kind and generous friend, Hilton Kramer was himself nothing if not serious. He is irreplaceable.

Original Publication
Information for Essays
in this Book

Part One: A Literary Education

"A Literary Education: On Being Well-Versed in Literature," the *New Criterion*, June 2008.

Part Two: Memoir

"Coming of Age in Chicago," *Commentary*, December 1969.

"Memoirs of a Fraternity Man," *Commentary*, July 1971.

"My 1950s," *Commentary*, September 1993.

"A Virtucrat Remembers," in John H. Bunzel, *Political Passages: Journeys of Change through Two Decades 1968-1988*, May 1988.

"A Toddlin' Town," originally published as "Reflections on a Toddlin' Town" in *Commentary*, November 2009.

"Old Age and Other Laughs," *Commentary*, March 2012.

Part Three: The Culture

"The Kindergarchy: Every Child a Dauphin," the *Weekly Standard*, June 9, 2008.

"Prozac, with Knife," *Commentary*, July 2000.

"You May Be Beautiful but You Gonna Die Some Day," originally published as "Nobody Gets Out of Here Alive" in the *Wall Street Journal*, January 29, 2011.

"Whose Country 'Tis of Thee," *Commentary*, November 2011.

"Stand-Up Guys," originally published as "Stand-Up" in the *Weekly Standard*, July 21, 2003.

"You Could Die Laughing: Are Jewish Jokes a Humorous Subject?," the *Weekly Standard*, August 19, 2013.

"Duh, Bor-ing," *Commentary*, June 2011.

"Nostalgie de le Boeuf," *Commentary*, February 2010.

"The Symphony of a Lifetime," *Notre Dame Magazine*, Spring 2010.

Part Four: The Arts

"What to Do about the Arts," *Commentary*, April 1995.

"Who Killed Poetry?" *Commentary*, August 1988.

"Culture and Capitalism," *Commentary*, November 1993.

"Educated by Novels," *Commentary*, August 1989.

Part Five: Education

"A Case of Academic Freedom," *Commentary*, September 1986.

"The Academic Zoo: Theory—in Practice," the *Hudson Review*, March 1991.

"Lower Education," the *Weekly Standard*, March 21, 2011.

"English As It's Taught," the *Wall Street Journal*, August 27, 2011.

"The Death of the Liberal Arts," originally published as "Who Killed the Liberal Arts?" in the *Weekly Standard*, September 17, 2012.

Part Six: Language

"My Fair Language," *Claremont Review of Books*, Summer 2012.

"Heavy Sentences," the *New Criterion*, June 2011.

"The Personal Essay: A Form of Discovery," in ed. Joseph Epstein, *The Norton Book of Personal* Essays, 1997.

Part Seven: Magazines

"*New Leader* Days: Can You Have a Political Magazine without Politics?," the *Weekly Standard*, September 18, 2006.

"*Commentary*," originally published as "The Jewish Encyclopedia" in the *Weekly Standard,* July 5/July 12, 2010.

"The *New York Review of Books*," originally published as "Thirty Years of the *New York Review of Books*" in *Commentary*, December 1993.

"The *TLS*," originally published as "A Bloody Trade" in the *Times Literary Supplement*, November 9, 2001.

"There at the *New Yorker*," the *Weekly Standard*, December 12, 2011.

Part Eight: Intellectuals

"Leo Lerman," originally published as "Man About Town" in the *Weekly Standard*, August 13, 2007.

"Walter Cronkite," originally published as "A Face Only a Nation Could Love" in *Commentary*, September 2012.

"Paul Goodman in Retrospect," *Commentary*, February 1978.

"Saul Steinberg," originally published as "Man With a Line" in the *Weekly Standard*, March 11, 2013.

"Hilton Kramer," originally published as "A Serious Man" in the *New Criterion*, May 2012.

Index

D